Praxis for the Poor

Stafford Library
Columbia College
1001 Rogers Street
Columbia, Missouri 65216

Praxis for the Poor

Piven and Cloward and the Future of Social Science in Social Welfare

Sanford F. Schram

NEW YORK UNIVERSITY PRESS
New York and London

NEW YORK UNIVERSITY PRESS
New York and London

© 2002 by New York University
All rights reserved.

Library of Congress Cataloging-in-Publication Data
Schram, Sanford F.
Praxis for the poor: piven and cloward and the future
of social science in social welfare / Sanford F. Schram
p. cm.
Includes bibliographical references and index.
ISBN 0-8147-9817-9 (cloth: paper) ISBN 0-8147-9818-7 (pbk.:paper)
1. Public welfare—United States. 2. Poverty—Government policy—United States.
3. Social justice—United States. 4. Political socialization—United States. 5. United
States—Social Policy. 6. United States— Economic policy. 7. Piven, Frances Fox.
8. Cloward, Richard A. I. Title.
HV95 .S367 2002
362.5'5'0973—dc21 2002009638

New York University Press books are printed on acid-free paper,
and their binding materials are chosen for strength and durability.

Manufactured in the United States of America
10 9 8 7 6 5 4 3 2 1

To Frances and Richard

The whole history of the progress of human liberty shows that all concessions, yet made to her august claims, have been born of earnest struggle. . . . If there is no struggle, there is no progress. Those who profess to favor freedom, and yet depreciate agitation, are men who want crops without plowing up the ground. They want rain without thunder and lightning. They want the ocean without the awful roar of its many waters. . . . Power concedes nothing without a demand. It never did and it never will.

—Frederick Douglass, 1857

Contents

	Acknowledgments	*xi*
	Introduction	1
I	The Theory of Practice	9
1	What Accessibility Can't Do: The Politics of Welfare Scholarship	11
2	The Future of the Past: Jane Addams and the Social Work of Politics	33
3	Radical Incrementalism Personified: The Piven and Cloward Legacy	49
4	Which Side Are You On? Rethinking Research and Advocacy in Social Welfare	109
II	The Practice of Theory	137
5	The Old Is New: The Racial Basis of Welfare Reform	139
6	Putting a Black Face on Welfare: The Good and the Bad	157
7	Success Stories: Welfare Reform, Policy Discourse, and the Politics of Research, *by Sanford F. Schram and Joe Soss*	186
8	Compliant Subjects for a New World Order: Globalization and the Behavior Modification Regime of Welfare Reform	201
	Appendix: Sources and Measures for Data in Chapter 5	241
	Notes	245
	Index	291
	About the Author	303

Acknowledgments

Two chapters of this book are based on earlier published versions: chapter 5 is based on research done for a co-authored piece by Joe Soss, Sanford F. Schram, Thomas P. Vartanian, and Erin O'Brien, "Setting the Terms of Relief: Explaining State Policy Choices in the Devolution Revolution," *American Journal of Political Science* 45 (April 2001): 378–95, chapter 7 is co-authored with Joe Soss and appeared in *The Annals of the American Academy of Political and Social Science* 577 (September 2001): 49–65.

A number of people commented on selected chapters in this volume. I want to thank Randy Albelda, Bruce Baum, Jim Baumohl, Stephen Bronner, Sam Chambers, Rosalee Clawson, Gary Delgado, Lisa Disch, Hilary Evans, Jenrose Fitzgerald, Richard Fording, Martin Gilens, Marissa Golden, Jack Gunnell, Ken Hoover, Jeffrey Isaac, Nancy Kirby, Steven Levine, Judie McCoyd, Connie McSherry, Carolyn Needleman, Phil Neisser, Ken Neubeck, Mary Osirim, Dave Osten, Joe Peschek, Frances Fox Piven, Adolph Reed, Brian Richardson, Marc Ross, Anne Sisson Runyan, Ryan Schram, Corey Shdaimah, Roland Stahl, Clay Steinman, Michael Tratner, Tom Vartanian, Ann Withorn, and Maureen Whitebrook. Hilary Evans's close and insightful reading of chapter 2 is also very much appreciated. Nancy Campbell, Ira Katznelson, Joe Soss, and Carl Swidorski read all the chapters and commented trenchantly on the manuscript as a whole. I also want to thank Joe for giving me permission to include our co-authored article as chapter 7. My collaboration with Joe goes well beyond this one piece and I have benefited greatly from working with such a thoughtful and skilled writer. The surplus benefits of this collaboration are reflected in all the chapters since Joe's critical readings of each led me to make significant improvements in all of them.

I want to make a special note of thanks to Brianne Wolfe for her meticulous and thoughtful editing of my chapter drafts. A top-notch wordsmith,

Briney is also an intelligent critic of social commentary—the perfect combination for this project. I also thank Tom Vartanian for providing carefully done calculations on the racial composition of families receiving welfare. I very much appreciate the excellent clerical assistance provided by Vicki Gerstenfeld and Lisa Kolonay. At New York University Press, Stephen Magro oversaw the completion of the book with skill and finesse, and Despina Gimbel managed its production with her usual meticulousness and style. I thank them both. At home, Joan and Jack Schram provided additional reflections that helped keep this book project moving along. I thank them for putting up with the inconveniences caused by my efforts to bring the project to conclusion. While these incidents were not unusual, they did grow in number in the closing stages. We are all glad that's over.

Finally, this book would not have been possible without the inspiration of Frances Fox Piven and Richard Cloward. Their work and life, as scholars and activists, individually and together right up until Richard's passing in 2001, have served as a testament to the hope that we all can make a difference. I dedicate this book to them.

Introduction

In 1996, after nearly three decades of gridlock, the stalemate over public assistance in the United States was dramatically broken when President Bill Clinton agreed to sign the Personal Responsibility and Work Opportunity Reconciliation Act. The 1996 law ended "welfare as we knew it," in Clinton's words, by repealing the sixty-one-year-old cash-assistance program to low-income families with children, Aid to Families with Dependent Children (AFDC). The old policy was replaced with a block grant program, Temporary Assistance for Needy Families (TANF), that gave states substantial discretion over the use of funds even as it imposed strict time limits and work requirements on recipients. A whole new world of "get-tough" welfare reform was initiated.[1] Access to assistance was tightened, and welfare shifted from an income support program to a behavior modification regime. Lawmakers created new rules designed to get low-income single mothers to augment their child-rearing work with paid employment outside the home.[2] Some families were helped; others found the reforms innocuous because they were already ready to move on from welfare to work. A large number confronted new bureaucratic complexities and the hardships of trying to survive without public assistance while working a low-wage job.[3] Still others fell through the cracks, leaving welfare, not working, relying more on family and friends, and hoping that charity and handouts could prevent them from succumbing to the oppressive weight of grinding poverty. Welfare reform has proven to be a milestone, though not the one that social justice advocates had hoped for back in the 1960s when the campaign for welfare rights had begun.[4]

In fact, the 1996 legislation could be said to represent several milestones, including the culmination of major changes in the relationship between welfare scholarship and politics.[5] During the 1960s, much of the best welfare scholarship was done in collaboration with social movements to create pressure from the bottom up to promote social change. Gradually, such work became marginal, displaced by a scientistic, technocratic social science that worked in service of the managers who fine-tune social policies.[6] While conservative critics of welfare, such as Charles Murray and Lawrence Mead, championed their political views in books and articles, the center of gravity for most social welfare research shifted to highly refined statistical analyses that sought to avoid being seen as political. From the 1960s to the 1990s, as corporate-sponsored campaigns to repudiate the welfare state ascended, conservative social welfare scholarship became increasingly vocal and explicitly political.[7] By contrast, liberal social welfare scholarship in this changed political climate increasingly adopted a depoliticized idiom and became limited in its political influence by being assimilated into the expert discourses of the bureaucracy.[8] In the process, the voices of dissent that opposed the deleterious effects of welfare reform were increasingly isolated.

Critical scholarship on social justice issues has long been vulnerable to marginalization. Nonetheless, there have always been some scholars who have sought to ground their scholarship in ongoing struggles for social justice, especially so in social welfare scholarship. In the 1960s, for example, practitioners of a politically engaged scholarship worked to connect theory and practice and to facilitate an informed challenge to the structures of power, the inequities of the political economy, and the deficiencies of social policy in the United States. This scholarship was best represented by the work of Frances Fox Piven and Richard A. Cloward. Their scholarship and activism reinforced each other as they worked on both fronts with others to push for social change. Piven and Cloward wrote sophisticated analyses that blended political economy, historical research, and strategic theorizing; they also worked directly with other activists to found the National Welfare Rights Organization and push for a guaranteed income policy that would eliminate poverty in the United States. While the guaranteed income narrowly missed getting enacted, the political agitation for welfare rights proved to be part of a larger set of social forces that led to the expansion of some social welfare policies and the development of others. Over the next few decades, billions of dollars in increased expenditures would be redistributed to low-income families and individuals. Piven and Cloward's role in all of this demonstrated how social science could inform social-policy politics in ways that helped energize a movement for a more just form of social provision. Their scholarship constituted a "praxis for the poor."

The phrase "praxis for the poor," I think, captures an important dimension of Piven and Cloward's work. By praxis, I mean theoretically informed

practice.[9] This Greek term was perhaps most famously championed by Karl Marx, who developed his own theory of praxis.[10] One theory of praxis holds that the ultimate truth of things cannot be known in advance, that theory cannot dictate practice, that knowledge arises within the context of struggle and is therefore historically and contextually contingent, and that the relationship of theory to practice is ultimately dialogical: theory takes ongoing struggle as its premise and works to help create the capacity for critical reflection within it. The ultimate test of theoretical work, then, lies more with the degree to which it is "true" to a particular struggle than with some idealized notion of what the world is or ought to be like.[11] Throughout their careers, Piven and Cloward have produced work that is entirely consistent with this theory of praxis. Social scientists should revisit their efforts and learn anew from them, not so much to uncritically accept their analyses as to develop new forms of critical social science that can help challenge the configurations of power that manifest themselves today.

In the essays that follow, I seek to do just that. The purpose of this book is to elucidate relationships between theory and practice, scholarship and politics, and social science and social welfare. The chapters that follow divide neatly into these two parts. The first four chapters, which develop the main themes of my perspective, offer a critical reflection on Piven and Cloward's work as a model of the relationship of scholarship to politics and, more critically, as a source of tools for building a better future for social science in social welfare. The last four chapters are animated by the spirit of Piven and Cloward's approach. In these later chapters, I seek to enact my own "praxis for the poor," building on the work of Piven and Cloward but focusing on the struggles of the current period.

In the first chapter, I take up the question of whether welfare scholarship has a role to play in mass politics and, if so, what forms this role should take. Specifically, I question ascendant notions of how to connect with the mass public that emphasize making theory and research, ideas and analysis, more "accessible." While the advantages of accessible language are widely known, the limitations and pitfalls of this popular strategy too frequently go unnoticed. After critically examining two contemporary examples of the "mass readership" strategy, I suggest that Piven and Cloward's work offers a different and better model. Rather than watering down their analysis or moderating their politics in order to enhance their mass appeal, Piven and Cloward have shown how highly sophisticated and openly critical scholarship can be inspired by, directed at, and useful for political action on the ground.

In chapter 2, I look to the past to consider Jane Addams as a protean but underappreciated model of how to connect theory to practice. Early twentieth century Progressive reformers such as Addams understood that there had to be a conscious effort to make research an explicit part of political struggle. Addams in particular was someone who distinctively understood the relationship of research to struggles for social justice. Addams gave priority to practice over theory, even as she sensitively theorized what was needed to realize democratic aspirations. She allowed research to grow out of the real problems confronted by persons living in poverty. Addams insisted that the primary goal of her poverty research should not be to advance the refinement of "sociological investigation" but rather to promote "constructive work" that could help push the progressive agenda to address the injustices of poverty.[12] Addams emphasized a "bottom-up" approach that started with the people, their hopes and dreams, their struggles and problems, and worked up from there to contextualize their situation and help create leverage for change. Practice had priority over theory; social science grew out of people's struggles. Addams's approach transgressed the boundaries between politics and social science, and worked in ways that did not reify distinctions within social science. The research was grounded in ongoing struggle and approached the subject of poverty as a multidimensional phenomenon. Addams and her colleagues used a variety of techniques, combining qualitative analysis with quantitative analysis, survey research with mapmaking, theoretical inquiry punctuated by empirical considerations.

Addams's life work offers a basis for imagining what a more politically engaged and methodologically diverse social science can be today. It suggests how research grounded in struggle forgoes rigid technicism and overspecialization in favor of the technical and tactical flexibilities needed to facilitate political change. Starting first in the community rather than in the academy is an important part of the critical insight Addams affords. And it is one that takes us farther than perhaps most social scientists are prepared to go today in trying to improve their craft. I conclude this chapter by suggesting how Addams's work anticipated insights that are being developed today by feminists, critical theorists, and even postmodernists. I suggest how Addams's efforts enable us to think seriously about the politics of scholarship and the possibilities for a better future of social science in social welfare.

The distinctive way that Piven and Cloward combined social science and politics bears many similarities to Addams's model. There are, however, differences as well. Piven and Cloward have emphasized the importance of a politics of dissent; Addams ultimately sought to get beyond conflict. Addams hoped the privileged would come to identify with the oppressed; Piven and Cloward emphasized that resistance to oppression by the oppressed was an important element of any equation for social justice. The dissensus politics that Piven and Cloward emphasized is an important missing ingredient in Addams's work.

It is in the third chapter that I examine Piven and Cloward's efforts to combine welfare scholarship with the struggle for welfare rights beginning in the 1960s. I examine how their theoretical work informed their activism, and vice versa. I suggest how their "praxis for the poor" can be understood as engendering what I call a "radical incrementalism."[13] Radical incrementalism involves accepting the strategic indeterminacy that arises from political contingency.[14] This means, as Piven and Cloward consistently emphasized in their own work, that political actors must work with what is available and figure out what can be done given the circumstances as they are presented. Like Marx's historical materialism, such a "praxis for the poor" accepts that social structures constrain what human agency can do at any one point in time. Like the pragmatism of John Dewey and Jane Addams, Piven and Cloward's "praxis for the poor" worked from immediate circumstances to realize a better future.

Radical incrementalism has implications not just for activism but also for the role of research within activism. Scholar-activists working in the radical-incrementalist mode orient their investigations toward what can be extracted from prevailing structures of power as they are constituted at a given point in history. Within a particular social order, they ask what can be won and how political action might be used to win it. In chapter 3, I suggest that such radical incrementalism also offers a particular model of politically engaged scholarship that is missing and very much needed in the relationship between social science and social policy today.

Social science, like social action, is context dependent. Social science is never disembodied or decontextualized, regardless of what social scientists might want to believe. It is already tied to structures of power, and therefore it is already implicated in politics. The relationship of social science to social context therefore implies the necessity of explicitly politicizing social science and highlighting how it is already implicated in power relations whether social scientists are willing to admit it or not. Social scientists therefore have no choice but to be political; they only choose whether to ignore the politics already embedded in their work or to struggle with it explicitly. Research that avoids explicitly confronting politics too often gets co-opted by it. Radical incrementalism, however, implies more than just challenging the dominant technocratic paradigm for doing research on social welfare issues.[15] It is not enough, for instance, to counter the quantitative modeling that has dominated so much of welfare research since the 1960s. It is not enough, say, to just add more politically engaged qualitative work to the mix of welfare scholarship. Instead, the only effective counter to the forces of depoliticization at work in social science is to contest politics from the very beginning by making it an explicit part of one's analysis, from topic selection, to perspective, to mode of analysis, interpretation, and so on. The necessity of not just adding politics but explicitly embedding research in politics means doing away with another precious distinction. Rather than segregating theoretical analyses of what should be from empirical examination of what is, empirical research needs to be grounded in theory. Empirical work can then be more effective at promoting alternative perspectives for understanding why things are the way they are and what should be done about them.

I pursue this issue further in chapter 4, where I focus on recent arguments in the field about the relationship between social welfare research and politics. I suggest that there is a tendency to deploy narrow notions of scholarly research in ways that end up reinforcing, rather than challenging, power. Such narrow definitions of research led to false accusations that Piven and Cloward and other explicitly political scholars were "against research" when in fact they simply embraced alternative models of research. I conclude that a growing technicism in social welfare research needs to be countered with research efforts that are more directly tied to ongoing political struggle. Rather than join the social scientists who ignore Piven and Cloward, or dismiss them for emphasizing the interplay of politics and social science, I seek to build on their model.

Chapters 5 through 8 do not argue for a particular version of a Piven and Cloward inspired future of social science in social welfare. Instead, these chapters enact that vision through a series of performances. Ranging across a variety of approaches, these performances do not emulate the methodology or even the theoretical orientation of Piven and Cloward in all respects. Instead, what these chapters share in common is that each is animated by Piven and Cloward's commitment to forge dynamic relationships between theory and practice, scholarship and politics, and social science and social welfare.

While arguments in the academy often revolve around issues of methodology and theoretical orientation, I suggest here that the more critical questions lie elsewhere. I do recognize that politics is involved in competing methodological approaches and theoretical orientations.[16] And I do accept wholeheartedly that there are political implications in emphasizing particular approaches to understanding specific subjects such as welfare and poverty. There are, to be sure, political implications to which side we choose in disputes over the advantages of quantitative and qualitative research, or between theorists who emphasize the importance of social structure versus those who stress the significance of the choices individuals make, or even in arcane debates between modernists who stress the priority of human consciousness for animating our actions versus postmodernists who emphasize the overriding significance of discourse, modes of representation, and the structures of intelligibility. In fact, that is why I try to choose carefully, picking from each approach and orientation what can best help inform my radical incrementalism, given where people in need find themselves now and what issues of welfare and poverty they confront demand the most attention. My radical incrementalism, grounded in the struggles of our time and the problems those struggles confront, determines my methodological approaches and theoretical orientations more than the other way around.[17]

My methodological agnosticism is therefore consistent with Piven and Cloward's animating spirit to appreciate the importance of context and accept the overriding significance of political contingency. Given the contingencies of politics, methodological flexibility is essential in order to adjust to what needs to be studied and how this should be done in different circumstances. My choice of topics is also consistent with giving priority to the role of context and the play of contingency.

Social welfare struggle in the current period, for instance, is one in which race plays a latent role that needs to be explicitly scrutinized. Therefore, two of the four chapters in the second half of the book focus on the racial dimensions of welfare politics today. Chapter 5 examines the significance of the racial composition of the welfare population in affecting the likelihood that states will take an aggressive approach to the new "get-tough" welfare reforms that have swept across the country. This chapter uses conventional quantitative analysis to address the overlooked if highly charged topic of racial bias in welfare policymaking. Chapter 6 examines the complicated politics that arise once we try to make the racial dimensions of welfare explicit. Important strategic issues come up in the context of race and welfare. This chapter itself employs quantitative, narrative, and visual forms of analysis to examine different dimensions of the problem of representing race in welfare.

The remaining two chapters broaden the analysis of welfare in the current period. Chapter 7 examines the political process by which welfare reform has been prematurely constructed to be the success it may well not be at all. This chapter employs a social constructionist perspective to critique the interrelationships among politics, research, and the mass media in reporting on welfare reform. Chapter 8 looks to the future to examine the relationship of welfare reform to globalization. Building on the work of Piven and Cloward, this chapter adds the consideration of poststructuralists to think through the ways in which welfare reform is helping create compliant subjects for a new world order.

My methodologically diverse performances on these different topics are united in one important respect. All reflect my commitment to build on Piven and Cloward's emphasis on grounding social science in social struggle in order to help realize more socially just forms of social welfare. In fact, it is important to note that the chapters of the book overall are organized around the three themes of social welfare, social struggle, and social science and how the three are related in important ways. I hope to demonstrate that a better future for social science in social welfare is to be formed in a more politically self-conscious research that is explicitly tied to ongoing political struggle, locally and globally. Readers will have to decide for themselves whether the approach offered here works for them. My hope is that they will find enough merit in what is offered to join in helping to realize a better future for social science in social welfare.

PART I

The Theory of Practice

1

What Accessibility Can't Do

The Politics of Welfare Scholarship

The call for compromise bulks large in welfare scholarship. This is especially the case when welfare scholars take on the role of "public intellectuals" who seek to influence public discourse on issues of social welfare policy. In several ways, a persistent tension runs through scholarship on social policy politics to moderate the level of abstraction and the critical perspective employed in order to reach a larger audience and mobilize a sufficient number of the mass public to support policy reforms. Write simply and propose feasible reforms: these are the edicts of responsible welfare scholarship today. They are often taken as givens, not subject to contestation. They combine to make for a preference for what we can call a "politics of blandness." The politics of blandness emphasizes clear and simple prose to offer basic facts that prove just how reasonable its proposals are. The hope is that this strategy will then lead reluctant Americans at least to support moderate improvements in social provision. The idea is to provide an analysis that both resonates with and is understood by the mass public.

In this chapter, I call this popular strategy into question. I examine two examples: one reflecting the belief that effective welfare scholarship should feature simple writing that focuses on a plain presentation of facts, and another emphasizing how a moderation in proposals is essential for welfare scholarship to connect effectively with politics. In both cases, I suggest that what seems patently obvious is less than meets the eye. Both examples point to what I call "dilemmas of accessibility," where moderation in terms of both writing style and policy proposals increases one's access to the mass public. However, this occurs at the cost of the ability to promote a critical perspective that might help get beyond the prevailing prejudices that hold down social policy. Both examples suggest how politically effective welfare scholarship requires something other than moderation of writing style and policy proposals. I conclude by suggesting alternative ways in which welfare scholarship can better inform ongoing struggle against the reigning structures of power and thereby can constitute a "praxis for the poor."

Middling Politics

One aspect of the accessibility problem for welfare scholars who want to inform public discourse is to make arguments that will resonate with the mass public. This is especially an issue for public intellectuals who seek not only to discourage elitism but also to promote democracy. From this perspective, it is imperative to couch a reform agenda in terms acceptable to the broad middle of the political spectrum. Without an effective pitch that will appeal to the middle classes, attempts to improve social provision are doomed to be ignored. For Theda Skocpol, no recent policy debacle more glaringly highlighted this necessity than the failure of health-care reform in the early 1990s under the Clinton administration.[1] In *The Missing Middle: Working Families and the Future of American Social Policy*, Skocpol focuses on the need to develop a way to hook the middle class into accepting a more generous and universalistic set of social welfare entitlements.[2] For Skocpol, a compelling hook, more than facts or an argument, is what is needed. While arguments and facts are important, to be sure, neither of them will matter much if they are not couched in terms that are appealing to the middle class. Welfare scholarship that seeks to be politically effective will go nowhere if it does not find a way to connect its proposals to middle-class values, ideologies, and interests. Such is the nature of scholarship that seeks to be effective in democratic systems. Skocpol writes:

> The call to reconfigure social supports to build a family-friendly America amounts to a moral vision, not just a laundry list of legislative prescriptions. This runs against the grain of politics today, because our national conversation seems increasingly dominated by policy wonks and economists mired in technical details or by media people focusing on short-term personal maneuvers and scandals. However, from the 1960s through the 1980s, conservatives showed that a politics of broad social mobilization around clearly articulated values, not just narrow policy prescriptions, could move the center of national debate and reshape the landscape of politics. Now it is time for Americans who believe government has a piv-

> otal role to play in building a just society to undertake a similarly bold and visionary strategy.
>
> A family-oriented populism focused especially on working parents can revitalize the tradition of successful social policy making in American democracy—generating civic dividends in the process. Americans believe in linking national support to important individual contributions to community well-being. Mobilizing government to work with nongovernmental institutions to better support parents is an endeavor very much within this vital tradition.
>
> Pursuit of supports for working families can strengthen Americans' sense of community—not just in particular localities, but also across lines of class and race.[3]

"Working families" is the key term here, and would be used by Al Gore in his bid for the presidency in 2000.[4] Skocpol preferred it as a way to create cross-generation, cross-class, cross-race, and cross-gender alliances on behalf of a more generous and inclusive system of social entitlements. Such cross-cutting alliances could create the needed public support for more universalistic forms of social provision. Skocpol adds: "A morally grounded appeal to shared concerns does better in American politics than any explicit call for class-based mobilization."[5] This goal could be achieved once we recognize that such alliances will come about only when we begin to build on the country's traditions and values for providing social assistance in terms of the contributions people make to the social order. Therefore, it is necessarily "working families" rather than children, the needy, or some other identity that takes the central subject position of such an agenda for social welfare reform.

This is in some respects a strategy of seduction designed to lure the middle class into supporting that which it would not otherwise support by tying more generous forms of social provision to an appealing metaphor. It is also, then, a strategy with real dangers that risks reinscribing hierarchies of privilege and deservingness in terms of who is working at what. There are other traps as well, which Skocpol recognizes others might want to emphasize. She writes:

> Many progressives who read this book will worry about my repeated stress on "family" well-being, and my claim that children ideally need the support of two married parents. In recent decades, many progressives have

> been unwilling to highlight family needs or champion two-parent households for fear of appearing to ostracize single mothers. But surely Americans of all political persuasions can acknowledge that children do best in two-parent families supported by the nation and local communities, without denying the single-parent families also deserve our support.[6]

Yet, it is just such privileging of the two-parent family that has led to denying aid to single-parent families on the grounds that it will just encourage family dissolution. In the United States, especially in recent years, public policy grounded in privileging the married two-parent family necessarily means denigrating the single-parent family. While it is surely possible that this need not be the case, it would be treacherous to ignore that this is the way social welfare policy gets made today.

It is somewhat ironic, then, that Skocpol in the end calls for public intellectuals to have the courage to offer a moral vision that will ground social welfare policy in supporting "working families." She writes:

> Americans who care about recentering our civic and political life must, in short, pursue strategies that look further ahead than the usual Washington time horizon of the day after tomorrow. With public intellectuals self-consciously taking a bolder stand than most elected politicians can be expected to embrace at any given moment, supporters of a more equitable society and stronger supports for families must frankly proclaim their moral vision, linking it to specific proposals. They must organize inside and outside the electoral system, and push politicians and other institutional leaders toward a bolder stand on behalf of all working parents and their children, even as broad swatches of Americans are brought together for action and discussion about the needs of communities and families.[7]

Where is the courage in couching appeals in terms that the middle class will find comforting? How will this create the capacity to think anew about how the class system re-creates processes of marginalization on a daily basis? Without sufficient attention given to questions like these, the strategy to offer a "moral vision" on behalf of "working families" risks reinforcing the privileges of the gender-race-class system as it is currently practiced.

Skocpol's effort here is laudable in its attempt to move beyond technicism and to speak more directly to the values that move the public to support or oppose social welfare policy. She says: "The policy specifics are less important than the principle."[8] Yet, less laudable, no matter how well intended, is her attempt to smuggle more generous and universal forms of social provision into the welfare state by way of legitimating that agenda as consistent with middle-class values. Such a strategy does not enhance our critical capacity to challenge the existing biases that constrain social welfare policy. And equally important, such a strategy is likely to reproduce those biases in whatever social welfare policy reforms it engenders. While welfare scholarship might prove to be politically relevant under such circumstances, its relevance should make us nervous.

Skocpol understands that welfare scholarship can only play a small role in mobilizing support for change: "American social policy will not change simply because people write books. . . . A new vision can help inspire the popular support to change the status quo. But people must be organized."[9] Yet, it seems that even its small role is here being mortgaged to the bank of political feasibility in ways that just pay more homage to the class, race, and gender hierarchies that go into making the social order. Her protestations aside, the consistent invocation of work and family values, the persistent focus on "working families," the constant need to shape policy to fit the predilections of some broad, imagined middle class, end up reinscribing the subordination and marginalization of low-income families who do not measure up to middle-class work and family standards. In the end, the universal policies that Skocpol supports become less realizable under the sign of "working families." Such are the risks when one succumbs to the lure of the siren of political accessibility.

Keep It Simple, Make It Popular

Another aspect of the accessibility problem for welfare scholarship is to make arguments that will be readily understood by the mass public. This strategy is extremely popular among welfare scholars. Every few years a book is published that is designed to be accessible to a broad audience and to state plainly that government is far more effective than it is often made out to be, or that social policy is really not destructive of basic work and family values, or that the time has finally come to push for a progressive agenda to guarantee access to a decent education for all, good jobs for those who can work, social insurance for those who cannot, and public assistance for those who for legitimate reasons are not able to have their needs otherwise met. These books usually are true to their word: accessible, demonstrating government's effectiveness, and outlining a modest progressive agenda. There was John Schwarz's *America's Hidden Success*,[10] *America's Misunderstood Welfare State* by Theodore Marmor, Jerry Mashaw, and Phillip Harvey,[11] and E. J. Dionne's *They Only Look Dead*.[12] There was also *America Unequal* by Sheldon Danziger and Peter Gottschalk.[13] More recently, a particularly pertinent example has been provided with *What Government Can Do* by Benjamin I. Page and James R. Simmons.[14] This book is in many respects similar to its predecessors: well written, well documented, and with a convincing plea for a real welfare state in the United States. It provides a noteworthy example of one prominent approach showing how to connect scholarship to social policy politics.

What Government Can Do has many virtues. It does not just reiterate or even update work that has preceded it: it is distinctive in its own right. Its distinguishing argument is that government social and economic policies are not just needed but are actually quite good at reducing poverty and inequality. Page and Simmons provide a survey of public programs to indicate that if only given the chance, government could reduce inequality and even begin to eliminate poverty. This is no small claim, but *What Government Can Do* largely delivers on it in the most concrete and straightforward way. Rather than offer a sophisticated theoretical argument, it makes its case by way of supplying an avalanche of evidence.

In three different ways, Page and Simmons address the issue of the need for government policies to attack inequality and poverty. First, they provide statistical evidence that inequality and poverty are serious problems for American society. Second, Page and Simmons effectively place the reduction of inequality and poverty among the major functions of government, highlighting how government policies that limit inequality and poverty buttress the fulfillment of other fundamental purposes of government to establish the foundations for a market economy, provide basic public goods that cannot be provided efficiently through the market, ensure economic growth and stability, and help promote a sense of fairness, community, and inclusiveness that is conducive to maintaining social order. Third and most impressively, Page and Simmons provide extensive coverage of all the major social and economic policies of the government today, highlighting their strengths as well as their weaknesses. They are especially effective in supplying concrete information that debunks myths about the supposed ineffectiveness of social and economic policies. Where there are weaknesses in current policies, *What Government Can Do* highlights how politics has often constrained policies so as to placate special interests and minimize interference with profit-making opportunities through the market or from government handouts.

What Government Can Do surveys tax policy, education, jobs policies, social insurance, and welfare programs. Its conclusion is that if serious political commitment were made to supporting policies that reduce inequality and poverty, the government's effectiveness in attacking inequality and poverty could shine through for all to see. The political explanation for problems in social and economic policies is not new. But Page and Simmons do a good job of updating it for various policies with the latest statistical evidence on such matters as who benefits from tax breaks, how corporate welfare is wasteful, and how social policies, whether for subsidizing incomes of single mothers or providing public housing, are constrained by the necessity to placate powerful political interests during the policymaking process.

Page and Simmons also use the latest empirical evidence to effectively demonstrate the solvency of Social Security and to question the supposed negative effects of welfare on work and family values. Using evidence to cut through the fog of deception regarding our most fundamental social policies is important political work and it is done in the most thoroughly documented way here. Yet, *What Government Can Do* is most especially effective not so much in debunking the opposition to social policies as in demonstrating the effectiveness of those policies, as they are operating in government today even before reform sets in to correct the distortions wrought by politics. The book is especially effective in doing this when it comes to social insurance programs; Page and Simmons use of the latest empirical evidence is also impressive in demonstrating the effectiveness of wage supplementation policies, education programs, and even much-maligned welfare programs such as the Food Stamp program.

In the end, Page and Simmons return to the progressive agenda that others have advocated. Consistent with the their method throughout, Page and Simmons want to emphasize how the facts basically speak for themselves and support the classic model of a social welfare state where everyone is guaranteed a quality education, a good job at decent pay supplemented by government policies where necessary, with social insurance benefits to cover those situations where people cannot work and public assistance for those whose needs remain unmet. And, given the evidence they supply, it is hard to question that, with sufficient political commitment, the U.S. government could quickly elaborate such a system even from existing policies.

What Government Can Do, therefore, replenishes the body of work written for a broad audience so as to plainly state the progressive agenda for social policy. This is a worthy cause and a needed exercise, in need of being updated periodically to provide the latest information documenting the good works in social policy. A book such as this is good scholarship, even if only in its own way, offering as it does a wealth of empirical evidence while trying to minimize theoretical insights in the name of keeping the narrative accessible to a broad audience. Its focus on a clear presentation of facts with a minimum of theoretical argumentation points to another way of trying to make the progressive agenda accessible to the mass public.

Yet, it is that latter goal of keeping it simple that points toward the flawed, unstated political premise of such books. These books do not matter much politically; they do not generate public support for the welfare state, and they do not result in the country getting any closer to adopting the agenda proposed. Mass-marketed books on the right have greater chances of being politically successful in part because they are more likely to be reinforcing prevailing prejudices of the individualistic, antistatist political culture ascendant in the United States. One need only think of Charles Murray's *Losing Ground,* which garnered a wide readership and in the process helped legitimize the assault on welfare.[15] But if lower sales are any indication, books on the left seem to be less effective. The left's ineffectiveness in this regard could very well be due to the fact that its advocates are challenging rather than reinforcing prevailing prejudice. I hold out little hope that Page and Simmons's book would, any more than the others of its genre, create a groundswell for its agenda. I fear that its impact on public discourse will be small compared with *Losing Ground*.

The question therefore needs to be posed: Who reads books like *What Government Can Do*? One suspects that it is less than the intended audience. Instead of attracting a wide readership across the political spectrum, these books are preaching to the choir. I feel there is value in such an exercise in spite of what the cliché suggests. Preaching to the converted helps keep the flock in place, reminding them of their shared vision and reinstilling commitment. Yet, the converted in this case are a small minority of the American public. And if simply attending to the flock is the only realistic goal to be achieved here, it needs to be said that this is a qualitatively far more limited vision than what I think is the one that informs this book.

What Government Can Do offers a narrative that forgoes making sophisticated theoretical arguments and eschews attempts to advance scholarship in the name of trying to put the facts before the mass public in order to inspire support for more progressive social policies. Page and Simmons have their arguments, but it is the facts that dominate. Their approach is to overcome their critics with an avalanche of facts. Still, facts are not dispositive when it comes to politics. Arguments grounded in no more than the best available facts do not make public policy. If they did, we would already have the progressive welfare state argued for in *What Government Can Do*. Instead, public policy is influenced by far more than facts. We need to consider also the role played by stories, rumors, and gossip as well as ideology and ideas.[16] We need also to account for the structure of power in our society and the ways it limits consideration of the facts and distorts the best ideas. Page and Simmons are aware of these matters and suggest at the end that reform of the political system will be a necessary ingredient of any strategy to realize the progressive welfare state.

Perhaps, then, the most important stage for a book such as this is not the public sphere so much as the undergraduate classroom. There, a new generation of citizens can be made aware of the basic facts concerning the necessity and effectiveness of social and economic policies. While this is hardly the dramatic stage of mass mobilization, it is a noble stage nonetheless; and Page and Simmons's book is deserving of that platform.

The Facts Never Speak for Themselves

There is, then, an important difference between *Losing Ground* and *What Government Can Do*. *Losing Ground* was not premised on the cliché that "the facts speak for themselves." Instead it reflected an almost casual relationship with facts, which many critics were quick to highlight.[17] Nonetheless, Murray's work remained influential among a wide readership and across the public policymaking community in spite of the factual refutations. What this comparison underscores is that it is never enough just to put the facts out there and hope that once they are disseminated, informed thinking will lead people to adopt the correct view of what needs to be done. Instead, public intellectuals who want their scholarship to connect to politics need more than facts.

If we return to Skocpol, we can pursue this issue further. For Skocpol, public intellectuals need more than facts, they need a hook. But not just any hook. They need a hook that will appeal to the middle class. They need a hook in the sense of an argument that is sufficiently arresting to get people's attention. More than facts, what mobilizes people are arguments that get them to think about an issue in a particular way. This is what Murray had in *Losing Ground,* in part because his argument against welfare resonated with prevailing prejudices about welfare recipients.

Leveraging political change comes not with disseminating facts in clear and simple prose. Instead, it comes from having an argument that people feel needs to be taken seriously. More than facts, a convincing argument is what connects welfare scholarship to mass politics. While this might come more easily for those who play to prevailing prejudices, it does not mean the other side can forget about this injunction. The fact that the injunction is more easily met by one side rather than the other does not mean it does not need to be taken seriously: it simply tells us that life is unfair. Once we get over the shock and relearn this particular truism once again, then we can begin the hard work of connecting welfare scholarship to politics in ways that might make a difference.

Part of the reason that facts are not enough is that people are smarter than scholars often give them credit for. Most people do not accept facts uncritically. They are sensitive to "how to lie with statistics." Even if they are not sure how the "lying" is being executed, they are often suspicious of facts and reluctant to believe the ones that are contrary to their preexisting beliefs. Without a compelling argument, clear and simple factual presentations will be insufficient.

Then again, part of the reason that clear writing about basic facts is not enough is that most people don't read—or at least are not likely to read serious scholarly works with footnotes and documentation. Even if the analysis is a clear and simply written presentation of basic factual information, the effort is likely to go unread by the bulk of the intended audience. And those who read it are most likely to be people already predisposed to believe it, making the idea of writing a straightforward factual presentation for the purposes of convincing the opposition somewhat beside the point. The argument that a simple narrative that clearly provides the facts assumes that political change is in good part something that comes when a literate public reads books, absorbs facts, and then, on the basis of reasoned deliberation, is motivated to mobilize around a reform agenda. This is a fabulous version of political mobilization, a fairy tale of how scholarship can play a critical role in politics.

Scholarship works best politically when it is part of a more ambitious attempt to champion a particular argument about why things are the way they are, and why they should change and how. At times, this means that scholarship best performs its political role not by trying to connect immediately with the mass public, but by helping to develop important arguments that over time are popularized by others, that are disseminated via social movements, and that are already circulating among the politically active but need further development in order to provide these arguments the depth and persuasiveness that only thoughtful scholarship can provide.[18] While the penchant to emphasize the facts tends to dominate, the need to go beyond them is also appreciated by welfare policy scholars. Nicholas Lemann suggests that even Skocpol's attempt to play to the middle is, in its own way, sensitive to the need to go beyond facts in order to energize the mass public around a particular policy agenda:

> To Skocpol politics isn't a matter of objectively determining the nation's most pressing needs and then devising government programs to meet them. If it were, then resulting programs would fail, because they would lack a strong-enough constituency, and the interests of working people would be ill-served, because they have no means of presenting themselves as a problem that must be solved. . . . Better to conduct politics differently, she implies, using as the central test of any proposal whether it will attract enough political support, rather than whether it will perform well in what Skocpol derisively calls "cost-benefit calculations."[19]

Skocpol saw a need to go beyond factual analysis when she developed the phrase "working families" as the implied subject position of her proposed social policy reform agenda. At one level, the emphasis on the catch phrase "working families" suggests that the two accessibility problems can actually be working at cross-purposes as much as they are working in sync. Proposing politically feasible reforms that resonate with the mass public sometimes may mean deemphasizing "hard" facts in favor of emphasizing "empty" clichés. Yet, at another level, the appeal to "working families" suggests more than an empty cliché that would legitimize moderate reforms. The "working families" gambit was not simply an attempt to ground social welfare policy reform in the work and family values of the middle class without logic or reasoning behind it. It was also not an attempt to be oblivious to factual evidence. It was instead perhaps better seen as an attempt to achieve a connection with the "missing middle" by offering them an organizing principle that showed how such social welfare policy reforms made sense. In this sense, "working families" was indeed a hook designed to appeal to the middle class but also, by way of giving them a reason to believe, a principle that made sense, an argument that was not easily dismissed.

Therefore, even if we do not buy Skocpol's desire to cut her policy proposals to fit the crammed confines of the political middle, I would suggest paying close attention to the additional message that Lemann says comes with her attempt to seduce the "missing middle" to support a social welfare reform agenda that supports "working families." The message has its own simplicity: for a public intellectual to be effective, you must provide more than facts; to make your case compelling; you must provide reasons why people ought to take your proposals seriously. As an important public intellectual herself, Skocpol has gone beyond academic technicism and an overemphasis on methodological specialization, to use a diversity of research approaches to build up a foundation for trying to speak intelligently to as broad an audience as possible. And when she has done so, she has sought to find ways to make her message compelling by providing more than just research findings. Therefore, while "working families" may or may not be an empty cliché strategically deployed to seduce the middle class into accepting social policies they would not otherwise endorse, the need to go beyond the facts comes through loud and clear.

In fact, Fred Block and Margaret Somers have convincingly argued that the whole of welfare policy discourse for the last two centuries can serve as an object lesson in just this insight. The central focus of Murray's *Losing Ground* that energized welfare retrenchment in the 1990s was the issue of welfare dependency. Yet, according to Block and Somers, for over two centuries the debate about welfare dependency has at significant junctures been most significantly influenced by one important argument. This argument is based on the selective dismissing of facts on the grounds that there is a need to take seriously the idea that appearances cannot be trusted; that we must look below the surface of factual reality and that underneath the flux of appearances was an unchanging natural order of things that should not be tampered with.[20]

In the 1980s, Murray successfully championed the cause against welfare dependency on just such grounds. He succeeded not because he had a strong factual foundation for his arguments about the alleged debilitating effects of welfare dependency, though he did seek to supply empirical evidence for his arguments. Instead, Murray's extremely successful campaign was in good part underwritten by his use of this age-old theoretical argument, which he put at the center of *Losing Ground*.[21] This argument was a replication of the conservative anti-welfare argument that had begun with Thomas Malthus and others approximately two hundred years before.[22] Albert O. Hirschman was to coin this argument "the perversity thesis."[23] The perversity thesis, as Somers and Block have effectively demonstrated, combined classical liberal economic theory and Christian morality to suggest that, contrary to the apparent reality that offering financial aid to the poor was a kind and charitable act of assistance, such interventions actually undermined the natural order of things. Individuals who took such succor would be corrupted, losing the ability to practice self-discipline and exercise personal responsibility. Thus, helping people in this way actually had perverse effects. For over two centuries, at varying points in time and to varying degrees, much success has come to the perversity thesis and its related cousin, the futility thesis—that is, "the poor will always be with us" no matter what we do. This success testifies to the ways in which such arguments can be persuasive independent of historical circumstances. The facts of welfare dependency at any time seem far less significant than the enduring power of the perversity thesis to appeal to ingrained moralisms of Western, liberal, capitalist societies claiming that public aid corrupts the individual and undermines self-discipline. The facts of welfare dependency in this sense are always already there, ready to be materialized in quotidian practices of welfare administration. All it takes is a less-than-active imagination willing to interpret unreflectively welfare participation as if it were without question a sign of personal deficiency. Sadly, the modern history of the Western world, especially in the United States and England, is replete with such instances of underutilized imagination placing whatever facts were offered about welfare use in terms of this argument about an unchanging underlying moral order.

And the facts of welfare dependency are less than apparent. No amount of piling up of facts about the myths of an alleged welfare dependency crisis did any good whatsoever in undermining the ideological juggernaut the right had developed to impugn the already sullied image of welfare recipients as malingerers and no-accounts, lazily living off welfare.[24] The mere recitation of factual evidence about contemporary welfare recipients was to prove woefully inadequate in the face of an argument that had endured for over two centuries and had convincingly encouraged people to ignore empirical information in order to appreciate the underlying natural order of things.

Assuming the Best: A Counterdiscourse

A major service to politics that welfare scholarship can perform is to provide a counterdiscourse that can effectively displace the dominance of the perversity thesis. This would be a real "praxis for the poor." This is no short-term project. This is not something that can be disposed of with a well-designed empirical research project. While short-term empirical efforts are valuable in their own right and can provide useful information relevant to ongoing political struggle, the real serious political work of welfare scholarship lies in attending to the discourse of dependency, challenging its suppositions, undermining its credibility, and displacing its dominance with the public. In fact, empirical work that highlights the myths about welfare and poverty will not by itself undermine popular ambivalence about assisting low-income groups via government aid. Instead, a convincing counterdiscourse is needed to make such empirical work something that people take seriously.

There is no reason to wait. For over two centuries, the perversity thesis has dominated. In the American context, its dominance has been near total, making the development of social provision for low-income groups an uphill struggle, occurring only episodically in response to economic crisis and political instability. Over that history, various writers have challenged the thesis, from Jane Addams beginning in the late nineteenth century to Frances Fox Piven and Richard Cloward in the later part of the twentieth century. Yet, the need to continue that challenge is apparent given the resurgence in influence of the perversity thesis with the welfare retrenchment of 1996.

Challenges to the perversity thesis can begin with questioning its assumptions—all of them, from how there is an underlying natural order to things that must not be tampered with, to how giving aid corrupts and undermines commitment to work and family values. A good empirical base can be invoked by pointing to the experiences of other advanced industrial societies that have far more generous terms of social provision and do not see the deleterious effects predicted by the perversity thesis. Yet, this factual base is hardly dispositive, since countries with stronger welfare states tend to have higher levels of unemployment.[25] Instead, what is needed is a counterdiscourse that can provide an alternative basis for interpreting the facts.

Comparisons with other countries are also pertinent in the quest for a counterdiscourse because they show the extent to which our forms of social provision are distinctively vindictive, given the high degree to which they are structured by the perversity thesis.[26] In comparison to other advanced industrialized countries, our social policies are to a far greater degree structured to "assume the worst" about people who receive aid. And ironically this "assume the worst" mentality ends up producing a self-fulfilling prophecy. Programs are designed to emphasize suspicion, surveillance, and a reluctance to provide aid except under the most extreme circumstances when people demonstrate that they are in desperate need for assistance. Cash, food, housing, and health assistance for low-income families all have operated under the "assume the worst" mentality. This leads to targeted, means-tested programs that are designed to guard covetously against providing aid to families with incomes above strict cut-off levels. As a result, recipients must of necessity restructure their identities, conform their behaviors, and fit themselves into the systems of assistance to make it seem that they are the most desperate of all and therefore should be provided with aid. Therefore, most ironically, the conservatives who most complain about how our welfare system creates dependency are in fact responsible for creating such a self-defeating mechanism that traps people in a system that forces them to prove their deservingness by keeping themselves poor so that they can tap much-needed aid.[27] Only when we begin "assuming the best" in people will we start to break the cycle of dependency that conservatives are so concerned about.[28] This then means moving to systems of assistance that rely less on suspicion and surveillance, less on targeting and means-testing. Instead, we need more universal programs like the ones championed by Skocpol and Page and Simmons.

This then is the beginning of a counterdiscourse that highlights how "assume the worst" is the self-defeating motto of a welfare system thoroughly grounded in the perversity thesis. It provides the initial outlines of an argument that not only points to the fallacious reasoning of the perversity thesis but offers a counterdiscourse that explains the same phenomenon in terms that create the basis for supporting more generous forms of social provision. Such a counterdiscourse does not so much try to convince by way of facts as provide an alternative basis for explaining facts. And it arguably ends up creating a potentially more enduring basis for achieving the progressive agenda endorsed by both Skocpol and Page and Simmons.

This is but an initial challenge to the dominance of the perversity thesis and the "assume the worst" mentality. Much more work needs to be done to build it into a compelling challenge that will resonate with the public and create the basis of support for more generous forms of social provision. Yet, it is my argument here that this is where the critical energy of welfare scholarship needs to be focused if it is to be politically effective. Politically effective welfare scholarship must challenge the reigning ideology of stinginess at its questionable intellectual roots. And planting alternative roots that will bear better fruit is also a big part of that work. This sort of critical work, more than accepting the prevailing discourse, the prevailing mindset, and the prevailing circumstances, is what is most urgently needed.

The Dilemmas of Accessibility

Therefore, there are good reasons to be sensitive to the problems associated with the two sides of the accessibility coin. Limiting arguments to those that are politically salable with the middle class can risk diluting the critical edge of scholarship so that it is of little value in challenging the existing state of affairs. Limiting presentation to the straightforward presentation of facts can seriously undermine the ability of scholarship to attract a following. There are then significant dilemmas of accessibility.

One alternative is to resist the insistence on accessibility, both in the sense of trying to appeal to what is allegedly the broad middle class as it is currently manufactured and of stating proposals for reform in the established vernacular of public discourse as it is currently constituted. This alternative involves donning the cap of a "public intellectual" while still adopting a critical stance in the name of those who are marginalized by the processes at work in producing the mass public as a reified entity that we are supposed to take seriously. To do this, scholars may need to risk being called elitists—in particular elitists of language. Christopher Hitchens has stated:

> I've increasingly become convinced that in order to be any kind of a public-intellectual commentator or combatant, one has to be unafraid of the charges of elitism. One has to have, actually, more and more contempt for public opinion and for the way in which it's constructed and aggregated, and polled and played back and manufactured and manipulated. If only because all these processes are actually undertaken by the elite and leave us all, finally, voting in the passive voice and believing that we're using our own opinions or concepts when in fact they have been imposed upon us. . . .

> [I]n the 18th Brumaire of Louis Napoleon, Karl Marx says, quite rightly, I think, "When people are trying to learn a new language, it's natural for them to translate it back into the one they already know." Yes, that's true. But they must also transcend the one they already know.
>
> So I think the onus is on us to find a language that moves us beyond faith, because faith is the negation of the intellect, faith supplies belief in preference to inquiry and belief, in place of skepticism, in place of the dialectic, in favor of the disorder and anxiety and struggle that is required in order to claim that the mind has any place in these things at all.
>
> I would say that because the intellectual has some responsibility, so to speak, for those who have no voice, that a very high task to adopt now would be to set oneself and to attempt to set others, utterly and contemptuously and critically and furiously, against the now almost daily practice in the United States of human sacrifice. By which I mean, the sacrifice, the immolation of men and women on death row in the system of capital punishment. Something that has become an international as well as a national disgrace. Something that shames and besmirches the entire United States, something that is performed by the professionalized elite in the name of an assumed public opinion. In other words, something that melds the worst of elitism and the absolute foulest of populism.[29]

On the issue of capital punishment, Hitchens effectively reverses the uses of elitism and populism in contemporary political discourse in order to make a point: elitists today cloak their dominance of the public policy process in the name of populism; and intellectuals can begin to help the oppressed have a voice in that process by acting as an independent elite willing to buck the tide of manufactured public opinion. For Hitchens, this intellectual work is not easy and involves careful attention to language. It most especially involves a willingness to challenge the language of power and how it masquerades under the cloak of populism. The public intellectual works with people to help them resist the powerful's use of language to erase the self-serving character of their actions. Repeatedly, this involves pointing out how things are often the opposite of what they are claimed to be. Inevitably, this raises the issue of how far we must go in providing an alternative vocabulary in a number of policy areas. To continually characterize things in the terms of ascendant discourse risks collaborating, if only unreflectively, in the processes of legitimation. Michael Shapiro has written:

> [T]here is a structural issue immanent in all critical argumentation. Criticism of systems of intelligibility must confront what I have elsewhere called "the dilemma of intelligibility," which necessarily hounds those who would distance themselves from canonical modes of thought. This dilemma arises especially in connection with the desire to create a politicized mode of apprehension. For to politicize something is, at once, to generate a frame with sufficient mutual intelligibility to allow for praxis or political engagement with what are recognized as problems in the predominant public discourse, and to distance oneself sufficiently from common views to allow for a frame that can disclose unrecognized commitments and forms of subservience to aspects of power embedded within what has seemed to be mere intelligibility, a natural structure of meaning. In this latter mode, one is interested not simply in addressing problems but also in showing the extent to which thinking tends to be confined within a set of problematizations.
>
> Like all dilemmas, this one has no simple resolution. All critical enterprises must operate partly within established conversations . . . and partly outside of them by showing that what is talked about is a limited mode of problematization.[30]

Shapiro practices what he preaches; his prose is intentionally designed to challenge us to think "at a distance," so that we can better appreciate the need to do so.[31] And so "the dilemma of intelligibility" points to how to get beyond the dilemmas of accessibility. Replacing the latter dilemmas with the former does not "solve" the problem; instead, the problems of the latter are transformed. As with most things, the question is not what will solve the problem as much as what problems are we willing to live with. I am suggesting that "the dilemma of intelligibility" is a better problem to live with. The issues of accessibility continually put scholars at risk of co-optation. The issues of intelligibility offer a better route to keeping alive the critical capacity to challenge power. If welfare scholars want their work to be politically effective in ways that do more than simply reinforce the prevailing structures of power, they need to risk being abstract and even unintelligible, all in the name of preserving their capacity for dissent. What will be gained in the process may more than compensate for the moments of confusion that will inevitably arise when challenging people to think anew, when helping people to unlearn the common sense of things, when disseminating a new vocabulary to give voice to that which has been marginalized. It seems that this is a better politics even if it has its own dilemmas.

Better to work at a distance so as to create new spaces for that which has been left out, than to work in the all-too-cozy environment of the safe and sanitized space of the already occupied public sphere and end up only reinforcing the terms of exclusion that keep the marginalized on the outside.

Therefore, ironically, the critical theorist or even the postmodernist theorist who works with a challenging vocabulary may be the one who is "closest" to the people, especially if "the people" are all those who have been regimented into the public sphere on terms that leave their concerns at the margins of public discourse and on the bottom of the public agenda.[32] Only a destabilizing counterdiscourse developed at a distance from the vernacular of the public sphere can help give voice to those marginalized concerns. By providing a means to name that which has been silenced, the lexicon developed from a distance provides an important public service. And as was mentioned earlier, this often involves renaming things as their opposite. In the case of welfare dependency, it involves renaming many of its instances as acts of independence, say by women who are escaping an abusive relationship by going on welfare or by women who are willing to apply for welfare in spite of the stigmatization and demonization that is heaped on them, all in the name of acting to save their children from the worst devastations of poverty. Working at a distance, such critical vocabularies re-mark these acts of passive welfare dependency as active assertions of independence enacted by women who are "heroes of their own lives."[33]

While working at a distance to give voice to that which has been silenced is potentially politically powerful work, it needs translation back into accessible modes of apprehension if it is to be politically effective. Traversing the lines of translation can get tricky. And so working at a distance presents its own dilemma. Yet, this dilemma is the better one, much to be preferred, for with it comes the hope of keeping alive the capacity to resist, dissent, challenge the sedimented ways of understanding and enacting social relations. The potential of supporting the oppressed in their challenge to power is greater when working at a distance.

In Struggle

While there is a role for writing that popularizes important ideas, the notion that welfare scholarship on its own can mobilize the mass public to support progressive change needs to be challenged as Skocpol suggests. I would add that politically effective welfare scholarship is more likely to occur when it is not written simply for a general audience. Politically effective scholarship is more likely to occur when it is tied to ongoing political struggle by the oppressed. In other words, critical distance need not mean disconnectedness. A good example is the writing of Frances Fox Piven and Richard Cloward.[34] They worked with low-income groups who already were struggling to resist oppression and offered new strategies for helping make those struggles more effective. Yet they wrote no simple pamphlets or brochures to disseminate their view beyond their immediate activist community. They used their theoretical writings in the 1960s and early 1970s to energize themselves and other activists and then work actively in face-to-face meetings and organized sessions to make the welfare rights movement a reality—one that almost resulted in the adoption of a guaranteed income policy for the entire country. The political effectiveness of their scholarship was the result of its ongoing connection to the welfare rights movement.

Their writing did not pander to the middle class with appeals that were bound to be co-optive. And with good reason. There are thousands of examples of how appeals to the middle class to "leave no child behind," to "invest in the next generation," to "do it for the children," to "put families first," to think of "us all as family," and so on, never work. It is time to give up on this failed strategy, which, if it were ever to succeed, would only end up reinscribing poor people's subordination for failing to measure up to middle-class standards. When it comes to poverty, the whole strategy of showing how "they" are like "us" goes nowhere that is good more often than not. A better approach is to write about welfare and poverty as part of ongoing struggle. Writing disconnected from struggle is of limited political value and is always vulnerable to falling into the trap of thinking writing can mobilize a broad population on its own. Such conceit leads to the self-defeating strategies of trying to appeal to the middle class in ways that end up reinforcing the very obstacles to change that ought to be attacked.

Conclusion

There are dilemmas of accessibility that haunt welfare scholarship today in its quest for political effectiveness. Some seek to make their work more accessible in the sense of appealing to the middle class so as to increase its political feasibility and heighten its chances of acceptance by the mass public.

Others seek to achieve that same result by writing in ways that make their work easier to comprehend, often by limiting their analyses to a relatively straightforward presentation of facts. While the first sacrifices all the concerns that do not resonate with the middle class, the second risks political ineffectiveness in spite of or even because of its simplicity.

Strategies that will assuage the middle class will only take us so far. Clear factual presentations will not by themselves provide people with a reason to believe. In both cases, the push for more generous forms of social provision will not be sufficiently served by such writing. This will not give us an effective "praxis for the poor." Instead, what is most urgently needed is a counterdiscourse that can challenge the prevailing "assume the worst" discourse on welfare recipients. What is needed is a counterdiscourse that undermines the basic assumptions of the reigning discourse of suspicion and provides the basis for a credible alternative interpretive framework. Welfare scholarship that can help disseminate an effective counterdiscourse will be attacking the problem at its roots and planting the seeds for a more tolerant political culture. Such work on discourse can help keep alive the capacity to dissent, and to do so effectively. And by standing outside the reigning structures of intelligibility, it creates the capacity to work more effectively within them. Work on a counterdiscourse more so than efforts that do not challenge the prevailing interpretive framework can end up creating a stronger basis for achieving the goals of more universal forms of social provision. The potential for welfare scholarship to help facilitate social change is perhaps better realized when such scholarship ironically seeks not to speak directly to the middle class in its accepted idiom. Rather than try to resolve the dilemmas of accessibility, it might be better to learn to live with the dilemma of intelligibility. Critical theory, offering challenging vocabularies, can perhaps better serve the oppressed in their attempts to give voice to their marginalized concerns. Politically engaged scholarship in this sense is neither moderate in its appeal nor simple in its presentation. Instead, it is challenging in both senses by forcing all who come across it to rethink beyond the bounds of acceptable political discourse.

The real potential for welfare scholarship lies in the process of changing conceptual resources available for thinking about social policy issues. Such work can make its contribution most forcefully at the very basic level of creating intellectual resources for changing the broader culture of society. It can help create new cultural resources for rethinking questions of social welfare in more critical terms. At this basic level, it can make its most effective contributions to inform other efforts geared toward political mobilization. Creating new vocabularies to give voice to marginalized concerns becomes the most important public service of welfare scholarship.

Working for social change involves many dimensions and must of necessity employ many different actors—some who give more emphasis to theory and some more to action. The role of welfare scholarship cannot be to do it all, at once, and for all, in writing. Welfare scholarship has its delimited roles to play. One important role is attending to the prevailing modes of apprehension that are ascendant in the public sphere. Creating the space to critique those modes is important work that should not be passed over in the rush to make welfare scholarship immediately accessible to a broad audience. And doing such work in the context ongoing political struggle is critical to ensuring its political effectiveness.

2

The Future of the Past

Jane Addams and the Social Work of Politics

Forging a better future for social science in social welfare necessarily involves rethinking the relationship of theory to practice.[1] In the late nineteenth and early twentieth centuries, Jane Addams was already demonstrating how social theory could be related to social practice in ways that engender fruitful connections between the two. While I do not agree with all of Addams's thinking, especially elements of her reformism, her work provides a model for thinking about theorizing practice and, in the process, suggests how we can better practice theory. A better future for social science in social welfare might well best be informed by revisiting Jane Addams as a theorist who was actively involved in practice and as a practitioner whose writings suggested alternative ways of doing theory.[2] In the process, Addams's combining of theory and practice points toward important dimensions of a "praxis for the poor" that grows out of a symbiotic relationship between social science research and social welfare politics.

Jane Addams's Feminist Theory of Democracy

There is renewed interest in Jane Addams as a theorist of democracy.[3] Long considered an important figure both in the development of social work as a profession and as an activist for world peace who won the Nobel Prize, Addams was vulnerable—throughout her career up until her death in 1935 and even long thereafter—to a variety of criticisms.[4] While the men of the Chicago School of Sociology dismissed her work as unscientific, later even as great a sociologist such as C. Wright Mills repudiated her as paternalistic in her treatment of the poor.[5] For a time, feminists derided her "maternalism" and her emphasis on the differences between men and women.[6] Yet, most important for my purposes here, for most of the twentieth century,

Addams was never really taken seriously as a theorist of democracy. She was considered a lowly settlement-house worker who concentrated on practical matters of social work rather than on the grand theories of democracy and social justice. This view is now changing, creating exciting opportunities for reexamining her activism and rethinking her role as a social theorist. The rediscovery of Addams as not only an important activist but also an important theorist raises profound questions regarding the meaning of democratic citizenship, the nature of social justice, the sources of knowledge and power, the relationship of theory to practice, and even the future of social science in social welfare.

The argument I make in this chapter suggests that Addams's work of the late nineteenth and early twentieth centuries, even as it was infused with the reformism of the social gospel of her time, parallels thinking that today falls under the rubrics of feminism, multiculturalism, and poststructuralism.[7] Addams did not live in a time when such terms were used, and she did not articulate her concerns in the contemporary vocabularies of these critical theories. Yet, her work shares much in common with these approaches and can be read using today's terminology. My central argument is that Addams's work in the past offers us a model for the future, especially in terms of her treatment of the question of "otherness." In what follows, contrary to her critics, I suggest that Addams's distinctive approach to working with oppressed people serves as a basis for a more "bottom-up" approach to creating knowledge about poverty.[8] I analyze how her thinking on "otherness" created the basis for what today might be called a critical-pragmatist and feminist conception of citizenship.[9] I suggest that Addams came to see this conception of citizenship as critical to promoting justice in a democracy. This conception of citizenship is dependent upon, and grows out of, everyday social relations necessary to sustain life in the immediate and concrete circumstances in which people find themselves. Addams provides us with a basis for suggesting that what is today being called "democratic justice"[10] is a justice contingent upon something other than choosing between the much-debated alternatives of a "politics of redistribution" and a "politics of recognition."[11] Universalistic justice holds all to the same standards irrespective of the circumstances that affect their ability to meet those standards. Democratic justice modifies such abstract standards of justice to account for difference and to allow it to thrive.

The role of the "other" in Addams's feminist theory of democracy highlights how "democratic justice" is better seen as being dependent for its realization on developing what Emmanuel Levinas refers to as an "ethic of alterity," one that accepts the other as other and does not insist on trying to understand the other in terms of the self.[12] Further, Jane Addams's work represents what today's feminist, postcolonial theorist Maria C. Lugones calls the "politics of loving," where the privileged go beyond just trying to understand the other to allowing themselves to be challenged by how the other sees them and their privileges, thereby providing the basis for more equitable encounters of mutual respect.[13]

In what follows, I analyze how these parallels suggest there is an affinity between Addams's treatment of the "other" and the way contemporary critical vocabularies suggest that democratic justice is dependent upon learning to live with rather than reject what Homi Bhabha calls the "anxiety of signification" and the impossibility of neatly categorizing the diversity of life in terms of any lexicon or taxonomy for ordering social relations.[14] From this perspective, our overriding concern should be to readdress the ways that these practices for ordering social relations inevitably instigate processes of marginalization. Informed by what William Connolly calls a "politics of becoming," a democratic justice of this sort is one that grows out of citizens' efforts of mutual aid, whereby daily encounters to address injuries and inequities engender an open-ended process of inclusion.[15]

Therefore, examining the role of the "other" in Addams's feminist theory of democracy creates an opportunity to suggest not only that she was an activist who was a theorist, but also that she was a critical pragmatist and cultural feminist who anticipated the need for what amounts to a poststructural political theory of justice.

Such an examination therefore suggests how the "social work" of everyday mutual aid is a critical dimension of the politics of state building and therefore how a "politics of survival" that grows out of everyday concerns is related to a "politics of social change" that focuses on long-run structural transformation.[16] In what follows, I argue that the major implication of the role of the "other" in Addams's feminist theory of democracy is that for citizenship to contribute to the promotion of justice, it must necessarily entail the ongoing engagement with others in their immediate circumstances and in terms of their concrete needs.[17]

The "Other" in Jane Addams's Feminist Theory of Democracy

Addams is a seductive writer. This is arguably the case because she is a feminist, a pragmatist, and someone who has a very conscious, well-developed understanding of democratic justice as something that grows out of engagement with others in their immediate circumstances and the concrete problems they confront. Her ostensibly simple prose is so directed at immediate problems and everyday circumstances that philosophical claims are stated as asides. She more often than not enacts her philosophy rather than defends it. Even in her most explicitly theoretical work, her first book, *Democracy and Social Ethics*, the big ideas of the philosophical tradition are not given attention at the expense of detailed examination of the requirements for good living in the face of burgeoning poverty in the industrializing city.[18] In fact, Addams's more philosophical claims are more frequently found in her memoir and the personal reminiscences in *Twenty Years at Hull House*.[19] Therefore, it is not entirely surprising that some wanted to dismiss her as a serious thinker[20] and others worked hard to denigrate the "applied" part of her work as not "scientific."[21]

Yet, there is ample evidence that Addams was a very serious thinker, deeply immersed in the intellectual currents of her time, and actively involved in exchanging ideas with like-minded women and men who visited Hull House, such as Charlotte Perkins Gilman, Florence Kelley, John Dewey, and George Herbert Mead.[22] Addams was influenced by and herself influenced developments in pragmatism just as she was influenced by and influenced the developing cultural feminism of the era.[23] As both a critical pragmatist and cultural feminist, Addams insisted that the sources of knowledge for democratically just citizenship were derived from active engagement with the immediate circumstances that confronted those struggling to survive. She wrote:

> Perhaps the last and greatest difficulty in the paths of those who are attempting to define and attain a social morality, is that which arises from the fact that they cannot adequately test the value of their efforts, cannot indeed be sure of their motives until their efforts are reduced to action and are presented in some workable form of social conduct or control. For action is indeed the sole medium of expression for ethics. We continually forget that the sphere of morals is the sphere of action, that speculation in regard to morality is but observation and must remain in the sphere of intellectual comment, that a situation does not really become moral until we are confronted with the question of what shall be done in a concrete case, and are obliged to act upon our theory. A stirring appeal has lately been made by a recognized ethical lecturer who has declared that "It is insanity to expect to receive the data of wisdom by looking on. We arrive at moral knowledge

only by tentative and observant practice. We learn how to apply the new insight by having attempted to apply the old and having found it to fail."[24]

As the foregoing suggests, the source of knowledge for democratic justice for Addams was derived from a relationship where theory was not given priority over practice.[25] In this vein, Addams wrote: "[T]he quite unlooked-for result of the studies would seem to indicate that while the strain and perplexity of the situation is felt most keenly by the educated and self-conscious members of the community, the tentative and actual attempts at adjustment are largely coming through those who are simpler and less analytical."[26]

Addams added: "Reform movements tend to become negative and lose their educational value for the mass of the people. . . . In trying to better matters, however, they have in mind only political achievements which they detach in a curious way from the rest of life, and they speak and write of the purification of politics as a thing set apart from daily life."[27] A profound understanding of the relationship of theory to practice was, therefore, implied by Addams's insistence that the way to usher in a more democratically just society was through working with the impoverished in their immediate circumstances. She also saw this as something that involved working citizen to citizen, in encounters of mutual aid and learning, thereby empowering themselves to build a better society that appreciated differences rather than erased them. Of relevance here is that Addams had her own version of the pragmatist's emphasis on experimentalism as the source of knowledge regarding democratic justice. Yet, she emphasized an experimentalism focused on active engagement with others in their immediate circumstances and in terms of their concrete needs. For Addams this meant that justice was more a process than an end result—a process that involved its own ethicality and sensitivity to how to go about working with others. Addams noted:

> Such a demand is reasonable, for by our daily experience we have discovered that we cannot mechanically hold up a moral standard, then jump at it in rare moments of exhilaration when we have the strength for it, but that even as the ideal itself must be a rational development of life, so the strength to attain it must be secured from interest in life itself. We slowly learn that life consists of processes as well as results, and that failure may come quite as easily from ignoring the adequacy of one's method as from selfish or ignoble aims.[28]

Therefore, instead of giving priority to theory, the primary source of knowledge about democratic justice quite explicitly for Addams derived from the encounter between self and other in their immediate circumstances and in terms of their concrete needs. Knowledge of democratically just citizenship arose from these encounters in a way that did more than simply invert the relationship of theory to practice. In the process, priority was given to the encounter itself as the source of knowledge for democratic justice. Such knowledge acted to produce community without conformity as people in the industrializing city were nurtured to respect the differences among what Addams called their "cosmopolitan neighbors."[29]

For Addams, the major way in which democratic justice could be activated was by equalizing access to the self-determining power of education. Yet, the inequitable circumstances of the industrializing city required that education and economic reform would have to work hand in glove. For Addams, education was a major source of empowerment needed in the struggle to achieve democratic justice. Addams wrote: "Doubtless the heaviest burden of our contemporaries is a consciousness of a divergence between our democratic theory on the one hand, that working people have a right to the intellectual resources of society, and the actual fact on the other hand, that thousands of them are so overburdened with toil that there is not leisure nor energy left for the cultivation of the mind."[30]

Yet, a democratically just education was especially education that instilled and encouraged not only self-determination but also community-mindedness. Addams, like Dewey, preferred what we can call "citizenship education" over the "character education" that she saw practiced in the schools. Addams wrote: "The educators should certainly conserve the learning and training necessary for successful individual and family life, but should add to that a preparation for the enlarged social efforts which our increasing democracy requires. The democratic ideal demands of the school that it shall give the child's own experience a social value; that it shall teach him to direct his own activities and adjust them to those of other people."[31] For Addams, education for democracy meant more than imposing dominant social norms on the lower orders of society; instead, it meant teaching one and all how to interact in ways that valued and affirmed difference and allowed democratic justice to flourish.

Yet, if education was the critical ingredient for creating a citizenship that could work toward democratic justice, it was then the encounter with the "other" that made democratically just citizenship come alive. In this respect, Addams went beyond the core pragmatism of Dewey and others.[32]

She was not content to simply put her faith in the people, to prize social intelligence, and to aspire to a democracy of inquirers who can learn from one another. She wanted more than what the pragmatists called the "cognitive division of labor."[33] While social intelligence was a critically important concept for Addams, she supplemented it with an ethic of otherness that was not emphasized by Dewey and other pragmatists. Dewey criticized liberalism for failing to appreciate how individuals need to be understood as embedded in social relationships; and he was suspicious of what we can call republican and communitarian ideas for assuming the extent to which people could be treated as all the same.[34] He emphasized that experience was the source of knowledge, intelligence was social, individuals were interdependent, and the community was made up of diverse people. Yet he did not go as far as Addams in grounding his call for a democratic community in the encounter with the other. This need to be in relation to the other was Addams's most distinctive contribution to the pragmatism and feminism of her day and a major part of her legacy.

Addams not only stated that "the cure for the ills of Democracy is more Democracy," but she added that democracy was a product of "diversified human experience and [its] resultant sympathy."[35] As with other pragmatists, for Addams citizenship was about more than rights; it was about relationships.[36] Yet, quite distinctively, for her, this involved a conscious attempt to value otherness on its own terms. She stressed that the local encounters of diverse peoples could even help usher in global movements for world peace.[37] Addams wrote:

> We are thus brought to a conception of Democracy not merely as a sentiment which desires the well-being of all men, nor yet as a creed which believes in the essential dignity and equality of all men, but as that which affords a rule of living as well as a test of faith. We are learning that a standard of social ethics is not attained by traveling a sequestered byway, but by mixing on the thronged and common road where all must turn out for one another, and at least see the size of one another's burdens. To follow the path of social morality results perforce in the temper if not the practice of the democratic spirit, for it implies that diversified human experience and resultant sympathy which are found and guarantee of Democracy. . . .
>
> We realize, too, that social perspective and sanity of judgment come only from contact with social experience; that such contact is the surest corrective of opinions concerning the social order, and concerning efforts, however humble, for its improvement. Indeed, it is a consciousness of the

illuminating and dynamic value of this wider and more thorough human experience which explains in no small degree that new curiosity regarding human life which has more of a moral basis than an intellectual one.[38]

Democratically just citizenship was built from the bottom up not the top down; it was grounded in the encounters of mutual aid necessary to sustain everyday life. Yet, more importantly, it required getting to know, and not just accepting but living with, the other on her or his terms. Addams wrote:

> We have learned as common knowledge that much of the insensibility and hardness of the world is due to the lack of imagination which prevents a realization of the experiences of other people. Already there is a conviction that we are under a moral obligation in choosing our experiences, since the result of those experiences must ultimately determine our understanding of life. We know instinctively that if we grow contemptuous of our fellows, and consciously limit our intercourse to certain kinds of people whom we have previously decided to respect, we not only tremendously circumscribe our range of life, but limit the scope of our ethics. . . . Thus the identification with the common lot which is the essential idea of Democracy becomes the source and expression of social ethics.[39]

In the process of emphasizing the importance of otherness, Addams is constantly destabilizing the reader's implied understanding of self and other. The most striking dimension of Addams's writing in this regard is how the reader is often caught off guard by the subtle way in which she alludes to her subject. While at times still using the male pronoun, the citizen is often the woman at home, forced to resort to a variety of means to make survival in the city possible for her family. Addams therefore anticipates effectively feminist arguments on citizenship and social welfare that suggest that, in order to overcome the prevailing gender biases operating in the political economy, we need to assume the woman as caregiver as the modal citizen and organize political and economic relations, social provision included, around that.[40] Addams writes:

> This instinct to conserve the old standards, combined with a distrust of the new standard, is a constant difficulty in the way of those experiments and advances depending upon the initiative of women, both because women are the more sensitive to the individual and family claims, and be-

> cause their training has tended to make them content with the response to these claims alone. . . . In considering the changes which our increasing democracy is constantly making upon various relationships, it is impossible to ignore the filial relation.[41]

The citizen/subject in need of education and uplift is also often the privileged, who would become real democratic citizens only if they began to live among the poor and, through their daily encounters, come to be educated in the needs of others as others in all their diversity. Addams's muted, understated, impersonal language jars and unsettles us, it afflicts us, especially when we come to realize she is talking more about "us" than "them." In this way, mutual aid and the equality that comes from shared learning come alive in these moments of realization. Addams underscored "our" need to learn from the "other" when she wrote: "There is a pitiful failure to recognize the situation in which the majority of working people are placed, a tendency to ignore their real experiences and needs, and most stupid of all, we leave quite untouched affections and memories which would afford a tremendous dynamic if they were utilized."[42]

The Politics of Social Work

Other expectations are upset while one reads *Democracy and Social Ethics*. Charlene Haddock Seigfried has emphasized Addams's purposeful shaping of the reader's response through the organization of her topics.[43] The first half consists of chapters on efforts of social amelioration in the context of everyday life, that is, personal and family relations. From there, the book broadens out to discuss issues of the community, the workplace, education, and political reform. Addams is structuring her argument on the need for a new social ethic to inform democracy by grounding that ethic, and the public participation it calls for, in the encounters of mutual aid that arise in everyday life. A new ethic of democracy necessarily then becomes an ethic of encounter. Citizenship moves from being about rights to being about relationships.

Yet, the most telling feature of the structure of the book is that it starts with the charitable relationship as the paradigmatic one for all the relationships that are to ground the new ethic for democracy. Addams could not be more explicit in her attempt to argue that democratically just citizenship is about relationships, encounters, engagements of mutual aid than when she follows the introduction of *Democracy and Social Ethics* with a chapter entitled "Charitable Effort." And her critique of the charity workers' ethics of measuring all according to the normative standard of individual success further underscores how it is "us" and not "them" who are the objects of inquiry, how the problem of education is as much one for the privileged as the oppressed, and how democratically just citizenship is about learning to promote our mutual interdependence so that we can all grow into a more equitable and democratically just set of social relations. Addams wrote:

> It is quite obvious that the ethics of none of us are clearly defined, and we are continually obliged to act in circles of habit, based upon convictions which we no longer hold. . . . It is largely in this modern tendency to judge all men by one democratic standard, while the old charitable attitude commonly allowed the use of two standards, that much of the difficulty adheres. We know that unceasing bodily toil becomes wearing and brutalizing, and our position is totally untenable if we judge large numbers of our fellows solely upon their success in maintaining it. . . .
>
> The daintily clad charitable visitor who steps into the little house made untidy by the vigorous efforts of her hostess, the washerwoman, is no longer sure of her superiority to the latter; she recognizes that her hostess after all represents social value and industrial use, as over against her own parasitic cleanliness and a social standing attained only through status. . . . The charity visitor finds herself still more perplexed when she comes to consider such problems as those of early marriage and child labor; for she cannot deal with them according to economic theories, or according to the conventions which have regulated her own life. She finds both of these fairly upset by her intimate knowledge of the situation, and her sympathy for those into whose lives she has gained a curious insight.[44]

Therefore, the encounter between the helping and the helped not only subverts our best intentions, revises our understandings of the sources of knowledge, and inverts the relationship of theory to practice, but it also opens the door to the possibility of appreciating "otherness" on its own terms according to its own needs and standards of judgment. Addams clearly suggests not so much that all citizens must become social work professionals, but that we, as citizens, must all recognize the need to execute the social work of politics if there is to be social justice. And just as she starts the book suggesting that there is a politics to social work and helping, so she ends the book by showing how there is a social work to politics.

The Social Work of Politics

For years, Addams had been interpreted as an educator of the poor who promoted moral uplift and personal self-reliance as the roads out of poverty.[45] Revisionist interpretations have since underscored how Addams was at pains to understand the poor on their own terms.[46] Yet, *Democracy and Social Ethics* is arguably not really as much about "them" as it is about "us." Its emphasis on education cuts both ways—the privileged need to learn from the oppressed as much as the other way around. Addams's arguments about good citizenship are grounded in promoting more and better encounters between the two as a way to begin to overcome the growing isolation and marginalization of the poor in the industrializing city. Citizenship is a duty, a duty that the privileged have abrogated.

The issue of role models brings Addams's concept of citizenship into the contemporary context. In recent years, much attention has been given to William Julius Wilson's hypothesis that with civil rights legislation prohibiting segregationist and discriminatory practices in housing, the opening of the suburbs to the African-American middle class has led to a decline of their presence in inner-city African-American neighborhoods and the resultant decline in available role models for poor black youths.[47] The increased marginalization and isolation of what is now called the "black underclass" has led to increased pathology in those neighborhoods with higher crime rates, greater school dropout rates, increased teen pregnancy, more mother-only families, and so forth.

The merits of this argument have been the subject of intense scrutiny and debate. The question of role models, however, is somewhat different for Addams, perhaps even inverted. For Addams, in *Democracy and Social Ethics*, the question of role models is not how the privileged can represent a standard for the oppressed but more the other way around. For Addams, the oppressed in their shared plight naturally resort to mutual aid and in that way give the privileged a model of the democratically just citizen. Addams wrote:

> [T]he young woman who has succeeded in expressing her social compunction through charitable effort finds that the wider social activity, and

> the contact with the larger experience, not only increases her sense of moral obligation but at the same time recasts her social ideals. She is chagrined to discover that in the actual task of reducing her social scruples to action, her humble beneficiaries are far in advance of her, not in charity or singleness of purpose, but in self-sacrificing action.[48]

Addams's concern for role models extended to the captains of industry such as George Pullman, who practiced a kind of paternalism that enabled them to claim superiority in knowledge and other respects because it was they who extended benefits to their employees. Addams called Pullman "a modern Lear" for his behavior during the strike of 1894. For Addams, Shakespeare's King Lear epitomized self-serving paternalism.[49] She wrote, in a passage that resisted explicitly naming Pullman as a "model employer," even as it is he who is being singled out:

> To perform too many good deeds may be to lose the power of recognizing good in others; to be too absorbed in carrying out a personal plan of improvement may be to fail to catch the great moral lesson which our times offer. . . . What he does attain, however, is not the result of his individual striving, as a solitary mountain-climber beyond that of the valley multitude but it is sustained and upheld by the sentiments and aspiration of many others. . . . The man who disassociates his ambition, however disinterested, from the cooperation of his fellows, always takes this risk of ultimate failure. . . . [T]he employer is too often cut off from the social ethics developing in regard to our larger social relationships, and from the great moral life springing from our common experiences. This is sure to happen when he is good "to" people rather than "with" them, when he allows himself to decide what is best for them instead of consulting them. He thus misses the rectifying influence of that fellowship which is so big that it leaves no room for sensitiveness or gratitude. Without this fellowship we may never know how great the divergence between ourselves and others may become, nor how cruel the misunderstandings.[50]

The role models for the "model" employer were ironically the very workers whom he oppressed with his paternalistic policies. The oppressed were the ones who knew best how the social order oppressed them. They also were the ones whose experiences gave rise to the knowledge of how to respond to such circumstances. They were the ones who developed an ethical sensibility for mutual aid and built that into their citizenship. The typical privileged "good citizen" was too disconnected from the politics of survival of the oppressed to be able to offer a model for a democratically just citizenship or its politics. Addams wrote:

> The wide divergence of experience makes it difficult for the good citizen to understand this point of view. . . . This results in a certain repellant manner, commonly regarded as the apparel of righteousness. . . . The success of the reforming politician who insists upon mere purity of administration and upon the control and suppression of the unruly elements in the community, may be the easy result of a narrowing and selfish process. For the painful condition of endeavoring to minister to genuine social needs, through the political machinery, and at the same time to remodel that machinery so that it shall be adequate to its new task, is to encounter the inevitable discomfort of a transition into a new type of democratic relation.[51]

Addams saw democratically just citizenship not in terms of rights but in terms of relationships—encounters that created the capacity to learn from the "other," whereby such a democratic knowledge, produced from the bottom up, gave rise to new forms of mutual aid. The result would be a greater sense of solidarity even as people learned to value their differences. And for Addams, the key to creating solidarity was rejecting the idea that antagonism or conflict is an ineliminable part of life and thought. By recognizing that antagonism need not exist and finding affinity in relationships beyond conflict, we can begin to work for a democratic justice.[52]

From Charity to Love

Addams's work was also strikingly visionary in that it anticipated the contemporary interventions of postcolonial feminist activists. Her efforts, I would suggest, most dramatically represent what today the feminist, postcolonial theorist Maria C. Lugones calls the "politics of loving."[53] A politics of loving builds on, but goes beyond, the idea of "walking a mile in someone else's shoes" to where the privileged not only see the world through the eyes of those who are marginalized, but also come to see how they themselves are seen by those marginalized. The recognition achieved through such encounters creates the basis for mutual respect and the foundation for moving beyond oppression. Addams's model for democratically just citizenship called for nothing less than a "politics of loving."

In this sense, Jane Addams's settlement at Hull House was never simply a place where the poor got help. It was an important social experiment in which the privileged were as much the subjects as were the poor. It was not solely a way of helping the poor but also a way of promoting a social solidarity that valued difference. Hull House was in part created as a place where women of privilege could do good work while they remained excluded from positions of influence in the academy and other major institutions. It also provided a way by which the classes could be brought together in relations of mutual aid; in so doing, it became a site for constructing democratically just citizenship. There is merit in highlighting, as David Wagner has recently done, how relations of aid, particularly in the form of organized charity, can be self-serving, functioning primarily to assuage the guilt and rationalize the status of the privileged.[54] Yet, there is arguably also much merit in Addams's more sophisticated understanding of how such relations, properly conducted, could form the basis of a "social work of politics" that would engender a democratically just form of citizenship.

Addams was late in life recognized to some extent as a model citizen on just the terms she was articulating. Her ability to do charitable work without being patronizing was a point that was emphasized when Addams late in her life was awarded, in 1931, Bryn Mawr College's M. Carey Thomas Prize for contributions to "American Living"—the same year she received word that she was to be given the Nobel Peace Prize.[55] Jane Addams died in 1935 still committed to making politics a form of social work and social work a form of politics, still committed to viewing the struggles of everyday life as opportunities to practice citizenship. From her understandings of the relationship of theory and practice to the relationship of public and private life, Addams was a cultural feminist and pragmatist whose writings pose important issues for those who seek to promote democratically just citizenship.

Beyond Antagonism

In life and thought, Jane Addams sought to transcend the dichotomies that hold us back from realizing affinity between ideas and among persons. She sought to move beyond the "either/or." Beginning with a rejection of the theory/practice dichotomy, her quest to highlight the affinity in superficial oppositions included that of mind and body, and self and other. The model

Jane Addams offers us today is one that we, as social workers, citizens, human beings, need to take seriously. Insisting on finding antagonism and pursuing conflict, for Addams, would only end in violence.[56] At the most basic of levels, this is where Jane Addams found her pacifism. The road to world peace was to be found in transcending antagonism, resisting dichotomous thinking, looking for affinity, and practicing reconciliation.[57] It is for this reason that, even though Addams was for all practical purposes a feminist and a socialist, she sought not so much to punish the privileged for the injustices of capitalism; instead, she sought to find ways for those of privilege to learn affinity for the people subordinated by the economic order. In this sense, Addams was not a revolutionary but a reformer. She sought to get beyond antagonism in order to engender cooperative efforts to overcome injustice.

Addams, however, may have failed to appreciate how revolution and reform are interrelated. For instance, Frances Fox Piven and Richard Cloward beginning in the 1960s consistently emphasized how a more dramatic and disruptive revolutionary politics of dissensus was always needed in order to get even more incremental reforms. Therefore, consistent with Addams's insistence that we transcend dichotomies, we might want to stress the interrelationships between antagonism and cooperation rather than their antinomies. It is then in her insistence to get beyond dichotomies that Addams was perhaps actually a revolutionary.

Conclusion

Applying a contemporary vocabulary to the writings of Jane Addams provides a basis for seeing the past as an important part of the future. It enables us to recognize Jane Addams as a profound social and political theorist even though she was not recognized as such from the time she wrote until this very day. It is likely that Jane Addams was not considered a serious theorist for many years for no other reason than that she was a woman. Yet, such an explanation oversimplifies the matter. As a woman and as a feminist, Addams grounded her considerations of how to achieve a democratically just citizenship in the particulars of everyday life and the struggles for survival that were enacted in the private lives of ordinary families. This approach, with its emphasis on the everyday, the ordinary, the concrete, made it far easier for those who did read her works to dismiss them as not directly focused on the matters of state building.

Yet, as a feminist, Addams knew that these private issues were critical to forging the public sphere, and in addition, that such ostensibly private issues suggested how care and mutual support were critical to social life broadly construed. And as a feminist, Addams knew that citizenship was more about caring relations of mutual support than it was about individual rights. Educating the privileged as well as the oppressed to a democratically just citizenship involved promoting an ethic of encounter that embraced the other on her or his terms and that struggled to communicate, cooperate, and coordinate social exchanges for the betterment of all. Such a democratically just citizenship involved more than the redistribution of material resources and the recognition of differences. It involved an ethics of encounter not just for those engaged in charitable work but for all citizens. An important chiasmus lay at the heart of Addams's political theory: the social work of politics required a recognition of the politics of social work. Yet, for too long the marginalization of Addams as a serious political thinker and the sequestration of social work in a specialized profession reduced the visibility of this recognition. We can hope that this is now changing.

The Addams model also points to the need for social welfare research to broaden its horizons, paying more attention to the social forces at work in reproducing poverty. And perhaps now moving beyond Addams, it should do this in a way that strengthens the capacity for people to resist those forces more effectively. In this way, Addams's work from the past contributes to, if it does not fully define, a future for radical incrementalism. Addams shows us that starting with the real, immediate problems of struggle is the necessary first step for better theories and a better social science. Addams points the way: first go to the people, be among them, and work with them, reflect on their conditions and constraints, gain perspective through identification, theorize practice, practice practice, continue to struggle, then resist, dissent, push for change that can make a difference in people's lives.[58] This is the better future of social science in social welfare. This is the future of radical incrementalism.

3

Radical Incrementalism Personified

The Piven and Cloward Legacy

Frances Fox Piven and Richard A. Cloward's work represents a distinctive alternative on how to combine welfare scholarship and politics. They were perhaps the most important people to have done so in the twentieth century. Piven and Cloward's work remains to this day among the most influential scholarship about issues of social welfare. Their first book, *Regulating the Poor*, published in 1971, has remained in print for over thirty years, being reissued in 1992 in an updated edition.[1] This book originally won the C. Wright Mills Award from the Society for the Study of Social Problems and over time has emerged as a modern classic in the field of social theory. Six more books followed, including *The Breaking of the American Social Compact*, published in 1997, in addition to scores of scholarly articles and essays.[2] Several of their works, particularly *Regulating the Poor* and *Poor People's Movements*,[3] have provoked continuing controversy among social theorists and activists. Their last book, *Why Americans Still Don't Vote*, revisits their successful effort in founding in 1983 Human SERVE, an organization that led the fight for the Motor Voter bill that was enacted in 1993 as the National Voter Registration Act.[4] Richard Cloward passed away in August 2001. Frances Fox Piven remains an active scholar and activist leading the fight over welfare policy.

Piven and Cloward consistently grounded all of their scholarship in the struggles for social justice, especially among the poor and oppressed. All their scholarship was directed toward understanding the limits and possibilities for social change. They pursued these studies always with an eye to helping make such change possible and worked tirelessly for social justice causes, movements, and organizations among the poor to make these changes more likely. Over the course of their careers, Piven and Cloward's combining scholarship and activism have been subject to intense criticism. In what follows, I defend them from much of this criticism and suggest that they do indeed offer a laudable model of how to combine scholarship and politics. I suggest how their approach contributes to what I call "radical incrementalism."[5] "Radical incrementalism" involves pushing for substantial change while learning to take what the powerful will concede. It is for me one major way a critical left can still be politically relevant in the face of entrenched power.

My analysis is in good part designed to make a contribution to the literature on the growing role of social scientists in the public policymaking process. Rather than focus on the increasingly noted rise of think-tank researchers inside the beltway of the nation's capital, I look at Piven and Cloward as offering a better model, one that is more powerful in its ability to resist the political co-optation to which think-tank research has proven so vulnerable.[6] Piven and Cloward's efforts to combine politics and scholarship offer a healthy antidote to the depressingly common pattern of social science being co-opted into rationalizing the powers of the state.

In what follows, I contrast their efforts to combine scholarship and politics on the issue of welfare rights in the 1960s with the efforts of Daniel P. Moynihan, a prominent politician who was also a social scientist, one who tried to have a political impact on issues of welfare and poverty. I also examine the efforts of David Ellwood, an economist from Harvard University's Kennedy School of Government who worked in the Clinton administration on behalf of welfare reform. I suggest how Piven and Cloward's work offers the superior model to those offered by Moynihan and Ellwood. Piven and Cloward's model obviates significant problems in combining scholarship and politics. It successfully combines a "politics of survival" that helped people in confronting the challenges in their everyday existence with a "politics of social change" that laid the groundwork for moving beyond the limitations of the existing social order. I suggest that such a combination is especially effective in mitigating asymmetries in power relationships between scholars and citizens that often arise when trying to combine scholarship and politics, theory and practice, social science and social welfare.

I follow this with an analysis that demonstrates that their model holds up even when examined in terms of its most controversial application—the "Crisis Strategy." This strategy, when advocated by Piven and Cloward in the mid-1960s, called for overloading the welfare system with as many recipients as possible in order to demonstrate its incapacity to meet the extant need and force evolution to something better, including the possibility of a guaranteed income.

Finally, I will deal with the issue of "radical incrementalism." I conclude by suggesting that Piven and Cloward's combination of scholarship and politics, especially in the controversial case of the Crisis Strategy, promotes a form of "radical incrementalism" that pushes for as much change as possible while recognizing that often the resulting changes that are implemented may only be modest improvements to the existing system. Their radical incrementalism is not conventional top-down interest group incrementalism designed to simply work with the powers that be in terms of what they will allow. Instead, it is very much a bottom-up strategy designed to push the limits of what is possible, but with the recognition that challenging power and the existing limits of public policy discourse does not allow for the expectation that blueprints for an ideal society will be what gets implemented.

Radical incrementalism challenges the existing constraints on the politically possible, recognizing that the changes forthcoming will be in the form of concessions at best. Yet, such concessions can improve the lives of the oppressed and marginalized and create the conditions for further incremental challenges and improvements in the future. Piven and Cloward's radical incrementalism is a commendable politics of contingency that emphasizes studying the possibilities for action and then exploiting them as best as possible. As Piven and Cloward once famously and subtly wrote: "A placid poor get nothing, but a turbulent poor sometimes get something."[7]

The Scholarship of Politics

The extent to which social scientists can and should help frame public policy is an important issue that has received attention at least since Max Weber and harkens back to issues raised by Plato in *The Republic*.[8] There is good evidence that social scientists were critical actors in the formative years when social welfare provision was being built into the modern state in a number of countries.[9] In the United States, social scientists in the years immediately after the World War II championed the idea that they could and should play a prominent role in the making of public policy.[10] By the 1960s, social scientists in the United States were increasingly participating in the making of public policy in general and social policy in particular.[11] Since then, the response has been dramatic, giving rise not only to a growing number of policy experts from within the academy but also a mushrooming of public policy think tanks.[12] The role of social scientists in the making of public policy has increased substantially to become itself a subject of social scientific inquiry.[13]

Our understandings of how public policy gets made continue to change in ways that increasingly allow for the consideration of the role of social scientists. Models of policymaking have evolved with the field moving beyond a focus on "policy triangles," "policy subsystems," "issue networks," and the like.[14] In all of these approaches, room is reserved for considering the role of experts, specialists, scientists, academics and others who can provide relevant information. A variety of pertinent issues arise in considering the role of social scientists in the making of public policy. In particular, there are important questions concerning what is the appropriate relationship between theory and practice, knowledge and power, as well as scholarship and politics.[15]

Therefore, on one level the case of Piven and Cloward should not be controversial. As "public intellectuals" whose scholarship and politics were interrelated, Piven and Cloward represented a venerable tradition committed to using knowledge to challenge power. The debates regarding Piven and Cloward's mixing of politics and scholarship therefore suggest other issues were at work. While Piven and Cloward's work remains profoundly influential and has garnered much praise, in recent years various commentators have suggested that their mixture of politics and scholarship has not been effective and has even led to perverse results.[16] Yet, it is not just questions regarding their strategy that have bothered critics. There are also questions regarding whether they, as academics, should have been willing to so tightly tie their scholarship to struggles for social justice. From the mid-1960s, Piven and Cloward were actively involved in the struggle for social justice in the United States. They of course have not been alone in this struggle. Yet, they do represent a distinctive example of combining of scholarship and politics as part of that effort, and it is this distinctive combination that underlies much of others' uneasiness with their work. Their political scholarship raises serious issues about how or whether knowledge and power and social science and social policymaking can or should be combined.

Modern social science was arguably founded on an explicit, if paradoxical, commitment to both the separateness and interrelationship of social science and politics. Max Weber's famous companion essays on "The Vocation of Science" and "The Vocation of Politics" at one level imply the need to separate politics from science; however, at another level they suggest that social science and politics need to relate to each other. Weber was deeply concerned that politics was devoid of a moral compass and in need of the tutelage that only social science could provide. The job of social science was very much, as later commentators were to have it, to speak "truth to power."[17] Yet, for Weber, social science could only come to such a state if it were to achieve legitimacy by virtue of its reputation as an authoritatively reliable source of nonpartisan and scientific knowledge. Therefore, ironically, for Weber, social science's political effect required that it remain apolitical.[18]

This paradox has played out in the twentieth century and, not surprisingly, it has remained irresolvable. Social science's tendency is to be aligned with power rather than to challenge it. The complicity of modern social science with the dominant centers of political and economic power is, I would suggest, hard to dispute. The evidence for this can be found in Dietrich Reuschemeyer and Theda Skocpol's 1996 edited volume of well-documented, if insufficiently critical, essays on the role of social science in the formative stages of the modern welfare state across a variety of countries during the catalytic years of the late nineteenth and early twentieth centuries.[19] According to several of the contributors to this volume, liberal, reform-minded social scientists, inside and outside of government, including both professional academics and amateur practitioners, as in England's "New Liberalism," promoted policies that helped rationalize a social order disrupted by a changing economy.[20] By the end of the twentieth century, noted Theodore Lowi in his 1992 presidential address to the American Political Science Association, the major fields of social science themselves had come to be assimilated into the state and were thoroughly preoccupied with meeting its needs.[21] Piven and Cloward, however, were to prove to be noteworthy exceptions to this problem.

Piven and Cloward: The Strategy of Crisis

As already noted, Piven and Cloward's writing together ranged across a number of issues that have led to a number of significant interventions in the public sphere—from helping to promote welfare rights to leading the push for the passage of the Motor Voter bill. One intervention that has received extensive commentary was their strategy in the 1960s to sign people up for welfare to overload the system and force consideration of a guaranteed income. I examine that strategy here as the critical test case for evaluating how they have combined scholarship and politics.

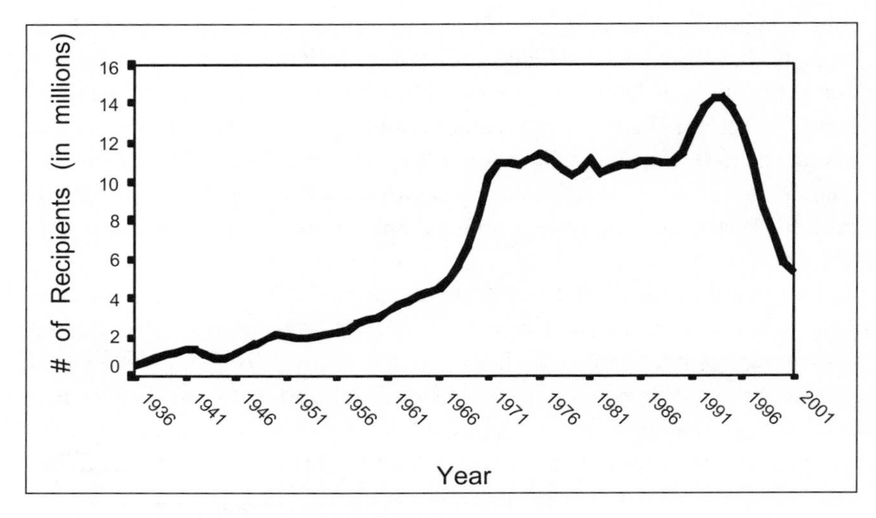

FIGURE 3.1 U.S. Welfare Recipients, 1936-2001
SOURCE: U.S. Department of Health and Human Services, http://www.acf.dhhs.gov/news/stats /newstat2.shtm. Monthly averages for each year, except for 2000 which is for October and 2001 which is for September.

The Personal Responsibility and Work Opportunity Reconciliation Act of 1996 (PRWORA) has quickly come to represent a watershed in the history of social provision in the United States.[22] In the least, it enabled President Bill Clinton to claim to have delivered on his 1992 campaign promise to "end welfare as we know it." That was more than rhetoric, for the 1996 law abolished the sixty-one-year old Aid to Families with Dependent Children (AFDC) entitlement derived from the New Deal landmark of social welfare legislation, the Social Security Act of 1935, and replaced it with the Temporary Assistance for Needy Families (TANF) block grant program.

In the process, a commitment to cash assistance to the needy was replaced with funding to move people off welfare as quickly as possible regardless of the quality of jobs and the effects on the well-being of children. The 1996 legislation time-limited welfare receipt and required work of recipients. It accelerated the already ongoing retrenchment of access to public assistance that led to massive declines in the welfare rolls from a high of 14.2 million in 1993 to 6.9 million in June 1999—the lowest level in over thirty years.[23] (See fig. 3.1.) The slide continued through 2001 with caseloads dropping to 5.3 million recipients by September.[24] This retrenchment has largely been heralded as a victory for reform even as reports from state-specific studies suggest that anywhere from one-fifth to over one-third of former recipients were not working and had reduced incomes one year after they had left welfare.[25]

The 1996 welfare reform therefore has been significant on many levels, from how it curtailed needed assistance for single women with children to how it has helped rationalize the reorganization of the United States into the rapidly emerging global political economy that heavily relies on low-wage labor. Yet, PRWORA was also an even greater milestone for some because it represented an end to what many had interpreted as an impasse over welfare that had paralyzed public policy in this area for three decades.[26] From the 1960s to the 1990s, the battle over creating income redistribution to eliminate poverty had been stuck in trench warfare over how to reform welfare. By the early 1970s, a relatively large population (in historical terms) of welfare recipients emerged. They were disproportionately persons of color who had been previously denied access to assistance in spite of their eligibility and high poverty rates. Largely through the success of litigation but also through other forms of political action, activists in the late 1960s were able to expand welfare rights.[27] In response to political agitation from below, the national government and the states took action to expand eligibility, welfare receipt lost some stigma, and as a result eligible persons became more willing to apply for assistance as welfare rights gained credibility.[28] Yet, the history of social policy since the 1960s suggests that once a program came to be seen as a "black program"—that is, a program for racial minorities—it would attract much controversy, become the center of policy debate, lose favor, and become increasingly subject to efforts aimed at retrenchment.[29]

This influx of new recipients also increased concerns about the costs to middle-class taxpayers and the consequences for low-income families of what came to be called "welfare dependency."[30] Welfare programs had never been popular in the United States, but an orchestrated campaign by corporate-sponsored critics of welfare focused on the growth in welfare participation, particularly by racial minorities. By the early 1970s, welfare policy had moved toward the center of political debate. And there it stayed for over two decades. Reform after reform during these years failed to move the welfare debate off the issue of "welfare dependency." There was no visible movement forward toward plans for a stronger welfare state, including especially a guaranteed income, or backward toward proposals for a more limited, decentralized system that relied more on private charity.

The push to scale back welfare, however, gained favor in the 1990s. It was almost as if, with the end of the Cold War, welfare, with its supposed deleterious effects on work and family, had come to replace "the scourge of Communism" as the new, if internal, enemy to the "American way of life." The social welfare policy debate increasingly moved from fighting a "war on poverty" to waging a "war on welfare" itself.[31] Popular attitudes increasingly indulged in the perspective that welfare is a program for the undeserving, especially those among racial minorities who resisted playing by the rules of middle-class white society regarding work and family.[32] The racialization of welfare reinforced the tendency of the "white" person to project repressed anxieties about the need to conform onto the "black" person. In this sense, "black" as a social construction probably always told us more about whites than it did about persons of color. Under these conditions, the proverbial "black welfare queen" represented how many whites feared their own inability to self-impose work and family values.[33] This anxiety crystallized in a growing concern about the "black underclass."[34] Such an intense process of racialization eventually succeeded in making welfare out to be a program for people who were "other" than the white and middle class. In this highly charged political environment, the 1996 law broke the deadlock in favor of the conservative approaches to eliminating the scourge of welfare dependency.

Therefore, when the dramatic changes of 1996 finally did come, it was clear that the United States would not be moving forward toward a more inclusive welfare state that provided income protection for the neediest families anywhere—white, black, or otherwise. Welfare reform that would overcome race, gender and class distinctions was not to be. Instead, the 1996 reform effort intensified such divisions.[35] It was rationalized by its proponents as necessary corrective medicine in the form of a "new paternalism" to treat a population that had grown ill with the disease of "welfare dependency."[36] The reforms were needed because "welfare dependency" was, for people like Newt Gingrich, a sure sign of how a "sick society" encouraged sickness with its failed welfare policies.[37] And once the efforts of Gingrich and others succeeded in making "welfare dependency" out to be a more important problem than poverty, they were then logically led to ask: Where did such a deleterious condition come from? Why had it created such an impasse over welfare reform? Who was responsible for this problem? The hunt for scapegoats was about to get personal.

In fact, it was not just conservative proponents of welfare reform who sought scapegoats, nor was it just politicians. This became apparent when a growing number of books reflecting various positions on the ideological spectrum appeared that also wanted to single out culprits for the failures of welfare and the years of gridlock. While many culprits were found, some were focused on more than others. In particular, for many of the critics, on both the right and the left, in the political arena and the academy, the impasse, if not the problem of welfare dependency, was largely the product of the efforts of two people—Piven and Cloward.[38] Piven and Cloward were undoubtedly preeminent scholars and activists who were very influential in contributing to the welfare rights movement that swept the country in the 1960s. More importantly, their call in the mid-1960s for a "Crisis Strategy" to overload the welfare system with as many eligible recipients as possible was a highly visible and much-discussed strategy within and without the welfare rights movement.[39] And the rolls did grow, and the country verged on replacing welfare with a guaranteed income in response to the crisis, just as Piven and Cloward had hoped. Yet, the guaranteed income did not get passed, the welfare rolls soon stabilized, if at high levels, and by the mid-1970s, political gridlock around welfare reform set in, lasting for two decades until the mid-1990s.

Piven and Cloward had also noted that tactics such as overloading the welfare system and other efforts to create political instability were basically all the political resources the poor had: "A placid poor get nothing, but a turbulent poor sometime get something."[40] Piven and Cloward subsequently wrote that civil disorder would lead to liberalization in welfare policies under the right conditions. And it is distinctly possible that that is exactly what happened in the 1960s. For instance, there is evidence that the states with the most intense rioting had the greatest increases in the welfare rolls in the late 1960s and early 1970s—a sign that civil disorder could under the right conditions be a tool for extracting concessions from the powerful.[41] In the eyes of many, however, this correlation only made Piven and Cloward vulnerable to the criticism that they encouraged the civil disorder in the form of riots by inner-city African Americans in the late 1960s. And riots and welfare would become very much interrelated in the minds of policy elites even to the point of connecting the 1960s to the 1990s.[42] In response to the Los Angeles riots in 1992 after the acquittal of the police who had beaten Rodney King, the Bush administration put out press releases indicating that the irresponsible behavior reflected by the rioters in the 1990s had been engendered by the liberal welfare policies of the 1960s.[43]

Yet, as strained as those connections were, the push to connect 1960s liberalism with 1990s policy objectives reached its pinnacle of strangeness when so many different people—politicians, social scientists, leftists—all chose to blame two specific individuals, Piven and Cloward, for the problems that have plagued welfare for three decades. Two scholars, no less. How could this be? While active in the movement, Piven and Cloward were by no means the leaders of the welfare rights movement.[44] They also were not that influential with the policymakers who increased access to assistance in those years. Their influence was very much limited to being activists in the welfare rights movement. And their focus over the next three decades moved from mobilizing welfare recipients to gain access to benefits to improving the ability of low-income people in general to be able to exercise political influence, particularly through the electoral process.[45]

Why then all the focus on these two scholars? For some on the right, the verisimilitude must have been overwhelming, for just as they tended to individualize the causes of poverty, they were preferring to locate the cause for the thirty-year impasse over welfare reform in two individuals whose political scholarship had helped promote the idea of welfare rights in the United States.[46] Like the thoughtless "modern men" Nietzsche critiques in *On the Genealogy of Morals*, these critics were in constant need to attribute personal responsibility for the events in question.[47] They could not think beyond a world in which individuals cause all things and for which individuals always must be held accountable. After all, the welfare reform legislation of 1996 was entitled the "Personal Responsibility Act." This mindset extended beyond holding recipients responsible for their own poverty to holding Piven and Cloward responsible for what had come to be called "the welfare mess." For others on the left, there was an overweening need to find someone to blame for the failure of the left to take the vitality of the '60s and convert it into significant policy advances by the '90s.[48]

The recriminations over welfare struggles, and the continuing tensions around race, riots, and reform, persisted from the 1960s to the 1990s. With the end of the century, people across the political spectrum pursued the hunt for scapegoats. What better candidates than two scholars who were not ashamed to combine scholarship and politics? What better candidates than individuals who did mobilize those in need of assistance and did contribute to their ability to gain access to that assistance? Those on the sidelines, in the back seat, on that proverbial Monday morning around the end of the century could proclaim that Piven and Cloward had taken us down the wrong path. Still others, of neither left nor right persuasion, the ever-present if equivocal liberals of social welfare policy analysis, could also blame Piven and Cloward for violating scholarly norms, for irresponsibly mixing politics with scholarship,[49] for promoting conflict where consensus was more effective, and, perhaps most damning, for making sure that their political scholarship was dedicated to empowering people on the bottom to force change in the way social welfare policy discourse was conducted.[50]

Perhaps it is this last point most of all that set Piven and Cloward apart and left them open to the scathing criticisms that were to come. More than most others in the contemporary period, they self-consciously tied their theoretical writings about the development of the welfare state and their strategies for combating its inequities to an explicit bottom-up approach that grew first and foremost out of a commitment to empower those who were already in their own time struggling to resist the oppression of welfare capitalism in the United States.[51] What do these striking responses say about how we construct historical explanation, and what does it say about the relationship of scholarship to politics, knowledge to power, social science to social welfare? These are questions that need attention if theory and practice are to make connections and if scholarship and research are to play roles in politics and public policy.

Daniel P. Moynihan: Playing Both Ends against the Middle

There are numerous examples today of persons, practices, and publications that represent the merging of social science and politics in less than critical ways. Former United States senator Daniel Patrick Moynihan from New York represents one example of what A. J. P. Taylor once called a "mass intellectual"—someone who combines scholarship and politics in the halls of power—perhaps even more forcefully than former secretary of state Henry Kissinger.[52] Moynihan achieved tremendous influence in the Senate, and earlier in the Executive Branch, as an academic expert on welfare even as his scholarly writings remain more stories of his attempts to influence social policy than systematic studies of poverty problems and welfare responses.[53] Moynihan successfully played both ends against the middle. He used his academic credentials to gain political influence and his political influencing to serve as the basis for his scholarly writings.

The Moynihan case raises several issues regarding the relationship of politics and scholarship. The first issue is whether we should see politics and scholarship as separate spheres. Another issue is if they are to be combined, then how. Moynihan represents still other possibilities in that he sought to keep them separate but in ways that were to redound to his advantage in each realm.

Moynihan's case also highlights another dimension of the relationship of scholarship to politics. Given the way he used social science and politics, his work often was geared to offering "secondhand" reporting of social science that could make his writing more accessible to a broader policy-oriented audience. *The Public Interest*, a popular neoconservative policy journal with which Moynihan is still closely associated, provides an excellent outlet for such "armchair" scholarship. Often reported here are stories, not just by Moynihan, about research. Yet, such secondhand reporting often makes serious assessment of the studies being discussed difficult. While such writing makes social science more accessible to the broader policy-interested community, for the general audience it has obvious defects that proponents of the "public scholar" overlook. Left-wing scholars such as Christopher Lasch have been outspoken as advocates of the "public scholar" as a paradigm for how academics ought to write in order to produce "common knowledge" for the general public.[54] Yet, their cries for relevance via simple prose have their own dangers, perhaps at least as great as right-wing calls for scholars to remain in the ivory tower, disconnected from political life. Dilution to the point of obscuring the methodological finer points of research is one rather glaring deficiency that is often associated with such secondhand reporting. The devil is indeed often in the details.

A rather striking example from *The Public Interest* is a short article entitled "Orphanages: The Real Story" by an economist, Richard B. McKenzie. The article reports the results of a survey of alumni of three homes for orphans, finding that "the results do seriously undermine some of the critics' most sweeping, if not reckless, negative assessments applied to all orphanages." McKenzie does note that the survey has limitations, including that respondents were not drawn randomly but from alumni mailing lists and that these mailing lists might be biased in favor of those who had favorable orphanage experiences. This caveat is probably an understatement given the richly detailed histories of abuse in orphanages.[55] By the time such secondhand reporting lands on the desk of talk-show policy-fabler Rush Limbaugh, the conversion of social science to politically tendentious rumor is complete.[56]

Therefore, the Moynihan approach to scholarship and politics is, I would suggest, problematic at a second level. Here, the attempt to combine scholarship and politics creates numerous opportunities to oversimplify and mischaracterize social science findings. Of course, Moynihan's greatest example of this sort of questionable social science—the infamous 1965 "Moynihan Report" entitled *The Negro Family*—was not published in *The Public Interest* (though he would publish several retellings of this incident there).[57] Written when he was on the staff of the U.S. Department of Labor, this report claimed to find an important change in the relationship between unemployment rates and welfare receipt by African Americans. It was ostensibly similar to other liberal analyses of the time in trying to indicate that racial barriers in society had led to the development of pathology in low-income African American communities.[58] Yet, the report ended up being championed by conservatives as proof that low-income African American families needed to assume personal responsibility for their own poverty.

Michael Katz and others have detailed that this appropriation came about in part because among the report's many deficiencies, it most egregiously and misleadingly reinforced the popular stereotype that all welfare families were black, by applying data on both white and black welfare families to just African Americans.[59] There has also been much critical scrutiny of the report's central statistical claim that an autonomous culture of welfare dependency was indicated by the fact that welfare caseloads were beginning to rise independently of changes in the black male unemployment rate.[60] Based on this questionable analysis, the "Moynihan Report" became most controversial for suggesting that the "Negro family" was wrapped in a "tangle of pathology." It was the misuse of social science research as part of an oversimplified and misleading analysis that helped, even if unintentionally, legitimize such "blame-the-victim" thinking.

Moynihan exemplifies a third level of the problem of scholarship and politics. Moynihan could combine politics and scholarship as successfully as he did because he was on the side of power—state power in particular. Bad social science can overcome its limitations and still achieve impact in the policy process when its findings reinforce the prejudices ascendant in that arena. Stanley Aronowitz has suggested that modern science, especially social science, has been at its most powerful when it is aligned with the dominant structures of power.[61] A compounding facet of this problem is that social science's quest for political influence via political impartiality has often resulted in its political co-optation. This often leaves even the sound research of objectivistic empirical studies to be subject to political appropriation by the powers that be. These two facets of the problem—bad social science that is favored by the powerful, and good, objectivistic social science that is appropriated by the powerful—can reinforce each other. In its quest to achieve political legitimacy via political impartiality, objectivistic social scientists have too frequently allowed bad social-scientific information to circulate in policy circles in relatively uncontested fashion. Unfortunately, for welfare policy, this is exactly what has happened to the "Moynihan Report." It was once vilified by social scientists and civil rights leaders as misguided liberal thinking that ended up encouraging a blame-the-victim approach to African American poverty. Yet, its claim that the "Negro family" is "wrapped in a tangle of pathology" has over the years achieved the unquestioned status of prophetic research that predicted the "welfare mess," the growth of "welfare dependency," and the rise of the "underclass"—three less than credible social science concepts themselves.[62]

While social scientists often resist recognizing the political character of their scholarship even when it is ostensibly directed toward addressing policy problems, the case of Daniel Patrick Moynihan should force reconsideration of the issue on several levels. The controversy concerning Piven and Cloward's role in the struggles over welfare from the 1960s to the 1990s also has several dimensions.[63] First, there is the issue of whether to combine scholarship and politics. Second, there is the issue of how. Third, there is the issue of whether social scientists have been constructive participants in the struggles over social welfare policy.[64] Yet, this third issue also involves a fourth one regarding the status of social scientists in the policy process and the extent to which they should have significant influence compared to welfare recipients, activists, and citizens in general.[65] This last issue has gained heightened intensity in recent years, as the battles over welfare reform have increasingly become battles over interpreting the research findings of social scientists.[66] All of these issues are exemplified in the controversy over Piven and Cloward's "Crisis Strategy" and the push to overload the welfare system as a means of achieving movement toward a more just form of social welfare policy.

Ambush inside the Beltway: The Case of David Ellwood

An even more conventional and more contemporary model than Moynihan is provided by David Ellwood, the Harvard economist who became a prominent expert on welfare. He went to Washington to work for Bill Clinton in 1993 on behalf of welfare reform, only to resign in 1995.[67] Ellwood would eventually resign over the direction that welfare reform was taking—because by then it was a freight train out of control, careening headlong into the draconian Personal Responsibility and Work Opportunity Reconciliation Act of 1996. The welfare reform law of 1996 time-limited welfare, imposed strict work requirements, and led to massive purges of the rolls, including sending scores of single mothers with children into a world of low-wage work and increased poverty, even as some others left with an improved economy and saw modest improvements in their incomes. Most who left remained poor. Many lost benefits, such as childcare, food stamps, and Medicaid, for which they remained eligible.[68]

As a social scientist and policy analyst, Ellwood in the Clinton administration was in the more conventional role of adviser to policymakers. And as is increasingly the case in recent years, his adviser status was in good part underwritten by his credibility not so much as a deep thinker on the topic, or as a person of profound judgments about what was right or wrong, but rather on the basis of his abilities to conduct methodologically sound quantitative social science research and his grasp of the supposed "facts" of the topic.

Yet, after resigning, Ellwood wrote with regret about his attempt to combine social science and social welfare policymaking. He noted that he had been too naive about the world of mixing social science and social welfare policy politics in the nation's capital. In retrospect, Ellwood suggests that his more supportive version of Clinton welfare reform was doomed to be overtaken by the more draconian version that became the welfare reform law of 1996 because the issue had been corrupted in public discourse, particularly by the pundits and the press. In 1997, Ellwood wrote:

> While many people complain about welfare, most are poorly informed and uninterested in learning or hearing much more. The press will do little to illuminate the real policy alternatives. There will always be an inside-the-Beltway dialogue carried out in the press with the premier reporters. But few papers will cover the issue, few people will read what they publish. Unless the issue is number one or two on the national agenda, the public will remain skeptical and alienated. Worse yet, the issues of race and class lie just below the surface, occasionally producing ugly stereotypes, often clouding the political dialogue.[69]

Ellwood stressed that politics was made of sound bites and limited attention spans. He cautioned that advocates for progressive welfare reform would have to proceed incrementally, choosing their words carefully, if they hoped to avoid debacles like the one that overtook the Clinton administration. Ellwood's analysis has merit; however, he leaves out too much. In particular, he minimizes the extent to which research like his own will most often get co-opted by the political process and highjacked for more conservative ends.[70] An earlier analysis of what happened to Ellwood by *New York Times* reporter Jason DeParle was subtitled "Mugged by Reality."[71] Frances Fox Piven herself had noted that Ellwood had been warned about the dangers of blithely mixing objectivistic social science with the politics of social welfare policymaking.[72] Piven had told Ellwood that his proposal in his 1989 book *Poor Support* to swap extensive social supports for time limits and work requirements would likely lead policymakers to drop the supports and keep the restrictions. As it turns out, that, in a nutshell, is how we got welfare reform.

Yet, Ellwood is perhaps even more complicitous in his own demise. His objectivistic social science research left itself open to political appropriation. His most prominent work had been co-authored with Mary Jo Bane (who also resigned from the Clinton administration over welfare reform). It consisted of empirical analyses that sought to show that welfare had created more long-term dependency than had been suggested by previous research. While the final verdict on this "dynamics study," as it came to be called, remains up for discussion, it swept like a firestorm through the welfare policy community in the late 1980s and early 1990s, vaulting Ellwood, and to a slightly lesser extent Bane as well, to national prominence. More importantly, it also energized calls to limit access to public assistance.[73] DeParle writes:

> The "dynamics study" had all the hallmarks of Ellwood's subsequent work: it was empirically grounded, nuanced, accessible and relevant. And *it allowed readers of varying ideologies to read into it what they would.* Though it was never published in an academic journal, the study went on to a samizdat life that changed the welfare debate of the 1980s. Though liberals still emphasized the considerable turnover, it became increasingly difficult, in light of Ellwood's data, to dismiss dependency as a figment of conservative bias.[74]

Yet these features of Ellwood's work were to prove less appealing once he was beyond the computer lab, the academic conferences, and even the talk show circuit. His work motivated Clinton to promise "to end welfare as we know it." Ellwood knew at that point that things were more complicated than predicting the average recipient's "welfare spell."[75]

Ellwood's work had been co-opted in at least two ways—first by jettisoning the liberal social supports he recommended should accompany time limits and work requirements, and second by assimilating his research written in objectivistic social science discourse into the growing campaign to vilify welfare dependency. Yet even with all these warning alarms going off in the public dialogue, Ellwood still went to Washington to work on how to use his research to remake social welfare policy. Ellwood would later say: "I was incredibly naive about a number of things."[76] Ellwood got a prominent position in the Clinton administration, and his research got a prominent place in the drive to cut back on welfare. Both got appropriated for political purposes. Both were "mugged by reality."

The Crisis of Strategy

Piven and Cloward's combination of scholarship and politics on issues of social welfare deviates in multiple ways from the models offered by Moynihan and Ellwood. Moynihan and Ellwood aligned themselves with those in power and offered a top-down perspective on how to "fix" the system of welfare. Piven and Cloward aligned themselves with those living in poverty and offered a bottom-up analysis of how things worked in terms of their effects on the people who had to live out the consequences of various welfare reform efforts. Moynihan and Ellwood grounded their recommendations in supposedly objective research about the real facts of welfare and poverty. Piven and Cloward unapologetically embraced an orientation that recognized how political values and research facts were entwined, and they self-consciously articulated their factual analyses in terms of a value-laden perspective informed by a commitment to empower low-income families to challenge their oppression.

Many examples can be used to highlight how Piven and Cloward's combination of politics and scholarship offers a laudatory model. The major example to be examined here is the 1966 proposal to sign people up for welfare and overload the system in order to force more progressive policies such as a guaranteed income—the "Crisis Strategy" discussed earlier. I focus on it because it is the most controversial. It stands at the center of the brief against Piven and Cloward as academics who irresponsibly combined scholarship and politics. The criticisms include the large claim that their strategy ended up producing a "welfare mess" that lasted for over thirty years and whose gridlock of high rates of welfare receipt was only finally broken in the 1990s with the passage of the Personal Responsibility and Work Opportunity Reconciliation Act of 1996. The connections between Piven and Cloward's scholarship and politics, between social science and social policy, the 1960s and the 1990s, and a lot more, have been pointed to in political speeches as well as academic writings.

In 1998, New York City's mayor, Rudolph Giuliani, said: "From 1960 to 1994, the work ethic was under attack in New York City. New York City viewed welfare as a good thing, as a wonderful thing. They romanticized it and embraced a philosophy of dependency, almost as if it's better to have somebody on welfare than to help somebody to work."[77] He called this a "perverted social philosophy" that needed to be overturned with a new social contract founded on the idea that you had to work first in order to qualify as a legitimate citizen deserving of support. His speech, given in the summer of 1998, had in an earlier draft attributed this "perverted social philosophy" to none other than Frances Fox Piven and Richard Cloward. In the *New York Times Magazine* at the end of 1998, Jason DeParle wrote:

> When the Mayor vowed to end welfare last summer, he did so pointer in hand, standing beside a chart that traced the exploding caseloads of the 1960s. At that decade's dawn, 250,000 recipients. *Thwwaaack*! Twelve years later, 1.1 million. *Thwwaaack*! "This wasn't an accident, it wasn't an atmospheric thing, it wasn't supernatural," Giuliani said. "This is the result of policies and programs designed to have the maximum number of people get on welfare." In railing against "the philosophy that was embraced in the 1960s," Giuliani is not just offering the standard deprecation of the age. In theory and practice welfare did undergo a revolutionary change.
>
> In an early draft of his presentation, Giuliani even rounded out his history by citing the two Columbia University professors whose audacious role in the welfare explosion is now all but forgotten. In plotting what they called the "flood-the-rolls, bankrupt-the-cities strategy," Richard A. Cloward and Frances Fox Piven literally set out to destroy local welfare programs. By drowning the cities in caseloads and costs, they hoped to build support for a more generous Federal solution, preferably a guaranteed national income. What's also all but forgotten now is that the strategy almost worked.[78]

The critics of the Crisis Strategy, however, too often ignore Piven and Cloward's goals and focus on their means. Even before the Crisis Strategy, Cloward had published a series of articles with Richard Elman and others highlighting the denial of basic civil rights that was an everyday occurrence in the welfare system. He had vividly demonstrated in detail how welfare was a corrupt system of arbitrary treatment of the poor,[79] which the critics tend to forget, especially when criticizing Piven and Cloward for doing little more than organizing a campaign that pointed out just how much poverty there was in the United States and then encouraged poor people who needed assistance to get it. Overlooking how this welfare rights strategy was only enabling people to get what they already were entitled to, the critics end up blaming Piven and Cloward for heightening the visibility of that need for assistance. It is no different from every other instance of blaming the proverbial messenger. In the process, Giuliani's mistake of identifying Piven and Cloward as supporters of the existing welfare system in the 1960s has been repeated again and again in the 1990s. The criticisms of Michael Tomasky are particularly noteworthy. He writes:

> [Piven and Cloward] may deserve credit for thinking dialectically, but not for much else. Who could seriously believe—even in an era of prosperity and possibility—that the government would react to a "furor" precipitated by the poor with anything other than a crackdown? It's not as if the idea that working is preferable to not working has been around only since Charles Murray. In 1964, reviewing a book on Appalachian poverty, W. Carey McWilliams, editor of the very journal in which the Piven and Cloward article had appeared, argued in *Dissent* that welfare "has become a dole, based on no sense of worth or contribution, accentuating the mountaineer's sense of weakness, depriving him of any sense of dignity. . . ." But Piven and Cloward's view was obviously quite a different one: in a 1967 *Nation* article, they actually described programs to find jobs for welfare recipients as "a serious threat to the movement." Finally, the authors' argument that dividing the middle class, the working class, and the poor would be a good thing was, of course, just the sort of disastrous cant for which the left is still paying a dear price (to say nothing of the poor people themselves).[80]

Yet, these criticisms that Piven and Cloward were concerned about the co-optive effect of make-work jobs and workfare programs miss their main point. The critique of Piven and Cloward's insistence on the need to create divisions and disruption overlooks that welfare was acceptable to the working and middle classes as an inferior program for people who did not deserve any better. If destroying the unjust welfare system was the goal, it would not work for the poor to play up to the dominant interest groups and go along with their agenda. Among the many things that Tomasky and the other critics of the Crisis Strategy overlook is that Piven and Cloward were critics of welfare bent on destroying a destructive system. This was their primary goal.[81]

Still today, this important and basic point is lost even on contemporary radical feminists such as Wendy Brown who have also joined the ranks of the critics of Piven and Cloward. Brown's criticism is that Piven and Cloward have lost faith and turned to defending welfare even as it continues to subordinate women with its coercive regulations and demeaning treatment.[82] It is questionable whether Piven and Cloward have been inconsistent. The issue for them has consistently been that welfare reform proposals have sought to make welfare either more punitive or less available. Neither approach replaces the deficiencies of welfare with public policy that will begin to address effectively the structural causes of poverty. Therefore, the issue for them has been that until alternative approaches begin to receive attention, standing up for welfare becomes the only thing advocates can do as part of the struggle to get beyond welfare to more progressive policies.

Piven and Cloward were never advocates for public assistance as it has existed; instead, they have been the country's leading critics of public assistance—something Tomasky and others easily forget. Given the implacable resistance to seriously considering alternatives, they argued that the only way to highlight the unworkability of welfare was to push for more welfare and thereby throw it into crisis by demonstrating its inability to handle the size and magnitude of the nation's poverty problem. The long-run end was to transcend welfare; the short-run means was to drive up welfare participation. In the process of proposing this strategy, Piven and Cloward came to be misidentified as advocates for welfare as it currently existed. Nothing could be further from the truth. DeParle writes:

> Though it has been much maligned in retrospect, it is easy to see, in the context of the times, the appeal of a relief expansion. Appalled at the racial terror of the South, Northern liberals saw the country's very future at stake in the their efforts to redress the nation's injustices. Providing the destitute

> with material relief seemed a logical place to start. But by 1966, Piven and Cloward had glimpsed the makings of something bigger.
>
> In an article in the *Nation*, they called for elevating the situation into a "profound financial and political crisis" through a "massive drive to recruit the poor onto the rolls." Tactically, they recommended "bureaucratic disruption in welfare agencies," "cadres of aggressive organizers" and "demonstrations to create a climate of militancy." Strategically, they hoped to place local officials in a box. If officials could not raise taxes (and alienate voters) or cut benefits (and risk riots in a riot-prone age), what would they do? They would call for a Federal guaranteed income, the two predicted, which could bring "an end to poverty."
>
> The article generated a sensation on the left with requests for reprints running 30,000 strong. Shortly after, the National Welfare Rights Organization was born, and the age of full-fledged welfare militancy was officially under way. . . . As predicted, the bureaucracy's first response was to open up the tap. . . . Likewise, as Piven and Cloward predicted, enthusiasm grew for replacing welfare with a guaranteed national income.[83]

It is therefore as misleading as it is convenient to label Piven and Cloward as welfare advocates in the narrow sense of the term. As DeParle clearly indicates, they were suggesting something much more profound. Rather than pushing for more welfare per se, they were pushing us to see how welfare was so thoroughly tied to the existing political economy and as such it could never do justice to the poor. Welfare was the co-optive and coercive practice used to get the poor to accept their plight as "the poor"—the people whose needs could not be met by the dominant institutions of society. The Crisis Strategy therefore recognized that appealing to ascendant cultural values, accepting existing economic practices, and participating in existing social welfare policies would only leave the poor behind as always, left out.[84] The Crisis Strategy therefore emphasized the need for "dissensus" and refusal to join in broader coalitions that would co-opt the poor into accepting welfare as the best they could get. For Piven and Cloward, dissensus politics was a much-to-be-preferred peaceful alternative to rioting and other forms of violent civil disorder, designed to get those in power to focus on making concessions to those who were radically "othered" by mainstream society. Overloading the welfare system was designed to provide a highly visible if peaceful way to highlight just how much need existed in society. That was the goal of the Crisis Strategy, rather than trying to make welfare a permanent reality. That welfare became gridlocked at high levels indicates more the resistance by the mainstream to structural changes than a preference for welfare by the poor. If anything, the failure of the Crisis Strategy revealed the mainstream's preference for welfare more than the poor's.

The poor hate welfare probably more than anybody else because they know the binds it put them in. Research by Kathryn Edin in recent years has effectively demonstrated that neither welfare nor the available low-wage work creates enough income for most poor single mothers. Piven and Cloward's Crisis Strategy was based on similar insights and sought to highlight how the existing political economy, low-wage labor markets, and welfare policies combined so that poor families found it near impossible to meet their basic needs.[85] The Crisis Strategy sought to bring this reality to a heightened visibility in a way that would require policy responses. The strategy, much maligned as it has been, nonetheless almost worked. The guaranteed income did indeed become a serious proposal that was pushed by no less a person than Republican president Richard Nixon.

The Cost of Good Intentions

A common criticism of Piven and Cloward's Crisis Strategy was that it sacrificed the well-being of the poor for the cause of social revolution. The criticism amounts to saying that Piven and Cloward were willing to pit the "politics of survival" against the "politics of social change."[86] The Crisis Strategy critic Fred Siegel suggests as much when he says:

> The advocates' compelling cry for justice led many at the time (and even subsequently) to downplay the disaster of welfare dependency as "the cost of good intentions." Some of the welfare radicals, however, saw the future all too clearly. "When attachments to the role of work deteriorate," wrote Piven and Cloward, "so do attachments to the family, especially the attachments of men to their families." They foresaw "the resulting family breakdown and . . . spread of certain forms of disorder," like "school failure, crime, and addiction." For most, this was a description of disaster, but for those like Piven and Cloward, who saw welfare recipients as the cat's-paws of the coming revolution, breakdown promised to unleash the furies of rebellion. "Unfortunately," wrote Roger Starr, a former member of the *New York Times* editorial board, "the exploitation of the Negro in America has

> been so thorough that a strain of it even runs through the movement to liberate him. . . ."
>
> The irony of New York's welfare revolution was that in the name of redressing old injustices that treated African-Americans as less than full citizens, it recreated their second-class standing through liberal paternalism. In eliminating invidious distinctions, it effaced the importance of character; in the name of the old Leninist dogma of "the worse, the better," it left the city far worse.[87]

This sort of criticism says much about Siegel's reluctance to defend his thesis that the political economy can work as well for the poor as everyone else if they only adhere to middle-class work and family values. Rather than offer evidence for his basic assumption, Siegel instead sticks to mischaracterizing Piven and Cloward's argument. Siegel attributes to Piven and Cloward things they did not say (all of which is made easier by Siegel's refusal to use any citations whatsoever) and then uses these quotes against them to suggest that they were cold, aloof, academic theorists who irresponsibly foisted their theories on the poor at the expense of the poor and only in service of their misbegotten ideas.[88] When Siegel quotes Piven and Cloward about the debilitating effects of nonwork on individuals and families, he is quoting them in passages where they are discussing the current reality, what has already happened, thanks not to Piven and Cloward's advocacy to accept welfare, but thanks to the less than "benign neglect" of the deindustrializing city. The reality of nonwork and its deleterious consequences had already arrived. If only Siegel gave more attention to this, he would junk his indictment as a bad case of reverse causality: welfare did not cause the nonwork and its negative effects; instead, nonwork and its negative effects of a more oppositional ghetto culture and less ability to sustain traditional family relations had already created the conditions under which growing numbers of people needed welfare.

Therefore, Piven and Cloward were not gleefully wishing that bad circumstances would flow from their strategy so that they would gain more enlistees for their cause. In fact, it was quite the opposite. Piven and Cloward valued their strategy because it thoughtfully and sensitively combined social work and social welfare strategies, helping people survive in the short run even as it built the basis for change in the long run.[89]

The Necessity of Dissensus Politics: Then and Now

Siegel also claims that this focus on mobilizing the poor on their own terms only ended up promoting widespread welfare dependency and that welfare dependency dragged down the public sector along with the poor. Siegel's point overlooks that before the Crisis Strategy came on the scene welfare was already needed by the poor whether they were mobilized to receive it or not. He writes as if nobody was poor before the Crisis Strategy, when in fact Piven and Cloward indicated in the Crisis Strategy article that sound social science research had forced them to conclude that "it appears that for every person on welfare in 1959, at least one more was eligible."[90] Piven and Cloward were bringing startlingly new research of dramatic import before the public. It would galvanize people into supporting their cause. If "welfare dependency" was to result, the cause was preexisting poverty that persisted in the face of the lack of economic opportunities, not a campaign to sign people up for public assistance. The problem was not that people were discouraged from following ascendant work and family values; the problem was instead that those values were already not working for the poor like they did for others. Therefore, a special strategy that focused on the poor as a distinctive population was all the more necessary. The goal was to highlight how the existing dominant values worked to marginalize the poor and relegate them to at best the inadequacies of welfare. This points toward what is really Michael Tomasky's main criticism.[91] His main argument is that the Crisis Strategy in the end is just what its name implies—bad strategy. For Tomasky, the Crisis Strategy was bad strategy for two reasons: (1) it emphasized always being *against* reforms and never *for* any, on the questionable grounds that reform always rationalized the existing inequitable social order; and (2) such an extreme "refusenik" position served in the end only to marginalize the left from the working and middle classes who wanted to find ways to make things work within the existing order.

Tomasky's criticism has parallels on the left. One version is the argument that the left needs to be less aggressive in standing up for those who have been marginalized as different. Instead, in order to avoid alienating the middle and working classes, advocates for progressive change need to demonstrate how they stand four-square with the mainstream, how they are committed to mainstream values, and how the left is seeking only to ensure that everyone who "plays by the rules" (of work and family) will not be unjustly treated.[92] Examples of this sort of argument are quite common among leftists. Some are better made than others.

This issue can arise even when denigration of the poor is the last thing that is intended. Examples can even be found among prominent allies of Piven and Cloward such as Joel Rogers. Rogers is himself an important public intellectual who combines scholarship and politics so that his intellectual work can inform his political activism. In the 1990s, he had been in the forefront of efforts to build the left-leaning New Party. Rogers basically single-handedly initiated the New Party and had been a prime mover behind its grassroots strategy to win elections at the local level and build up from there. He has since deemphasized this strategy. Yet, the New Party had some limited success electorally, in part from gaining cross-endorsements for its candidates in local elections. Its efforts to help support local "living wage campaigns" also paid off with an increasing number of cities requiring local government and its contractors to pay a livable wage. In this important campaign Rogers at times stated his argument in ways that risked implying that the left needed to distance itself from a politics of confrontation on behalf of welfare recipients. For Rogers, such a strategy would only marginalize the left and make it seem that it is not a movement designed to get economic and social justice for upstanding citizens who play by the rules.[93] Rogers's work in recent years has reflected a nuanced understanding of these issues that includes recognition of the need to stand up for the welfare poor.[94]

Another parallel, if of a different sort, is between Tomasky's argument and Thomas Edsall and Mary Bryd Edsall.[95] The Edsalls argued that the liberal wing of the Democratic party had ruined its electoral chances because it had become consumed with placating "special interest" groups such as African Americans and women. Advocating for special interest legislation, such as Affirmative Action, was alienating the party's natural constituency—the white male working class. The Edsalls forgot to note that the white working class was being transformed with postindustrialism, making it less a coherent block of unionized blue-collar workers, just as demographic and social changes were making it less white and less male.

In the process of criticizing Piven and Cloward for being insensitive and irresponsible toward the poor, Siegel also provides his own version of the argument that the Piven and Cloward strategy had deserted the traditional left position of working to ensure fair treatment for those members of the working class who "played by the rules."[96] Siegel himself believes that Piven and Cloward's strategy did more than get people on welfare; in fact, for Siegel the strategy also became the critical factor that led to the bankrupting of New York City. Worse, Siegel says, the Crisis Strategy laid the groundwork for the deterioration of work and family values in the City because it told people they could be irresponsible and still get government aid.[97] Siegel goes so far as to suggest that Piven and Cloward's Crisis Strategy undermined public morality to the point that New York City went into decline because people did not make the effort to work and raise families as they should, thereby simultaneously producing less wealth while draining the public coffers. In particular, Siegel refers to what he calls "the riot ideology" that began to take hold in big cities across the country after the civil disorder of the 1960s. He claims it encouraged low-income African Americans in particular to feel that their plight merited protesting and creating havoc and that they no longer had to aspire to hard work and discipline to get out of poverty.[98] For Siegel, only when Giuliani began to stand up for work and family values did New York City begin to turn around. It should come as no surprise that Siegel had been an adviser to Giuliani on welfare and related matters.

Siegel's critique illustrates how far the mainstream-values argument can go. His claims that left-wing politics brought down New York City have been thoroughly repudiated as gross exaggerations about the power of the left to set policy and change values.[99] His arguments about what really weakened the economy of the City have also received a critical eye for exaggerating the effects of welfare on economic activity and neglecting the role of the banks, real estate speculators, corporations and other monied interests.[100] I do not want to revisit these criticisms. Instead, I am interested in how Siegel contributes to the complaint that the Crisis Strategy is bad strategy. Siegel represents the extreme among the critics in suggesting that if everyone just "played by the rules" we would be better off and those who did and were still disadvantaged would be seen as "deserving poor" and would be compensated.

Siegel joins a growing group who forget that Piven and Cloward did not create poverty in New York City, or around the country for that matter. They merely helped people enduring persistent poverty combine a "politics of survival" with a "politics of social change." They simply helped people who were already poor exercise their rights to public assistance (a "politics of survival") in a way that helped dramatize the inadequacy of welfare in the face of massive need (a "politics of social change"). People were already playing by the rules and were still being left behind in the deindustrializing city; they needed assistance. Encouraging them to take welfare was not causing their poverty; they were already poor. The Crisis Strategy therefore did not undermine mainstream values as much as show that those values were already bankrupt and were being unfairly applied to the poor to deny them needed assistance on the grounds that their immorality on matters of work and family had made them "undeserving."

This rebuttal suggests that another critic of the Crisis Strategy is not so much wrong as he is putting things backwards. Steven Teles criticizes Piven and Cloward's Crisis Strategy for promoting an alienating and debilitating "politics of dissensus."[101] He ideally wants to replace it with a "politics of consensus"—less confrontational, more geared to showing how the poor are like everyone else, and more focused on creating a supportive social welfare state that would reward people for "playing by the rules" and compensate those who did but still remained poor. Yet he suggests that this will be hard given how competing elites have come to use welfare as a convenient site for fighting out their cultural differences. In this regard, Teles, like the rest of the Crisis Strategy critics, seems to look nostalgically to some supposed time in the past when advocates for the people on the bottom of society were more interested in showing how the poor were no different from everyone else; to the extent that they played by the rules concerning work and family, they should be protected by the welfare state.[102] The recurring question is: How can advocates for social reform make their proposals more appealing to the mainstream? Of necessity, this goal implies appealing to the same values, often work and family values, that are ascendant in the broader society. This is what I have previously called a "politics of incorporation," and it has its merits in particular circumstances.[103] Not all marginal and oppressed groups can afford always to reject or ignore the dominant culture but must find ways to negotiate with it. Yet, all strategies that arise from this reality have their risks, especially for the poor. The risks of active negotiation with the dominant culture include neglecting to address how the dominant values are working to undermine what you are trying to achieve. In the case of Piven and Cloward and their push for welfare rights, Tomasky claims their strategy of standing up for marginal groups on their own terms will only isolate them further by alienating the mainstream.[104]

Yet, welfare is to the poor what social security or unemployment insurance is for the nonpoor—it is their safety net. For already isolated poor populations, residing in marginal neighborhoods, cut off from mainstream educational and occupational opportunities, often as single mothers caught in the difficulties of extricating themselves from abusive relationships, welfare is a critical economic resource. Under these circumstances, insisting that the poor forgo welfare is like telling the retired to forgo social security or the jobless to forgo unemployment benefits.

If you are going to stand up for the poor as an already marginalized population, you need to consider how they got marginalized and constructed as "the poor." It could well be that mainstream values, economic practices, and public policies contributed to their marginalization as less than deserving, less than productive, and less than virtuous citizens. If that is the case, as it surely has been to at least some appreciable degree in the United States of the last fifty years, then simply expressing adherence to mainstream values of work and family will not suffice. Nor will an emphasis on creating more jobs. Neglecting welfare as a program for the undeserving will hurt even more. In his critique of Piven and Cloward's "dissensus politics," Steven Teles admits as much. He recognizes that welfare politics erroneously, if easily, slips into "othering" the poor as different because they fail to adhere to middle-class values. Teles emphasizes how welfare politics conveniently uses the poor as a scapegoat rather than criticizing people in general for failing to live up to the society's dominant moral values. Teles writes:

> Welfare is extraordinarily susceptible to dissensus politics because it permits issues of social value to be debated without directly judging the behavior of the majority of citizens. Family decomposition, the decline of the work ethic, and the erosion of personal responsibility are social trends occurring throughout American society. However, to discuss them directly would inevitably lead to fingers being pointed at a large group of American citizens. The politics of morality are generally more effective when the finger can be pointed at someone else.[105]

Teles, however, has it backwards because his argument actually underscores the need to resist the consensus politics he prefers, for it is that sort of politics that feeds into the very scapegoating of the poor that he decries. Claiming that we all agree on universal values is more likely to promote the idea that the poor have failed to "play by the rules" that we all should live by. Such an approach singles out the poor because they end up needing public assistance for the same situations (unmarried births, absent fathers, single mothers with children) that the upper classes are more likely to handle without prolonged use of public assistance.

Resisting the trap of basing welfare on shared values of work and family creates the basis to see how the poor are and are not different from everyone else. They are no different from everyone else, just forced to appear that way because they are operating under distinctly more adverse conditions that lead them to rely on public assistance more frequently. Teles's criticism notwithstanding, Piven and Cloward's "dissensus politics" very much anticipated Teles's concerns about how the dominant values are biased against an increasingly nonwhite poverty class of single mothers, and how "the rules" of work and family operated to leave black single mothers in particular marginalized in the ghetto of welfare.[106] Until the built-in biases of work and family values were made open for reconsideration, a politics of dissensus was what we needed in order to address the marginalization of the poor. That still holds today. Welfare reform imposes work requirements and time limits on all recipients alike even while there is growing evidence that nonwhite recipients are finding it much harder to find jobs so they can work their way off welfare, and that most of the white and nonwhite single mothers who do are still finding their incomes are not enough to support their families.[107]

What Teles is missing here is that dissensus politics is actually on the side of universal values and neutral standards rather than demanding special treatment. It seeks to insist that the state give up its *falsely* universal standards and *false* neutrality by coming to recognize the built-in biases that are embedded in public policies that are said to be in the name of society's fundamental values. Dissensus politics seeks to highlight how ostensibly neutral standards are actually biased, as in the case of social welfare policies that are based on work and family values that end up unfairly privileging two-parent families over single mothers who have been deserted. The argument of dissensus politics is not so much that we should have special standards and programs for other individuals and families, for instance single mothers with children, as much as it is to get the state to stop unfairly privileging the traditional two-parent male-headed family as somehow more deserving of support. Such policies help perpetuate the family wage system that unfairly assumes all families, regardless of how they are positioned in the social order by class, race, and gender relations, are expected to be able to provide for themselves through the wages of a primary wage earner. For instance, dissensus politics seeks to disclose that widows are given more favorable treatment by the two-tiered welfare state that allows them to receive social insurance in the form of survivors' benefits under social security while deserted mothers are relegated to a second tier of inferior public assistance benefits.

Dissensus politics asks why one mother is more deserving than the other. Is this practice really fair, neutral, and consistent with universal values? Or does it reflect the biases of the welfare state to privilege families that are seen as helping perpetuate the existing political economy in spite of the injustices such distinctions re-create? Dissensus politics pokes holes in the false neutrality of the welfare state and the false universalism of the work and family values on which it is based. Dissensus politics has parallels in what Lisa Duggan has called "queering the state,"[108] a strategy grounded in recognizing the embedded biases in falsely neutral public policies, as in the case of policies that favor opposite-sex marriages over same-sex marriages. In response, activists make visible the embedded biases of falsely neutral public policies and push to insist on the neutral standards that the state claims it wants to uphold but does not.

Piven and Cloward's dissensus politics therefore was very much dedicated not so much to opposing universal values, neutral standards, and "playing by the rules" as much as it was focused on making visible just how much the state was biased against the poor and was not applying values, standards, and rules in any way that could be called fair. The goal was to put a stop to these unfair practices at all levels, from the way welfare caseworkers applied the law to how the laws were framed. The end result envisioned would be a more just welfare state that came much closer to actually treating individuals and families more fairly and in a less discriminatory fashion. Only then would the universal values championed by a consensus politics begin to be realized in a more just welfare state.

The dissensus politics of the Crisis Strategy was therefore nothing less (and actually a whole lot more) than what today theorists would call a "politics of theater," or better, a "politics of spectacle."[109] It was designed, however, not just for show but to highlight how low-income families were suffering due to their marginalization in the affluent United States. Just as the Crisis Strategy combined a "politics of survival" with a "politics of social change," so it also combined a symbolic politics of theater with a material politics of accessing basic economic resources.[110] Just as the civil rights protests in the South were highlighting for a national audience how white southerners were mistreating African Americans, the campaign to flood the welfare rolls was also designed to highlight for the whole nation how local welfare systems were denying needed aid to the poor.[111] In both cases, the goal was to move beyond the local level to force the involvement of the federal government on behalf of national policies that would ensure basic rights—to vote in one case, and to have access to basic economic resources in the other. In both cases, there was a strategy to promote what E. E. Schattschneider, in his classic book, *The Semi-Sovereign People* (1960), had called "the socialization of conflict." In "the socialization of conflict," groups outside the state and locality are made aware of the injustice being done inside a jurisdiction and would support the elevation of a policy problem to a higher level of government.[112] Dissensus politics in those days was necessary in order to symbolize injustice, to highlight the false neutrality of universal standards that allegedly guaranteed equal treatment, to galvanize national audiences to push for federal action, and to indicate in no uncertain terms that the price of acquiescence was much higher than those in power had previously thought.

As theorists of the contemporary "new social movements" on behalf of women's rights or gay and lesbian rights remind us, those politics are no less necessary now than they were then.[113] The need for dissensus politics persists today across a variety of areas. The issue of whether to join a broad-based movement committed to change in terms consistent with common values versus pursuing a dissensus politics that challenges those values has been most significantly raised in recent years over debates about what strategy should be pursued by African Americans. William Julius Wilson has consistently championed the former strategy as a way to build a "bridge over the racial divide."[114] Yet, Wilson's approach risks forcing African Americans to forgo pointing out how they are distinctively marginalized by racism, and how government responses to racism need to attend specifically to that. Wilson's call for "race-neutral" social policies in the past implied opposition, for instance to affirmative action. He in fact has moved to supporting affirmative action for persons of color but wants to augment this with other policies that will compensate poor whites.

While both policies are needed, there are reasons to suggest that African American coalition building needs to emphasize the ability of African Americans to dissent from consensus politics, common values, and majoritarian strategies so that their distinctive concerns about the persistence of racism and the inequities of racial discrimination are not lost in the push to build a majority coalition. As a necessary strategy for a political minority, this might even mean pushing for policies that heighten awareness of problems such as racism by increasing divisiveness in the country about how to handle that problem.

Dissent and the Repressive Hypothesis

The forgoing suggests that Wendy Brown misses the point when she criticizes Piven and Cloward for shifting from being critics of welfare to being its defenders. Brown accuses Piven and Cloward of participating in a "retreat from the politics of domination within capitalism."[115] Brown's concern is that Piven and Cloward were allegedly once sensitive to the ways state power, particularly in the form of the welfare bureaucracy, perpetuated gender domination. For Brown, this is the problem of "the man in the state." Relying on welfare instigated a "politics of protection" that simply shifted male domination from the private sphere of the family to the public sphere of the state. Women were still subordinated by relations of gender domination, this time by the gendered welfare state that privileged the male "breadwinner" and the male-headed family. The result was that they often qualified for social insurance benefits over the female "homemaker" and the mother-only family, which were most often relegated to receiving inferior welfare benefits under highly regulated conditions. Yet, as Barbara Cruikshank has noted, Brown overlooks that state power is neither univocal nor exhaustive—it neither simply subordinates women nor does it definitively determine their subject positions in the social order.[116] Women indeed risk further subordination, in terms of class, race, sexual identity as well as gender, when they enter into power relationships with the state as well as other social formations; however, this state power can be empowering as well, providing, say, the ability to escape patriarchal relations in the family. Women can resist how the state subordinates them because their identity is never solely determined by their participation in government programs. They can use government benefits subversively to empower themselves in terms of alternative identities other than the identity the state imposes on them as the "good mother," the compliant woman, and so on.

A case can therefore be made that Piven and Cloward have consistently recognized the contradictory power relations embedded in welfare, making welfare an object of defense as well as attack, depending on the circumstances. For them, welfare is always something that can help the impoverished even as it is something that regulates them. It provides social assistance even as it operates as a form of social control.[117] It is something to be defended even as it is opposed, sometimes more one than the other, depending on how those with power are treating it at any one point in time. When welfare is offered as a concession, it needs to be challenged for its inadequacy. When welfare is made more restrictive, it is time to defend its potential to assist those in need. In both cases, the approach is to highlight how welfare relations are unjust, reflecting the contradictory purposes of the state, and how struggle for a more just set of social relations involves trying to work through these contradictions.

There are reasons, then, to question Barbara Cruikshank's own criticism of Piven and Cloward and the welfare rights effort in the 1960s as allowing an overly essentialistic form of identity politics to inform their campaign to "empower" low-income citizens as "the poor."[118] Cruikshank suggests that one mistake of Piven and Cloward's dissensus strategy was that it tended to overly invest in and uncritically accept the government-sponsored invention of "the poor" as a distinct group of people with identifiable interests and concerns associated with their particular circumstances and way of life. This reification of the poor was promoted by the government during the War on Poverty, not so much to pacify low-income neighborhoods as much as to actively mobilize them into government in particular ways. The specific purpose was to establish these individuals as a group or population that was to be treated in a specific fashion. Rather than pacifying the poor during the turbulent 1960s in order to re-create the conditions of political stability, the War on Poverty's invention of "the poor" was undertaken to actively mobilize low-income persons into the public sphere in ways that ensured their domestication and the return of domestic tranquility. Cruikshank writes:

> The popular thesis on the left that CAPs [Community Action Programs] were invented by the government primarily to divert, co-opt, repress, and undermine the legitimate opposition to the state assumes that "the poor" do indeed have objective interests that can be co-opted. I have shown that "the poor" cannot have interests of their own until and unless they are constituted as a group. That did not happen until the War on Poverty was waged; government did not repress the poor but invented the poor as a group with interests and powers. Before government intervention—and I mean that in the broadest sense—"the poor" were disparate, isolated, and often in conflict with one another; they were Appalachian coal miners, urban single mothers, illiterate, unskilled black migrants from the South, southern fundamentalists, the elderly, "delinquent" youths, and the unemployed. The assumption that people do not know their own best interests is politically suspect, but that their interests do not divide them as much as they promise to unite them is unfounded. Nevertheless, the implicit elitism of the will to empower, claiming to know what is best for others, does

> not condemn it to failure or necessarily to a reactionary status. Empowerment is a power relationship, a relationship of government; it can be used well or badly.[119]

Cruikshank therefore criticizes what she calls the "will to empower" for naively assuming that the attempts to mobilize economically and socially disadvantaged groups as "the poor" can take for granted that all low-income persons are already grouped as a coherent population with unified interests reflective of that consolidated identity. "The poor," however, do not preexist government intervention but are an artifact of it. Therefore, mobilizing the poor qua poor as "the poor" only buys into the government's reification and unreflectively risks reinforcing the marginalization of low-income citizens as that distinctly troubled population, "the poor." Piven and Cloward therefore were dangerously risking helping the government do its own mobilization work, leading to the regimentation of low-income families into the welfare state as a marginalized group to be sequestered in their own separate inferior programs reserved for "the poor." And AFDC did indeed continue to be an inferior track of social policy after the mobilizations of the 1960s were finished.

Therefore, Cruikshank has a point. Her perspective is a sophisticated one, drawing as it does on the work of Michel Foucault. In particular, Cruikshank is using Foucault's critique of what he calls the "Repressive Hypothesis,"[120] which suggests an alternative conception of power. Foucault was critical of the prevailing conceptions of power that saw power as an external force operating from the outside to repress individuals from realizing their true interests by becoming empowered autonomous subjects who could achieve their own emancipation and liberation. He saw this definition of power as too old-fashioned, tied to older eras of centralized sources of authority in which a sovereign source of power such as a king ruled over his subjects. This sort of definition of power saw it in negative terms as something that constrained individuals, repressed them, and limited their ability to act.

Instead, Foucault saw power as more diffused throughout the social order, pulsing through various social practices, operating positively by working internally through forms of self-discipline, internalization, and what he called "bio-power." Power operated not so much through external forces preventing people from doing things as much as through internal forms of self-regulation, self-monitoring, and self-surveillance that encouraged individuals to positively enact or perform various personal practices. Sexual repression, for instance, occurred not so much through how society discouraged sex but instead through the ways that it encouraged it. By encouraging only particular forms of sex and actively campaigning for the valorization of those forms, people would then forgo other kinds. Heterosexual, monogamous, procreative sex would crowd out its alternatives. Encouraging low-income individuals to identify as "the poor" at the expense of other identifications could prove to be indifferent to their diversity and the variety of circumstances and problems that they confront.

Cruikshank's critique also effectively draws on another Foucaldian idea—that of "governmentality."[121] As Nikolas Rose has described it, governmentality involves the proliferation of state power throughout society not so much by means of direct intervention and control but by the elaboration of various private practices across a variety of institutionalized settings. These encourage the development of particular populations of individuals who are expected to practice various forms of self-discipline, self-monitoring, and self-surveillance appropriate to their population and necessary for producing a self-regulating society.[122] Governmentality begets individualization where society is increasingly seen as composed of various types of individuals who have successfully internalized the particular forms of individual practice appropriate for their type of person and determined as necessary for the managing of the social order.

The arts of governmentality, for Cruikshank, came in the 1960s in the United States to include the creation of the population called "the poor." The state became interested in peopling this population with individuals who internalized this identity. In this way, "the poor" would be constituted as a population that acted accordingly, making their behavior as individuals more predictable and their management as a population less difficult. "The poor" would be constituted in ways that were consonant with the established state of affairs and the existing constellation of powers operating in society. In order to make "the poor" safe for society they had to be actively invented, constructed, mobilized, enlisted, and regimented into that society via the arts of governmentality. We called this the "War on Poverty." It was for Cruikshank more like the consolidation of the poor as "the poor." It was more the "Consolidation of Poverty." State certified, U.S.-approved poverty, stamped, registered, and with its own legally copyrighted trademark. Official poverty, for official purposes.

Keeping low-income people down was, therefore, to be achieved not by repressing them with negative external acts of power, but by positive, internalized forms of self-regulation. Actively mobilizing low-income individuals as "the poor" ensured their continued existence on terms defined by the government.

There is value in preferring constructivist over essentialistic approaches. Essentialistic approaches emphasize "the poor" as a preexisting reality that needs to be examined in terms of their identifiable characteristics. Constructivist approaches emphasize the process by which the poor get constructed as "the poor." Constructivist approaches resist naturalizing and reifying "the poor" as an othered group of those "other people" who are distinct and different by virtue of their membership in that group.

Could it be, then, that Piven and Cloward were unreflectively doing the government's bidding by reifying low-income people as this group of other people who were "the poor," "welfare mothers," and so forth? I agree with Cruikshank that this was indeed always a risk; however, Piven and Cloward and others doing the work of encouraging low-income mothers to stand up as welfare recipients and demand their rights were sensitive to the ways in which recipients were demonized as "welfare queens" and "dependents." There is nothing essentialistic in the calls to empower "the poor," or if there was, it was more of what Gayatri Chakravorty Spivak has called "strategic essentialism," a consciously crafted, socially constructed, strategic-deployed essentialism adopted by low-income single mothers in a way that could be dropped at a moment's notice once that identity lost its power to exercise leverage over the welfare state and extract needed benefits.[123] "[Strategic essentialism entails] consciously choosing to essentialize a particular community for the purpose of a specific political goal. Strategic essentialism ideally should be undertaken by the affected community, which is best situated to undertake the process of selecting the appropriate circumstances in which to offer cultural information."[124] A nonessentialistic essentialism crafted strategically from the bottom up by the oppressed themselves in their own voices to create identities that can highlight their oppression is what was arguably at work in Piven and Cloward's call to mobilize "the poor."

A close reading of the organizing efforts of the welfare rights movements suggests that low-income women were organized around "the poor" as an alternative to the already delegitimated state-imposed category of "welfare recipients."[125] And both "the poor" and "welfare recipients" were, according to ethnographic accounts, dropped in favor of "mothers" when the actual organizing was going on.[126] Further, Piven and Cloward themselves would go on to write *Poor People's Movement*. Here they underscored the dangers of organizing low-income groups into the pluralist lobbying system where they were inevitably slotted as second-class, low-budget political actors doomed to lose out in the attempts to exercise conventional political leverage in the policymaking process.[127] Instead, they called for a movement politics that resisted the ossification of "the poor" as an organized lobby. They sought to stress the importance of resistance, dissent, and a refusal to be pigeon-holed in ways that accommodated power. For Piven and Cloward, a politics of dissensus that resisted the way power positioned "the poor" was of supreme importance. In this sense, their efforts were very much appreciative of how contingency reigned supreme, and the movement needed to think strategically about how to get what it could, when it could, from those in power. A politics of dissent was a politics of contingency, adapting itself to what circumstances allowed, not insisting on fixed plans or even fixed identities. "The poor" was as strategic as later appellations such as "the homeless," designed to highlight injustice and leverage concessions from those in positions of power.[128]

The organizing of the poor as "the poor" can also be criticized as incorrectly assuming that mass activation as an identifiable group is necessary for engaging in the politics of the public sphere and the realm of action as such when in practice the "public sphere" is itself another questionable social construction for which marginal groups are slotted an inferior status politically.[129] It can also be added that with the collapse of the "social" as a space for acting in solidarity to realize rights as individuals, such mass organizing becomes even more questionable and puts organized social groupings of marginal persons at greater risk of being assimilated into the disciplinary practices of the welfare state.[130] These positions also have merit for they effectively underscore the need to think differently about politics as better focused on interventions that problematize the disciplinary practices of the state. Yet, these issues do not really pose criticisms for Piven and Cloward because their attempt to organize the poor as "the poor" was itself specifically designed to challenge the disciplinary state as manifested in coercive welfare policies.

Backlash and Gridlock: Contingency and Dissent

A politics of dissent is a politics of contingency. It suggests that there are times to be against the pitifully inadequate and often punitive welfare system and times to defend it from retrenchment and repeal. When the guaranteed income proposals had finally failed in the 1970s, it became necessary to turn to continuing the struggle for social justice in terms of what welfare could provide for those who could now receive it. The welfare rolls gridlocked at historically high levels and remained there for several decades as people made do with the limited rights to welfare they had achieved. In the face of these persistently high rolls, "the welfare mess," as it came to be called first in the Nixon administration, became an increasingly heated topic. Reform attempts increased in their intensity to restrict access to assistance and curtail rights to welfare. Defending welfare now became more important than criticizing it. Welfare became the lesser evil compared to draconian workfare policies that force people into low-wage jobs most often without sufficient preparation, training, and education to escape poverty.

When proposing the Crisis Strategy, Piven and Cloward knew that gridlock and backlash were always possible but were worth the risks given the circumstances. The circumstances, as they subsequently were to theorize them in *Regulating the Poor*, were structured by a capitalist political economy that made the prospects for progressive change limited and contingent upon agitation from below. The best that could be done was to push for improvements beyond welfare and to hold on to whatever gains could be made until the next opening. This included the possibility of enrolling people on welfare and then helping them keep their benefits if nothing better could be developed. In that sense, circumstances called for the seeming contradiction of both opposing welfare as inadequate and defending the right to access it.

Writing immediately after the assassination of Martin Luther King, Jr., Piven and Cloward noted that activists could not entirely ever know for certain how to overcome this contradiction. This was unavoidable, they insisted, because political reality always presents itself to us as something that we inevitably can never entirely control. In spite of or even because of the contingent nature of politics, dissensus was what the marginalized needed to practice because it held out the hope at least of creating new openings to get beyond existing power relations.

> It will be said that dissensual politics may so aggravate the working class that it moves further to the right, or even out of the Democratic coalition altogether. While this danger exists, it must be said that the working class is now being held securely in coalition by policies which work against the black poor. It has opted for specific and limited economic reforms, and has now become a major impediment to economic advances by the Negro.

> It will be said that disruptive tactics may spur greater violence in the cities, arousing so strong a backlash that politicians can no longer ease conflict by making concessions to different groups in a coalition. Violence is a *danger*, but since the conditions which breed violence already exist, the occasions which provoke it are manifold. To assume the burden for keeping the peace by refraining from disruptive tactics may be to forego the major reforms upon which a more enduring, less volatile peace depends.
>
> A dissensual political strategy is risky for another reason. The poor who generate disruption have little control over the responses to it. Still, the only recourse of an impoverished minority is to create the kinds of crises to which political leaders must respond, hoping that reforms will follow. In Martin Luther King's words, "We are aware that we ride the forces of history and do not totally shape them."[131]

Piven and Cloward's dissensus politics was nonviolent; however, there were risks that backlash would not be. While the United States could not be accused of practicing state terrorism against welfare families, the backlash took the form of welfare retrenchment and a shift to more intense efforts to rely on aggressive incarceration practices as the way to exercise social control over the low-income population.[132]

The Welfare Pendulum: From the 1960s to the 1990s

Given the necessity of an indeterminate dissensus politics, the foregoing suggests that the critics of the Crisis Strategy fail to properly assign responsibility for welfare gridlock. Yet, the critics also fail to assess the consequences of the growth of the rolls. For some like Tomasky, backlash is a problem because it has led to reduced support for public initiatives. For others like Siegel, the gridlock of welfare led to spending on welfare that diverted resources away from more needed programs and encouraged disinvestment from the city as an excessively expensive place to do business given the need for high taxes to support increased welfare spending. For still others like Teles, paralysis most seriously affected public discourse and our inability to imagine consensual approaches to attacking poverty. None of these perspectives has as much validity as Piven and Cloward's theory on the role of public assistance in the contemporary political economy.

Piven and Cloward's theory was most forcefully articulated in *Regulating the Poor.* There, they offer the basis of understanding how the reforms of recent years reflect that welfare is a contradictory phenomenon. The contradictions of welfare are due to its serving competing political and economic purposes. These help re-create the conditions for maintenance of the existing political economy by (1) gaining political acquiescence from the poor while still (2) enforcing their willingness to participate in low-wage labor markets. For Piven and Cloward, welfare is a secondary institution calibrated to be consonant not with the needs of the poor but with the contradictory needs of the primary institutions of the polity and of the economy to re-create political stability and reinforce the willingness to take low-wage work.[133] As such, welfare is itself wrapped in contradictions and over time would change not so much to get better as to swing in pendulum-like fashion alternating to serve political and economic objectives as conditions dictated. The possibilities for progressive change under these conditions were small and only likely to occur to the extent that agitation from below could force more substantial concessions than policymakers would normally make. Piven and Cloward were in this sense neo-Marxists: dialectical thinkers who recognized the contradictory character of social formations such as welfare; structuralists who recognized that the relationship of structure to agency did indeed constrain what was politically possible at any one point in time, but who were perhaps more open for the capacity of actors to push for change than Marx himself had allowed.[134]

Piven and Cloward's perspective was, at the time it was introduced, a startling theoretical development in the historiography of social welfare. Within a short time, it singlehandedly forced a reconsideration of the received wisdom in the field challenging the idea that social welfare history is best seen as linear, developmental, progressive, and cumulative. Piven and Cloward's *Regulating the Poor* forced us to consider that the history of social welfare provision in the United States is not something that has inexorably gotten better. This analysis upset the prevailing common sense of the social welfare scholarship at the time as represented most prominently by Harold Wilensky and Charles Lebeaux's 1958 book, *Industrial Society and Social Welfare*. In its 1965 edition it still suggested that even in the racially divided "reluctant welfare state" of the United States, their functional analysis underscored the necessity of an expanding social welfare state for an industrializing society.[135] Walter Trattner's 1974 book, which did not cite *Regulating the Poor*, reflected the consensus in its very title suggesting that the development of social welfare was a linear, cumulative, developmental process moving *From Poor Law to Welfare State*.[136] Piven and Cloward's thesis was the sociological equivalent of a scandal suggesting the blasphemous idea that in the area of social welfare policy, things had not necessarily, in all respects, all the time gotten better in a linear, developmental, progressive fashion. Instead, the history of social welfare was a lot like race relations, which today are arguably better in some respects, with less systematic job discrimination, and worse in other respects, with more segregation and opportunity hoarding in the suburbs, cordoning off persons of color from the economic resources outside the central city.

Instead of following a linear, developmental trajectory, the history of social welfare moved, for Piven and Cloward, more like a pendulum. It moved back and forth over time as it tried to work out the contradictions embedded in it. In particular, the tensions between what we can distinguish as "social assistance" and "social control" historically continued to move social welfare policy in a more cyclical fashion. Admittedly, each time the pendulum swung back it was never the same as before. Medicalization in the 1990s, criminalization in the 1950s, demonization a century before may each represent a different form for a different time in which the pendulum swung more toward social control. Still, the old wine of social control was in new bottles of social construction. The more things changed, the more they stayed the same. The old tensions persisted.

Piven and Cloward therefore in 1971 radically disrupted the consensus over the linear-developmental perspective on how social welfare policy had gotten better over time by becoming more inclusive and tolerant, moving from the poor law to the welfare state.[137] Trattner in particular, but many others as well, had a visceral reaction to Piven and Cloward's analysis.[138] This probably occurred in no small part because Piven and Cloward's clear-eyed, realistic analysis stripped away the sentimentality associated with social welfare as a kindly service toward the poor. It probably did not help that Piven and Cloward ripped away the supposed autonomy associated with social welfare provision and from a structural, neo-Marxist point of view explained how social welfare was a secondary institution calibrated to serve the purposes of the economy and the political system. From this perspective, capitalist societies had capitalist welfare—an idea that could not have sat well with the scholars of social welfare who most often were proponents of the growth of the welfare state and who saw their efforts in opposition to the harshness of capitalist practices. Worse, Piven and Cloward demonstrated that social welfare, especially in the highly capitalistic United States, tended to be very much capitalist welfare that was designed to ensure that people were offered only the limited assistance that was consistent with the needs of that particular hyper-capitalist political economy.

Under these constraints, welfare served its contradictory economic and political functions, economic by enforcing work norms and political by co-opting the poor into going along with a social order that left them out and on the bottom. Welfare tended to modulate back and forth in cyclical fashion, giving more emphasis to political co-optation during times of political instability, as during the Great Depression and the 1960s, and more emphasis on enforcing work norms during times of stability. Welfare was more liberally distributed when it was needed to re-create political stability but during times of stability it returned to being more restrictively structured to be consistent with the old principle of "less eligibility" to be below the lowest-paying jobs, to enforce the incentive to take whatever work was available.[139] Change in social welfare was historically not linear and developmental as much as it was cyclical. Things did not necessarily get better as much as they went back and forth in emphasizing political and economic functions.

Regulating the Poor was distinctive in another regard. It combined functionalist or conflict theory perspectives. In the functionalist register, it suggested that, realistically speaking, irrespective of people's motivations or intentions, welfare as a secondary institution historically served political and economic functions consistent with the needs of the primary institutions of the polity (i.e., the state) and the economy (i.e., the market). Welfare was "functional" for the existing social order in modern societies in the Western world generally. The functionalist idiom suggested that regardless of whatever humanitarian value welfare may have in providing assistance to people historically, welfare had served to rationalize the existing order by getting people to take whatever work is available, especially by operating according to the age old idea of "less eligibility" (i.e., keeping welfare benefits below the lowest-paying jobs). Welfare historically also served a political function by providing enough aid to mollify the poor and get them to go along with the existing order in spite of its inability to enable them to escape poverty.

Piven and Cloward's analysis was not a conventional functional analysis that suggested that welfare served consensually agreed upon purposes. Instead, this functional analysis was combined with its alter ego of the time—conflict theory—which suggested that in a stratified and divided society conflict was the basis for understanding all social formations, which unavoidably in all cases arose out of and were imbued with conflict. Welfare was functional for elites but less so for the masses in class-stratified societies of the Western world such as the United States. Welfare reflected these divisions and was itself riddled with conflict. Welfare simultaneously served conflicting purposes by promoting political stability in providing assistance to the needy but only doing so in ways that reinforced the need to take the lowest-paying jobs offered by the market system.

Welfare therefore made sense not just from a functionalist point of view but also from a conflict theory perspective. Welfare was very much the product or the result of conflict between the classes in capitalist societies. Historically, it has represented a compromise between the classes, part of the social contract that serves to bind people to the social order. It is a concession that the dominant classes make to the poor, and the poor, by accepting welfare, go along with the existing state of affairs. In this sense, welfare is not so much functional as it is a product of class conflict. Welfare has contradictions reflecting its attempts to fulfill both economic and political purposes. For example, it tries to enforce the work ethic but it also tries to care for families, it tries to ensure that single mothers will be personally responsible parents who work even as it provides aid so women can fulfill the role of the good mother. These contradictions are reflected in attempts to limit assistance only to the deserving poor and truly needy. As a result, welfare often seems schizophrenic regarding issues of work and family, trying to support families even as it enforces work requirements in ways that undermine them. As a result, these contradictions suggest that welfare can be a source of empowerment for single mothers (as when it offers the ability to escape an abusive relationship) even as it tends to stigmatize and demean them (as when home inspections or interrogations of their sex lives take place).

It is important to note that for Piven and Cloward there was supreme political significance in the fact that welfare also alternated in how it gave stress to these conflicting political and economic functions. The economic function was stressed during times of political stability, and, of necessity, the political function was stressed during times of unrest. For Piven and Cloward, the poor lacked enough political power to operate like a conventional interest group and derived what influence they had from being disruptive and remaining unorganized so that they could not easily be coopted. From Piven and Cloward's perspective, the poor rarely could exercise influence over social welfare policies except when they were disruptive—and even then that did not always work. By creating disorder, under the right conditions, the poor could force a shift toward more liberal forms of assistance. Yet, once order had been re-created, the pendulum was likely to swing back again. The shift in England from the guaranteed income of Speenhamland of the 1790s to the Poor Law of 1834 illustrates this dramatically. So does the shift in the United States from AFDC as it had been liberalized in the 1960s to time-limited TANF in the 1990s. After years of deadlock over persistently high welfare rolls, welfare was finally reformed in dramatic fashion with the passage of the Personal Responsibility and Work Opportunity Reconciliation Act of 1996. This readjustment of welfare dramatically reduced access to assistance by imposing work requirements and time-limiting federally funded assistance to no more than five years in a lifetime for a family. The legal gains in "welfare rights" that had been developed in the 1960s were thrown into doubt by this legislation. The growth in the rolls that had developed since the 1960s was reversed with unprecedented declines. Whereas since the 1960s states often felt obligated not to impede people's access to assistance, now states actively engaged in "diversion" programs that sought to discourage people from going on public assistance in the first place.[140] The law represented stark evidence that welfare tended to change in cyclical fashion.

Yet, not everyone has agreed that the pendulum has shifted back toward a more draconian welfare system. Some doubt this because they say welfare spending has continued to increase.[141] Piven, however, has suggested that the case can be made that the 1996 reforms represent a shift back toward more coercive forms of assistance even if we consider evidence that welfare spending has continued to increase.[142] This topic undoubtedly forces us into the quagmire of what counts as welfare spending. If we define welfare broadly, say to include social security to the nonpoor and poor elderly alike, then it will always be the case that the federal government, or the public sector in general, spends a hefty percentage of its expenditures on "welfare." Yet, if we focus the definition of welfare on only those expenditures that go to low-income persons, then the percentage drops radically. Cash assistance to poor single mothers with children is less than one percent of government spending, even adding food stamps and medical assistance keeps the percentage under five percent of total government spending. Far more money goes to the nonpoor in tax breaks alone just for child-related and housing benefits.[143]

Even within the more circumspect definition of welfare, we need to distinguish between policies that are designed to enforce work in low-wage labor and those that are more supportive of families and their needs. Spending on education and training programs for welfare recipients would be expenditures that perhaps would have to be examined closely to see where they would fall. This is Piven's point: there are arguments being made that suggest welfare spending continues to grow even with the 1996 reforms; however, these analyses fail to distinguish sufficiently among the kinds of welfare expenditures. As a result, what is being missed is that the state is cutting back on welfare benefits while it is increasing services and supports for those who take low-wage work. For Piven, this means that the cyclical movement of welfare might be better termed recommodification rather than retrenchment. The state is moving back to enforcing low-wage work requirements on the poor; it is recommodifying labor especially as it is reducing support for single mothers who stay home with their children. The net result is that the growth in welfare spending that is being detected is misleading and does not constitute evidence against the cyclical theory or evidence that the reforms of 1996 are positive. It may very well be the case that the "mean season" has returned even though social welfare expenditures are rising, for new expenditures focus more on promoting work and are part of a diversion of funding away from supporting families and ensuring their well-being.

There Are Cycles and There Are Cycles

Piven and Cloward's emphasis on the cyclical nature of welfare policy change continues to have much credibility even if the gender and race dimensions of their perspective need to be made more explicit. It could well be that the cyclical aspect of their theory of welfare, like the regulatory dimension, can be amended, if not rejected. Given the foregoing, we might want to accept that the existing political economy has profound class, race, and gender biases that prevent it from allowing state support for parents as parents. We might also want to stress that welfare historically has oscillated within a fairly constrained orbit that has allowed it to provide only limited benefits, often only at the state or local level in ways consistent with local culture, politics, and labor market needs.

Given these constraints, it is worth considering that the cyclical pattern of welfare policy change occurs because programs are initiated to fit within this context. However, as they expand over time, they are retrenched when they begin to conflict with the constraining environment. Retrenchment in turn eventually gives rise to new programs to compensate those who have been seen as unfairly excluded. Then the cycle repeats with a new round of expansion and retrenchment. Rather than there being a "welfare trap" for recipients that prevents them from becoming "self-sufficient," there is a welfare trap for society where the policy process is stuck in this vicious cycle.

This thesis is perhaps best represented by Deborah Stone's *The Disabled State*. This book focuses on the historical development of disability policy in the United States in particular but which can be used to suggest that welfare programs in market-centered societies are prone to go through such cycles.[144] For Stone, in market-centered societies such as the United States, most people are expected to provide for themselves and their families via what Stone calls the "work-based system," which is most heavily centered in the private labor markets where people are said to "earn" their income and benefits.[145] Not everyone can do so, however, so the work system needs to be supplemented with what Stone calls the "need-based system."[146] The needs system is concentrated in the public sector in government entitlement programs where, if people can gain legitimacy as deserving of being exempted from the work system, they can receive access to the income and benefits offered by this safety net. The old and the young are most likely to qualify for exemptions. The "disabled" are a much-contested category that is continually under scrutiny for being exempted from the work system and qualified to receive assistance from the needs system.

For Stone, the battles over disability demonstrate that the major way in which people can qualify for the needs system is by proving their "innocence" in the sense of showing that they are not personally responsible for their inability to participate in the work system.[147] Some groups find this harder to prove than others: say, alcoholics and drug addicts compared to those with physical impairments. Disability purges arise periodically to rid the rolls of people whose "innocence" has come under suspicion. This purging occurs in response to program growth that is often interpreted negatively as undermining the importance of the market. Examples from disability policy over the last decade bear this out, as in the case of program growth that provoked purges of persons with chemical dependencies. Yet, as the example of disability purges amply indicates over time, concern arises that some of those who have been cut off are really "innocent," and the need for new programs or opportunities to regain assistance under old programs builds. Stone basically is suggesting, given her model, that this cyclical process of qualifying and purging people for assistance is endemic to welfare states in market-centered societies where concern about the growth of government is perennial.[148]

The contemporary welfare retrenchment is therefore likely to give rise to two new kinds of programs: (1) compensatory treatment programs for people with personal issues that prevent them from being "job ready"; and (2) educational programs for those who are trying to live on more than the inadequate wages offered for entry-level jobs. Neither of these compensatory responses addresses the work biases of welfare policy. For those who are seeking support for parenting, improvements in child support will help some, including increased efforts to support noncustodial parents in improving their employability. Yet, many poor single parents, mostly mothers, will still not be supported in this mix of responses. After education and treatment, this is the frontier of welfare reform: how to support single parents who need to stay at home with their children. Case advocacy can only go so far, working, as it must, with the policy options in existence. Eventually, we need to expand the mix of policy responses to welfare reform to include either revising existing programs, such as child support, unemployment compensation, social security, or even tax exemptions, or to develop new programs to support the ability of mothers to be effective parents.

This becomes especially the case if we look at ethnographic data concerning women on welfare. Kathryn Edin has highlighted the variety of issues that discourage poor single mothers from marrying or remarrying.[149] Based on a study of 320 women in the Philadelphia area, she has found that issues of finances, control, and trust are large for many of these women such that they often are "forced" to "choose" to stay unmarried. With neither low-wage work nor welfare able to support them enough, the dilemmas over marriage are particularly painful. In the background are the changes in the broader political economy that make it more difficult for the fathers, partners, or other men who might become partners to earn enough to support these families. As welfare passes away and the low-wage job market becomes the prevailing reality, the nation must begin to address this issue in some other way. As Matthew Crenson has pointed out, historically, basing welfare policy on children has been one of the few acceptable ways to legitimate assistance for low-income families.[150] From orphanages, to mother's pensions, to Aid to Families with Dependent Children, children have been the "innocents" we have been prepared at least to consider supporting through public aid on the basis of need rather than through private labor markets based on work.[151] Child support assurance therefore seems likely to be part of the next swing in this cycle as the pendulum of policy indecisiveness and lack of commitment to all families turns back from the cruelties of the 1996 welfare reform.

Big Bangs versus Incremental Reforms

Another source of reconsideration of the cyclical theory comes from scholars who emphasize historical approaches that lead them to reject the idea that social welfare policy change is wrought by a "big bang" of dramatic action. Part of the cyclical theory is that welfare shifts back to being more accessible when there is the need to re-create political stability. Political instability is associated with agitation from below. Agitation from below instigates political instability, which in turns leads to a dramatic liberalization of welfare. As a result, real improvements in welfare tend to be dramatic leaps forward that occur episodically under conditions of extreme political instability and mass agitation. The most dramatic instances of this in the United States are the movements agitating for change during the Great Depression and the 1960s. Yet, in a thoughtful and important book, *Building the Invisible Orphanage: A Prehistory of the American Welfare System*, Matthew Crenson writes:

> This effort to understand the evolution of social policy and social welfare institutions draws some of its guidance from recent research on the development—or underdevelopment—of the American welfare state. Like Theda Skocpol and Michael Katz, I have departed from the "big bang" theory of the welfare state, which locates the origin of modern social policy in the legislative explosion that occurred in the early years of the New Deal. Instead, I look for the roots of welfare in institutional developments of the late nineteenth and early twentieth centuries. But I carry the investigation in somewhat different directions from Katz or Skocpol. Unlike Katz, I emphasize the formative role of the orphanage rather than the poorhouse in the development of welfare. Unlike Skocpol, I am concerned not so much with explaining the adoption of social policies like the mothers' pension, but with accounting for their formation or "invention."[152]

Crenson raises an important issue. While the contrasts with Michael Katz and Theda Skocpol are interesting, the more important contrast is between them and Crenson on the one hand and Piven and Cloward on the other.[153] Crenson rejects what he calls the "big bang" approach to explaining the development of the modern welfare system. He specifically cites the New Deal legislation as the focus of this perspective. He uses an approach that he implies is more historically informed and gradualist. It traces how the accumulation of institutional practices lays down the context that will eventually, in a less dramatic if more powerful way, create the basis for the elaboration of the modern welfare system. He stresses the ways in which welfare under these conditions is "invented." By this, I take him to mean that he is using a more genealogical approach of Michel Foucault that focuses on the ways in which the dissemination of practices, discursive and otherwise, across a wide swath of society's disciplinary institutions are insinuated into personal relations that help make some ways of providing social welfare seem plausible and possible while others are not. This sort of genealogical approach can be contrasted with Piven and Cloward's more structuralist approach. This approach emphasizes how at specific points in time, when conditions allow for it, social change can take the proverbial "great leap forward." In this sense, Piven and Cloward were in their own way "big bang" theorists of social welfare policy change. Their Crisis Strategy in particular was a bold application of such a perspective. It was a stunning and brilliant example of making the connection between theory and practice.

Crenson's gradualist perspective seems to be at odds with the "big bang" approach of Piven and Cloward and would likely make him an opponent of the Crisis Strategy, even though he never addresses this issue. Yet, there are both empirical and theoretical issues that need attention in this contrast. First, there is the empirical question of whether orphanages, poorhouses, mothers' pensions, or the accumulation of institutional practices of this sort over the long haul were critical in the formation of the modern welfare system in the United States. On this point, there is likely to be much debate, as already witnessed by the differences among the gradualists like Crenson, Katz, and Skocpol. Yet, that debate aside, there is the larger theoretical issue of whether the gradual accumulation of institutional practices in orphanages or elsewhere was more important than more dramatic events, including mass insurgency undertaken under the appropriate structural conditions.

This second empirical issue points toward a larger theoretical question. As Piven and Cloward emphasized in *Regulating the Poor* and especially in *Poor People's Movements*, irrespective of whether structural conditions, societal values, or even the accumulation of institutional practices had created the basis for progressive social welfare policy change, such change was not likely to occur without agitation from the bottom when the time was right. This was especially true when elites were fragmented and vulnerable, making them open to granting concessions in order to re-create the conditions for political stability.[154] Orphanages may have put the focus of social welfare on children and therefore helped lay the basis for mothers' pensions. This outcome in turn influenced the development of Aid to Dependent Children in the Social Security Act of 1935. Yet, that does not mean the Social Security Act of 1935 had to be passed when it did. Nor did it mean that the Social Security Act had to be liberal in extending benefits to the poor. Agitation from below may have indeed been necessary for that to happen. Gradual developments may have incrementally created the conditions for change, but that change might not have happened as it did without agitation from below.

An additional theoretical issue concerns what I would suggest is a question of perspective. Crenson's interest in history, in particular his interest in what Skocpol has referred to as "historical institutionalism," may encourage him to overemphasize how the historical accumulation of institutional practice lays the foundation for social welfare policy change. Crenson is following Skocpol here in emphasizing the importance of an interdisciplinary approach that combines social theory and historical analysis. Yet, this approach may encourage the overemphasis on historical details to the neglect of broader structural forces at work in laying down the context for social welfare policy change. Capitalist political economy may have operated as a structural constraint on both institutional practice and the elaboration of social welfare policy.

Piven and Cloward have not been ones to neglect the importance of history. Yet, their history is discussed in terms of an explicit theory of the way social welfare has operated as a secondary institution calibrated to be consonant with the overarching political and economic institutions. Crenson is cognizant of this perspective and cites Piven and Cloward favorably as offering an example of theorists whose work explains the role of social welfare policies in society as forms of social control. Their work can therefore be seen as consistent with Foucault's emphasis on the ways institutions elaborate practices in order to discipline the subjects of the social order.[155] Therefore, Piven and Cloward's work suggests that an emphasis on history need not necessarily lead either to a gradualist perspective or one that is inconsistent with an emphasis on the ways social welfare institutions work to enforce discipline and promote social control.

The historical-institutional approach need not promote a particular political orientation. Skocpol has thoughtfully emphasized this point in a discussion of her methodology.[156] It can promote even graduations of gradualism. It does seem that the historical orientation has, however, made gradualists of both Crenson and Skocpol, though in different ways. Crenson's emphasis on a more genealogical approach that examines how the elaboration of institutional practices allows for the "invention" of modern social welfare policy ties Crenson's gradualism to a rather limited perspective on the possibilities for social change. His approach is limited in its tie to a Foucauldian kind of struggle against the micropractices of disciplining institutions. Skocpol's gradualism arises from a perspective that emphasizes how, historically, change comes in terms of what the institutional framework allows. Yet, as opposed to Crenson, she is more optimistic since it turns out she has come to be supportive of the basic work and family values emphasized by that framework.[157]

The gradualist perspective therefore may to varying degrees and in different ways in different cases be a self-fulfilling prophecy that discourages consideration of the possibilities for dramatic policy change via political agitation from below. As Piven and Cloward themselves have emphasized, a historical perspective is critical for understanding how social welfare policy gets made. However, considerations of history need not mean that welfare policy change must always result from the gradual accumulation of institutional practices. Nor do such considerations necessitate neglect of how political economy operates both to constrain and to make change possible. In writing about how historical circumstances shape popular mobilizations for social change, Piven and Cloward have noted:

> [The] conditions for the realization of class power, and the ability of groups to manipulate them, depend on very specific and concrete historical circumstances. To appreciate this, we have to forgo our tendency to speak of classes and systems. For some purposes, these abstractions are of course useful. But the interdependencies which sometimes make assertions of popular power possible don't exist in general or in the abstract. They exist for particular groups, who are in particular relationships with particular capitalists or particular state authorities, at particular places and particular times.[158]

Therefore, there are reasons to question the growing tendency to replace Piven and Cloward's structuralist perspective and its own version of a "big bang" approach with more gradualist perspectives of either the genealogical or historical-institutional kind.[159] A better response would be to examine the ways that genealogical and historical-institutional approaches to change relate to the "big bang" perspective.[160]

Given the foregoing analysis, it would be a mistake to criticize Piven and Cloward as if they were strict theorists or practitioners of "big bang" politics. For critics who prefer a strong emphasis on institutions or organizations, it has long been tempting to paint a caricature of Piven and Cloward as unflinching partisans of the "inchoate uprisings of anomic masses."[161] But this criticism is based on a polarity that Piven and Cloward have consistently identified as false. They never suggested that mass disruption—on its own, undertaken in ignorance of structural, institutional, and organizational circumstances—could be counted on to yield victories for the poor. On the contrary, they have consistently argued that the origins and consequences of mass disruption depend, first and foremost, on historical and structural circumstances.

Mass disruption, in Piven and Cloward's account, is more appropriate and effective in some historical circumstances than in others. They have never favored dramatic, momentary spasms of mass unrest *to the exclusion of* more gradualist developments. Instead, Piven and Cloward have argued that protest politics and more reformist approaches need to work in tandem. When conditions are right, mass disruption can contribute to making worthwhile reforms more realizable; institutional reforms, on the other hand, can establish the conditions needed for effective protest. In this sense, it may be said that their approach is no less historical or institutional than those of the other theorists considered here.

Radical Incrementalism

Recognizing the interrelationships between gradualist and more dramatic approaches to social change strategy creates an opening for considering how Piven and Cloward's laudable model for combining politics and scholarship is consistent with what I call "radical incrementalism."[162] Radical incrementalism is like conventional incrementalism in that it leads to small changes in public policy, taking what can be feasibly given by the political system at any one point in time. It also shares with conventional incrementalism a disinterest in relying on plans, blueprints, and comprehensive visions for informing what should be done. Its similarity with conventional incrementalism, however, stops there.

Conventional incrementalism pushes for small, remedial, technical corrections in existing public policy in ways that fine-tune and reinforce the existing state of affairs. Conventional incrementalism works within the existing bounds of acceptable political discourse, does not question its underlying assumptions, and works within that context to make minor improvements in existing public policy. Conventional incrementalism is at risk of making changes that do not begin to address the ways in which policy problems are built right into the very foundations of the current structure of society, the distribution of power, and the terms for elaborating change.[163]

Radical incrementalism, by contrast, does not accept the conventional bounds, assumptions, context and limits that inform established policy. Instead, it explicitly challenges them, pushing for different sorts of changes than can usually be squeezed from the policy process. Yet, not any changes are acceptable for a radical incrementalism. Instead, radical incrementalism pushes for the reluctantly granted concessions that not only improve the immediate circumstances of those most harmed by existing policy, but also lay the basis for building upon that success for even greater changes in the future, which can over time cumulatively result in the transition beyond the current limits-constraining policy. This then is an incrementalism that can over time cumulatively amount to more significant challenges to embedded biases of existing policy.[164]

Incrementalism is also often contrasted with comprehensive policymaking.[165] A related distinction in the area of social welfare policy involves targeted categorical programs for discrete populations with specific needs versus broad, universalistic policies where eligibility is not tied to membership in a specific group. Social Security retirement insurance is often pointed to as a universal program where public assistance to families with children is offered as an example of a targeted categorical program. Part of the criticism of Piven and Cloward is that their work with the welfare rights movement focused too narrowly on short-run political gains for low-income families with children so that, in the end, these families were only further marginalized in an inferior categorical program just for them. The argument therefore faults Piven and Cloward for eschewing both comprehensive decision making and universalistic policies. As a result, welfare became increasingly isolated and delegitimated as a public program. Eventually, it was retrenched in 1996.[166]

Yet, as Piven and Cloward have themselves noted, the success of the reformers in undermining welfare to low-income families was hardly due to the fact that welfare rights activists failed to think about universalistic programs comprehensively. The welfare rights movement grew out of the more broad-based civil rights movement and was initially part of efforts to push for more dramatic broad-gauged policies to create jobs, increase wages, and promote social justice for low-income persons in general. It only became more focused on improving access to welfare as those more dramatic calls for change failed to move liberal policymakers to take action. And, we should not forget, when the welfare rights movement pushed for policy change at the national level, it emphasized a universalistic guaranteed income. It is important to distinguish the orientation of the activists from the concessions government makes. Calls for universalistic policies often result in the adoption of categorical policies. And comprehensive thinking about what needs to be done often results in incremental actions being taken.

Piven and Cloward can therefore be seen as radical incrementalists not because they contented themselves with small changes but because they recognized that dramatic political mobilizations, from below, in the name of comprehensive policy change and universal social policies, often result in more modest concessions being extracted from the powerful. For this reason, they were less concerned about plans and blueprints for the ideal society. Their radicalism derives instead from the fact that they were willing to challenge the fundamental premises of existing social policy. Their incrementalism derives from the fact that they were savvy enough to recognize that incremental concessions would often be all that they could get. Their radical incrementalism emerges when we appreciate how they focused on pushing for concessions that actually made for improvements in people's lives in their immediate circumstances and did so in a way that could empower people to demand even more in the future.

As radical incrementalists, Piven and Cloward pushed for universalistic policy change recognizing that they might only get categorical reforms, but emphasized that such reforms should create the conditions for more inclusive policies in the future. As they themselves put it:

> We think, in fact, that the welfare rights movement actually did move the categorical programs in the direction of universalism. For one thing, welfare rights agitation and litigation helped bring the rule of law to AFDC and other means-tested programs which had been designed in the 1930s to allow enormous discretion to state legislatures and local officials, the better to mesh practices with local labor requirements and local political animosities. . . . But the goal of universalism aside, we estimate that the enormous expansion of the means-tested programs meant that something on the order of a trillion dollars flowed to the poorest people in America over the past three decades. It was not enough, and the flow is now dwindling, but it was not negligible.

> Someone will say, indeed many people will say, that the liberalized means-tested programs didn't last, and universal programs would have lasted. As to the first, true. People got what they could, while they could. But the more universal programs that the Left favors were beyond their political reach. . . . Anyway, even if, universal solutions had not been beyond reach, there isn't much reason for confidence that they would have survived the right-wing juggernaut of the 1990s, either.[167]

The Piven and Cloward Legacy

Piven and Cloward were distinctive intellectuals in an age when most people who accept that label have been assimilated into institutions of higher learning and have assumed the role of academics. As academics, institutional constraints limit political involvement and funnel scholarship toward theory building, theory testing, and the growth of knowledge as an end in itself. Academic politics is often conflict over theoretical orientations rather than conflict over public policy positions.

Among scholars who do want their work to connect to ongoing struggles outside the academy, two different sorts of institutional constraints often limit that connection. First, much politically relevant work still seeks, as its first commitment, to make a difference within a particular specialized area of scholarship—a particular school of thought, theoretical orientation, or specialized area of study. The relationship to informing, empowering, or aiding in any ongoing political struggle becomes secondary. Often the hope remains that the academic advances will trickle down to serve as the basis for political advances as ideas are influenced, thinking gets changed, and people generally come to question established understandings of the topic in question whether it is gender relations, the role of the state in perpetuating the market system, or whatever else. Yet, this hope for the realization of this "trickle down" theory of intellectual work is in most cases infinitely deferred. The weaknesses of the ideas and the unwillingness of people to hear them are two prominent hypotheses for this infinite deferral.

Second, for the more empirically oriented researchers, being an academic first often means couching one's research in ostensibly neutral terms and allowing the "facts to speak for themselves." The political implications of the research is left to others to decide. The hope here is the one most forcefully expressed by Max Weber in the early days of modern social science around the turn of the last century, to wit: social scientists will achieve their greatest political impact by establishing first their bonafides as impartial researchers. In other words, the best way to have political impact as a social scientist is not to be political. Yet, this wish is also often unfulfilled. The case of welfare scholarship has often dramatically demonstrated in recent years how easy it is to misappropriate neutral research to serve politically tendentious purposes of across-the-board retrenchment of public assistance programs.[168]

Piven and Cloward never allowed the institutional constraints of higher education and the exclusionary practices of academic research to intrude on their model of combining scholarship and politics. Surpassing Weber's hopes for a politically relevant social science, they did so by rejecting his injunction for self-censorship and enforced neutrality. Ellwood was closer to Weber's model and he was co-opted seriously by the Clinton administration—"mugged by reality," as DeParle has said.

Piven and Cloward of course paid a price for rising above the petty constraints of the academy. Piven was rejected for appointment at Columbia University, forcing her to leave Cloward in New York; and Cloward, in an attempt to join Piven in the Boston area, applied for a professorship at Brandeis University, only to be turned down. As a subsequent report from the American Sociological Association indicated, Brandeis faculty on the governing body responsible for deciding tenure treated Cloward improperly according to their own guidelines, politicizing his case and resisting his appointment on a partisan basis.[169] Cloward remained at Columbia, while Piven subsequently took a professorship at the Graduate Center of the City University of New York.

Piven and Cloward also went farther than most to articulate relationships between their theoretical and empirical studies, on the one hand, and their activism and the needs of the movement for social change, on the other. They found ways to remain intellectually honest and were still able to offer insightful critiques even as they spoke and wrote consistently in ways that provided useful strategic thinking for organizers and activists alike. Sometimes their positions were resisted, as with the arguments in *Poor People's Movements*, which called for the poor to exercise their only political leverage—the ability to create disruption and cause instability in the political system—rather than pretend they could join other groups in forming formalized organizations dedicated to the traditional interest group lobbying process.[170] They found ways to question established understandings inside and outside the movement even as they worked to make the movement more effective.

Piven and Cloward were also willing to shift gears, as when welfare rights organizing began to falter as a strategy for creating more dramatic changes than simply giving increased access to the existing inadequate system of public assistance. They turned to voter registration as another means to destabilize the existing political system—this time by creating the conditions under which large numbers of low-income citizens could come into the electoral process for the first time, thereby upsetting the established campaign strategies of playing strictly to the middle and upper classes. They founded Human SERVE and it led to the passage of the Motor Voter bill, which has increased low income voter turnout and makes possible future increases.[171]

While some on the left, including Stanley Aronowitz and others, criticized this shift as contradictory, they were as mistaken, it seems to me, as those such as Wendy Brown who criticized Piven and Cloward for the alleged contradiction of first attacking welfare and then defending it.[172] Voter registration was not in contradiction with protest politics; it was a related way to revise the structural conditions that establish the mix of barriers and possibilities for future confrontational politics. A crucial point in Piven and Cloward's analysis is that the success of dissensus politics hinges on the vulnerability of public officials; this vulnerability in turn depends on low-income people's access to the electoral process.[173]

By creating the possibility that low-income groups could more readily mobilize electorally and have an influence in elections, Piven and Cloward hoped that Motor Voter registration would heighten the capacity for protest politics to be seen as having a potential impact on the political system beyond "causing a scene." With these changed conditions, protesters could also be seen as raising issues of concern to a larger pool of potential voters. They would not be seen as one or the other but as people who could be both. Piven and Cloward had previously emphasized how African American civil rights protesters could be more effective once they had the right to vote.[174] Now, they were making a similar argument for welfare and low-income groups more generally.

Therefore, it is not only a mistake to criticize Piven and Cloward for being contradictory on shifting from a protest to an electoral strategy, it is a mistake to now criticize them if it turns out that increases in low-income voter turnout under Motor Voter have not been as dramatic as some had hoped. Both the before and after criticisms fail to appreciate that Piven and Cloward never saw protest politics and electoral politics as mutually exclusive. They saw them as interdependent.[175] Protest politics would be more effective where the electoral threat could potentially be actualized, and electoral politics would be more effective where groups that are traditionally marginalized by that process were willing to exercise other sources of influence. In both cases, Piven and Cloward were working to revise the structural conditions under which the oppressed's capacity to act[176] and what they came to call their "repertoires of power"[177] could be expanded. For Piven and Cloward it was critical to diagnose the structural conditions in terms of the capacity for action that would force more attention to the needs of those in poverty. This always required giving attention to how structural conditions did and did not allow the marginalized to get heard in the political system.

Motor Voter was another bottom-up strategy for pursuing a radical incrementalism. In their quest to allow people on the bottom of society to rise and be heard, to make their own history as it were, Piven and Cloward were not to be deterred by precious academic distinctions between "radical" protest politics and "conventional" electoral politics. They recognized their interrelationships. In the real world of political struggles in the late twentieth century United States, there was nothing conventional about low-income people voting. Ending the class bias of the electoral system was radical and fraught with numerous political possibilities, which the people who ensured George W. Bush his "stolen" electoral victory knew all too well. That is why they took various actions to disenfranchise large numbers of newly registered low-income African American Florideans in the 2000 presidential election.

Therefore, Piven and Cloward's legacy is very much as "radical incrementalists" who were willing to move their scholarship in new directions and revise their focus as the contingencies of movement politics necessitated. In-depth study of the inequities of the election system followed probing analyses of what made for effective protest movements. The shift followed the turns in the movement as it moved from pushing for a guaranteed income to trying to develop new energies to challenge established power in other ways. Piven and Cloward allowed their scholarship to be true to their most basic insight—that worthwhile political change on behalf of those on the bottom of the social order never came unless the people on the bottom rose up and demanded it themselves. Piven and Cloward allowed those on the bottom to inform their scholarship as much as the other way around. And when they did so, they recognized this meant forgoing blueprints, comprehensive plans, and grandiose schemes for change in the name of pushing for what concessions they could extract from power.

I think Piven and Cloward at times bemoaned the failure of the left to continue to articulate a vision of a universal welfare state, and in this sense they were more foundationalists than their actions suggested.[178] They recognized the role of utopian thinking in providing motivation to want to do better.[179] They were perhaps more modernists than postmodernists. At times, their writing failed to capture how they worked with the contingencies of politics. Their efforts reflected scholar/activists who pushed for what was needed not for all time, but for what was called for in any one point in time. In this sense, Piven and Cloward remained radical incrementalists perhaps more than they themselves would allow.

Yet, if what I have suggested here has any merit, we can see that Piven and Cloward thoughtfully and intelligently eschewed blueprints for politics even as they recognized the role of idealistic and utopian thinking among the oppressed as a source of inspiration and energy. They recognized that the "Promised Land" was infinitely deferred, never fully realizable, and something after which we constantly strive. In its wake, politics called for making the best of the current predicament. In so doing they practiced radical incrementalism: their orientation was radical, while their strategy was incremental. In the end, their legacy is a model not just for welfare scholarship but all scholarship.

Conclusion

There are reasons to suggest that Piven and Cloward's political scholarship was both good social science and sound political strategy. They courageously put their scholarly reputations on the line. They did so in service of the struggle for social justice. They recognized that their chances of succeeding were not great; however, they remained committed to the necessity to combine scholarship and politics and contribute efforts to promote progressive change as best as they could. Their own theories, stretching back before the publication of *Regulating the Poor* in 1971, alerted them to the fact that this struggle was not likely to succeed, even if those same theories suggested that they had no alternative but to try nonetheless. Yet, they did so knowing the alternatives were worse.

When asked about whether he felt that the welfare reforms of 1996 were a backlash to the Crisis Strategy, Cloward simply stated: "We knew that trouble was coming. Our view is the poor don't win much, and they only win it episodically. You get what you can when you can get it—and then you hold onto your hat."[180] This casually worded summation, however, subtly suggests the profundity of Piven and Cloward's work as scholar-activists. It reflects how their intellectual and political work involved working through the contradictions built into welfare by combining theory and practice, scholarship and politics, in a way that sensitively integrated a "politics of survival" with a "politics of social change." This was all done recognizing that politics was a contingent practice and that dissensus politics was the only real tool that persons living in poverty could wield in the contingent world of politics. While such work itself recognizes that it will not produce a smooth and linear road to social justice, it still holds intellectual and political merit that the critics have all too often missed.

The real genius of Piven and Cloward's work is that they showed how scholarship could contribute to activism without compromising its intellectual integrity. They not only analyzed the conditions of structural domination in order to promote greater understanding, they did so in ways that elaborated how the oppressed could challenge those structures of domination. They were able to do this because of the centrality they gave to politics as a force for making change happen. They were neither theorists without implications for practice nor determinists without hope that politics could make a difference. Whatever the topic, their work reflected an enduring theme of demonstrating how politics was important, how activism could make a difference, how theorizing and analyzing the conditions of oppression could be done in a way that suggested opportunities to dissent, resist, mobilize and work for change.

Piven and Cloward's work therefore has offered us a laudable model of how to combine politics and scholarship in ways that can promote a "radical incrementalism" that challenges the existing limits of power while working to produce whatever change can be obtained under such circumstances. It eschews dreaming of blueprints for the struggle to gain concessions from power. It is simultaneously more radical and more realistic than its alternatives. Over the long haul, Piven and Cloward's work has not only helped low-income families by the legions to receive needed assistance, it has done so in ways that have kept alive the basis for taking action on behalf of building a more socially just welfare state in the United States. And when the time is right, the next moves can build on what came before, in no small part due to the efforts of Piven and Cloward.

4

Which Side Are You On?

Rethinking Research and Advocacy in Social Welfare

The politics of scholarship in recent years highlights the difficulties of articulating politically productive and socially progressive relationships between social science research and social welfare politics. These difficulties are demonstrated in several recent calls for reconfiguring the relationship of social science to social welfare. Pleas for both a more political and a more scientific social science have rung hollow to me. A good part of the problem is their failure to give a priority to political struggle.

In what follows, I examine two calls for changing the relationship of social science to social welfare—one that calls for more politics in the social science of welfare and poverty, and one that calls for less politics in research on social work practice. While I find the former more appealing and therefore spend less time criticizing it, both are, in my mind, inadequate. Both fail to give sufficient priority to political struggle as the first order of business, the unavoidable starting point for analysis, and the ineliminable reality of the relationship of social science to social welfare policy and practice. Both fail to appreciate the importance of resisting the pitfalls associated with a "top-down" approach to connecting research to politics and of giving more emphasis to a "bottom-up" approach that starts with the people who are struggling to challenge the power that oppresses them.[1] Both take what should be a debate about which different types of research should be seen as making significant contributions to knowledge and turn it into a basis for implying that "research" is by definition appropriately limited to a highly select group of conventional qualitative and quantitative analyses. And for this reason, both in the end are unlikely to encourage forms of research that are consonant with "radical incrementalism." In what follows, I suggest why and offer some thoughts on research that is more consistent with radical incrementalism.

Political Contingency: The Ineliminable Reality

In *Poverty Knowledge*, Alice O'Connor offers a meticulously researched and thoughtfully composed history of the role of social science in social welfare policy.[2] Her examination of the history of social science research on poverty suggests that it has increasingly become a highly technical field dominated by quantitative modeling grounded in economic reasoning. As a result, the field has become more narrow, less critical, and more in service of state power. She recommends more methodological diversity and encourages a politicized scholarship that is more attentive to how its research gets appropriated for political purposes in the public policy arena.

Yet, I can offer only qualified support for O'Connor's call for a politically engaged, methodologically diverse social science of poverty. Her call for methodological diversity and political engagement is only the beginning of the kind of thinking needed to promote a better future of social science in social welfare. *Poverty Knowledge* is a work of history and is not to be faulted for not demonstrating in detail what the new and improved social science would look like. Nor should it be criticized for not clarifying how the role of social science in social welfare would be different if its recommendations were followed. These are not valid criticisms for me. I do have concerns that by not specifying the proposed alternative social science and its role in social welfare, O'Connor leaves the door open for less than favorable versions of her suggestions to be emphasized by others.[3] Yet, I have additional concerns that I want to emphasize here. I am interested in offering the kind of criticism that is consistent with the spirit of O'Connor's call for a more methodologically diverse and politically engaged social science of poverty. I want to criticize O'Connor for not going far enough in calling for a new poverty knowledge. Simply put, my main criticism is that calling for methodological diversity and political engagement are not enough if we want to engender a more politically progressive role for social science research in social welfare politics.

More than methodological diversity and political engagement, we need to invert the relationship of social science research to social welfare policy. We need to challenge the assumption that social science in theory precedes social welfare advocacy in practice. We need to challenge, therefore, the assumption that research is the foundation for policy, and that there is a logical order to things where thought comes first and action follows based on rational plans.

Actually, even this is not enough, we need to go even farther to challenge the whole linear paradigm and the categorical distinctions that underlie it. We need to see theory and practice as entwined and we need to give up the idea that social change proceeds in linear fashion on the basis of thought-out plans of action. Instead of continuing to cling to the linear paradigm, we need to consider the possibility that a better relationship of theory to practice and social science research to social welfare policy lies in seeing them in a more dynamic relationship.

Embracing this alternative perspective allows for consideration of how thought and action, theory and practice, scholarship and politics, and social science and social welfare are inextricably entwined, actively and continually influencing each other. On the issue of moving to a more dynamic model of the relationship of social science to social change, there are parallels to what Bent Flyvbjerg has written about the relationship of rationality to power:

> I have found that modernity and democracy have a "blind spot" in their reflexivity regarding the real relationship between rationality and power. Ideals seem to block the view to reality. Modern democratic constitutions typically prescribe a separation of rationality and power, much like the untenable separation of fact and value in conventional social and political thinking. The ideal prescribes that first we must know about a problem, then we decide about it. For example, first the civil servants in the administration investigate a policy problem, then they inform their minister, who informs parliament, who decides on the problem. Power is brought to bear on the problem only after we have made ourselves knowledgeable about it.
>
> In reality, however, power often ignores or designs knowledge at its convenience. A consequence of the blind spot is that the real relationship between rationality and power gets little attention both in conventional constitution writing and in the research literature. There is a large gray area between rationality and power, which is under-investigated.[4]

Further embracing this more dynamic model means also accepting the ineliminable reality of political contingency.[5] A full embrace of the dynamic model includes accepting the radically political character of the social world and how it is something that grows out and returns to political contingency and the indeterminacy that comes with it. The full embrace of the dynamic model includes accepting that we do not have all the answers, that rational thought, whether in the form of science or philosophy, cannot supply them, and, most critically, that the problems of the social world are politically constructed and must be responded to in kind—that is, through politics. The answers to any one social problem are inevitably multiple and only politics can settle which answers work best. Political struggle is therefore essential and unavoidable. It has priority over everything else when it comes to deciding what to do about social arrangements.

Therefore, by implication the dynamic model also requires recognition of how social justice itself is something that must be continually redefined, as an ever-reconsidered, never fully realized socially desired state. From this perspective, social justice is not to be seen as an end state that can ever be fully defined or even ever fully achieved. Instead, it too is an artifact of political contingency and subject to reevaluation depending upon what circumstances are before us.

No matter how ineffable social justice is in the dynamic model, once we embrace this perspective on the relationship of social science to social welfare, we can see how struggles for social justice have priority, how ongoing action provides the basis for thought, how practice gives rise to theory, and how social science should grow out of the real problems that confront those working for better social welfare policies. Under these conditions of political contingency, emphasis is given to trying to research and understand what is needed to be known in order to better facilitate change as it is currently being pursued. Research is not something that provides definitive answers to what social welfare policy ought to be like as much as it becomes another useful device for leveraging political change. Under these conditions, researchers perform an underlaborer's role, but it is an underlaborer for those struggling to overcome the oppressions of the existing social order. And research helps perform this role by providing politically contingent, historically contextualized, socially bounded knowledge that can help strengthen efforts for social change. This is still knowledge, not mere opinion; but it is hardly universal, timeless, objective, and disinterested. Instead, it is a situated, partial, and interested knowledge tied to political struggle and efforts to change social conditions.

Therefore, when we accept the ineliminable reality of politics, we must start by deciding which side we are on, by being involved in political struggle, by working to help the oppressed more effectively confront oppression and to develop responses. This must be done recognizing that the process is inherently political in still another sense of the term—that is, in the sense that the "solutions" are ones that oppressed people make through their own participation in collaborative processes. It is a political process, then, in this best sense of the term that suggests there are no scientific or philosophical truths that can tell us what is the right thing to do in all instances. Instead, theory and research can help us fashion our own collective responses, taking into account the contingencies that we currently confront.

The process is political in the sense that people have to decide for themselves, collectively and collaboratively. In other words, in order to promote a better role for social science in social welfare, we need to rethink the relationship of scholarship to politics in its entirety. O'Connor's *Poverty Knowledge* fails to do this. Her analysis suggests she is for the most part content to continue with the implied linear paradigm and its foundational logic, which assumes social science research precedes the making of social welfare policy. It is very telling that O'Connor's critique of the social science of poverty and welfare excludes consideration of alternatives that have existed for much of the history she considers. After noting in her first chapter how people like Jane Addams did reflect her alternative model, she becomes preoccupied with criticizing the ways mainstream, liberal social science addressed issues of poverty and welfare. Her criticisms are good for as far as they go, but her exclusion of more critical-minded social scientists and their work suggests that she has not given sufficient attention to the alternative models that are already available. Worse, her failure to consider alternative models might suggest that she does not consider them worthy of serious consideration. In either case, her failure to consider already-existing alternatives is related to the insufficiency of her own recommendations.

Particularly noteworthy for its absence in a book on the history of the relationship of social science to social welfare is the work of Frances Fox Piven and Richard A. Cloward, arguably the most politically influential scholars writing about social welfare in the 1960s and 1970s.[6] *Poverty Knowledge* does devote some attention to the early work of Cloward, especially his work with Lloyd Ohlin in *Delinquency and Opportunity* and their theory of "differential opportunity structures" as the primary cause of poverty.[7] O'Connor, however, ignores the subsequent substantial body of work that Cloward was to do with Piven from the mid-1960s right through the end of the century. Part of the reason is most likely that this work was not, strictly speaking, social science research in the sense that it was not "studies" as in experiments, surveys, field projects, or ethnographies. Instead, Piven and Cloward, along with a number of other scholars whose work was excluded from consideration in *Poverty Knowledge*, might be seen as having supplied works of political analysis that drew upon available research of others to supplement their own assessments of policy politics. Yet, this perspective overlooks how Piven and Cloward were simultaneously social scientists and social activists involved in the National Welfare Rights Movement and the push for a guaranteed income and subsequent social welfare struggles. O'Connor's perspective does not envision this sort of hybrid role as part of her recommended alternative form of poverty knowledge. As a result, her call for a more politicized social science of poverty and welfare rings hollow.

In some sense, therefore, O'Connor's analysis is a bit tautological. Confining the study of poverty knowledge to only the mainstream, quantitative, or other objectivistic analyses, she finds what her reduced sample gives her. Yet, the alternatives, in the work of Piven and Cloward and others, have been available but were not included. I understand this in part, and in part I do not. Not quite "real" social scientists with "real" studies, these other scholars and their work could be excluded. But that is the point, to get beyond the artificial boundaries, to include more hybrid work, to fashion better relationships between social science and social welfare. O'Connor accepts, if only by default, the conventional definition of research and therefore is trapped into answering the question of a successor science in overly scientistic terms. It seems to me it is going to require taking seriously at a minimum the idea that this alternative work is an already existing form of alternative social science that needs to be embraced. Not to mention it and not to embrace it is to suggest it is not a model for a successor science of social welfare.

To overlook this already-existing alternative work is to suggest by default that the preferred form of a successor is one that is more like the existing poverty knowledge, with only perhaps minor changes added in to create more political sensitivity and greater methodological diversity. Yet this "mix and stir" approach will largely leave in place the prevailing commitments in social science to what I am calling the linear paradigm. And as a result, the granting of priority to politics will remain deferred, and the undeserved privilege accorded selected conventional forms of social analysis will remain unchallenged. The quantitative survey and qualitative field studies on welfare and poverty will continue to be preferred over historical and political-economic analyses that take a broader and more contextualized perspective. O'Connor's call for a successor science that allows for a full consideration of politics might well go unanswered in good part because she ignored the models already available.

What's Research Got to Do with It?

The failure to accord priority to struggles for social justice is also an issue in another recent call to reconfigure the relationship of social science to social welfare. In this second case, the call is in the opposite direction; instead of suggesting that politics play a larger role in social science, it asks for science to play a larger role in social work practice. Allen Rubin made such a plea while serving as president of the Society of Social Work and Research in 1999. Rubin's concern is actually a persistent one in social work where for much of its history various leaders of the profession have worried out loud that the field is without professional legitimacy because it lacks a scientific foundation to underwrite its interventions.[8]

Rubin was prompted to make his plea for the importance of building a scientific base for social work practice in response to the comments of Richard Cloward. Cloward had stressed that research was being overemphasized by the profession at the expense of the wisdom that comes with experience in the field. Cloward's remarks set off a firestorm within the profession, and Rubin was at the center. The reaction was quite remarkable given that Cloward only stated his concern once at a "summit" organized by the National Association of Social Workers (NASW) and subsequently in a letter to the journal *Social Work* in its special issue commemorating the centennial of the founding of the profession.[9] The letters to the editor in the subsequent issue of the journal were for the most part focused on Cloward's comments, especially his concern that an exaggerated sense of what research can tell us was undermining the profession's commitment to practice education. Rubin's letter was among them.[10] Rubin had been so concerned about Cloward's comments about research that he had already taken the extraordinary step of using the pages of his association's journal to criticize Cloward in two separate editorials—this in a journal that normally does not have editorials![11] Part of the reason for the strong reaction was that Cloward did not mince words:

> What I see on social work's centennial is a divorce between professional education and professional practice, and it alarms me. Graduate schools of

> social work, especially the better-known ones, are taking on the attributes of research institutes, with faculty venturing into the field of practice only to collect data. The leaders of this transformation charge that the schools of social work have never given sufficient emphasis to research, especially quantitative research. I think this charge was once true. But the remedy is not to make research faculty dominant, as practice faculty once were. We need balance between practice and research, and as much integration as possible. What is happening instead is that the practice traditions of graduate social work education, including the tradition of close integration with social agencies, are being superceded, even extinguished, by this growing research movement. . . . The leaders of the research movement that is sweeping social work higher education are like all rising elites. They want more than a place at the top; they want total dominance. . . . I find the intellectual conceit of this movement very troubling. It promises to prove whether particular policies and professional practices work or do not work. But social work research, like social science research more generally, is subject to so many theoretical and methodological conflicts and uncertainties that it is hard to say anything has been proved. . . . I think research faculty should show some humility. . . . They are perpetuating a fraud on students, and the profession should not be an unwitting accessory to it.[12]

Rubin was less interested than others in the practice education issue and more interested in Cloward's comments about research. Rubin interpreted Cloward as wanting to minimize the role of research in telling social workers how to advocate for their clients. Rubin also interpreted Cloward's comments as suggesting that the research movement was threatening to replace value choices in politics and political struggle with factual research as the central basis for animating social work advocacy. It is this complaint, more than the concern of how research was devaluing of practice education, that Rubin took issue with. And it is the one about which I myself have a few things to say.

More than anything in the centennial letter Cloward had written, Rubin was concerned that Cloward had allegedly said at the NASW "summit" that he was "insulted by the notion that we need to research the outcome of our efforts to provide care."[13] Rubin also noted that he was most especially disappointed that Cloward's alleged attitude was influential, especially among the leadership of the National Association of Social Workers. He feared that this sort of dismissive attitude would only lead to the neglect of needed research, and, by implication, in the long run, would lead to the denigration of the social work profession as one founded more in politics than science.

Rubin's position is on the surface quite logical. Objective scientific research should be the basis for knowledge of what makes for effective practice in social work. Otherwise, therapies will fail and programs will not work. Yet, this position can be taken too far. Rubin's own missteps start with his mischaracterization of Cloward's appreciation of the importance of research, something Cloward makes explicit in his letter as quoted. Long an advocate for more and better research in the field of social work, Cloward was for a time the chair of the research committee in his Columbia University School of Social Work. As Cloward himself emphasized, research should play a role in informing social work practice and social struggle more generally.

Rubin therefore commits an error similar to O'Connor's. To an even greater extent, he accepts the conventional definition of research as limited to a select group of forms of quantitative and qualitative analyses. He too, then, is basically converting a debate about what role different forms of research should play in contributing to knowledge into a basis for claiming that his opponent is against all research. Totally ignored is Cloward's commitment to research that grows out of practice on the front lines and can be funneled back to contribute to such field work; in fact, this commitment is transformed in Rubin's characterization as being "against research." Rubin implies: If you do not agree with my form of research, then you are against research in general. Rubin frames the research question as a trap that ends up reinforcing the privilege accorded the more conventional forms of objectivistic social science that are disconnected from the exigencies of practice.

There are, however, more problems with putting undue emphasis on research. Regardless of which type, I doubt that research can or should by itself tell us what policy goals to advocate and how to achieve them. In fact, I would suggest that social justice is only in small part an empirical question.[14] In addition, the idea that facts and values, or for that matter science and politics, are separable is not only naive but pernicious. It leads to social welfare research that ends up reinforcing the established relations of power.[15] Relying on research too heavily will lead us down the road to technicism—a place where allegedly social work can avoid political commitments and stay above political struggle.

This is already happening to a frightening extent. Over the course of the second half of the twentieth century, social work research had gotten pulled out of communities and away from taking a "bottom-up" approach to working with clients on their own terms.[16] It has over time increasingly become in service of the state and the programs and policies designed to control those communities and regulate the behavior of individuals in them. Now, as a new century unfolds in which state responsibilities for control and regulation are being privatized, we face the prospect of social work research increasingly being tied to corporate, for-profit interventions. The need for social work to break its growing assimilation into the apparatuses of control begins with listening closely to Cloward's call for better integration of research and field work rather than dismissing it as "anti-research."

Managed Research

At risk is nothing less than the future of social work as a profession. If the technicist position becomes the influential one, then social work will be over as the profession it once was. In its place will be a new profession of technical experts who administer scientifically proven therapies and run positively evaluated service programs.[17] Gone will be the profession that worked with individuals, groups, and communities to empower them to realize their social, economic, and political goals. At that point, we could then say: good-bye social work, hello managed care.

The dark side of the future of social welfare provision is visible in the emerging systems of managed care. Managed care regimes for containing costs in health insurance are in their present forms at risk of primarily serving agents of capitalism and economic efficiency first and foremost.[18] Research has special value in such a regime to the extent that it can help decide which practices can be imposed from the top down so as to ensure their use in a standardized, routinized, and most efficient fashion. The connection between a growing reliance on research to emphasize allegedly "validated" practices and the growing role of insurance companies in supervising and approving clinical interventions is quickly emerging on the horizon. As the long shadow of managed care has been extended over time from traditional medicine to behavioral health services, to psychological counseling and various other forms of psychological therapy, social work has come increasingly under that shadow.[19] And with that pall has come the growing interest in the already thriving movement to validate "best practices" so as to decide which ones are worthy of reimbursement.

None of this is very surprising, given that for several decades the center of gravity in the social work profession has been shifting from political advocacy on behalf of clients to clinical treatment.[20] As the profession becomes more situated in treatment settings, it comes to be associated more with the medical model of intervention, relying more on research to suggest which treatments, which medications, which therapeutic regimens will produce the desired cognitive and behavioral changes in clients. With the center of gravity in the profession situated in medicalized practices, it is not surprising that social work comes to be increasingly preoccupied with how it, like medicine, can fit into the world of managed care. It is also not surprising that social work comes to be increasingly preoccupied with researching its practices as if they are analogous to medical therapies and drug treatments.[21] While these developments are indeed not in the least surprising, they pose real risks for emphasizing forms of research that undermine social work as a form of political advocacy. This is especially the case given that effectiveness research tends to promote a "one size fits all" mentality because of an undue focus on what works for the modal subject, leaving concerns about outliers and marginal groups to the side.

While it is understandable that drug interactions be studied according to predictive models, just because more and more social work takes place in clinical settings where drugs are dispensed, it does not follow that predictive models are the most appropriate for studying the effectiveness of social work practice interactions.[22] Further, the increased tendency to study social work interventions as if they were "like a new drug" contributes to the tendency to emphasize more of a clinical therapeutic approach.[23]

Managing Best Practices

Related developments regarding the deleterious effects of scientism are now running rampant throughout the profession of social work. For instance, in recent years social work professionals' political commitments to advocate for the oppressed (an already beleaguered ideal) are increasingly at risk of being overtaken by calls for grounding social work practice in documented "best practices."[24] "Best practices" is a buzz word reflecting a trend that has spread from more technical professions such as engineering and environmental management across the whole spectrum of expert fields including even "softer" ones such as clinical and community social work practice specialties. In social work and related fields, it is now more often aligned with efforts that go under various names, including "evidence-based practice."[25] "Best practices" connotes scientifically validated interventions that can be disseminated throughout the profession. This is in many ways a misnomer since much "best practices" research is basically bad social science where anecdotes, vignettes, and isolated examples of "success stories" are latched onto as evidence of service excellence. Such "best practices" research often amounts to no more than selecting on the dependent variable to highlight instances when the desired result has occurred. Such claims often fail to be accompanied by evidence that exogenous factors other than the treatment, intervention, service, or program were the reason for realizing the desired result. In addition, such selective reporting also creates numerous opportunities for just the sort of politics advocates of "best practices" are seeking to avoid. Without appropriate accounting for why success has occurred in particular instances, claims that a treatment or intervention is a "best practice" can easily serve to promote a political agenda and particular value biases.

Yet even if "best practices" research is based on sound principles of conventional social science, as is stressed in "evidence-based practice," other problems persist with this idea. The term "best practices" troublingly masks two major dimensions of difference. First, if years of meditation on the insights of social conflict theory have taught us anything, it is that we need to ask: "Best practices" for whom?[26] "Best practices" suggests value neutrality and consensus about matters over which there is usually much conflict. "Best practices" for managers may not be the same for front line workers or clients. "Best practices" can become a way of instituting changes in treatment, intervention, or program administration while silencing consideration of the value conflicts associated with such changes.

Second, "best practices" suggests that dissemination is an unproblematic matter in which validated practices can be emulated in different agencies, settings, and contexts.[27] Yet, this flies in the face of some of the most important insights scholars like Piven and Cloward have emphasized about the importance of accounting for context and appreciating the significance of contingency in social interventions. Just as Piven and Cloward showed us that context and contingency greatly affect what social welfare political strategies need to be pursued and when, we need to recognize that "best practices" in some situations are totally inappropriate in others.

There is an interesting parallel here with research on another buzz word. The research on "risk and resilience" often seeks to discover the distinguishing characteristics of resilient individuals among populations at risk.[28] The problem here is that resilient individuals, say child survivors of abuse who succeed as adults, often are by definition fairly unique, and their capacity to survive and thrive is not easily emulated by others even after we learn what these capacities are and how these individuals developed them. Decontextualization of political strategy at the structural level and decontextualization of emotional well-being at the individual level are fraught with pitfalls. So is the decontextualization of "best practices" at the organizational level. The decontextualization of "best practices" is especially chilling if we are interested in encouraging creativity and flexibility in professionals to work with their clients on their own terms given their immediate circumstances.

The effects of the growing interest in consolidating practice around "best practices" in social work are therefore deeply depoliticizing. Research on "best practices" can be informative, but the "best practice" movement's tendency to promote "one best way" to execute various practices threatens to squeeze out innovation and discretion to advocate for clients beyond established practice in clinical as well as community settings.[29] This need not be specific to social work and would be true in any field that succumbs to a technicism of preestablished practice guidelines. This tendency to legislate "best practice" is growing in social work in remarkable ways. The "best-practice" movement has even reached Congress, where proposed legislation would create a national social work research center that would research best practices and disseminate them throughout the profession.[30] The "best practice" movement easily fits, if even unreflectively so, with the role of insurance companies under managed care systems to regulate what practices will be supported and what interventions will receive coverage that qualifies them for insurance reimbursement.

Given the increasing role of the insurance companies in determining what best practices will or will not be funded, there is the potential for social workers, especially in clinical settings, to have decreasing discretion to find ways to advocate for clients. The potential grows that research validating best practices will work hand in glove with insurance schemes to manage care such that the political dimensions of social work will be squeezed out. One clinical social worker has noted the following:

> We all know the picture today. Managed care has "carved out" the field of providers. Each managed care organization has its preferred provider list. Treatment has shortened still further, and medication has become a

> routine part of many treatment plans. Some employer benefit plans have reduced rates for the clinical hour. Some employers are talking about reducing the types of diagnoses to be covered. After all, they say, we are concerned about restoring an employee to productivity in the workplace. Is it necessary to include "growth therapies"? Treatment works. We know it. Clients know it. Adjusting the family dynamic benefits the family and the workplace. As managers, both in hands-on care and in making decisions about care, it is up to us to keep our clients' best interests in mind. We who have been their strongest allies might, in the future, be their only allies.[31]

From my perspective, research on best practices is at risk of helping prematurely shorten the list of covered treatments. Best practice research can lead to delegitimizing worthwhile interventions in clinical settings. We may lose the ability to offer forms of intervention on behalf of clients simply because they have not been given the funding that would enable them to demonstrate their effectiveness.[32] Other interventions might get ignored because they are too challenging to established practice. In their place, we might, for instance, get excessively "brief" treatment, an overreliance on medicating clients, and other forms of intervention that appear in the short-term as palliative responses that enable diagnosed conditions to be "managed" but not really effectively treated. Social work in various settings risks becoming just another "Band-Aid."

The insistence on research as opposed to politics as the basis for deciding which interventions ought to be emphasized is undoubtedly a false choice. Yet, even proponents of the more competently researched "evidence-based practice" overinvest in the ideal of facts generated by research to the point that their campaign risks undervaluing values generated by politics. Carol Swenson has written:

> The modern scientific tradition has held that theories and practices should be evaluated on the basis of empirically measured outcomes. The view is widespread that theories are "value free" and that choosing among them is not a question of match with values but of the "explanatory power" or "rigor." One unfortunate result has been that social workers, perhaps especially clinical social workers, have been burdened with theories that are not particularly congruent with social work. Fortunately, some important contemporary views recognize that all theories embody values. These include postmodernism, critical theory, hermeneutics, or interpretive social science. Social constructionism has alerted the profession to the ways that

> knowledge is socially created, as people filter "data" through the lenses of their experiences, values, and prior knowledge. Hermeneutics directs attention to the complexity of meanings inherent in supposed "facts." And postmodernism and critical theory have emphasized that ideas that become privileged as "knowledge" are those that support power interests. All of these perspectives challenge the belief in the objectivity and neutrality of data. They offer support for using values as a standard for evaluating the adequacy of theories and practices. . . . Sadly, in the contemporary world, social justice-oriented clinical practice is under assault. Managed care and other cost-cutting measures appear to be increasing social injustice, rather than increasing social justice.[33]

The Weakness of the Strong Program

Those who argue for research-based practice are often arguing from a generally shared perspective. I call this perspective the "Strong Program" on research-based practice.[34] My critique is based on distinguishing between the Strong Program for a research-based practice and an alternative "Weak Program." The Strong Program assumes that facts and values can be separated in research, and that science and politics can be kept apart. It also assumes that research should be the primary basis for policy and practice and that thinking and writing about social justice strategies should only play a secondary and distinctly separate role. The Weak Program assumes that facts and values are inseparable and that politics is not only always intermixed with science, but that science needs politics if it is ever to have any meaningful role to play in the creation of socially just institutions, policies, and programs.

What I am calling the Strong Program is appropriately named in another sense. Some researchers write as if the leadership of the profession were recalcitrant and reluctant to sign on to their push to give greater emphasis in creating a research-based practice. Yet, one could just as easily argue that advocates of the Strong Program have basically won and have for several decades been turning schools of social work into places where students learn more about how to research practice than about how to practice practice.[35] The Strong Program is in a position of strength even if its advocates act as if it is not. Yet, the Strong Program has conceptual deficiencies that make for serious problems in emphasizing research as the foundation for practice. These problems are epistemological and methodological as well as professional and political. I consider each in turn, and I conclude with suggestions regarding how my Weak Program can offer a more credible way to combine research and politics in social work practice today.

Social Work's Epistemological Quandary

Those championing a strong version of the commitment to a research-based practice have a questionable theory of how knowledge is constructed.[36] This theory of knowledge embraces what Wilfrid Sellars long ago called the "myth of the given," or the questionable idea that facts exist on their own and can be known independent of value-laden interpretive processes.[37] Sellars's myth of the given became but one entry in a long list of devastating criticisms of scientistic and objectivistic epistemologies such as the one ascendant in social work today. The continuing popularity of the myth of the given provides the misleading basis for suggesting that facts can be separated from values, and from there it becomes easier to suggest that science can be separated from politics. As a result, proponents of the Strong Program can be indignant about how politics is contaminating social work as a profession as well as undermining the role of research. Politics and science are in this epistemological universe to be kept separate, and we can do this by keeping values away from facts and studying the facts on their own terms as they exist in the real world.

Yet, whose world is this? Is it the white, middle-class world of capitalist democracy with its pretensions of liberalism as a political philosophy of tolerance and equal opportunity? Is this a world where false neutrality implicitly privileges a specific type of diet, exercise regime, psychological outlook, aging process, and cultural value system, as well as a world of a very specific set of understandings of self-worth and economic productivity? Is it a world of one kind of family, several, or many? If we accept that there is not one world of objective facts, but instead many worlds based on differing cultures, values, and understandings of the relationship of the individual to society, then which of these worlds is being researched by objective "facts"? Do these objective facts speak to all worlds when they recommend particular ways of living and relating, and if they do, do they do that effectively? I suspect not in either case. Instead, the myth of the given promotes "one-worldism," and everyone, regardless of their culture and values, is encouraged to fit into that one world. Such a perspective mistakenly overlooks the role of values in not just interpreting facts but also creating them. Such neglect helps engender a form of practice that is the social work equivalent of cultural imperialism.

This "one-worldism" allows for the idea that there are both facts and values and that both play a role in research. Yet, this perspective suggests that they are separable and that they play different roles at different stages of the research process. Values are most influential in topic selection at the beginning and are again to be given due influence in interpretation of findings at the end. Factual analysis of one's data, however, is to be done in a way that is insulated from the corrupting biases of values. Best practices for whom? The question lingers.

The failure to consider this question reminds me of how civic reformers during the Progressive Era mistakenly thought they could build a firewall between the value-laden political choices in policymaking and the factual decisions of administration. They thought they could take politics out of the running of government programs. They used the old slogan that there was "no Democratic or Republican way to clean the streets." Years later, the futility of trying to separate politics from administration and facts from values was underscored when in response to threatening civil disorder the city manager of the city of Oakland, California, sought to constrain police from overreacting.[38] When criticized for taking what some saw as a politically charged policy decision, he responded that the policy decision was whether the police would carry guns, and administrative decisions concerned such things as how they would use them. Just as the policy/administration dichotomy can often seem evanescent, so does the fact/value dichotomy when it comes to research. Upon close inspection, all research concepts are value-laden, and the facts that come to represent them are therefore constructed in ways that are value-laden as well. Facts are just like "proper gun use," and their biases can in particular instances backfire as well. That is why the ethical dimensions of research extend beyond how one collects one's data to issues of what one takes to be data.

Take the issue of "welfare dependency." As Michael Katz has reminded us, the Progressive Era reformers were not very interested in providing economic assistance to low-income families but were more interested in finding ways to "improve" them.[39] The same is very much in vogue today as welfare has been converted into the social welfare policy equivalent of a 12-step program designed to help welfare recipients to "recover" from their bouts with that dreaded addiction of "welfare dependency."[40] Welfare programs are now designed to treat welfare dependency as if it were like chemical dependency. And, like drug addiction, welfare dependency had by the early 1990s come to be seen as reaching crisis proportions and necessitating emergency action by the federal government to track down its causes and root it out. Welfare dependency became subject to statistical measurement according to federal legislation in the name of trying to reduce its prevalence in society.

Building on early 1990s state demonstration projects, the Personal Responsibility and Work Opportunity Reconciliation Act of 1996 reformed welfare to impose time limits and work requirements so successfully that welfare rolls have been cut by more than half, from 14 million in 1993 to less than 5.3 million by September 2001.[41] The net result is that the country moved from a "war on poverty" in the 1960s to a "war on welfare dependency." We gave up the winnable battle to eliminate poverty for the questionable battle to abolish welfare dependency. During all this frenetic welfare-related activity from research to demonstrations to reforms, however, very few researchers or policymakers ever asked: What is welfare dependency? Is it an objective reality, is it really a form of dependency, or is it a profoundly biased conception of welfare receipt, marginalizing consideration of the issues of poverty and powerlessness that lead some single mothers to rely on welfare for extended periods of time. In other words, some people created facts of welfare dependency, produced studies detailing its causes and consequences, and even went on to make historically significant social welfare policy in its name without ever sufficiently recognizing that values were embedded into the very facts they took at face value. In the end, the alleged facts of welfare dependency were highlighted in the preamble to the welfare reform law of 1996 and spewed across the newspapers of the country again and again as an undisputed reality.

What was measured quantitatively as welfare dependency, however, could often be called "welfare independency" since other, less-noticed studies have in recent years indicated that as much as three-quarters to four-fifths of single mothers on welfare have suffered physical and sexual abuse and as many as one-fifth to one-third are either currently in an abusive relationship or have just left one.[42] For years, the simple empirical question of what percentage of women on public assistance are survivors of domestic violence was not studied, let alone asked in research circles. And when the question finally got some attention, the results of the studies have only made a marginal impact. The 1996 welfare reform law did come to include the Family Violence Option that allows women at risk for domestic violence to be exempted from time limits. Yet, this has proven to be a very difficult option to extend to recipients, and many women suffering from domestic violence continue to face termination from public assistance.[43]

This is not to say that the correct reaction to the biases of welfare dependency facts would be to create more objective ones either of the same name or some other. This is rather to say that the facts are always value-laden, that facts and values cannot be separated, and that attempts do so will only result in the insidious effects of allowing biases to work their way into ostensibly objective analyses without challenge.

The facts of welfare dependency are highly contestable and have always needed theoretical supplementation to be credible.[44] From Thomas Malthus in the late 1700s to Charles Murray in the 1980s, the most effective way to make the case about welfare dependency has been to interpret whatever facts have been available in terms that Albert O. Hirschman called "the perversity thesis."[45] The perversity thesis argued that providing assistance to people in the long run sapped them of their self-discipline. The perversity thesis has proven resilient, serving as the basis for welfare reform in the 1990s.

With the perversity thesis firmly in place, welfare reform has been imbued with a sense of moral urgency to refashion systems of public assistance into therapy programs that help wean people from the "dole." The veritable reams of evaluation research coming out on self-esteem workshops, "job-readiness" training, postemployment intensive case-management counseling services, and the like, all to a great degree never question the value premise that reducing welfare dependency is ipso facto a good thing.[46] These evaluations rarely consider how values not only frame these studies but how they socially construct the facts studied and their interpretations as well.

For instance, improved self-esteem as an outcome for "job-readiness" counseling and training may receive not only exaggerated attention but may often get manufactured more through how questionnaires get constructed than through how recipients come to see themselves over time. And these artifacts of questionnaire construction can come to take on a life of their own as they are tracked through repeated querying in longitudinal studies. They even come to have careers of their own as studies tend to engage in replication using validated measures of such things as low self-esteem, dysthymia or low motivation, pessimism, depression, post-traumatic stress disorder, and so forth. It is not uncommon for whole cottage industries to grow up around such constructed entities with their energies focused on demonstrating what boosts scores on self-esteem scales and other related measures to the point that these efforts become ends in and of themselves, irrespective of whether client well-being in a more robust sense is being improved in one or another localized setting. Such are the real risks of objectivistic, top-down research in an era of medicalized social work practice.[47]

Research that does question value premises for the facts that are being studied is nonsensical in the top-down research world, where value questions are bracketed for the purposes of providing an allegedly objective assessment of the program. Yet the failure to question such premises allows the lie that welfare use is a form of dependency that needs treatment to go uncontested.

A better epistemology, therefore, is to give up the myth of the given and accept that facts are human creations constructed from the ground up in terms of implicit as well as explicit, unconscious as well as conscious, value commitments. From there, we can begin not so much to allow values to run amok but to begin to recognize that they are present and need to be accounted for in all stages of the research process, including the construction of facts. This then presents the possibility of "factual parallelism" where there can be competing differing facts for the same subject and where each set of facts emerges out of a differing value-laden perspective.

The possibility of competing worlds, competing realities, becomes something that needs to be taken seriously. Welfare receipt can be both a form of dependency and independency simultaneously, and no amount of factual accumulation will necessarily ever end that parallelism. Objective, factual research, therefore, not only does not exist, but cannot tell us which of these parallel realities is the one we ought to take most seriously. And if it cannot do that, it certainly cannot tell us what to advocate.

Not only does science not exist independent of politics, but when we pretend that it does, it leads us astray. While apolitical, ostensibly objective, factual, empirical research can be suggestive and informative, it needs to be examined for its implicit politics. And even after that exercise is consummated, research can still only play a small role in telling us what is right and what is wrong and how to help realize the former while resisting the latter. In other words, science not only has politics, it needs it. Without politics, science cannot serve society.

Epistemic Privilege in Social Work: Methodism Meets Technicism

The credibility of the Strong Program as the foundation for a research-based practice is further weakened when we see how it ultimately produces a most unproductive dilemma. The Strong Program is vitiated once it comes to be caught between the Scylla of its own understanding of science and the Charybdis of its equally questionable understandings of politics. On the one hand, the Strong Program of research for practice ends up tending to produce research that will never be scientifically acceptable. On the other hand, such research tends to encourage the idea that practice should proceed only on the basis of scientifically validated research results.

There is merit to the idea that research should inform practice. Joel Fischer made this point effectively on the issue of casework years ago and helped generate the long-running campaign to develop single-subject designs for documenting casework's effectiveness.[48] While single-subject designs have evolved, their credibility as "scientific" remains highly contestable.[49] For some, therefore, who embrace the Strong Program, it could be suggested that practice remains without legitimation until scientifically credible forms of evaluation are in place.

This is William M. Epstein's position in his ambitious book *Welfare in America: How Social Science Fails the Poor.*[50] In this book, Epstein goes beyond most other researchers' commitment to the Strong Program and puts forward the very large argument that what is wrong with social welfare policy and programs is that they have never been based on scientifically credible research. Epstein suggests that this is true even for the best of studies, such as the Families First Project, which evaluated the success or lack thereof of Family Preservation programs in reuniting parents and children in cases of abuse and neglect. Epstein suggests that this state-of-the-art social welfare research project failed to meet his standards of good experimental design. For Epstein, the conclusion is that until we have real experiments—those that can pass scientific muster—that can serve as the basis for making informed public policies and creating well-designed public programs, the social welfare institutions of this country will remain fundamentally flawed. Epstein wants the social policy equivalent of B. F. Skinner's *Walden II*, where science replaces politics as the basis for public decision making, and experts rely strictly on scientific tests for determining how society should be structured.

Yet, if Epstein is taken seriously, then there will be no social welfare programs. And perhaps that is fine by him. We will never have perfect research, and waiting for it is an excuse for indefinite delay. Whether it is his intent or not, his extreme commitment to perfect research as the basis for practice and policy is a politically convenient position for those who want to minimize the role of social welfare in the existing society. It reminds me of the persistent claim by opponents of environmental regulation that policy change needs to wait until more research is done to understand better the causes and consequences of acid rain. These same opponents often accused the environmentalists of producing "analysis paralysis" when insisting that environmental impact studies be done before major development projects were undertaken. Waiting for the definitive research to underwrite public policy is like waiting for Godot. At some point, we have to decide to act even though we have less than perfect information. Research can never definitively underwrite social policy.

There are two major problems with Epstein's exaggerated version of the Strong Program. First, Epstein not only embraces the fallacy of the myth of the given, but he also invokes what can be called "epistemic privilege."[51] This is the idea that practice follows knowledge rather than vice versa. In other words, Epstein goes where Fischer not only dared not go but had no interest in going. He goes to a very strong version of the Strong Program and commits to the very questionable idea that knowledge precedes and informs action or that research is prior to and the source for practice.

Fischer could be said to be a proponent of the Weak Program, suggesting that research could improve the quality of information used for deciding what forms of casework, counseling, and therapy were effective. Yet, in the Weak Program, research is not superior to, prior to, or even the source for practice. Research often is best done within the context of ongoing efforts to improve social welfare policies and programs. In this context, it can play an underlaborer's role and help flesh out details that can be useful in improving social welfare provision. This is a secondary role, where research follows after policy. Where it is best limited to answering technical questions of "how" and not the important advocacy questions of "what" and "why." Research of this sort is actually best limited to answering specific empirical questions of a descriptive sort, such as how many people have a specified condition, what are the major reasons for people initiating contact with a service, what are their needs, who drops out of the program, and so on. These are in good part technical questions. And at that level research can be very informative. Yet, this is hardly research that would reflect the hubris of "epistemic privilege," and it would not be research that is claiming to serve as the sole basis for advocacy. Research, as an underlaborer's activity, as a secondary phenomenon, coming after the fact, being informed by practice more than informing it, that would be putting research in its rightful place. The Weak Program is committed to such a role for research.

There also is a second feature of the Strong Program that is devastatingly unrealistic and dangerously politically naive. It too is illustrated with a contrast between Fischer and Epstein. Fischer's support for single-subject design research suggests that issues of scientific meticulousness were secondary to creating sources of credible information in a more general sense. This does have its pitfalls if standards of research are relaxed too far. Yet, since research is in an underlaborer's role and is trying to help serve rather than rule over practice, it is understandable that it is going to have to make concessions in order to fit into and be relevant to ongoing practice. In their popular research methods textbook, Allen Rubin and Earl Babbie provide extensive discussion of these matters and provide helpful guidelines for how these concessions should be made.[52] None of this will do for Epstein, who goes too far in the other direction with his insistence that policymaking and programming cannot proceed unless based on research that always is in strict adherence to those standards. Epstein's insistence on rigor and design standards throw into doubt his claim that he is interested in research that can inform contemporary policy.

I would suggest that one laudable genre of research in the Weak Program is not program evaluation per se but rather forms of what some people call "Participatory Action Research" (PAR).[53] Participatory Action Research accepts the politically contested nature of facts and the critical role of values in constructing facts. It is research that is grounded in the community, that takes its cues from people on the ground who are actively involved in struggle against the constraints that limit their capacity to live better. Participatory Action Research sides with these people, adopts their value orientation, seeks to work for and with these people in order to empower them to better fight the power they are challenging. Participatory Action Research seeks not to treat the people on the ground as passive objects of study but as acting subjects. Participatory Action Research seeks not so much to teach in a patronizing way what people in the community need to know or what they should think, rather PAR seeks to inform and facilitate the realization of goals that community actors are already working, if only furtively, to achieve.

Fact Consensus and Value Conflict

In the end, the most troubling dimension of the Strong Program is demonstrated in the contradiction between the role of facts and values in social work. The Strong Program justifies the need for research to validate practices on the assumption that seeking factual agreement in social work is a good thing while promoting such agreement over values is not. For instance, Allen Rubin's editorials stress this theme when criticizing the NASW for misleadingly presenting itself as representing a consensus among social workers on key social issues.[54] Rubin wants us to assume that, warts and all, in spite of the less than perfect nature of empirical research, we can still basically put aside value differences and consider facts on their own terms. On the other hand, he insists that value differences are real to the point that the NASW is never presume to suggest that members of this professional organization agree on fundamental value issues. Therefore, Rubin concludes that the leadership of the NASW is wrong for suggesting that values can serve as the basis for policy positions but factual research can fulfill that role. In criticizing a member of the NASW leadership, Rubin wrote:

> I was struck by the relevance of her comments to [the] position that our values are a sufficient basis for our activist aims and that research is an unimportant resource. If specific activist proposals flow exclusively from our values and don't require scientific evidence as to their impact on social welfare, wouldn't it be logically consistent to censure conservative social workers for deviating from our professional values? Don't get me wrong. I am certainly not proposing that we do that. I am merely trying to show the implications of current notions embraced by NASW leaders that broad professional values can be defined in terms of specific liberal policy and legislative proposals and that it is not important to investigate these proposals scientifically regarding their effects (both intended and unintended) on the folks we are trying to help.[55]

Rubin fails to consider that, given the unavoidable intermingling of facts and values, the conflicts of one necessarily spill over into the other. Therefore, the NASW cannot really ever expect to claim consensus on the most important issues of social work and social welfare regardless of whether it uses facts or values. Substituting factual research for value-laden argumentation will not solve the problem of politics as an obdurate reality. Creating a national center on social work research to disseminate validated findings on so-called best practices will undoubtedly just be perpetuating this misunderstanding. Yet, the unavoidability of politics should not stop the NASW from trying to offer value-laden proposals for action on which its membership can at least compromise. Nor should it stop it from supporting research that can help better promote various value positions. In the end, Rubin fails to appreciate that his concern to protect value differences in the profession applies to his much-vaunted factual research as much as anything else. There is a need to protect diversity—about facts as well as values. Only then will social workers be given the credential as professionals that they justly deserve—as critical-minded, knowledgeable specialists who can combine their own facts and values and help empower clients to challenge the constraints and barriers society has placed in front of them. One way to do this is by letting bloom a thousand flowers of Participatory Action Research. One suspects that a national center on social work research will not engender such a blossoming, especially not if the Strong Program continues to dominate the profession's journals and its curricular resources.

The value question underscores the need for an alternative model of how social research relates to practice in ways that recognize the ineliminable entanglement of facts and values rather than their artificial separation. In my mind, this underscores the need to emphasize the importance of practice. Value questions need to be the starting point for any worthwhile social research, and these value questions need to come from those who are struggling to address problems. Recognizing the role of values in imbuing research with meaning, purpose, direction also means giving priority to practice as the basis for our research endeavors.

Bent Flyvbjerg's call for a social science grounded in the Aristotelian concept of *phronesis* sums up nicely what I see is the need to eschew illusions of a top-down, objectivistic science that can tell others what to do.[56] His vision for better social research is to start with value questions grounded in the struggles of ordinary people and to remain dedicated to being of service to them. Such research does not pretend to be Olympian, above the fray. Such research is embedded in the community, in client populations. It grows from the bottom up. It starts with the value questions that people in need have. It therefore recognizes the role of values in influencing research from the very beginning and throughout the entire process. It also recognizes how research is in a dynamic relationship with practice. Research does not monopolize the position of knowing and therefore does not relegate practice as a second-order activity. Instead, dialogical research learns from practices as much as vice versa. *Phronesis* is translated as practical wisdom, something that research cannot supply on its own and something that is only learned from ongoing practice and the iterative activity of constantly revising what is known in terms of what works when and how in the real world when trying to make a difference in people's lives. Flyvbjerg has written:

> I . . . present . . . a conception of social science based on a contemporary interpretation of the Aristotelian concept of *phronesis*, variously translated as prudence or practical wisdom. In Aristotle's words *phronesis* is a "true state, reasoned, and capable of action with regard to things that are good or bad for man." *Phronesis* goes beyond analytical, scientific knowledge (*episteme*) and technical knowledge or know-how (*techne*) and involves judgments and decisions made in the manner of a virtuous social and political actor. I will argue that *phronesis* is commonly involved in social practice, and that the attempts to reduce social science and theory either to episteme or *techne*, or comprehend them in those terms, are misguided.
>
> We will see that in their role as *phronesis*, the social sciences are strongest where the natural sciences are weakest: just as the social sciences have not contributed much to explanatory and predictive theory, neither have the natural sciences contributed to the reflexive analysis and discussion of values and interests, which is the prerequisite for an enlightened political, economic, and cultural development in any society, which is at the core of *phronesis*.[57]

Conclusion

Recent calls to make the relationship of research to policies and practices either more political or more scientific have not always been convincing. Nor are they likely to promote a politics of radical incrementalism. Part of the problem is the failure to accord priority to political struggle. Simply adding political considerations to conventional "top-down" research is inadequate, for it will still leave people on the ground and involved in struggle as passive objects of study. Insisting on a more scientific research base for informing program interventions will only deepen this problem further. While research has a real role to play in struggles for social justice and better social policies, it can only begin to fulfill this role by taking a "bottom-up" approach, starting with the people on the ground involved in struggles over social justice issues. Only by allowing their value orientations at least to inform research and to frame it to some healthy degree can factual research be expected to be relevant to the issue of social welfare. This is as true, I would argue, for social work in clinical and community settings as anywhere else. There are indeed already models for such "bottom-up" research. Activist scholars like Piven and Cloward serve as one model of how to do this on the stage of national policy politics. Researchers working with community groups to create Participatory Action Research is another. Creating a national center to disseminate "factual recipes" for social work practice is not.

PART II

The Practice of Theory

5

The Old Is New

The Racial Basis of Welfare Reform

What is the future for social science in social welfare? Will it be a quantitative future or one focused on the narratives of policy discourse? Will it be dedicated to illuminating the iconography of social welfare and the role of representations in shaping the public imaginary on matters of social assistance? Perhaps social welfare scholarship will increasingly be involved in all of these, as I think it should. No one idiom will definitively represent all the power relations involved in making social welfare policy what it is. Work needs to be done in all registers of welfare policy discourse for social science to have political import.[1]

The future of welfare scholarship lies beyond tired debates about which mode of analysis is superior. Narratives, numbers, and visual depictions all offer potential and pitfalls for producing insight regarding the politics of welfare. All have their exclusionary practices that must be interrogated for how they construct their subject matter in ways that limit what can be considered.[2] Critical scholarship has rightly highlighted in particular the historical ties of statistics to the state and has effectively demonstrated how numbers erase their own political construction.[3] A good case can be made that welfare scholarship today is more than ever overly quantitative in ways that obscure the political biases of such analyses, the decision rules for deciding what to count and how, and the interpretations of those counts.[4] Nonetheless, part of this critique recognizes the power of numbers in policy debates. Employing numbers in ways that are sensitive to their political character and with an eye toward how they can have political impact should therefore be part of the future of welfare scholarship.[5] This might mean critical scholars agreeing to work in multiple media, perhaps simultaneously. Or it might mean that more theoretically oriented welfare scholars need to be prepared to work in teams with more empirically oriented scholars. In what follows, I attempt to do just that by drawing on previously published, co-authored work that resulted from teaming up scholars with different kinds of skills, some more narrative in focus, others more numerical.[6] The increased effort needed to combine different orientations produced a product that could speak to different audiences simultaneously. This added value of hybrid scholarship may suggest its increased potential impact within and without the academy.

Where is the radical incrementalism in this inquiry? There is radical potential to be exploited here, I would suggest, by working with rather than against social statistics as long as this is done in a critical fashion at a distance and attentive to the pitfalls of such work conducted as it is inside the existing forms of social representation.

Using Statistics to Examine the Racial Underside of Welfare

The research reviewed in this chapter underscores the value of quantitative analysis of politically volatile topics. The subject in question is the role of racial bias in welfare reform. Racism, racial discrimination, and racial disparity are issues that easily lend themselves to polemics and polarization, as in the case of debates about race and welfare reform. While sophisticated critiques of quantitative research have effectively shown that it is never objective, statistical documentation is nevertheless not easily dismissed. This is especially true for the state, which relies so heavily on statistics for legitimating its actions. Refutation is still possible but must usually proceed by supplying alternative statistics and interpretations in ways that can been seen as no less convincing. There are, to be sure, limits in using what Audre Lorde called the "Master's Tools," including especially the fact that most of the readily available statistics have been constructed with political biases already built into them.[7] Government statistics, including the U.S. Census and other sources, are prominent examples.[8] Nonetheless, sensitive use of these and other statistics that is done in a way that accounts for these limitations and biases can challenge their less reflective use by others. Such sensitivity can create a basis for highlighting racial bias in ways that get beyond polemics. Sensitive use of quantification can help critical arguments survive in the especially statistically dependent world of policy debate about welfare.[9] Quantification can be particularly useful in suggesting that there is an empirical basis for claims of racial bias under welfare reform. With such evidence in place, it becomes harder to dismiss claims of racial bias as overheated rhetoric.

State Discretion under Welfare Reform

In 1996, the Personal Responsibility and Work Opportunity Reconciliation Act was passed. This law dramatically reformed the system of public assistance in the country by giving the states great latitude especially in the area of moving recipients off welfare. From the beginning there has been a growing concern that the latitude afforded states could be abused. In particular, there has been growing concern that states have been freed to such a great extent, and federal oversight has so diminished, that states can use their discretion in ways that will reintroduce old forms of arbitrary and discriminatory treatment that existed in the welfare system before legal protections were established in the late 1960s and early 1970s. In the last few years, evidence has in fact been mounting that this law has created numerous opportunities for states to act in ways that reflect racial bias in the adopting and implementing of welfare policies.[10] The research reported here indicates that there is reason to be concerned about racial bias under welfare reform. The findings presented below indicate that race has been a factor influencing whether states adopt an aggressive approach in trying to move recipients off welfare.

Part of the problem with the current situation starts with the fact that the 1996 welfare reform legislation gave states substantial discretion beyond what they had before. It abolished the Aid to Families with Dependent Children (AFDC) cash assistance program and replaced it with the block grant program, Temporary Assistance for Needy Families (TANF). Under AFDC, states had discretion in setting benefit levels and selected features of their programs, but the federal government exercised oversight to ensure that state AFDC programs conformed to federal standards. In 1996, with the repeal of the AFDC program, the welfare reform law ended what had essentially become an entitlement for cash assistance for low-income single parents with children. States were given great latitude in using TANF block grants—they did not even have to provide cash assistance if they chose not to and could even turn all the money over to "faith-based" service programs under the charitable choice option. Portions of some state block grants have been used to cut taxes.[11] The 1996 welfare reform law is therefore said to have produced a "devolution revolution" that has reduced federal authority over public assistance programs, providing states more freedom to fashion their own solutions to the problems of poverty and welfare dependency.[12] While this freedom can serve as an opportunity for states to be innovative "laboratories of democracy," it can also lead to states to compete in a "race to the bottom" in trying to outdo one another in cutting back on public assistance. In both cases racial bias may end up influencing how states choose to adopt and implement welfare reforms.

The welfare reform legislation was, however, not entirely an act of devolution. The 1996 law lays down standards for a "get-tough" approach to welfare reform. It specifies that no TANF block grant funds can be spent on assistance to any recipient who has received aid for two years or more and is not working. The law also prohibits the use of TANF funds to aid any family for more than five years. It imposed strict quotas on the percentage of adult recipients who must be participating in "work-related activities," starting at 25 percent of the targeted caseload working twenty hours a week in 1997, and rising to 50 percent of the caseload working thirty hours a week by the year 2002. The federal goal of reducing access to public assistance was made explicit in the law, and states were expected to follow suit.

In the spirit of emphasizing "welfare dependency" as a problem that had to be attacked, the law allowed each state to set even stricter work requirements and time limits as conditions for aid in that state. States are also given other options, including perhaps most controversially the "family cap" option to deny additional aid to any child born to a mother who is already receiving family assistance. The last major option for adopting a get-tough approach to welfare was that states can impose varying degrees of sanctions on families, reducing their cash assistance for failure to conform to program requirements designed to get recipients to leave welfare for paid employment outside the home. One of the most significant changes developed under welfare reform was associated with what the legislation referred to as "individual responsibility plans," which states can require adult recipients to sign as a condition for receiving assistance. An individual responsibility plan included steps that the recipient promises to take to get off welfare, most especially by taking paid employment. States could adopt sanctions procedures to penalize recipients who do not fulfill the steps in their individual responsibility plans or are otherwise deemed negligent under the new welfare regime. For instance, failing to keep an appointment with your case manager (now often called a job coach or counselor) can be grounds for the imposition of a sanction. Sanctions normally involved deductions in benefits, and they can be imposed initially or only after a number of violations. They also can involve only the recipient's part of a family's assistance check, or they can be what are called "full family sanctions." The strictest sanctions would be "Initial Full-Check Sanctions" where the benefit check for the entire family is terminated with the very first failure to conform to program requirements.

The Past Is Prologue

States have numerous options to vary how restrictive they choose to be in adopting a get-tough approach to limiting access to welfare. One important question is whether states allowed race to influence their choices in adopting get-tough welfare reforms. If past practices of the states are any indication, there is reason to believe that this just might in fact be the case.

There are reasons to suggest that in the past race has played a significant role in how states go about establishing their welfare policies. While systematic statistical research on the factors that affect state adoption of welfare policies in the past did not always emphasize the role of race, several important studies did.[13] Larry Orr found a correlation between low benefits in states and the percentage of the welfare population that was African American. Based on his multivariate analysis, he concluded that this was not simply the result of state inability to fund higher benefits or anti-welfarism in southern states with more poor African Americans. Instead, racial hostility and resentment against African Americans receiving welfare was more likely to be the problem. Gerald Wright also examined differences in average AFDC benefits across states.[14] Wright used the proportion of blacks among each state's population as a proxy for the extent to which welfare benefits in each state would flow to African Americans. He included a measure of the scope of each state's civil rights laws as a way of tapping the racial liberalism or conservatism of the state. Even after controlling for a host of other factors, Wright found that states with the smallest proportions of blacks and those with the most progressive civil rights laws offered the highest average AFDC benefits.

More recently, Christopher Howard has found that while the percentage of the state's population that is African American is negatively related to state AFDC benefit levels, it is unrelated to state unemployment benefits.[15] This suggests that racial concerns are associated with welfare but not unemployment insurance.

The findings from these studies provide support for examining the state's percentage of welfare recipients who are African Americans as a measure of the extent to which a state program is vulnerable to being given less support due to racial hostility. Public opinion analyses suggest that hostility toward African Americans and opposition to welfare are intimately connected.[16] The racial resentment hypothesis is that white citizens will be less supportive of welfare the more the rolls are comprised of nonwhites. A related hypothesis would be the political vulnerability hypothesis, which suggests that a welfare program that is viewed as a program for minorities will be treated less sympathetically by the white majority and their representatives. Jill Quadagno in particular has argued that when a social welfare program comes to be seen as a program whose beneficiaries, recipients, or clients are disproportionately nonwhite but especially African American, the program becomes less popular and more subject to retrenchment.[17] This suggests a racial indifference hypothesis as well, where programs that are seen as "minority" or "black" programs are considered less important.

On the issue of whether opposition to welfare is more related to African Americans than other minorities, Martin Gilens compared attitudes toward African Americans and other ethnic groups with opposition to welfare. He found that negative attitudes toward African Americans were the most important predictor of opposition to welfare. He did find a weak relationship between attitudes toward Hispanics and opposition to welfare but no relationships for attitudes toward other groups. Gilens wrote: "As the country's Hispanic population continues to grow, attitudes toward welfare and poverty may become as strongly associated with perceptions of Hispanics as they are now with perceptions of blacks."[18] Therefore, analysis should examine whether welfare reform policy adoption is tied to racial indifference, resentment, or vulnerability for both African Americans and Latinos. An effective way to measure this is to test to see if there is a relationship between the racial composition of the welfare population at the time of policy adoption and the restrictiveness of the policies adopted. If a relatively high percentage of recipients being African-American or Latino is associated with a higher probability of adopting get-tough welfare reforms, then there is reason to suspect that race is playing a role in affecting the propensity of states to pursue an aggressive get-tough approach to welfare reform.

Welfare Retrenchment and Get-Tough Reforms

The first years of welfare reform have already provided a record for assessing how states have chosen to use their discretion under welfare reform. It is true that all states have basically followed along with the program to emphasize a get-tough approach to welfare reform. They really do not have much choice given that the federal government has imposed time limits, work requirements, and other conditions on the use of TANF block grant funds. States were, prior to 1996, experimenting with selected reforms by receiving waivers from the federal government. Yet, with the 1996 law, states can choose to what degree they want to buy into the get-tough approach to welfare reform across a number of policy options. They can go along with the federal limits and requirements or they can set even stricter ones. So far, the state responses to the welfare reform law of 1996 have varied, with some states choosing to go beyond what the federal government imposed, putting in place even tougher standards for recipients.

Table 5.1 indicates that in the first year under welfare reform states did indeed vary in the extent to which they chose to adopt get-tough policy options. In 1997, twenty-one states had adopted a time limit shorter than five years, and twenty-six states adopted a work requirement sooner than two years, with thirteen states choosing to adopt an immediate work requirement. In addition, twenty-one states chose to adopt the family-cap option, and fourteen states had adopted full-family immediate sanctions.

One initial issue is whether there is reason to suspect that these get-tough policy choices were likely to have had any impact on access to assistance. There is no mystery, however, about whether or not there has been a decline in welfare rolls. The welfare roll declines in the initial years of welfare reform were indeed steep. As a result, attention focused on why. Economic growth and welfare reform have both been credited with contributing to the decline in the rolls. Studies have been done to determine the more important factor in affecting the declines. It is important to note that these declines began in most states in 1993, before the welfare reform legislation was enacted, and can in part be attributed to experimentation by the states authorized through the waivers they received under the old AFDC program.[19] Later reports gave greater stress to improvements in the economy.[20] Still more recent reports suggest that states have indeed been using their newfound discretion in a variety of ways, including discouraging people from applying for assistance as well as imposing sanctions on families that fail to fulfill new requirements.[21] The welfare rolls have declined 63 percent nationwide, from 14.28 million in January 1994 to 5.33 million in September 2001.[22] All states and Washington, D.C., have had welfare roll declines, suggesting that the national changes in policy and/or national economic growth have been influential.

TABLE 5.1

States with Get-Tough Welfare Reform Policies, 1997

	TANF Limit < 60 Months	Work Requirements < 24 Months	Family Cap	Initial Full-Check Sanctions
Arkansas	X	X	X	X
Arizona	X	X	X	
California			X	
Connecticut	X	X		
Delaware	X		X	
Florida	X	X	X	X
Georgia	X	X	X	X
Idaho	X	X		X
Illinois	X	X	X	
Indiana	X		X	
Iowa		X		
Kansas				X
Louisiana	X			
Massachusetts	X	X	X	
Maryland			X	
Michigan		X		
Minnesota		X		
Mississippi			X	X
Montana		X		
Nebraska	X		X	X
New Hampshire		X		
New Jersey			X	
New Mexico	X	X		
New York		X		
North Carolina	X	X	X	
North Dakota		X	X	
Ohio	X			X
Oklahoma		X		X
Oregon	X	X		
South Carolina	X		X	X
South Dakota		X		
Tennessee	X	X	X	X
Texas	X	X		
Utah	X	X		
Virginia	X	X	X	X
Washington		X		
Wisconsin		X	X	X
Wyoming			X	X

SOURCE: See Appendix, items 11–14, for policy sources.

Yet, the declines have not been uniform. In some states the declines have been much higher, exceeding 75 percent in Colorado, Florida, Idaho, Mississippi, South Carolina, and Wisconsin and Wyoming. In others, the declines have been less—under 50 percent in Alaska, Delaware, District of Columbia, Hawai'i, Nebraska, New York, Rhode Island, and Washington. The declines have also not been uniform within states.[23] Whites have exited from welfare faster in most states, leaving the welfare population to become increasingly nonwhite. This evidence also includes findings suggesting that nonwhites are more likely to leave welfare due to sanctions rather than because of employment.[24]

Given these state variations in roll decline, there is reason to suggest that state variation in welfare reform may be a significant factor. Robert Rector and Sarah Youssef found that states that had Initial Full-Check Sanctions had significantly greater roll declines compared with other states. They concluded that sanctions, more than the economy (as measured by the unemployment rate), were affecting roll decline. My own research suggests that while the economy cannot be dismissed as a factor for welfare roll declines in the first years of welfare reform, sanctions were indeed a significant factor in influencing state welfare roll reductions.[25] I compare here states with Initial Full-Check Sanctions with all other states. Figure 5.1 indicates that that the fourteen states that had adopted the strict sanction policy of initial full-check sanctions had an average welfare roll decline from January 1996 until June 1999 of 61 percent, compared with a 44 percent average decline for other states with less restrictive sanctions policies. I did not find comparable effects for the other major get-tough policy options—a time limit less than the federal limit of sixty months, a work requirement sooner than the federal requirement of twenty-four months, or a family-cap policy. (See table 5.2.)

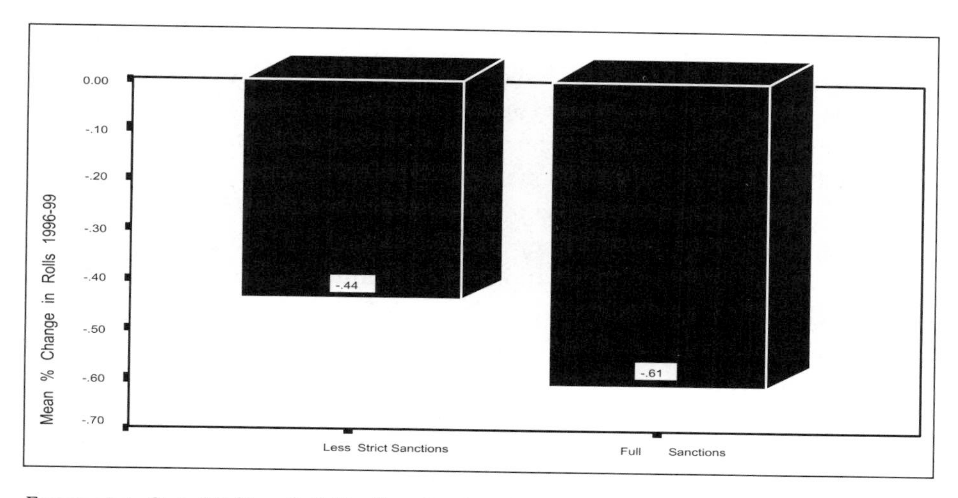

FIGURE 5.1 State Welfare Roll Declines By Sanction Policy, 1996-99 SOURCE: See Appendix.

TABLE 5.2

Welfare Roll Declines by Time Limit, Work Requirements, and Family Cap Policies, States, 1996–1999

Policy	Average Change, TANF Rolls 1996–99	Number of States
Time Limits		
< 60 months	-49%	21
All other states	-49%	29
Work requirements		
< 24 months	-50%	26
All other states	-48%	24
Family cap		
Yes	-51%	21
No	-46%	29
Sanctions		
Initial full-check	-61%	14
All other states	-44%	36

SOURCE: See Appendix, items 11–14, for policy sources. Welfare roll data are from the U.S. Department of Health and Human Services (http://www.acf.dhhs.gov/news/stats/recipientsL.htm).

While these findings are largely consistent with those of Rector and Youssef, they also point to serious differences in interpretation of the effect of reforms on roll decline. Rector and Youssef assume that roll decline is ipso facto good. They emphasize that a finding that sanctions are more important than low unemployment in reducing the rolls implies that a get-tough policy works. The implicit suggestion is that recipients can be forced to leave welfare and find work regardless of whether unemployment is high or low in a state. Yet, this assumes that everyone who was leaving welfare got jobs. More recent research indicates that this is not the case, and that people who had been sanctioned off welfare were less likely to be working than others who left.[26] Instead, the effects of get-tough welfare policies on the rolls may well indicate a source of concern in that these policies are having the negative effect of forcing people off the rolls even when they still need assistance and even when they end up not working after leaving.

This alternative interpretation is all the more troubling given that the roll declines in the initial years of welfare reform occurred during a relatively strong economy. Rector and Youssef's failure to find an association with the unemployment rate and welfare roll declines is in part most likely due to the fact that unemployment was declining in most, if not all, states. Therefore, in spite of their lack of finding a relationship between unemployment levels and roll declines, there is merit in taking seriously the widely held assumption that the relatively strong economy helped reduce the rolls in the initial years of welfare reform just as a strong economy normally reduced the rolls in other periods of the history of public assistance.[27] The evidence we have reviewed, however, also indicates that get-tough welfare policies, especially strict sanctions, have also contributed to the roll declines and may have done so in ways that forced people off even while they still needed assistance. This occurred during a relatively strong economy; with a weaker job market the effects of forcing people off assistance are likely to be even worse.

These findings are a cause of concern especially regarding the potential role of racial bias in welfare reform, because more recent research indicates nonwhites are more likely to leave welfare due to sanctions.[28] Still other recent research indicates that people who had been sanctioned off welfare are less likely to be working than others who left for other reasons.[29] Therefore, get-tough policies are arguably having a more negative and frequent effect on nonwhite welfare recipients. The finding that initial, full-family sanctions are related to roll decline should therefore be considered a major issue of concern that get-tough welfare reforms are forcing people off assistance when they still need it and might be doing so in a way that has disparate racial effects.

Therefore, there is evidence that get-tough welfare policies are adversely affecting large numbers of welfare recipients, and this is more likely to be the case for nonwhites than whites. These developments point to a persistently troubling racial dimension to public assistance that has plagued it throughout its history. Nonwhites, African Americans in particular, have historically been subject to more punitive treatment by the welfare system.[30] These issues suggest there are important reasons to move beyond the debate concerning what drove down the rolls. The issues extend beyond whether, for instance, the economy or welfare reform was the more important factor affecting roll declines. There is evidence that sanctions, in particular initial, full-family sanctions, are contributing to a welfare retrenchment that pushes people off the rolls regardless of their continuing need for assistance. There is evidence that this is happening in ways that have disparate racial effects, reinforcing historic tendencies in the welfare system to treat nonwhites less favorably, African Americans in particular. These issues then add additional significance to the questions of whether race was a factor in affecting the likelihood that states would adopt get-tough policies. It is to this issue that I now turn.

Race in State Get-Tough Welfare Policies

Previous research in which I have participated has documented the effect of race on state welfare reform policies for the first year of the new program.[31] This research focused on the get-tough choices states made in the first year of welfare reform. We examined what type of sanctions policy a state adopted, whether the state established a family cap, and whether the state would put in place work requirements and time limits stricter than those set by the federal government. While some states had policies such as these under waivers preceding welfare reform, all states had the option to choose whether to adopt these policies statewide when the 1996 welfare reform law was first being implemented. We looked to see which states chose either to continue or to initiate an aggressive approach to get-tough reforms during that first year of welfare reform. We found that the percentage of recipients who are African American significantly affected the probability that a state would adopt a time limit stricter than the federal government's sixty-month limit. We also found that the percentage of recipients who are African American is also related to the probability that a state would adopt a family-cap policy. Last, we found that the probability of a state adopting Initial Full-Check Sanctions was significantly related to the percent of recipients who are African American. We also found that the percentage of recipients who are Latino also affected the probability of adopting stricter time limits and the family cap. The results for the percentage of recipients who are Latino were not quite as strong as the results for the percentage of recipients who are African American; however, they were statistically significant. Neither the percentage of recipients who are African American or the percentage who are Latino achieved statistical significance regarding their effect on the probability that a state would adopt stricter work requirements than the twenty-four-month requirement set by the federal government.

These relationships were found even after controlling for a variety of other possible influences. All tests included the percentage of recipients who were African American, the percentage of recipients who were Latino, the unemployment rate, the rate of increase in the incarceration rate, the ideology of state-elected officials, interparty competition, low-income voter turnout, the recipient/population ratio, the out-of-marriage birthrate, and a measure of how early each state began to get involved in welfare reform by applying for waivers from the federal government.[32] None of the variables proved to be as consistently significant as the race factor in affecting the probability that a state would adopt an aggressive approach to adopting get-

TABLE 5.3

Predicted Probabilities for Strict Policy Choices at Selected Levels of Significant Predictors

	Adopting Strong Sanctions (Probability)	Adopting Stricter Time Limits (Probability)	Adopting a Family Cap (Probability)
Average Probability	.12	.36	.34
Predictor Value:			
Percent African American			
Low	.05	.14	.09
High	.27	.66	.75
Percent Latino			
Low		.22	.19
High		.61	.63
Caseload-to-Population Ratio			
Low	.43		
High	.03		
Unmarried Birthrate			
Low	.05		
High	.28		
Government Ideology			
Low	.35		
High	.04		
Interparty Competition			
Low	.26		
High	.05		
AFDC Waiver Innovation			
Low	.35		
High	.04		

NOTES: All predicted probabilities are for the highest category of each dependent variable. "Low" refers to results when a predictor is set at one standard deviation below its mean. "High" refers to results when a predictor is set at one standard deviation above its mean.
SOURCE: Joe Soss, Sanford F. Schram, Thomas P. Vartanian, and Erin O'Brien, "Setting the Terms of Relief: Explaining State Policy Choices in the Devolution Revolution," American Journal of Political Science 45, 2 (April 2001): 385.

tough welfare reform policy options. Several factors in addition to the percentage of African Americans did affect sanctions policy: government ideology, interparty competition, the recipient/population ratio, the unmarried birthrate, and how early a state started to adopt welfare reform by getting waivers from the federal government. Yet even here the racial composition of the recipient population was prominent among the factors that mattered.

Table 5.3 indicates the predicted probabilities associated with the different factors for the three policies that we found were affected by race.[33] The table presents the probabilities for states in adopting the get-tough policies that were found to be affected by race—sanctions, time limits, and family caps. (Work requirements were not found to be affected by race, and therefore I focus here on the other policies.) These predicted probabilities provide a more easily interpretable way of demonstrating the relative effect of race compared with the other factors. The table indicates the overall probability for the average state and then the change in probability when the value of the significant variable increases for one standard deviation below the mean (Low) to one standard deviation above the mean (High).[34]

Table 5.3 indicates there is a 12 percent chance that the average state will adopt Initial Full-Check Sanctions. That means there are only twelve chances out of one hundred that the average state would adopt such a strict sanctions policy. The probability, however, increases from a 5 percent to a 27 percent chance when the percentage of recipients who are African American increases from Low to High. Tracking the same change from Low to High for the other variables, the following changes occur in the probability of adopting strong sanctions: 43 to 3 percent for the Caseload-to-Population Ratio; 5 to 28 percent for the Unmarried Birthrate; 35 to 4 percent for Government Ideology; 26 to 5 percent for Interparty Competition; and 35 to 4 percent for Welfare Innovation. Higher caseloads decreased the probability of adopting strong sanctions, higher unmarried birthrates increased it, more liberal government decreased it, increased party competition decreased it, and an earlier start to initiating welfare experimentation increased it. The race factor is undoubtedly one of several factors affecting the adoption of strict sanctions, but it is definitely a significant one.

In comparison, there is a much higher chance of the average state adopting stricter time limits, and here there is also a significant race effect. There is a 36 percent chance of stricter time limits being adopted in the average state. It increases, however, from a 14 to a 66 percent chance with a change in the Percent African American from Low to High. It also increases from a 22 to 61 percent chance with a shift in the Percent Latino. Only race and ethnic composition significantly affect the probability of a state adopting stricter time limits, and these factors do so in a big way.

There is a 34 percent chance of the average state adopting a family cap, but it increases from a 9 to 75 percent chance with the increase in Percent African American and from a 19 to 63 percent chance with an increase in the Percent Latino. Again, only race and ethnic composition affect the probability of adopting a family-cap policy.

Race is therefore a very significant predictor of whether a state will adopt an aggressive approach to get-tough welfare policies. More than any other factor, it is associated with large increases in the likelihood of adopting stricter versions of get-tough reforms across a number of policy options. The probability of adopting the family cap, for instance, moves up 66 percentage points with a shift in the percentage of welfare recipients who are African American from one standard deviation below the mean to one standard deviation above. The same shift in the racial composition of the recipient population increases the probability of adopting stricter time limits by 52 percentage points, and it produces a 22-point increase in the probability of adopting strong sanctions. Like no other factor studied here, race matters in affecting the likelihood of adopting the more restrictive versions of the get-tough welfare reforms.

Disparate Racial Effects

The quantitative analysis presented here indicates that race is indeed a significant factor in influencing states to adopt an aggressive approach to get-tough welfare reforms. While the probability of adopting stricter work requirements is not tied to race, the probability of adopting strong sanctions, stricter time limits, and the family cap are consistently affected by the racial composition of the rolls. Ideology is important in adopting strong sanctions, so is interparty competition, family formation, and past welfare practices. Yet race is a greater influence in affecting more policies. Race casts a much longer shadow than any of the other factors considered in this analysis over the state adoption of get-tough welfare reforms.

And not only does the racial composition of the rolls increase the likelihood of adopting get-tough policy options, there is evidence of disparate racial effects for African Americans as well. African American recipients are more likely to live in states that have tougher policies, and therefore they face a greater probability of being affected adversely by these policies. This might be one reason why nationally African American recipients are more likely to leave welfare because they have been sanctioned. They are more likely to confront strict sanctions, and therefore it follows that they are more likely to be sanctioned.

The disparate racial impact of get-tough welfare policies is statistically documented. We can begin to demonstrate this just by examining the percentage of African American and white recipient families living in states with strict policies. Twenty-three percent of white recipient families, compared with 29 percent of African American, participated in welfare under strong sanctions; 39 percent of white recipient families, compared with 50 percent of African American, participated in welfare under time limits less than sixty months; and 45 percent of white recipient families, compared with 57 percent of African American, participated in systems with a family cap.[35] African American families on welfare were more likely to have to endure a more aggressive get-tough policy regime. Race not only affected the probability whether a state would adopt stricter welfare reforms, stricter welfare reforms were more likely to affect families based on their race. Where African American single mothers predominated on the rolls, the chances were much higher that the state would pursue an aggressive approach to choosing stricter get-tough policy options. And stricter get-tough policy options were more likely to affect African American mothers than their white counterparts. Race mattered at least twice-over when it came to imposing the get-tough policies of welfare reform.

Conclusion

Therefore, there are reasons to be concerned about the ways that the "new day" of welfare reform has freed states to exercise discretion. This "new day" has freed states to return to some "old ways." These research findings suggest that under welfare reform, states are freed to allow race to influence the choices they make in adopting welfare reforms. The past history of race-based welfare policy resurfaces under welfare reform.

Quantitative analysis can play an important critical role in highlighting a troubling underside to welfare reform. The evidence presented here raises the issue of the role of race in welfare reform. The findings suggest that under welfare reform, states continue the old practice of allowing the racial composition of the rolls to affect the extent to which they adopt more or less restrictive welfare policies. These findings indicate that welfare policy in the states remains racialized in ways that are troublingly reminiscent of the checkered past of public assistance in the United States.

These findings, however, do not answer exactly why this is the case; instead, they point to a series of difficult questions that need to be asked about the processes behind the adoption by states of get-tough policies under the contemporary welfare reform system. What are the specific reasons why the racial composition of the welfare population has affected the willingness of state policymakers to choose get-tough policy options? Are state policymakers more willing to get tough with welfare recipients when the recipients are seen as "other," or as a group of different people who do not have standing as mainstream participants in the white middle-class society? Is it that state policymakers are more likely to adopt get-tough welfare reform when the welfare population is comprised of people from backgrounds that are seen as more marginal to the political process and without political clout? Or even more bluntly, we need to ask: Does racial hostility increase the likelihood of adopting get-tough welfare policies? If race is thus an important factor affecting welfare reform policy choices, what is the precise nature of its effect on state implementation of welfare reform? The research reported here cannot answer these questions definitively; however, it does suggest that these are not rhetorical questions posed for polemical effect. There is a race-welfare reform connection that needs to be highlighted, scrutinized, and understood. And quantitative analysis can play an important role in bringing this troubling topic to the public in a way that suggests there is credible evidence for taking this issue seriously.

It is important, then, to stress that the race-welfare reform connection is not just a statistical curiosity. Dramatic declines in the welfare rolls have taken place in recent years. Debates have centered around whether the economy or welfare reform has been the primary factor producing the declines. The findings reported here suggest that state policies under welfare reform are indeed an important factor affecting roll decline in recent years. Sanctions, in particular, are strongly associated with roll declines. Yet a neglected dimension of this issue is the factors that have influenced states to adopt get-tough policies that have contributed to these steep declines in the rolls.

When we examine this issue, we find support for several hypotheses as to why states adopted these potent get-tough policies. Stricter time limits were strongly associated with the percentage of recipients who were African American and the percentage who were Latino. Adoption of the family cap was also strongly associated with the percentage of recipients who were African American and the percentage who were Latino. The important policy change of adopting stricter sanctions was more likely to occur in states where a number of relevant factors were at work, including a welfare population that has a relatively high percentage of African Americans. Overall, in states where the welfare population is heavily composed of African Americans and also Latinos, there will be less reluctance to adopt the strictest policies that will promote a concerted effort to purge the welfare rolls.

These findings suggest the need to examine the ways in which race is related to get-tough welfare policy adoption. Is it racial vulnerability, resentment, or just plain indifference that is driving the tendency of some states to more aggressively pursue the get-tough welfare reform strategy?

What these findings say about the true character of welfare reform now needs to be given serious attention. The implications of these findings for understanding state welfare policymaking is equally significant. Race continues to be significant in welfare in deeply troubling ways. The findings presented here suggest that while welfare reform has been instrumental in reducing the rolls, it has often done so by way of get-tough policies that force needy families off assistance, in some cases even when they are not able to work. More troubling, the findings presented here indicate that the new day of welfare reform has largely freed states to return to old practices, including allowing race to influence how punitive the states will be in treating welfare recipients. Welfare reform in this sense is a return to the past more than an innovation for the future. And it is a racialized past that needs to be challenged.

6

Putting a Black Face on Welfare

The Good and the Bad

"Everyone who knows anything about welfare knows that most recipients are white." This is a common statement among people concerned about racist representations of welfare in the mass media. It often goes unchallenged. In fact, in recent years it seems to have taken on the status of an unquestioned truth known by all those who know better than to buy into the myths and stereotypes that are associated with welfare in the popular culture. This statement has been used repeatedly in attempts to undermine the prevalent notion that welfare is largely a "black program" and that welfare use is largely a result of low-income African Americans being trapped in a "black underclass," mired in a "culture of poverty," bereft of "personal responsibility" and unable to break out of an intergenerational cycle of "welfare dependency."[1]

Yet, this statement increasingly is factually questionable; and it is politically problematic. In what follows, I argue that failing to acknowledge the racial composition of the welfare population today serves to "whitewash" the racial disparities in the U.S. economy that often force low-income African Americans and Latinos to rely on public assistance far more than whites. In other words, contrary to the conventional understandings about the best way to depict welfare, it might be important to recognize that there is both a good and a bad to highlighting the race issue in welfare. I suggest how the issue of putting a "black face" on welfare is not as clear-cut as it is often depicted.[2] There are pitfalls either way. White or black, the face of welfare that we project poses political risks to which we need to alert ourselves.

In this analysis, I note the importance of recent scholarship on the ways racial representations of welfare undermine support for public assistance, but I also suggest that such scholarship all too often fails to appreciate the political complexities involved regarding the issues of race and welfare. The problems of racial representations of welfare therefore spill over into questions of advocacy. I conclude that issues regarding racial representations of welfare involve layers of political consideration and pose a variety of strategic problems for political activism. I recommend that more stress be given not so much to the frequency of racialized depictions of welfare in the mass media, but to how the broader society, the culture, and the prevailing modes of perception prime people to interpret issues of race and welfare in nonsalutary ways.[3] It is important to recognize that while putting a black face on welfare risks reinforcing racial stereotypes, only by acknowledging the disproportionate numbers of persons of color relying on welfare can we challenge this as an effect of racial inequality that is built into the economy.

Where is the radical incrementalism in this inquiry? The radical potential here lies in challenging prevailing modes of racial representation and then exploiting their ability to highlight social injustice. By discussing the issue of racial composition of the welfare population and taking the issue on more forthrightly can perhaps more effectively address issues of racial bias. Such reworking of prevailing forms of representation conducted from a critical distance, invoking discourses of interrogation, can provide voice to alternative perspectives so that ongoing struggles within the political process need to account for them. And that is exactly my hope for this analysis. I undertake this inquiry to suggest how understanding of the racial dimensions of welfare can help promote racial justice. In other words, it may well be that in order to get more racial justice, we need to be willing to ask hard questions and break with conventional wisdom.

The Moynihan Problem

Asking hard questions and breaking with the conventional wisdom on racialized depictions of welfare have their own political pitfalls, to be sure. The risk here is what I call "the Moynihan Problem," that is, looking into welfare use along racial lines might lead to results that will be associated with the most controversial work on the subject—Daniel P. Moynihan's *The Negro Family*. This work was an internal U.S. Department of Labor report completed in 1965 that Moynihan himself leaked to the press.[4] It ended up not being seen as an effort to highlight racial unfairness in the broader society, even though that might have been part of its author's intention.[5] Instead, the "Moynihan Report," as it was quickly dubbed, was criticized for serving to essentialize race differences, reinforce racist attitudes, and generally promote the idea that low-income African American families were mired in a "culture of poverty" that was of their own making and therefore made them responsible for their own plight. This was a widely accepted interpretation of the report by civil rights advocates and others concerned about poverty among African Americans. The Moynihan Report quickly fell into disrepute. In particular, it was criticized for unfairly stressing racial background as the key factor in producing poverty among African American families to the neglect of the political and economic roots of that poverty. Although Moynihan was rarely labeled a racist, his work was seen as being part of a broader perspective that encouraged "blaming the victim" for poverty.[6]

There is reason to think that the report did in fact deserve such an interpretation, in effect if not necessarily in intention. It was rather quickly appropriated by conservatives to justify cutbacks on welfare on the grounds that public assistance was a major contributing factor in promoting "welfare dependency" and a lack of "personal responsibility" among low-income African American families.[7] This was a campaign theme of the right for three decades until they succeeded in 1996 in ending welfare as an entitlement. In spite of Moynihan's own pained resistance to that act of disentitlement, the seeds for the Personal Responsibility and Work Opportunity Reconciliation Act of 1996 and its abolition of the welfare entitlement were therefore sown in the release of the Moynihan Report.[8]

The Moynihan Report's conclusions not only created a bad impression, they did so on the basis of bad research. The most often cited statistical claim in the report was premised on a supposed weakening of the ostensible link between African American male unemployment rates and welfare caseloads. The Moynihan Report seized on this shift to suggest that while the number of families on welfare was in the past tied to the black male unemployment rate, the welfare participation rate for African Americans in the early 1960s was starting to become "unglued." It was therefore interpreted as turning into an autonomous problem disconnected from the status of the economy and indicating that the black family was becoming wrapped in a "tangle of pathology."[9] To underscore its importance as a finding of social science, Moynihan would in time proudly call this the "Moynihan Scissors."[10] Yet, this analysis has been consistently critiqued for inappropriately tying the unemployment of black males with the welfare caseload for all races; subsequent research has shown the correlation to be unsubstantiated.[11]

William Julius Wilson has most prominently highlighted the problems with this statistical claim.[12] Yet, Wilson himself was to go on to trumpet Moynihan as a prophet who was unfairly castigated for pointing out the growing problems of social breakdown among what Wilson called the "black underclass."[13] Wilson in particular laments that the firestorm of criticism over the Moynihan Report may have induced a long-term wave of self-censorship among social scientists who feared being labeled racist for raising issues of family formation among African Americans. Adolph Reed and others have questioned whether this self-censorship ever really happened, finding no evidence for Wilson's concern.[14] A more compelling explanation for this self-censorship might be that in the wake of the controversy over the Moynihan Report, researchers who, like Moynihan, had previously followed the "culture of poverty" argument were now more sensitive about avoiding the racist canard that low-income African American families were the source of their own poverty. Researchers instead sought to find new ways to understand how poverty could create conditions that at times made it difficult to adhere to conventional moral standards of personal responsibility. Rather than speculate that an underclass had come to indulge in a culture of poverty, they found more meaningful ways to understand the causes of what was previously called "pathology." The Moynihan controversy therefore was not, as Wilson suggested, a cautionary tale about the premature dismissal of good research that prophetically predicted the demise of the traditional, nuclear family among low-income African Americans. Instead, the Moynihan controversy was more about the risk that emphasizing race as a factor in welfare receipt might be correctly interpreted as a sign of blaming the victim.

Still, the controversy surrounding *The Negro Family* does provide a cautionary reminder of the dilemmas associated with raising issues of race and welfare. The Moynihan Report was nothing more than an unevenly written, short (78 page) government document that emphasized the then well-accepted theme of pathology among economically marginalized African Americans.[15] Its own distinctive claim was that welfare dependency among low-income single-parent African American families was starting to spiral out of control due to a breakdown in values in low-income black communities. It was this thesis of cultural pathology that immediately touched off a firestorm when the report was leaked. Subsequently, the report was roundly criticized for imputing to African Americans a lack of commitment to what today policymakers call "family values."

There are good reasons, then, for wanting to be sensitive about introducing race into the analysis of welfare. There is the chance that your research can be associated with the Moynihan Report and its blame-the-victim outlook. Yet, there are problems in the other direction as well. While Reed is correct to dismiss Wilson's unsubstantiated claims about self-censorship, there are legitimate reasons to fear that analysis of the disproportionate use of public assistance by African Americans will be left in the dust. It could be a casualty of another kind of self-censorship grounded in a concern not to reinforce racist stereotypes about who uses welfare and why. There are pitfalls to not putting a black face on welfare, as I will demonstrate in the following section.

Myths about Myths

In 1996 the Personal Responsibility and Work Opportunity Reconciliation Act was enacted into law, ending welfare as an entitlement. As part of the battle to prevent this from happening, numerous efforts were made to inform the public about the real facts on welfare.[16] Most of this work was quite good in pointing out misunderstandings circulating among the public about welfare. Yet, analyses that were sound in other respects often mischaracterized the racial composition of the welfare population. For instance, one scrupulously researched and clearly presented publication was *Welfare Myths: Fact or Fiction? Exploring the Truth about Welfare,* published in 1996 by the Welfare Law Center.[17] Yet, even this publication was prone to parsing its statistics on race and welfare in a problematic way. *Welfare Myths* stated:

> MYTH: Almost all of the families receiving AFDC are Black or Hispanic.
> FACT: Many more White families than Black families or Hispanic families are helped by the AFDC program.

In the Internet version, to the left of "MYTH" is a button to push for "More Info." That "more info" turns out to be several paragraphs providing statistics that cover the "facts," such as "the percentage of Black families and of Hispanic families that receive cash assistance is larger than the proportion of White families who do, as is the proportion of Black and Hispanic families that are in poverty." Yet, the main point here that is emphasized is that even though poverty forces African Americans and Latinos to rely on welfare more frequently than whites, the facts still indicate that whites make up the majority of welfare recipients. The factual basis for this claim is reported as follows:

> A study of families receiving AFDC between January 1990 and June 1992 found that less than 3 in 10 women receiving AFDC for the first time were Black and 1.6 in 10 were Hispanic. Looking at all families receiving aid during a given period of time, White families still outnumber Black families, although the percentage of Black families in the total caseload is higher than the percentage among first-time recipients. White families make up 38.3% of the caseload, Black families 36.6%. Hispanic families account for 17.8% of all families receiving aid while Asians and Native Americans amount to a total of 4.2%.[18]

There are numerous problems with this factual claim. First, the study from which these calculations are drawn is cited nowhere in the publication. Second, the primary statistic reported is about the percentage of first-time users of welfare; this measure neglects to count people who are reapplying or cycling back onto aid after having been off. This measure also does not count people who are still receiving assistance they initiated before the start of the time period studied. In short, this particular statistical claim that most recipients are white is highly selective.[19] There are, however, many other ways to measure the racial composition of the welfare population. While none is perfect, several are an improvement over simply looking at first-time users. One common approach is to examine the racial composition of the rolls in a representative month (say January or June, or better, the average monthly breakdown for 12 months in that year). This approach is reported in figure 6.1.

The data in figure 6.1 are the more commonly reported data from the federal government and indicate that for the decade before welfare reform, about equal proportions of recipients at any one time were white or African American, with Latinos at a lower but increasing rate during the 1985–1999 period. These data are by no means consistent with the claim that most welfare recipients are white, indicating as they do that whites and blacks received welfare in approximately equal numbers for most of the years since 1985, and the number of Hispanic recipients was somewhat lower. Data on the number of recipients indicate that since the mid-1990s, the number of

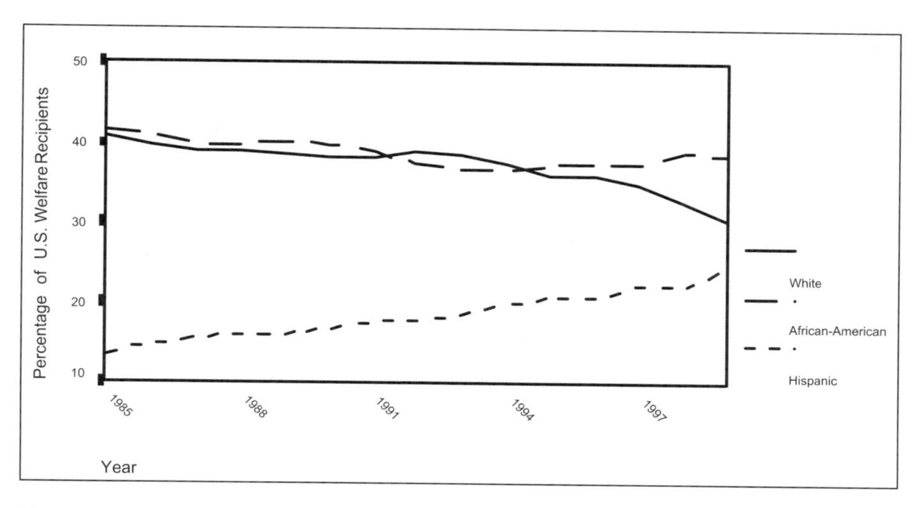

FIGURE 6.1 Distribution of U.S. Welfare Recipients by Race, 1985–1999
SOURCE: U.S. Department of Health and Human Services, http://www.aspe.os.dhhs.gov/hsp/leavers99/race.htm.

recipients for all three groups has declined, fastest for whites and slowest for Hispanics, so that blacks were the largest group by the end of the 1990s. A major part of the explanation for the disparity between these data and those reported in *Welfare Myths* is that the federal government data include the people on the rolls at any one point in time, regardless of whether they are using assistance for the first time.

The federal government, however, is excluding people who have gone off the rolls but had received welfare during that year. Therefore, we might want to try still another method that estimates the racial composition all family heads that received any assistance during a calendar year, regardless of whether it was their first time or not. Table 6.1 presents data from the Panel Study of Income Dynamics (PSID) on the racial breakdown of welfare recipients. The PSID is a national longitudinal study, with a sample population in any one year exceeding two thousand families.[20] The data are weighted to ensure representativeness by race.[21] The figures in table 6.1 are from the annual PSID waves for selected years 1970–1993. The figures presented are the percentage of all the PSID married women or independent female heads of households with children who indicated receiving any amounts of public assistance at any time during the preceding calendar year.

TABLE 6.1

Welfare Receipt by Race, 1980–1993. Percentage of Married Mothers and Independent Female Heads of Households Who Received Welfare during the Calendar Year

Race	1970	1975	1980	1985	1990	1991	1992	1993
Black	46	44	46	50	54	57	53	50
White	45	50	50	49	45	42	43	46
Other	9	6	4	1	1	1	4	4
Total	100	100	100	100	100	100	100	100
N	281	361	350	304	301	302	314	292

SOURCE: University of Michigan, Panel Study of Income Dynamics (PSID), annual waves. Calculations provided by Thomas P. Vartanian.

In these figures, blacks slightly outnumbered whites in 1970. Whites slightly outnumbered blacks in 1975 and 1980. Blacks outnumbered whites in each year after 1980. For 1991, 57 percent of all the mothers who indicated receiving any public assistance were black, 42 percent were white, and 1 percent were other races. In 1992, 53 percent were black, 43 percent were white, and 4 percent were other races. In 1993, 50 percent of recipient families were black while 46 percent were white and 4 percent were other. These calculations sort by race identification alone so Latinos, for instance, are sorted into either Black or White categories, and the Other category refers to Native Americans, Asians, and other racial groups designated neither white nor black. The calculations are based on all the married women and independent heads of households who had children and had received any welfare benefits in the preceding calendar year. Therefore, this is an inclusive sample that maximizes the chances of counting even a middle-class suburban woman who received only a partial welfare benefit for one month while, say, making the transition from being in a marriage to being divorced. This calculation therefore does not systematically exclude whites. Still, the percentages indicate that *in each year examined from 1985 on, more black than white women received assistance.*

These larger PSID numbers for blacks were for essentially the same time period covered by *Welfare Myths* data. During that time period, the average number of whites and blacks receiving welfare at any one point in time (e.g., in any one month) was essentially the same according to government statistics.[22] Yet, according to the PSID data, the total number of blacks who had received assistance during the calendar year exceeded the number of whites.

These data are therefore different from both the *Welfare Myths* data and those reported by the federal government. Part of the explanation is that the government and the *Welfare Myths* data report Latinos separate from race.

Another difference that is important for the contrast with both the *Welfare Myths* and federal government data is that the PSID data account for recycling back onto welfare. Looking only at first-time uses ignores the fact that compared to whites, African Americans who have left public assistance are more likely to return later (largely due to lower marriage rates).[23] Therefore, presenting a racial breakdown of the first-time users, as is done by *Welfare Myths*, cuts out more African American than white families. In the case of the federal data, not counted are all the people who are not currently receiving assistance, including recyclers who are disproportionately nonwhite.

Another difference with the *Welfare Myths* data is that by only concentrating on people who initiate the receipt of welfare, those data miss people who began using welfare before the time period covered. This leaves out longer-term users who are already welfare recipients. According to available research, these people are more likely to be nonwhite.[24] This is critical especially since long-term use has for years been the main source of concern about welfare in the mass public. Therefore, looking only at first-time receipt or only at who is on welfare at any one point in time takes the focus off the more controversial, long-term welfare population, which happens to be even more disproportionately comprised of nonwhites.

The PSID data, however, do not fully solve these problems. These data produce a very small sample, making their generalizability suspect. In addition, the inclusion of anyone who receives welfare for even the shortest period of time and the smallest amounts fails to address the claim that longer-term users are the more significant population. An even better estimate would weight the population by how long each family received welfare and how much they received. When this is done, the racial composition of the welfare population would in all likelihood be shown to be even more disproportionately nonwhite because, as indicated above, nonwhites are likely to have longer spells of welfare receipt.[25]

Therefore, I would suggest that the data on the racial breakdown of those receiving welfare is subject to much debate. One thing is clear: in the run up to welfare reform it was questionable to claim, as many did, that most welfare recipients were white. This claim operated as its own unquestioned myth among those seeking to repudiate the equally suspect notion that welfare was a "black program" for those "other" people who were not conforming to white, middle-class work and family values.

There was, however, at least a good rationale for the myth-busting about race even if it was factually suspect. Martin Gilens has effectively demonstrated that, beginning in the 1960s, the mass media—both print and electronic—began to overrepresent African Americans in negative stories about poverty and, to a lesser extent, about welfare.[26] Gilens also notes that beginning at that time, the mass public began to regard welfare as a "black program" that coddled low-income black families and rewarded them for not adhering to middle-class work and family values. Gilens goes on to demonstrate persuasively that both the mass public and journalists were likely to grossly overestimate the proportion of welfare recipients who were black. There came a need to challenge the highly racialized image of welfare recipients that was and continues to be ascendant in the culture and among the people in positions to influence opinion.[27]

Gilens's work is important in highlighting the role of the mass media in providing a racially distorted image of the welfare population. He is effective in suggesting that this role encouraged the denigration of welfare as a program for "other" people who were different and not adhering to white middle-class work and family values. Yet there is a need to consider how the problem transcends the mass media and its racialized depictions of welfare. There is a need to consider what to do when mass media depictions of the welfare population become accurate when they indicate that the welfare population is disproportionately nonwhite. There is a need to go beyond discussing whether accurate or distorted mass media depictions are affecting attitudes toward welfare as Gilens and others have demonstrated. There is a need to consider why the mass public is reluctant in the first place to see black welfare recipients as deserving. In other words, there is a need to examine why some segments of the white population are predisposed to looking negatively upon blacks receiving welfare and are therefore already primed to respond negatively to media depictions of them. Gilens's work gives insufficient attention to this issue. His version of the story also reinforces the tendency to want to insist that welfare recipients are no different from everyone else in their social lives. In that sense, it provides no defense for the disproportionate need among low-income single mothers of color for public assistance. In the end, Gilens participates in squelching discussion of the disparate racial effects of the political economy that make it necessary for low-income African American single mothers to have to rely on public assistance more than other families.

This is exactly what can happen with the dissemination of the factoid that "everyone who knows anything about welfare knows that most recipients are white." As this mantra becomes a more and more popular myth-busting claim among antipoverty advocates, less attention is given to how welfare recipients are "different" in racial composition and other ways, especially in terms of how society treats them. As a result, less attention is given to examining how this relatively distinctive group came to require assistance.[28]

The lure of "almost all recipients are white" is the prospect of unracializing welfare, of "whitening" it. If that can be accomplished, it creates an opening for developing more equity in the treatment of welfare recipients. For if the racial composition of the welfare population is no different from that of the society overall, there is a stronger empirical base for insisting on more equitable treatment of recipients because they really are not different from everyone else and do not need to be treated as some alien "other" group to be looked down upon and singled out for distinctive treatment under some punitive welfare system. The goal of equitable treatment is laudable and well established among advocates for a more progressive welfare state. But trampling over basic demographics and creating a distorted image of the racial composition of the welfare population is a strategy that is doomed to fail. It will founder on the shoals of factual disputation, which will not help realize the larger goal of equity.

In addition, while we might want to downplay race as socially constructed, it has real consequences as a way of organizing social life. Ignoring the racial composition of the welfare population on the grounds that race should not count unfortunately overlooks that it does count. Therefore, we need to recognize how it does and deal with the consequences. As much as we want to sweep the fictions of race into the dustbin, they continue to haunt social life. A disproportionately black welfare population is a subject that needs to be addressed for no other reason than to resist racist interpretations of welfare. And when the welfare population becomes increasingly composed of nonwhites to the point that the myth busters' myth about a white welfare population can no longer be sustained, where are we then?

One answer is: the present. That is exactly where we are right now. Today, we confront the prospect of having to argue for equity on grounds other than the distorted image that the demographic profile of welfare recipients mirrors the general population. It has not for a long time, and it increasingly does not. While during much of the 1980s it at least might have been true that whites and blacks were about equal in the government's monthly tabulations of welfare recipients, it is no longer the case. As Michael Brown and others have emphasized, with welfare reform in 1996, the welfare rolls declined dramatically through 2001, with whites leaving welfare faster than other groups, making the welfare population even more disproportionately nonwhite and creating an even greater prospect that welfare will be marginalized as a "black" program for "other" people.[29]

The main source for tracking this change has unfortunately been the federal government's statistics on the characteristics of the welfare population.[30] These data combine race and ethnicity to report not only on "whites" and "blacks," but also on "Hispanics," which is not a racial designation. Nonetheless, these data supply the evidence that, since welfare reform was enacted in the mid-1990s, there has been a rapid increase in the proportion of welfare recipients who are nonwhite, even if one makes the conservative assumption that about half of Hispanics on welfare are nonwhite.[31] In 1985, for the average month, 40.8 percent of adult recipients were white, while 41.6 percent were black and 13.6 percent were Hispanic. In 1999, the percentage of whites had fallen sharply to 30.5, while the percentage of blacks had only dropped to 38.3 and the percentage of Hispanics had risen to 24.5.[32] (See table 6.2.) The U.S. Department of Health and Human Services noted in its report on these figures,

> The racial composition of welfare families has changed substantially over the past ten years. In 1990, it was 38 percent whites, 40 percent blacks and 17 percent Hispanics. In 1999, however, it was 31 percent whites, 38 percent blacks and 25 percent Hispanics. In addition, the small percentage of the welfare population which is Asian has grown slowly but steadily over the period from just under 3 percent to about 3 and one-half percent. Viewed over the decade there has been a shift from white to Hispanic families which is consistent with broader population trends. This shift has been accelerated since 1996 and is particularly pronounced in California, New York and Texas. Thus, in 1999, 70 percent of all Hispanic welfare families were in three large States (California, New York and Texas), as compared to 65 percent in 1996. In California, the proportion of Hispanic welfare families increased to 46 percent in 1999 from 38 percent in 1996. In addition, black families which had been a declining proportion of the caseload have trended up slightly since 1996. The upshot of these changes is that the proportion of welfare families that were minorities has increased from three-fifths to just over two-thirds over the decade, primarily driven by the growth in Hispanic families.[33]

Given the racial diversity of the Latino population, we can conclude that part of its growth as percentage of recipients further adds to the increase in the nonwhite proportion of the welfare population. With welfare reform,

TABLE 6.2

Percent Distribution of TANF Families by Race, October 1998–September 1999

	Total Families	White	Black	Hispanic	Native American	Asian	Other	Unknown
U.S. Total	2,648,462	30.5	38.3	24.5	1.5	3.6	0.6	1.0

SOURCE: U.S. Department of Health and Human Services, Administration on Children and Families, Office of Family Assistance, National Emergency TANF Datafile as of 4/14/2000 (http://www.acf.dhhs.gov/programs/opre/characteristics/fy99/tab06_99.htm, last updated on 08/27/2000). Figures are for the average month.

blacks have increasingly been established as the largest group, and nonwhites as the majority, of recipient families at any one point in time. (See table 6.2.)

These figures, however, point to an even less discussed dimension of the issue. Comparing these figures to raw population numbers, we can suggest that the probability that African Americans rely on welfare is much greater than it is for whites. We can estimate that approximately, on average, in any single month in 1999 *1* out of *100* whites and *8* out of *100* blacks were receiving welfare.[34] While the probability is low for both racial categories, persons designated as black had an eight times higher probability of using welfare than those designated as white.

What are we to do now, under these circumstances, with a welfare population as racialized as this one? The welfare population remains diverse but increasingly composed of nonwhites more so than the U.S. overall. Arguments for equity based on a distorted image of the welfare population as a largely white population that is essentially no different from the society overall were always questionable; now they are irrelevant.[35] How are we now to build the case for equitable treatment of welfare recipients? For a long time, equity arguments should have been made on other than the misleading grounds that most welfare recipients are white; for a long time, they needed to be made not by neglecting race but by explaining how African Americans in particular, but other racial minorities as well, especially including Latinos, were more likely to be living in poverty and in need of public assistance at higher rates. Equity arguments need to be urgently made now on the basis of taking race into account, indicating that African Americans and Latinos need to rely on public assistance more frequently and that there are good reasons why they should be seen, if only in this regard, as "different." They confront different circumstances, often facing greater need and more often requiring the assistance of welfare. The situation is critical since research indicates that blacks constitute a large majority of the recipient families that are predicted to be affected by the new time limits under welfare reform. Greg Duncan, Kathleen Harris, and Johanne Boisjoly estimate that blacks constitute over two-thirds of the families who will reach the newly imposed sixty-month federal limit for the receipt of welfare.[36] Taking race into account is now perhaps more than at any other time in the history of the welfare program an unavoidable necessity.

Yet, as long the myth of a white welfare population persists, and as long as advocates cling to it as the basis for arguing for equity, we are at risk of neglecting to attend to the problems of racism, the issue of racial barriers, the extent to which there are race-related differences that need to be addressed. Such neglect is dangerous; it can ignore the systemic sources of poverty for low-income families of color. This failure, however, is not just a conservative deficiency but part of a pattern of political inadequacy among liberals unwilling to discuss what they see as potentially troubling facts about welfare recipients.

While this gentility is understandable, it is also hurtful. The unwillingness to address more forthrightly the racial composition of the welfare population springs in part from a fear that conservatives will use such information to reinforce their arguments that welfare recipients are "different." This reticence extends to discussing the "differences" associated with all single mothers on welfare, black or white, yet often leaves the field open to conservatives to decide how these differences are interpreted.[37]

There are many parallels for this sort of reticence by liberals. For instance, for years liberals were reluctant to examine seriously what was misleadingly alleged to be "welfare fraud" when poverty-stricken recipients were not reporting all of their other small sources of income. For years, the topic was dominated by conservative viewpoints that led to the development of obsessive practices by states to hunt down and punish violators who failed to report all of their income from all sources even if they were marginal. "Welfare fraud" had become another way to smear and harass economically distressed welfare recipients and depict them as undeserving.[38] Finally, after decades of campaigning to crack down on these alleged abuses of welfare, studies such as the one by Kathryn Edin and Laura Lein offered an alternative perspective which showed that low welfare benefits left recipients no choice but to supplement their welfare checks with unreported income just to survive.[39] Unfortunately, by the time that Edin and Lein published their findings it was 1997 and the campaign to combat fraud and withhold aid from "cheaters" had held down welfare benefits for over two decades so that they had on average declined in real value by over 40 percent since the early 1970s.[40] The prior failure to join the discussion about the issue of "welfare fraud" was therefore at best unhelpful. At worst, this lapse in political courage provided an opening for conservatives to frame the issue of unreported income in the worst possible light as "welfare fraud." This in turn enabled states to tighten access and reduce benefits to, in effect, punish people in most cases for just trying to survive by combining inadequate welfare benefits with small amounts of unreported income.

Reluctance to discuss particular issues about welfare and poverty can have its negative effects. But the whole point of getting involved and discussing potentially difficult issues about welfare and poverty is to prevent those issues from being framed in tendentious ways. Talking about the disproportionate numbers of nonwhites receiving welfare does not have to involve buying into the Moynihan "tangle of pathology" perspective that ends up blaming the victim. Yet, if only the Moynihans of the world get involved in highlighting the racial composition of the welfare population, that is just what might happen. Others need to engage these issues not just to check the facts about the racial composition of the welfare population, but more importantly to check how the facts are being framed and how assumptions of otherness are informing the interpretation of those facts.

Visualizing Race

The issue of racialized depictions of welfare recipients is not just a problem of numbers. It is perhaps an even greater problem when we turn to issues of visual culture. For a long time, there has been great concern that showing pictures of African Americans on welfare only serves to reinforce the stereotype that welfare is strictly a "black" program. Such pictures inevitably risk reinscribing the notion that only blacks use welfare because there is something different about them, not so much about their social and economic conditions, but about their personal characteristics, behavior, and culture, leading them to be more likely to rely on welfare. Images of blacks on welfare unavoidably reinforce the worst racist stereotypes about why African Americans use welfare.

There is a cultural dynamic that underlies racialized images. The denigration of "black" supports the privileging of "white." The socially constructed designation of "black" is continually manufactured and given life largely in order to sustain the privileges associated with the equally suspect category of "white." Therefore, if "black" had not existed, then in the quest to validate "white" identity and culture, something else would have been created. Hortense Spillers has written: "Let's face it. I am a marked woman, but not everybody knows my name. . . . 'Sapphire' . . . or 'Black Woman at the Podium': I describe a locus of confounded identities, a meeting ground of investments and privations in the national treasury of rhetorical wealth. My country needs me, and if I were not here, I would have been invented."[41] In a more abstract register, Slavoj Žižek has seconded this assessment and pointed it toward how the "black welfare queen" has been constructed out of need for an "other" to legitimate the middle-class white man of virtue who practices personal responsibility and has no need for assistance from the government:

> [E]ach universal ideological notion is always hegemonized by some particular content which colours its very universality and accounts for its efficiency. In the rejection of the social welfare system by the New Right in the US, for example, the universal notion of the welfare system as inefficient is sustained by the pseudo-concrete representation of the notorious African-American single mother, as if, in the last resort, social welfare is a programme for black single mothers—the particular case of the "single black mother" is silently conceived as "typical" of social welfare and of what is wrong with it. . . . Another name for this short-circuit between the Universal and the Particular is, of course, "suture": the operation of hegemony "sutures" the empty Universal to a particular content.[42]

Žižek emphasizes that the abstract categories need to be filled with content from the existentially experienced world of social relations. The idea of a welfare queen is one of black single mothers who rely on public assistance, making the abstract idea seem more credible and consistent with real life. Yet, most women on welfare are not as the stereotype depicts—that is, they are not lazy, unmotivated, irresponsible, promiscuous, and so on. They are often actually "heroes of their own lives," exercising initiative and independence by putting themselves on welfare in order to make the best of a bad situation and provide for their children.[43] Furthermore, most white middle-class "men of virtue" rely on the government for various tax advantages, subsidies, and other forms of assistance. Nonetheless, the contrast between "black welfare queen" and white middle-class "man of virtue" resonates very strongly in popular culture, scholarly critiques notwithstanding.

The images of women on welfare help reinforce this biased distinction and in the process reinscribe notions of black inferiority and white su-

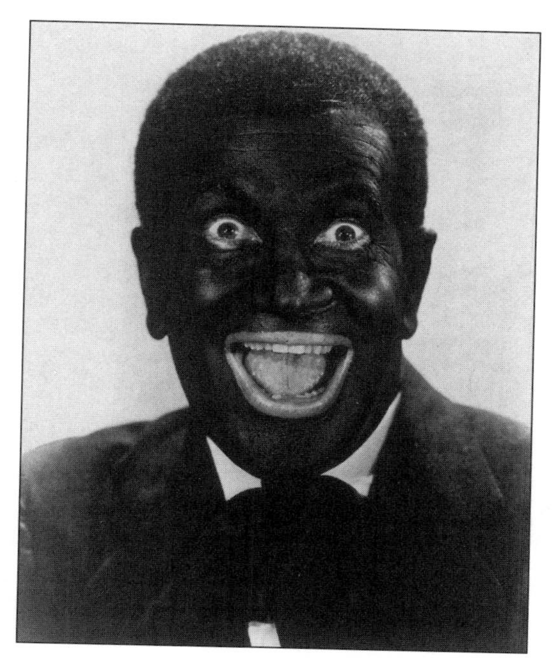

FIGURE 6.2 Using Blackface to Reinscribe Otherness and Legitimate the Self Al Jolson Publicity. Reprinted courtesy of Movie Star News @ Warner Bros.

premacy. The history of racist depictions of African Americans in the United States creates a rich reservoir of racist iconography that reinforce stereotypes. The exploitation of black images in order to access white privilege is a recurrent theme in our culture. We need reach no farther than the well-established, if now repudiated, practice of white entertainers practice performing in "blackface," beginning in the 1840s in minstrel shows and becoming popular first among Irish, and eventually among Jewish, entertainers. (See figure 6.2.) Michael Paul Rogin has written:

> Blackface is a form of cross-dressing, in which one puts on the insignias of sex, class or race that stands in binary opposition to one's own. . . . Assimilation is achieved via the mask of the most segregated; the blackface that offers Jews mobility keeps blacks fixed in place. Rabinowitz turns into Robin, but the fundamental binary opposition nevertheless remains. That segregation, imposed on blacks, silences their voices and sings their names.[44]

FIGURE 6.3 Another Form of Blackface Associated Press Photo. Reprinted by permission.

Rogin stresses how the "blackface" facilitated assimiliation for white immigrants, demonstrating that they must be white because they had to paint their faces in order to make them look black. The Jew becomes white by way of demonstrating he was not black until painted. The Jew in this sense uses blacks to become white. The cultural dynamic of invoking black in order to privilege white is enacted all over again.

The social, cultural, and historical significance of the creation of whiteness via the denigration of blackness is an immense topic that has only been beginning to receive serious study by white scholars in recent years.[45] Yet, African American intellectuals have been commenting on this issue for decades, highlighting that becoming white was the goal of many immigrants. This made the American Dream something that was not accessible to African Americans in ways it was for other groups. James Baldwin once emphasized:

> No one was white before he/she came to America. . . . It took generations and a vast amount of coercion before this became a white country. . . . There is an Irish community. . . . There is a German community. . . . There is a Jewish community. . . . There are English communities. There are French com-

munities. . . . Jews came here from countries where they were not white, and they came here in part because there were not white. . . . Everyone who got here, and paid the price of the ticket, the price was to become "white."[46]

The use of "black" to legitimate "white" has at times even in recent years turned horrific. (See fig. 6.3.) How does white, female Christie Todd Whitman, former governor of New Jersey, legitimate herself by frisking an African American male? In this recently released controversial photo, Governor Whitman is caught on film frisking an innocent man, for what exact purpose remains unknown.[47] One possible explanation is the imbrication of race and gender and how a female Republican governor felt the need to prove she was as tough as some of her white, male conservative party members when it came to the issue of cracking down on crime. Dressed in white, this female governor was intentionally or not claiming access to white male privilege. As a woman, she was adopting the traditional role in American society of the white male overlord. She was perhaps too thoughtlessly and inexcusably exploiting a black man in order to prove she was tough enough to be like a white man herself. She erased her gender on the back of a black man. With this visual display, her wish to be not just Governor Whitman but also Governor Whit_e_man was fulfilled.[48]

In the process, Whitman unreflectively ratified the practice of racial profiling by the New Jersey state troopers. The systematic stopping and harassing of African American motorists on the New Jersey Turnpike was to continue even after the state settled out of court in a controversial case on the matter. In that case, the state all but admitted responsibility for the shooting of two black and one Latino young males. Sufficient evidence had been produced, including the picture, about the state's willingness to allow racial profiling to continue.[49] The racist practices of the state police were not to be repudiated until Whitman left to assume the head of the federal agency that was dedicated to making our environment clean. The racial connotations from white clothes to white environment make the Whitman photo all the more troubling.

Therefore, racialized images have a long history of reinforcing white privilege in the broader society and not just in welfare. This perhaps makes some thoughtful people understandably reluctant to put a black face on welfare. The book cover in figure 6.4 is for Martin Gilens's book telling how the media from the 1960s promoted the racialization of welfare. His editors probably did not put an African American woman on the cover in part because his main thesis is that beginning in the 1960s, the overrepresentation

FIGURE 6.4 *The Act of Visualizing Race*
The cover of *Why Americans Hate Welfare: Race, Media, and the Politics of Antipoverty Policy* (Chicago Universtiy of Chicago Press, 1999). Reprinted by permission.

of African Americans in stories and accompanying pictures about welfare led to increased opposition to the welfare program.

Yet Gilens's cover suggests something else is at work as well. The hand shown is multishaded, suggesting ambiguity and highlighting how viewers are forced to make their own judgment about who is taking welfare and why. In this sense, this picture is what W. J. T. Mitchell calls a "metapicture"—a visual representation that refers not so much to some visualized subject but more importantly to the process of visualization.[50] This metapicture highlights how all representations require the work of viewing subjects to make the viewed object coherent and that these judgments are to varying degrees grounded in the prevailing culture.[51] White viewers were often thinking negatively about persons of color on welfare even before reading slanted news stories. As it turns out, the racially ambiguous hand proved to be too troublesome an image and was removed from the cover with the publication of the paperback version of the book.[52]

I tap into this issue of the relationship of the viewing subject to the viewed object with an analysis of racialized representations of welfare in my book *After Welfare*. Inside the book, I show the photo in figure 6.5 in order to demonstrate how racialized images of women on welfare are often interpreted in ways that reinforce prevailing cultural prejudices against persons of color, against women, and against public assistance.[53] In that book, I argue that such images are critical to reinforcing white privilege in society. Yet, my major point is that these pictures do not do this all by themselves. They require an act of supplementation. Paul de Man once defined reading as supplying what is missing to a text.[54] Texts are inert until they are read; reading breathes lives into making them interpretable through the very act when they are interpreted. The net result is that each reading supplies its

FIGURE 6.5 Visualizing the Welfare Queen
Valerie Watson of Memphis, who complained of back pain, was cut off welfare last fall after missing training classes. She then sold her appliances and now uses a backyard grill to cook for her family, including son Jeremy, 18, at right. Reprinted from Barbara Vobejda and Judith Havemann, "Sanctions: A Force behind Falling Welfare Rolls; States Are Cutting Off Tens Thousands Who Won't Seek Work or Follow Rules," *Washington Post*, March 23, 1998, p. A1. © Troy Glasgow.

own text, making the idea of one objective reading of any text unattainable and the definitive meaning of any text something that is infinitely deferred and ultimately undecidable. And we are in turn shaped by texts in less than predictable ways. The same is true with pictures. Pictures are nothing until they are seen. What we see is an act of visualization, as multivalent and polyoptic as texts are undecidable. Every picture produces as many visualizations as the number of people who see it. Maybe more. This is Mitchell's point about what the metapicture tells us. It teaches us about visualization in the abstract, overall, in general; and part of that act of visualization is its unavoidably subjective character, inevitably destined to produce multiple readings that loop back to influence the viewers in multiple ways.

A larger point here is that visualization is a dynamic process; it is not one in which pictures impose their imagery on passive viewers. Viewers must be enlisted into the viewing process in order for visualization to occur. Pictures of black women on welfare do not necessarily in and of themselves mean anything in particular. They need to be visualized; they need viewers to interpret them before they can become meaningful representations. And when viewers draw on the rich cultural traditions of reconstructing white privilege on the backs of black people, then pictures of African American women on welfare take on an added significance, signifying black inferiority in the name of consolidating white supremacy.

Therefore, we need to go beyond Gilens's analysis. It is not enough to emphasize that the mass media exaggerate the extent to which the welfare population includes African Americans. We need also to explain how our culture primes people to read news reports and images in a certain way.

Of the woman in figure 6.5, I wrote:

> The woman depicted . . . had in 1997 been sanctioned to the point where she was being removed from the welfare rolls. Reduced to cooking family meals on an outdoor grill, she sits outside and stares blankly away from the camera while her teenage son looks on. She seems to be an enigma, refusing to work and claiming undetectable maladies, though not even trying to defend herself against a welfare bureaucracy that rejects her story. Her inscrutability creates doubts in our minds, allowing us to decide that she is incorrigible in her insistence on taking welfare. Her passivity becomes a form of active defiance. Her blank face is a blank slate on which welfare discourse can write its stigmatizing story of the welfare queen. Her body language is therefore not of her own making but a discourse that reads her a

certain way. Simply being there, in poverty, on the welfare rolls, in the backyard, cooking on the grill, she is open to being read by welfare policy discourse. Without knowing anything about her life, her personal experiences, or her hopes and fears, welfare policy discourse appropriates her body and judges her passivity as a willfully chosen dependency.[55]

Therefore, for me, it is important to emphasize how the preexisting prejudices operating in society prime people to read racialized images of welfare recipients in particular ways. I also want to highlight how the prejudices of the culture not only reinforce negative views of welfare-taking by persons of color but also necessitate the greater frequency with which persons of color are forced to rely on public assistance. I feel it is necessary to put a black face on welfare *and* to make more visible how those prejudices are operating and to what effect. I requested that my editors place the photo of the woman sitting by the grill on the cover of *After Welfare*. My editors rejected the photo as "too negative" and offered a new picture (see fig. 6.6). Here, an African American woman on welfare is at a job site stopping to pose while cleaning a bus. Whether this cover was an improvement is surely subject to debate. She is on welfare but she is working. She is on welfare working at a menial job, but she can be interpreted as having a proud and dignified look. Facing the camera, she is not ashamed. She is at the front of the bus.[56] This picture is qualitatively different from the one in figure 6.5, yet one has to wonder whether such a difference amounts to anything. It is still a black face at risk of being read tendentiously by a white society that freely draws on a rich cultural reservoir of racial bias. And as a black face, it risks reinforcing stereotypical understandings of welfare in ways that do not challenge viewers to change how they might think.

Such a picture may have several redeeming features. It highlights how race and welfare are often connected. It also reminds us that the act of viewing demonizes welfare recipients at least as much as the picture itself. Here is a woman at work on the cover of a book about welfare. What is this supposed to tell us? If the photo is frequently read as a tale of black insufficiency, then we need to ask how a woman at work, with a dignified gaze, is read in such a demonized way. The answer, one suspects, will be found more in our hearts and in our heads than on the page or in the photo. And until we are willing to interrogate the rich cultural reservoir that funds such prejudice, the manufacturing and demonizing of black welfare queens will surely continue.

FIGURE 6.6 Putting a Black Face on Welfare
The cover of Sanford F. Schram's *After Welfare: The Culture of Postindustrial Social Policy* (New York: New York University Press, 2000).

Putting a Face on Advocacy

The issues of representation spill over into questions of advocacy. A common dilemma among advocacy and welfare rights groups is who should represent welfare recipients in public forums. One response is to choose white, single mothers who have been divorced, who have only one or two children, who are in transition from welfare to work.[57] The goal is often to suggest that welfare recipients are no different from the average middle-class family and that all families should be supportive of welfare because it is really a program for all of us, and all our families may need to rely on it at some time in our lives. This of course is not true. Most families will never need welfare, even during divorce. Many women do go on welfare for short periods of time during divorce; however, they do not comprise a majority of divorcing families, let alone all families, nor do divorced families make up a sizable proportion of welfare recipients.[58]

Yet, there are more serious problems than the factual misrepresentations. Putting a white face on welfare and then pretending that recipients are just like middle-class families risks encouraging policymakers to reform welfare on the basis of that assumption. Then, we face the prospect that welfare policies will be even less attuned to the real circumstances and struggles that the families who need welfare actually confront. If we represent welfare mothers as people who are "job ready," who are only going to need to rely on welfare for a short period of time while they make the transition to paid employment, then we are more likely to get public policies that are insensitive to the fact that some mothers will need to rely on welfare for extended periods of time. Our policies may then neglect that many are not able or ready to secure employment that can pay them enough while they maintain full responsibility for their children on their own. This is exactly the kind of welfare reform we have been getting—reform that seems to be oblivious to the realities that most welfare mothers, of any color, confront. Presenting the welfare population as being just like the middle class leads to public policies that assume that welfare mothers can begin acting middle class tomorrow, when in fact many confront dire circumstances that make that assumption ludicrous.

The more effective responses lie in recognizing the diversity of welfare recipients. Neither white nor black, divorced or unmarried, "job ready" or not, will do. Only when we begin representing welfare families in all their diversity, in all their colors, highlighting how many of them are confronting numerous social and economic obstacles, will we begin to convince others to join us in trying to remove those barriers. In particular, we need to highlight that large numbers of welfare mothers are in very difficult circumstances that are often the result of having been marginalized by class, race, and gender discrimination. They are not ready to act middle class because the structure of society has ensured that their inequitable access to education, their lack of opportunities to form traditional families, their lack of economic opportunities, and their overall poverty were not of their own making but a result of being left out of the mainstream of society. Only when welfare recipients in all their diversity get to articulate in their own voices that they have been marginalized will we begin to see how putting a full face on welfare is a better alternative than whitewashing the welfare population with strategic misrepresentations.

Conclusion

There is merit in the idea that the United States has a bifurcated welfare state.[59] In this bifurcated state, citizens qualify for the more generous social insurance programs on the basis of their participation in the labor market, requiring others to settle for the inadequate benefits of public assistance programs. The privileged under this system can qualify for retirement benefits, survivor benefits, disability insurance, and unemployment compensation; those who have not worked enough in the right jobs or were not married to someone who worked enough in the right jobs must rely on welfare.

There is also something to be said for the notion that this bifurcated welfare state is based on invidious distinctions, socially constructed to achieve the political effect of privileging some families as more deserving than others. The deservingness of top-tier families is not the result of politically neutral, fair economic processes. Instead, the distinctions between deserving and undeserving are politically suspect, reinforcing long-standing class, race, and gender biases about which types of people and families are more appropriate for our social order. The traditional two-parent family with a "breadwinner" and a "homemaker" is privileged, especially families where the breadwinner worked in an appropriate job long enough to qualify for benefits. This privileged status was more often accessible to white middle- and upper-class families. It is no surprise, then, that the bottom rungs of the welfare state are disproportionately populated with low-income, nonwhite single-parent families where a mother is left to do the double duty of being a breadwinner and a homemaker for her children, in ways that make her less likely to qualify for top-tier benefits.

Writing about the conservative push for welfare reform in the early 1980s, Frances Fox Piven and Richard A. Cloward wrote:

> [W]hen the several major policy initiatives of the Reagan administration are laid side by side, something of a coherent theory can be detected. . . . [T]he coherent theory is about human nature, and it serves the class interests of the Reagan administration and its business allies. It is the archaic idea the people in different social classes have different human natures and

> thus different basic motivations. The affluent are one sort of creature and working people are another. It follows that these different sorts of creatures require different systems of incentives and disincentives. The affluent exert themselves in response to rewards—to the incentive of increased profitability yielded by lower taxes. Working people respond only to punishment—to the economic insecurity that will result from reductions in the income support programs.[60]

There are therefore institutional roots behind the concern of reinforcing the idea that welfare recipients are these "other" people. Highlighting that welfare recipients are different in any relevant way, including their racial composition, is at risk of being appropriated in service of the right-wing agenda to construct welfare recipients as these "other people." This easily slides into more ambitious attempts to "other" welfare recipients as deviants who fail to conform to white middle-class work and family values. Focusing on differences between welfare recipients and others can reinforce attempts to blame welfare mothers for their own poverty, allegedly attributable to their failure to try to be like the rest of us.[61]

Yet, there is also the risk that if we fail to indicate how welfare recipients are different and why, those differences will not be taken into account when fashioning welfare reforms. Social policy becomes even more obtuse than it normally is, imposing an intensive set of assumptions on recipients and expecting them to live up to them immediately. Welfare reform becomes focused on enforcing work and family values on welfare recipients when they are not always ready immediately to take a job and work their way off welfare and out of poverty. Obtuse welfare reform that fails to account for difference can end up insisting that welfare recipients be "job ready," make "rapid attachment" to the labor market, take paid employment, and so on, without noting that recipients might, for instance, face race and gender biases and barriers in the workforce and on the job. In fact, that is what we have today: obtuse welfare reform that fails to account for difference, fails to understand how the welfare population is disproportionately comprised of people of color, and fails to try to do anything worthwhile to address the racial dimensions of our social and economic life that make race the salient reality of welfare today.

We need to learn to be able to walk and chew gum at the same time. One would think we could do that. We need to learn to see the differences among welfare recipients, including the racial difference, but not be so blinded as to assume immediately that traits specific to these different individuals account for their being on welfare. We need to challenge how we see and how we think. Otherwise we will remain blind and ignorant.

For centuries, men have found ways to sexualize any act by a woman. An acting woman is itself a performance open to be read in sexualized ways. A woman's active stance is even suggested to be, at times, a sign of her passive availability for the realization of male sexual fantasy. The viewing subject can invert the viewed object converting its active performance into a passive receptacle for that which is wished for. The male gaze, however, is not the only gaze. The passivity of women on welfare can be inverted into active defiance encouraged by a deviant underclass committed to resisting conforming to the work and family values of white, middle-class society. Then again, no amount of pictures of passive women on welfare will necessarily undercut well-entrenched assumptions that these women are outlaws, defiantly resisting assimilation into the dominant culture. To reverse it one more time, we also need to be alert that depictions of women on welfare, black or white, are often automatically interpreted as signs of their "dependency." We need to think about the ways in which those readings about passive welfare dependents obscure that these welfare recipients are often asserting their independence and courageously taking action to respond to dire circumstances, ranging from economic need to abusive relationships. We need to recognize how the viewing subject is implicated in the construction of the visualized representation. We need to interrogate the assumptions used to visualize welfare recipients, passive as well as active, as the "other."

In other words, it takes more than images to create racism. It takes more than pictures of black women on welfare to reinforce that they are undeserving. The racist premises that inform such interpretations must already be available before these pictures can do their work. Yet, given that those prejudices are there, racial representations of welfare need to be sensitive to the fact that they will possibly tap those reserves and reactivate such tendentious interpretations of why some people need to use public assistance more than others.

As with images, so with numbers. In either case, there is a need to acknowledge that race does figure into the use of welfare. The difficulty is in introducing such topics in a culture that is predisposed to talk about such issues in the worst possible ways, serving to further reinscribe the prejudices and racial barriers that create the racial injustice in the first place. Yet, until we find ways to talk about race and welfare, the predicament will continue. Persons of color, African Americans and Latinos in particular, will continue to be overrepresented in the welfare population; however, our willingness to openly discuss the racism and racial barriers that put them there will remain off the public agenda. The dilemma is that if we take race into account, we risk reinscribing racial prejudice; however, if we do not, we risk not calling such prejudice into account for the crimes of poverty that it has inflicted on some groups more than others.

As the welfare population becomes increasingly nonwhite, the dilemma intensifies and the situation becomes even more urgent. In order to get equity for welfare recipients, we need to begin highlighting their differences and their often inequitable situations. We cannot afford not to talk about race. In particular, we cannot afford not to talk about the assumptions about race that infiltrate discussions of welfare. Just as it takes more than numbers and images to create racism, it takes more than numbers and images to undo it. Examining these assumptions more so than waging wars of images and numbers becomes critical to advocacy for racial justice in welfare in particular and in social relations more generally. In order to be "against race," as Paul Gilroy has aptly termed it, it may well be that we need first to account for it and take responsibility for it, in the most explicit terms possible.[62]

7

Success Stories

Welfare Reform, Policy Discourse, and the Politics of Research

Sanford F. Schram and Joe Soss

We live in a forest of symbols on the edge of a jungle of fact.
—Joseph Gusfield, *The Culture of Public Problems* (1981), p. 51

Our understanding of real situations is always mediated by ideas; those ideas in turn are created, changed, and fought over in politics.
—Deborah Stone, *Policy Paradox* (1997), p. 282

Welfare reform is a success! Or so one might think based on a majority of evaluations coming from leading public officials and media sources. After five years under the new policy regime, initial anxieties have given way to a rough consensus that welfare reform, up to this point, has succeeded. As the architects of Temporary Assistance for Needy Families (TANF) had hoped, the welfare rolls have declined precipitously from 12.24 million recipients in August 1996 to 5.33 million recipients in September 2001, a decline of 63 percent.[1] In addition, a number of studies have suggested that many people leaving welfare are faring well.[2] To many observers, these facts suggest that the success of welfare reform is self-evident, indisputable among reasonable people.

The goal in this chapter is to question the prevailing consensus on welfare reform by showing how TANF's status as a "policy success" may be viewed as a political construction.[3] Evaluations of public policy inevitably require political choices regarding which facts will be valued as indicators of success and which interpretations of facts will serve as a basis for judgment.[4]

Welfare reform is now widely viewed as a success, not because of the facts uncovered by researchers (which paint a murky picture), but because of a political climate that privileges some facts and interpretations over others.

Judgments of policy success and failure are built on the backs of what Joseph Gusfield once called "public facts"—statements "about an aggregate of events which we do not and cannot experience personally."[5] Although any one of us may have personal experience with poverty or welfare, it is impossible to draw from such experience a conclusion about whether welfare reform in general is "working" or whether poor people in general are faring well. To arrive at such judgments, we must rely heavily on what media stories, public officials, and experts report about general states of affairs. Such reports serve to establish the success or failure of government policy as an authentic fact for the public.

The popular belief that welfare reform has succeeded can be traced chiefly to positive interpretations of two public facts: declining caseloads and outcomes for program "leavers." In what follows, we explore the politics that surround these two facts. We argue that the meanings of caseload decline and leaver outcomes remain far from clear and ask how alternative criteria might point to less sanguine evaluations of reform.

Welfare Reform as a Success Story

That the new welfare policies have succeeded where earlier, more liberal efforts failed is now taken by many to be an irrefutable fact. Writing in the *Washington Post*, Michael Kelly states, "In all arguments of policy and politics, there comes sooner or later the inevitable moment when it becomes simply undeniable that one side of the argument is true, or mostly so, and the other is false, or mostly so."[6] "The inevitable moment," Kelly writes, "arrived for liberals on . . . welfare reform."[7] As early as the summer of 1997, President Bill Clinton was ready to conclude, "The debate is over. We now know that welfare reform works."[8] Three years later, the debate really did seem to be over. The 2000 presidential campaign included almost no significant disagreement over issues of poverty and welfare, as the Democratic and Republican nominees both touted the achievements of reform and pledged to build on its successes.

Media stories on welfare reform have been more measured in their tone, but have largely bolstered the image of success. Because welfare reform has produced so many new policies and outcomes in such a diversity of places, it has been a difficult story for news media to cover. Some journalists have made great efforts to meet these challenges. Jason DeParle's year-long series in the *New York Times*, for example, was an admirable piece of journalism.[9] In the main, however, media stories have tended to forgo investigative journalism and critical inquiry in favor of presentations that rely heavily on statistics and interpretations proffered by government. Such stories are typically written in a traditional journalistic idiom that emphasizes balance, impartiality, and presentation (rather than critical interrogation) of facts; but in a majority of cases, these stories portray new TANF policies as a success.

Between January 1998 and September 2000, the top fifty newspapers in the United States ran 250 stories on welfare reform and caseload decline.[10] Examining these stories, we found that only 28.4 percent offered an unmitigated positive or negative view of reform; most assessments came with some counterpoints. Over half the articles in our sample were either wholly positive (19.6 percent) or generally positive with caveats (32 percent). By contrast, only about a quarter were wholly negative (8.8 percent) or generally negative with caveats (15.6 percent). Twenty-four percent gave equal weight to the pros and cons of reform.[11] The modal story on welfare reform raised concerns about families leaving the TANF program and about what might happen if the economy sours; but with these caveats in place, it went on to suggest that welfare reform so far has had remarkably positive results. (See fig. 7.1.)

Media stories on welfare reform have tended to be framed in terms that establish and dramatize the success of new TANF policies. By this claim, we do not mean that journalists have disseminated incorrect facts, exhibited overt bias, or colluded with those who have a stake in welfare reform's success. Rather, our argument is that media coverage has been shaped by policymakers' concern with the problem of dependence and, hence, has focused on a set of facts and interpretations that support a verdict of policy success. The roots of this focus, we argue, lie in an anti-welfare discourse that not only produced policy retrenchment in the 1990s, but also defined the terms on which this retrenchment would be judged. As we describe below, the current framing of welfare evaluation in terms of caseload levels and leaver outcomes is far from natural or neutral. The "inevitable moment" described by Michael Kelly was not inevitable; it was and is an outcome of political battles fought on the contested terrain of public discourse.

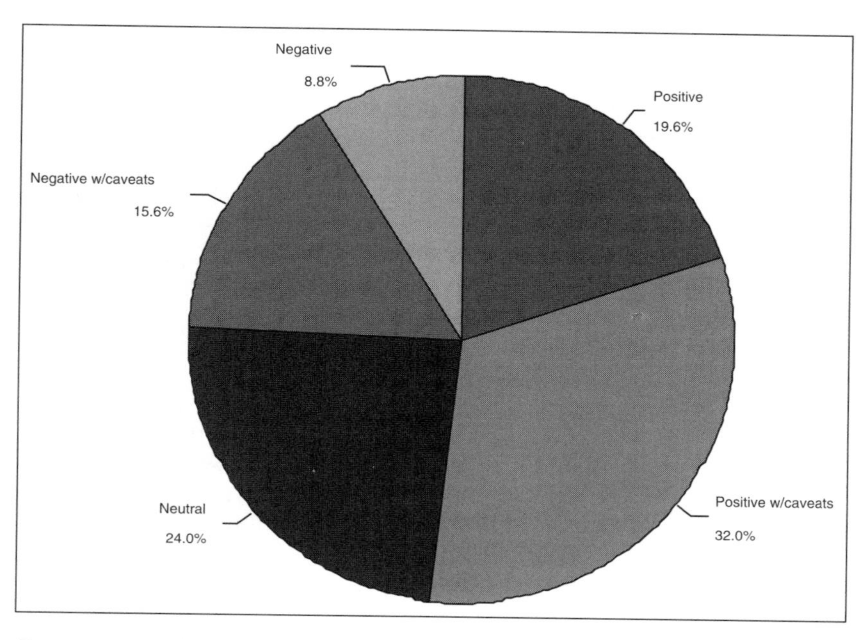

FIGURE 7.1 Media Coverage of Welfare Reform, 1998-2000
SOURCE: This chart is based on an analysis of welfare reform stories that ran in the top 50 newspapers in the United States between January 1, 1998 and September 1, 2000; N=250.

Constructing the Standards of Policy Success

Constructivist political analyses suggest that any object or event, however real, can take on diverse meanings, and it is these meanings rather than brute facts alone that form the basis of political thought and action.[12] Political information is inherently ambiguous; the public that receives this information is typically ambivalent. Thus, when citizens evaluate a complex political object such as welfare policy, they are likely to hold a variety of conflicting, potentially relevant considerations. A major way in which political actors shape public responses is by advancing issue frames that highlight some of these considerations while obscuring others. When consensus emerges on an issue such as welfare reform, it suggests that some political group has succeeded in constructing what Dennis Chong calls a "common frame of reference"—a frame pervasive and powerful enough to focus diverse publics on a shared set of considerations.[13] The TANF program is now perceived as a success, in large part because caseloads and leavers have become a shared frame of reference for evaluating reform. Some well-known characteristics of mass media arguably have contributed to the construction of this common frame. Social networks, organizational routines, and shared work pressures invite a kind of "pack" journalism in which reporters focus on the same "top stories."[14] Forms of objectivity encourage reporters to build these stories out of information provided by a small stock of "credible" government officials and experts.[15] Narrative conventions push reporters to dramatize and then normalize these stories in similar ways. Concentrated ownership and the use of wire stories increase the likelihood that a small number of reports will run repeatedly in different media outlets.

Perhaps most important, the diversity of frames presented by mass media on a given policy issue usually depends on the extent to which public officials generate competing flows of information.[16] In recent years, leaders of both major political parties have been committed to new welfare policies, and activists have generally failed to disrupt this harmony with pressures from below. In such a "bipartisan" context, elite consensus usually gives rise to large numbers of media stories that paint a relatively consistent portrait of reality.

The implicit frame of reference for most recent reporting on welfare reform can be traced to a discourse of dependency that grew influential in the 1980s and 1990s. Dependency discourse identifies reliance on public assistance as an important social problem and defines transitions from welfare to low-wage work as steps, however perilous, toward self-sufficiency. Within this paradigm, champions of welfare reform point to roll decline as clear evidence of policy success, while critics use evidence from leaver studies to suggest that former recipients are not actually achieving self-sufficiency. Only marginal voices seem to raise the possibility that the TANF program might be better evaluated by other criteria. To explain how welfare reform got labeled a policy success, one must investigate how this discourse came to prevail and how it obscures evaluative criteria that might cast reform in a different light.

Beginning in the 1970s, conservatives waged a disparate but effective campaign to change the terms of debate on welfare. Moral conservatives entered the fray as part of a broader countermovement against changes in gender and race relations, consumption patterns, and sexual and familial norms that they saw as evidence of moral decline.[17] Business interests had more material goals: by pushing the poor out of welfare and into low-wage work, employers hoped to lighten their tax burden and, more importantly, prevent tight labor markets from enhancing the bargaining position of labor or pushing wages upward.[18]

Throughout the 1980s and 1990s, foundations with funds supplied by corporate interests and moral conservatives promoted a string of influential critics whose books charged that welfare encouraged perverse behavioral choices, flouted the obligations of citizenship, and undermined the voluntarism of civil society.[19] Soon, such critics were joined by government officials who saw political capital to be made in attacking federal welfare programs and shifting control over welfare resources down to the state level. Liberal and left advocates, suddenly forced to defend an unpopular program that they perceived as inadequate, failed to establish a positive alternative to dependence and devolution as grounds for debating the future shape of welfare policy.

The achievements of the political campaign against welfare are easy to miss if one accepts the one-sided myth that Americans are selfish individualists who oppose government assistance on principle. Most Americans do place a high value on personal responsibility and the work ethic, but these commitments are balanced by a belief that government has an obligation to help those in need.[20] Seventy to ninety percent of Americans say they support government assistance targeted at the poor and believe government has a responsibility to guarantee every citizen food to eat and a place to sleep.[21] The campaign against welfare did not persuade the public that aid to the poor was undesirable; it simply reframed "welfare" in terms that highlighted alternative considerations. Dependence and personal responsibility were central to the new frame, but there were other elements as well. Critics evoked anti-statist and anti-elitist sentiments in the public by attacking welfare as a self-serving creation of liberals in government and the "intelligentsia."[22] Welfare, in this frame, was not a hard-won protection *for* poor workers and their families; it was a policy imposed *against* workers' values as well as their bank accounts. Second, "welfare" also got reframed in racial terms by coded political rhetoric and distortions in media coverage.[23] In media stories and in the public mind, black people (especially black single mothers) became the most damnable and most frequent welfare recipients. As a result, racial resentments and old stereotypes of black laziness became fuel for hostility toward welfare.

All these frames contributed to the demise of the AFDC program, but the effort to reframe welfare debates in terms of the issue of dependency arguably played the most crucial role in shaping later evaluations of welfare reform. Here, it is important to recall that in an earlier era liberals had framed "troubling" behaviors among the poor as products of poverty and used images of social disorganization as evidence for the necessity of extending aid.[24] The crucial move made by conservatives was to reframe these same behaviors as products of "permissive" social programs that failed to limit program usage, require work, and demand functional behavior. Long-term dependency became a keyword in welfare debates, usually treated as part of a broader syndrome of underclass pathologies that included drug use, violence, crime, teen pregnancy, single motherhood, and even poverty itself. Gradually, permissiveness and dependency displaced poverty and structural barriers to advancement as the central problems drawing attention from those who designed welfare policy.

The discursive turn to dependency had important political consequences. First, welfare dependency and its effects on the poor set the agenda for poverty research in the 1980s and 1990s.[25] To distinguish myths from realities, researchers expended great effort identifying the typical duration of participation spells and the individual-level correlates of long-term program usage.[26] Structural questions received less attention as defenders responded to critics in a debate that focused on work effort, program usage, and poor people's behaviors. Second, as dependency came to be seen as a cause of intergenerational poverty, it became a kind of synecdoche—a single part used to represent the whole tangle of problems associated with the poor. To fight dependency was, in essence, to fight a kind of substance abuse that led to unrestrained sexuality, drug problems, violent crime, civic irresponsibility, and even poverty itself.

As a synecdoche for diverse social ills, dependency became the basis for a powerful crisis narrative in the 1980s and 1990s. Critics spoke of a "crisis of dependency," often in conjunction with fellow travelers such as the "teen pregnancy crisis" and the "underclass crisis."[27] As Murray Edelman explains, such crisis language evokes perceptions of threat, conveys the need for immediate and extraordinary action, and suggests that "now is not the time" to air dissent or seek deliberation.[28] Claims about the prevalence of long-term program usage were often overblown, and images of wholesale social disintegration depended on highly selective readings of poor people's attitudes and behaviors.[29] But by applying the label of crisis, critics turned ambiguous trends among the poor (many of which also existed in the rest of society) into a fearsome threat to the values of "middle America."

Just as the "drug crisis" seemed to require a tough, incarceration-minded "war on drugs," the crisis of dependency called for nothing short of an assault on permissiveness. In this environment, poverty advocates who tried to direct attention toward issues other than dependency were seen as fiddling while Rome burned. Long-term program usage was a major social problem requiring a bold solution; it called for extraordinary measures, not tepid liberal palliatives. The only suitable response was to attack dependency at its root by imposing a new regime of welfare rules designed to dissuade and limit program usage, enforce work, and curb unwanted behaviors. In 1996, that is exactly what welfare reform did.

The key point for our purposes is that when advocates established dependency as a synecdoche for underclass pathology and as the central target for reform, they simultaneously highlighted caseload decline and employment among leavers as preeminent standards for judging the success of reform. One point to note about these standards is that they are not very demanding. Compared to improving material conditions in poor communities, it is relatively easy to pare the welfare rolls and push the poor into low-wage work. When these outcomes are treated as *ipso facto* evidence of policy success, they make it easier for the architects of TANF to deflect criticism for current hardships, gain standing to make future policy decisions, and claim credit in front of their constituencies.

The second point to note about these standards is that they direct attention away from criteria that might suggest policy failure. One such criterion, of course, is poverty reduction. Antipoverty effectiveness served as a primary measure of success for public assistance programs through most of the twentieth century.[30] Yet the TANF program does not offer benefits sufficient to lift recipients out of poverty, and (despite a strong economy) the majority of families who have moved off the TANF rolls have remained in poverty.[31] Consideration of another traditional economic goal, reduction of inequality, only makes matters worse. Welfare reform has coincided with massive growth in income and wealth disparities; it has done little to slow the expansion of inequality and may have actually accelerated the trend.[32] Has welfare reform created job opportunities for the poor? Has it promoted wages that allow low-wage workers to escape poverty? In all these areas, the economic story remains the same: we have little evidence that reform has produced achievements that warrant the label of success.

Introduction of less market-centered criteria creates even more uncertainty about the success of reform. For at least a century, liberals have hoped that welfare programs might ease the social marginality of the poor and, thereby, enhance the solidarity of the national community. Participatory welfare programs have also been viewed as opportunities to build political efficacy, engagement, and leadership in poor communities.[33] With TANF recipients now being hassled, fingerprinted, forced to work in public settings wearing distinguishing clothing, and otherwise made into objects of public scorn, it is difficult to see how welfare reform has been successful in relation to these criteria.[34] Alternatively, consider the long-standing goal of providing aid in a manner that is equitable across categories of race and gender. Welfare reform has applied a profusion of new rules to poor women that are not applied to men in any sector of the welfare state;[35] and the toughest TANF rules have been disproportionately implemented in states where people of color make up higher proportions of the caseload.[36] A more inclusive society, a deeper democracy, a more just and humane system of provision—we have little evidence that reform is meeting any of these standards of success.

A narrow focus on caseload reduction and leaver outcomes obscures not only liberal measures of welfare success but also traditional conservative tests. Before 1996, conservatives routinely cited waste, fraud, and incompetence in the administration of welfare funds as evidence of "policy failure." Such a standard of evaluation has rarely been applied to welfare reform despite well-documented cases in which clients have been unable to gain access to remaining entitlements[37] and corporate welfare providers have used public funds for profit-enhancing purposes.[38] Likewise, the old permissive welfare was deemed a failure because it did little to end social problems in poor communities, but there are good reasons to believe that such problems have not waned under the new welfare.[39] Proponents touted TANF as a form of "moral tutoring," a way to instill responsibility and other desirable values in the poor; but client studies under TANF report that "paternalist reform seems to be a lesson about power, not responsibility."[40]

This list of alternative criteria could go on indefinitely, but our point by now should be clear. The success of welfare reform has seemed indisputable primarily because of how the TANF program's achievements have been evaluated. What must be underscored is that the public does not necessarily view alternative criteria as less important than caseload reduction. Rather, these criteria have been obscured by a discourse that focuses attention narrowly on the contrast of dependency and self-sufficiency.

From Possible Interpretations to Authentic Facts

Thus far, we have made two arguments about the current focus on caseloads and leaver studies. First, it is chiefly a political outcome: a victory for those who sought to frame the goals of welfare policy in terms of dependency, and a loss for those who valued other objectives. Second, it renders welfare reform a success by obscuring evaluative criteria that would otherwise complicate or perhaps reverse public assessment. In this section, we make a third point. Even if one ignores other criteria, the belief that caseload decline and leaver studies demonstrate the success of welfare reform depends on a particular framing of the evidence. Roll decline and leaver outcomes are facts *and* fictions.[41] The facts are that caseloads have dropped, leavers have experienced outcomes, and researchers have produced measures of each. The fictions are that such measures offer an unambiguous rendering of reality and that they do so in a way that establishes the truth of welfare reform's success.

Consider the fact of caseload decline. As Wendell Primus, former Deputy Assistant Secretary of Health and Human Services, observed in August 1999, "The conventional wisdom here in Washington is that welfare reform is an unqualified success because caseload reductions have been so dramatic."[42] Welfare rolls had declined by 53 percent between 1996 and June 2000.[43] With concern over dependency as a backdrop, observers have tended to interpret this figure as evidence that TANF policies are motivating and assisting program users to leave the rolls. Such an interpretation, however, can be maintained only by isolating one possible meaning of roll decline and minimizing the play of alternative readings.[44] Mainstream media stories typically recite a list of important but limited questions regarding the meaning of caseload decline. Most point out that a significant portion of the 53 percent drop can be attributed to an unusually strong economy.[45] A small number do even better, noting the impact of policies that augment the earnings of low-wage workers, such as the Earned Income Tax Credit (EITC). Most stories highlight the need to evaluate roll decline by studying leavers, and many suggest that caseloads could rise again if the economy takes a dive.[46]

What these reports rarely do, however, is question the underlying premise that the TANF program's contribution to lower caseloads has consisted primarily of encouraging and helping dependent recipients to leave welfare for work. Such an interpretation may seem self-evident, but a closer look at the evidence reveals that it is based on faulty assumptions about the sources of continuity and change in welfare caseloads. Before the 1996 reforms, large numbers of recipients always left the welfare rolls each year; continuity was maintained because these recipients were replaced with a new cohort.[47] Of the people who entered the old AFDC program each year,

56 percent left within a year (averaging 5.3 months), and only 18 percent stayed on continuously for more than five years.[48] Even among long-term clients who accumulated in the annual caseload, significant numbers would leave each year to enter jobs or relationships or because children became too old to qualify for benefits. Caseload levels were maintained through a process of cohort replacement: new and former recipients would enter AFDC, taking the places of those who left.

Thus, over the four years since 1996, we would have expected a large number of program exits even if the "permissive" AFDC program had remained in place. Given the imposition of tough new TANF rules, roll decline since 1996 undoubtedly reflects *some* increase in program exits, but a significant portion of the decline may also be traced to a decline in the number of replacements entering the rolls. Our ability to distinguish between these processes is hampered by the fact that, under TANF, states have not had to report exit and entry figures.[49] Several observations, however, suggest that a significant portion of TANF's impact on caseloads can be linked to a decline in *new* cases rather than movement of long-term recipients into work.

First, although we do not have good TANF data, we do know that roll decline under AFDC between 1994 and 1997 was based more on a drop in new and recent cases than on a decline among long-term recipients.[50] The nationwide roll decline of 28 percent from 1994 to 1997 cannot be accounted for by the 2.5 percent *increase* in the number of long-term recipients during this period; it is far more plausibly tied to the 37 percent decline in new cases.[51] Second, under TANF, a majority of states have added new diversion policies that deflect claimants toward job searches or private assistance rather than adding them to the rolls.[52] Third, although evidence is sparse, many observers suggest that the cultural and administrative climates that have accompanied welfare reform have functioned to deter eligible families from claiming benefits.[53] Fourth, recent data on the remaining TANF caseload suggest that long-term recipients with barriers to work make up a disproportionate number of clients who are *not* exiting TANF.[54]

Despite these facts, public discourse on caseload decline focuses primarily on leavers, paying little attention to those who do not or cannot gain entry to public aid. Of the 250 media stories we analyzed (see notes 10 and 11), only 7 mentioned diversion as a possible source of roll decline; 114 discussed people leaving welfare in conjunction with roll decline. The fact that prevailing interpretations of roll decline emphasize leavers and exit rates rather than diversion and entry rates has major political implications. Moving long-term recipients out of welfare and into jobs that raise them out of poverty would be widely hailed by the public as a major policy achievement.[55] By contrast, we suspect that paring the rolls by shutting the gates on needy families would be viewed by many as a small and ignoble feat.

Beyond the issue of take-up rates, there is an additional reason to question the use of caseload statistics as symbols of policy success. If roll decline primarily resulted from TANF policies helping recipients to move toward self-sufficiency, one would expect to find the largest declines in states that have the strongest work promotion, training, and opportunity-producing policies. This is simply not the case. The welfare rolls have dropped the most in states that impose immediate, full-family sanctions—that is, states that punish a client's first failure to comply with a program rule by eliminating aid for an entire family.[56] From 1997 through 1999, an estimated 540,000 families lost their entire TANF check due to a full-family sanction for such things as failing to report to a work site due to complications in child care or even other less significant reasons;[57] yet only 24 of our sample of 250 media stories raised questions about the impact of sanctions policy.

Our purpose here is not to suggest that caseload decline should be interpreted solely as bad news. Rather, it is to recover the lost frames of reference that could and should make observers uncertain about what roll decline really means. Some of the decline can be traced to a strong economy; some is due to wage supplements such as the EITC; a portion can be traced to diversion and deterrence of income-eligible families; and some percentage can be attributed to sanctions that simply cut families off the rolls. How much of the remaining portion really reflects "successful" movement of clients from long-term dependence to self-sufficiency? Our best answer is that no one really knows and too few people are asking. Instead, caseload decline is assumed to be about people trading in welfare checks for paychecks and, hence, is evaluated almost primarily in terms of leaver outcomes.

Since TANF was implemented in 1997, a welter of studies have attempted to track families who have left the TANF rolls.[58] Mass media have given heavy coverage to these studies and have treated them as key arbiters of claims that welfare reform is succeeding. Leaver studies provide important information on a particular set of outcomes for poor families. But like reports on caseload decline, these studies supply ambiguous evidence that must be framed in particular ways to support claims of policy success. The key leaver outcomes cited as evidence that welfare reform "is working" are that 50 to 60 percent of former recipients have employment one quarter after exiting the program; such former recipients generally experience a modest increase in income; and they tend to make wages equivalent to those of other low-income women.[59] Do these statistics suggest success? It depends what one uses as a baseline for judgment. That 40 to 50 percent of first-quarter leavers are trying to survive without a job and without cash assistance hardly seems like good news—especially since this percentage rises over later quarters and, eventually, almost a third of leavers have to return to TANF.[60] The evidence of success becomes even less convincing if one uses outcomes under the old "permissive" welfare as a baseline for comparison: about 46 percent of AFDC recipients left the welfare rolls because of employment earnings.[61] This is a lower percentage than one finds under TANF but, given that unemployment rates have been at historic lows and TANF workers have been promoting employment of almost any sort, the shift hardly suggests a stunning policy achievement.

Turning to the evidence on income increases, one finds the same story. The baseline most frequently used to frame leaver incomes is previous income as a TANF recipient. By this standard, leaver earnings are almost guaranteed to suggest success. To encourage work, welfare benefits have always been set well below the lowest wages in the labor market.[62] Moreover, the real value of welfare benefits has declined by about half since 1970 and is currently too low to cover basic family necessities, let alone lift families out of poverty. Thus, TANF income provides a very low bar for gauging leaver success.

A comparison of leaver earnings to those of *low-income* women poses an equally lax test. In 1998, the poverty threshold for an adult and two children was $1095 per month; the median earnings for TANF leavers in a study of eleven states ranged from only $665 to $1083 per month.[63] In fact, leavers have incomes so low that 49 percent report that often or sometimes food does not last until the end of the month and they do not have money to buy more; 39 percent report a time in the last year when they were unable to pay rent, mortgage, or utility bills.[64] Whether leaver earnings indicate positive program outcomes depends, critically, on how much hardship one sees as acceptable for disadvantaged families to endure.

Finally, the claim that welfare reform is a success rests, to a significant degree, on the idea that leavers are now being provided a stronger system of support to smooth the transition to self-sufficiency. As in other areas, there is a grain of truth here. Public assistance prior to 1996 provided clients with limited resources to facilitate a lasting transition into work and out of poverty.[65] TANF policies have arguably expanded these resources. But while many forms of transitional assistance are now on the books, survey-based leaver studies show that large numbers of former recipients are not actually receiving benefits. Despite widespread need, 53 percent of children in leaver families are not receiving Medicaid assistance, 66 percent of adult leavers do not receive Medicaid coverage; and 69 percent of leaver families do not receive Food Stamps.[66] Among those making the initial transition to work (in the first three months), 81 percent do not receive child care assistance; 89 percent do not receive any help with expenses; and 85 percent do not receive help finding or training for a job.[67]

None of these figures should be taken as unambiguous evidence that welfare reform, as a whole, is a failure. There is some nontrivial number of former welfare recipients who have been well served by new TANF policies—who have been encouraged *and* assisted to find jobs that lift them out of poverty and who are now doing well enough not to need transitional or ongoing assistance. The problem is that recent leaver statistics have been framed to misleadingly suggest that such experiences (a) rarely occurred under the old AFDC program, (b) characterize a majority of TANF leaver outcomes, and (c) account for the bulk of caseload decline.

Conclusion

> It is official: the reform of the welfare system is a great triumph of social policy.
>
> —Michael Kelly, "Assessing Welfare Reform," *Washington Post*, August 4, 1999

Although one can find significant dissenting voices in government, the press, and advocacy organizations, welfare reform is now widely viewed as a policy success. The backdrop for this assessment is a causal story suggesting that "permissive" welfare policies from the 1960s to the 1990s produced a crisis of long-term dependency that, in turn, bred behavioral pathologies and intergenerational poverty. Over a twenty-five-year period, promotion of this story turned the size of welfare caseloads into a key indicator of policy performance and established transitions off the rolls as a central policy goal. Accordingly, in the current era of welfare reform, caseloads and leaver outcomes have become the most salient measures of policy success—even for many who doubt that cash assistance was ever the root cause of poor people's problems. The secret of success for welfare reform has been a frame of reference that suggests positive interpretations of roll decline and leaver outcomes while simultaneously obscuring alternative criteria that might produce more critical assessments.

The discursive processes that we have highlighted in this chapter merit close attention because judgments of policy success and failure are more than just political outcomes; they are also political forces. Beliefs about which policies are known failures and which have been shown to succeed set the parameters for a "reasonable" debate over the shape of future legislation. Reputations for developing successful ideas confer authority, giving some advocates greater access and influence in the legislative process. Public officials who are able to claim credit for policy success hold a political resource that bestows advantages in both electoral and legislative contests. For all these reasons, politically constructed beliefs about the successes and failures of welfare policy can be expected to play a key role in determining the fate of TANF reauthorization in the 107th Congress. Such beliefs, and the political actions that sustain them, constitute major influences on the shape of social provision in America.

8

Compliant Subjects for a New World Order

Globalization and the Behavior Modification Regime of Welfare Reform

There is an important debate about whether globalization needs to be taken seriously, especially in terms of its implications for social and economic life in the United States.[1] There is also another important debate about whether welfare reform's new behavior modification regime is more about imposing cultural values regarding family morality than enforcing labor discipline.[2] A third issue I would suggest is whether welfare reform is related to globalization. My thesis for the following analysis is that welfare reform's behavior modification regime is related to globalization in ways that are cultural as well as economic.

My argument is that globalization's undermining of social institutions requires the elaboration of surrogate means of social control to promote adherence to family as well as work values. Welfare reform therefore almost inexorably gets caught up in efforts to stave off the demise of the basic institutional structure of what various theorists have called the family-wage system, founded on a set of relationships between the traditional two-parent family, the market, and the state. Welfare reform in this sense is a critical component of the contradictory impulses of globalization. Economic processes of globalization create new forms of economic exploitation and domination, including the proliferation of new low-wage labor markets, heightened job insecurity, the increase in overwork, the rise in dual-earner families, and growing inequality between families that are benefiting financially from economic change and those who are not. In the process, the fabric of basic social institutions, including most especially the family, is worn increasingly threadbare.

As more and more individuals, especially on the lower ends of the socioeconomic order, find the need to deal with the social consequences of economic globalization, the state is forced to intervene to create surrogate means for promoting adherence to traditional cultural values regarding work and family.[3] Welfare reform's new, intensified behavior modification regime contributes to this surrogate process in two ways—both of which reflect the historic role that welfare has served in the United States. Welfare, as reformed, imposes work and family standards on recipients in ways that are particularly demeaning and stigmatizing. Such treatment punishes recipients in ways that discourage them from deviating from family as well as work values. And such treatment of welfare recipients sends a loud symbolic message to other low-income individuals that they too will suffer such denigration and marginalization should they fail to toe the line in adhering to the work and family values that underpin the political economy. These historic twin purposes of welfare take on a heightened significance in the era of globalization and its disruptiveness to social life and its destructiveness of basic social institutions. Today, the macroprocesses of globalization call out for the micropractices of increased behavioral regulation—just like the ones found in the new welfare reform regime.[4]

The analysis that follows, therefore, seeks to demonstrate that the Personal Responsibility and Work Opportunity Reconciliation Act of 1996 is a quintessential example of "postindustrial social policy."[5] This law represented the culmination of years of campaigning by conservatives against the supposed epidemic of "welfare dependency."[6] Welfare dependency had been emphasized for some time as the primary focus of postindustrial social policy. According to this perspective, counteracting the economic processes that produced poverty was the primary focus of industrial social policy, but now that has been replaced in the postindustrial era by the need to reduce the behavioral patterns that produced an overreliance on welfare.

Moving adult welfare recipients, mostly single mothers, into the workforce was now the pressing issue to be addressed in the emerging postindustrial order. Attacking welfare dependency had come to be seen as the major purpose of welfare reform in order to fashion a policy appropriate for the emerging postindustrial economic order. Welfare had to shift to being primarily a therapeutic intervention designed to treat people so that they will learn to do without welfare assistance. Only by reducing its welfare burden could the domestic political economy remain competitive, and only by promoting greater work-effort among low-income families could they be expected to have a chance at a decent life in the rapidly globalizing postindustrial economy. In the process, both the society and the individual would become more effective and efficient competitors in the emerging global postindustrial political economy.

An interesting question arises with this alleged connection between treating welfare recipients to wean them of their alleged dependency on welfare and the need to do this in order to have a welfare policy more consonant with the alleged inevitability of an emerging global postindustrial economic order. Is there a relationship between the "micro" focus of treating individuals to get them to change their behavior and the "macro" concerns of retrofitting the domestic economy to respond to the pressures for globalization? In this chapter, I try to demonstrate that in fact there is a strong connection, if not the one suggested by the proponents of "postindustrial social policy." I will suggest that there is such a real connection in spite of the fact that the treatment of welfare dependency is largely chimerical and economic globalization is not natural, inevitable or even good, given the way it is being promoted.

Therefore, while I disagree about the way both welfare reform and globalization are being championed, I do think there are strong connections between misguided attacks on welfare dependency on the microlevel and the misplaced glorification of globalization on the macrolevel. There are interrelationships between the microtherapeutic orientation of the new behavior modification of welfare reform and the macrodevelopments associated with economic globalization. In fact, my thesis is that there is such a strong relationship between the microprocesses of welfare reform and the macroprocesses of economic globalization that there is value in thinking about how that relationship may well be pointing to the emergence of new forms of power and domination.[7] These new forms of power and domination highlight how the micro-macro connections between the behavior modification regime of welfare reform and the processes of globalization are about more than economics and enforcing labor discipline. This new configuration between the micro of welfare reform and the macro of globalization suggests that welfare policy has always been about reinforcing both culture and economics, family values and work ethic. This time the cultural economic hybrid that is being reinforced is in the service of social relations influenced by processes of globalization.

In the following I will elaborate on my definitions of the micro of behavior modification and the macro of globalization, and I will then examine the three specific ways in which they are related.

First, I suggest that the micro of welfare reform and the macro of globalization are linked via "neoliberalism." I define neoliberalism as the hegemonic ideological perspective that informs much of contemporary public policymaking, not only in the United States but increasingly also around the world.[8] The neoliberal perspective emphasizes the need to reduce the welfare state, cut back on the size of the state, free the market to operate more on its own terms, and require people as much as possible to make their livelihood through the market with little help from the state.[9] Neoliberalism suggests that a lean and mean political economy will be more competitive globally and will more effectively produce wealth from the emerging postindustrial global economy. Neoliberalism therefore reemphasizes that all able-bodied adults, even single mothers with young children, reorganize their lives so they can make their livelihood from the jobs that are created in such a market-centered society. In some countries more than others, neoliberalism promotes a transnational interest in "workfare" as a program for getting the poor regimented into the emerging global low-wage labor markets.[10]

Next, I seek to modify the critique of neoliberalism as primarily about laissez-faire economics to show it to be about more than scaling back government to free the market. Instead, neoliberalism implies privatizing government in order to disseminate disciplinary practices and promote social ordering that serves in building the emerging economic system. I then suggest that there is value in examining the connection between the microprocesses of behavior modification and the macroprocesses of economic globalization to understand that welfare reform's new privatized system of behavioral modification is a stark example of the hybrid nature of neoliberal welfare policy. Here, I show that welfare policy has historically served both cultural and economic purposes simultaneously because both are entwined beyond the world of welfare, as well as within it.[11] I suggest that welfare policy has historically served to promote both the cultural value of family morality and the economic value of work incentives. Welfare policy can do this because its contemporary objective has not been the culture or the economy but the cultural-economic hybrid that various commentators have termed the "family-wage" system.[12] This system operates via the assumption that adherence to work and family values is the best road to social stability and economic success for the individual and for society. Even in the face of historic contradictions, the family-wage system assumes that the modal family is a traditional two-parent family in which the male "breadwinner" earns enough money via the paid-labor market to support a female "homemaker" and children.

In the name of propping up the family-wage system, welfare policy has historically served the broader symbolic purpose of reinforcing the role of the working poor in the political economy even as it had material effects on those who receive welfare. The demeaning conditions under which welfare has historically been provided discourages the formation of single-parent families without a wage-earning "breadwinner." Both work and family values are reinforced for the population as a whole via symbolic means as denigration and stigmatization is imposed on welfare recipients who are given inadequate benefits under the most demeaning conditions. Welfare reform's behavior modification regime is the latest installment in welfare's long history of using low-income families for Durkheimian rituals of stigmatization, operating to promote labor discipline for the general population. In the process, the old practices of work and family discipline are retrofitted for a new U.S. economy in the era of globalization and all the more effectively via a privatized system of disciplinary practices.[13]

Finally, I show how the microprocesses of behavior modification in welfare reform and the macroprocesses of economic globalization are connected via emerging scientistic discourses of control that are increasing globally in prominence. These expert discourses are part of emerging "transnational knowledge regimes."[14] I suggest how these expert discourses facilitate regimentation on global terms in part because they offer an ostensibly abstract and decontextualized knowledge that ignores issues of culture, context, and community.[15] As "transparency narratives," such expert discourses make the labor discipline of welfare reform seem to be objective and grounded in science, while masking class, race, and gender biases.[16] They have become crucial in connecting new forms of self-regulation of individuals, often instigated through therapeutic modalities of thought and the need for assimilation, integration, and coordination in the emerging global postindustrial economic order. I suggest how therapeutic interventions focused on "governing mentalities" help to create the conditions for compliance within a new world order of global capitalism.[17]

I compare the ostensibly neutral discourses of individual development to the discourses on collective economic development and suggest that they operate in similar ways to rationalize the emerging global regime of production. I show that they propagate their rationalizations via a false neutrality that masks their ties to power and the reproduction of hierarchies of privilege along class, race, and gender lines. In the end, I suggest that critiquing the twin logics of "development" and their relationships becomes critical to challenging power in the current period. In this sense, fighting the micropractices of behavioral modification of welfare reform at the local level is an important ingredient in contesting the push to global empire, and vice versa. In the end, there may be no more important political work than recognizing the chiasmatic character of the micro/macro divide and working to resist one in terms of the other. This, I suggest, is a "radical incrementalism" for the new world order.

I conclude this articulation of the microprocesses of behavior modification in welfare reform and the macroprocesses of economic globalization by theorizing their connections. To do this, I first turn to the work John Gray on the destructiveness of globalization and how it requires increased forms of social control to substitute for the social institutions it undermines.[18] Then, I examine the work of Michael Hardt and Antonio Negri.[19] Hardt and Negri suggest that the new postindustrial globalized economy thrives without central direction. Power for sustaining this system operates more from the bottom-up via what they call networks of "cooperative production," by which individuals are enlisted in constructing themselves as compliant subjects of the new world order largely out of fear of suffering the consequences of being left out. The macropower of the globalized economy is built on the backs of microprocesses of self-discipline. I suggest that there is merit in considering that welfare reform may well be a quintessential example of microprocesses that serve to facilitate the regimentation of people into an emerging globalized system of cultural as well as economic production.

Globalization as Macrodiscourse

There is much debate today about whether or not we need to take economic globalization seriously.[20] Commentators have noted that there are signs of growth in transnational economic exchanges in recent decades.[21] Beyond that, others have argued that a globalized economic system is emerging, having profound implications for the structuring of political power and social relations.[22] Others contest the idea that there is a distinctively new global economic order.[23]

There are good reasons to suspect that economic globalization is not an inevitable outcome of capitalist development. The better theories of political economy, whether from the left by major thinkers like Karl Polanyi or from the right from a prodigious theorist like Joseph Schumpeter, have historically emphasized how the market in general is neither natural nor deterministic.[24] Markets, like all other social creations, are the result of power relationships. Markets are embedded in cultures and social systems; they operate in institutional frameworks and rely on social institutions for their reproductions and survivability.[25] The globalization of capitalist markets therefore is not something that must happen, and if it does, it does not mean that it must follow a deterministic economic logic.

Then again, an even better argument is to appreciate the political potential of what Frances Fox Piven and Richard A. Cloward have called "the globalization hoax."[26] In criticizing arguments on behalf of globalization, Piven and Cloward have written the following:

> [W]e think this analysis is entirely too simple. It treats globalization as a set of economic changes which have necessary and inevitable consequences for politics and the terms of the social compact. This economic determinism ignores the dimensions of globalization which are in fact political and strategic. Expanded global markets for goods, labor, and capital may make exit or the threat of exit *possible,* at least in some industries and in some capitalist regimes. Even this is only a possibility, its realization usually contingent on government policies which facilitate exit. Less obvious but very important, exit threats are political strategies constructed by power-seeking agents who draw variously on the actual reality of exit, on exit as an ideological ruse, and who also may invoke state authority to expedite the threat of exit or to suppress countervailing threats.[27]

Therefore, for Piven and Cloward, globalization is as much ideological as it is economic. It is in good part a political strategy to threaten capital flight across nation-state borders in order to intimidate labor into submitting to increased discipline and declining wages. It is neither inevitable nor deterministic.

There is, however, more to their argument. While globalization may in part be a hoax, it has several dimensions that make it quite real. Even though globalization may exist largely as an imagined reality, it is an imagined reality that can have real consequences when it successfully intimidates labor to submit to capital's demands. In addition, in order for the threat of global capital flight to carry a punch, it must at least have the prospect of actually occurring. In discussing how labor confronts new forms of discipline in the current era, Piven and Cloward write as follows:

> Incessant talk about globalization and downsizing figures indirectly in all of this, as the rise of an ideology that asserts the necessary and inevitable autonomy of markets and therefore of capital, a resurrection of nineteenth-century laissez-faire doctrines about the unregulated market now expanded to world scale. But none of this talk would be especially forceful by itself. The ideology is frighteningly persuasive not only because it is heard on all sides, but because it appears to explain the decline of concrete and particular working-class groups. Globalization talk gains force not from abstract generalities about trade and capital movement, but when jobs are cut or restructured, when trucks labeled "Mexico" pull up to a striking plant, or simply when a business moves across the state line.[28]

Therefore, globalization is a political strategy that threatens capital flight and exploits the possibilities emerging in the changing economic landscape. It does so in ways that can have real consequences in material deprivation for the laboring populations who are subjected to such political strategies.

Not all nation-states, however, have succumbed to the threats of global capital flight. The United States is particularly distinctive in this regard. Corporate campaigns to whip up fear and promote economic insecurity in the name of globalization have been more aggressive and more successful in the United States than in other western industrialized countries. So much so that the United States is now offering a "model U.S.A."—something that needs to be replicated by corporations in other Western industrialized societies if they want to squeeze as much profit from labor as U.S. corporations.[29] And in the United States, welfare retrenchment has been more dramatic as a response to campaigns over fears about globalization. Piven notes:

> The welfare state is under attack in all of the rich countries where it flourished over the course of the 20th century. Rollbacks are said to be imperative. The big argument for why this is so emphasizes globalization and technological change which together have heightened international trade and investment competition. But rather than a widespread "race to the bottom" which these economic determinants would suggest, welfare state outcomes have been very different from country to country. These variations, and in particular the fact that the U.S. has been the rollback pioneer, argue that politics plays a large role in contemporary welfare state policies. American developments are best explained by paying attention to the political mobi-

lization of business over the past two decades on the one hand, and the uses of the politics of resentment and marginalization on the other hand.[30]

Globalization therefore can be usefully seen as a macrodiscourse that exploits changes in the international political economy in order to pose the threat of capital flight that can impose labor discipline and welfare state retrenchment. While it has been most aggressively and successfully pursued in the United States more than other Western industrialized countries, it is a political strategy of increasing popularity. As its popularity grows, it may well become a self-fulfilling prophecy. In order to sustain the threat, capital must be willing to act on it. As corporations and governments in one and then another country follow suit, the threat of economic globalization materializes right before our eyes in an international "race to the bottom." In fact, there is reason to think that the globalization threat is already materializing itself into a real system of transnational dominance.

Welfare Reform as Microdiscourse

There is also much debate about whether the welfare reforms of the current period are significant. The 1996 law abolished the preexisting Aid to Families with Dependent Children (AFDC) cash assistance program and replaced it with the Temporary Assistance for Needy Families (TANF) block grant program, whereby states are given a lump-sum of money each year and need not spend it on cash assistance if they so choose. Some have suggested that the law did not represent a significant change, since states retained much of the discretion in setting benefit levels and eligibility requirements that came with the 1996 welfare reform law.[31] Yet, others emphasized that the shift from AFDC to TANF was a major move that, in the process of producing a shift to greater state latitude, also ended what had become a federal entitlement guarantee for low-income families with children.[32]

As important as this debate is, there are other features to welfare reform that are distinctive. Among the more noteworthy developments is that the welfare reform law of 1996 derives from an inflection in the preoccupation with welfare dependency as a debilitating condition from which welfare recipients must recover. With this increased preoccupation has come a shift in emphasis in welfare away from providing cash assistance to aid families with children toward intensifying the focus on modifying the behavior of parents. What is remarkable, I would argue, is the degree to which this shift has occurred away from what would seem to be the unimpeachable good of helping children avoid living in destitute circumstances toward focusing on getting parents to change their work and family habits. This shift moves welfare from an economic to a therapeutic policy. Welfare reform has transformed welfare into the social policy equivalent of a 12-step program.[33]

While the new welfare regime has demonstrated its ability to slash rolls and reduce costs, it does so by an intensive set of procedures designed to get recipients to change their work and family practices. In the process, a corresponding dramatic shift has occurred in the way welfare agencies operate, how they are staffed, what the relationships to clients are, and how much is now given over to "case management," where recipients are moved through a series of activities and programs to accelerate their departure from welfare, either by taking paid employment, forming two-parent families, or both.[34]

Welfare policy includes time limits, work requirements, and sanctions in lost benefits for failure to comply with program rules. A major vehicle for the regulation of recipient behavior are Individual Responsibility Plans that recipients sign, promising to take various steps (sometimes more than twelve) in order to leave welfare. Enforcement of these plans along with the other time limits and requirements introduces unprecedented levels of behavior regulation into the administration of welfare. In addition, all of these enforcement devices are administered at the caseworker level, reintroducing a form of discretion that had been repudiated thirty years earlier as prone to arbitrary application. This sort of individualized administration of surveillance and monitoring further intensifies the therapeutic character of the administration of welfare today.[35]

Welfare reform's behavior modification regime goes well beyond enforcing labor discipline among welfare recipients. As Jodie Levin-Epstein notes, many states have aggressively pursued the option to impose family life obligations on welfare recipients as part of their signing of Individual Responsibility Plans or Individual Responsibility Agreements (IRAs) and the corresponding promise to take steps to demonstrate "personal responsibility." In 1998, Epstein wrote:

> [In] . . . 37 states . . . it appears a family life obligation may be made of the recipient. Some states' obligations are more explicit on the form than other states. About 30 state IRAs explicitly target family life obligations and appear in the text as well as the chart; the other seven appear to expect a fam-

ily life obligation (3 states expect the counties to establish an IRA and 4 states include information about family life obligations within the agency responsibilities and sanction sections). . . .

The majority of states—30—have an IRA which contains some type of explicit family life obligation.

In addition to the 30 states which have an explicit family life obligation defined in the IRA, 3 county-established IRAs (Colorado, Ohio, Maryland) may also mandate family life obligations. Several states have open-ended forms which may also result in family life obligations.

Family life obligations range from life skills/parenting training to family planning to child support cooperation.[36]

Table 8.1 indicates what Epstein found were the most common family life obligations identified in the thirty states with explicit IRA family life obligations in 1997.[37] In Georgia, for instance, adult as well as teen parents could be sanctioned for failure to attend parenting classes if caseworkers had determined attendance was a prerequisite for demonstrating personal responsibility.[38] This sort of micromanaging of families is the norm under welfare reform, and the repercussions for failure to meet such family life obligations can be devastating. Epstein has noted:

In Tennessee, over 3500 families lost assistance because they did not sign the state's individual responsibility plan. The Tennessee form includes TANF obligations related to minor teen parents and child support; it also includes three additional obligations: regular school attendance by all chil-

TABLE 8.1

Common Family Life Obligations

Family Life Obligation	# of States
School participation	22
Child support	20
Immunization	17
Health visits	17
Life skills/parenting	13
Drug assessment	10
Family planning	9
Teen living arrangement	9

dren, immunization of children, and well-child health check ups. It is not known why these families did not sign the IRA.[39]

Welfare reform discourse is therefore quintessentially micro in its orientation, focused as it is on the alleged personal failings of recipients who, by definition, are deemed to be deficient and lacking in their ability to exercise personal responsibility due to their supposed inability to live without public assistance. Primary among the concerns that animate welfare reform discourse may well be the desire to reduce welfare burdens and cut costs. It is also in good part animated by pressures to impose labor discipline. Yet, also at work is an insistence that welfare work more effectively to promote family norms. While welfare policy has historically emphasized all of these concerns, it does so today in an inflected therapeutic discourse that rationalizes its social control functions in a highly medicalized way. While welfare policy at other times in the history of the United States might have been as punitive, it is doubtful that the social control apparatus of welfare has ever relied so much on therapeutic discourse for its justification.

Neoliberalism: The Ideology of the Market

Welfare reform's behavior modification regime and economic globalization potentially have some very strong links. One way in which they may be connected is via the growing ideological dominance of what many people are calling "neoliberalism." Elizabeth Martinez and Arnoldo Garcia define neoliberalism effectively:

> "Neo-liberalism" is a set of economic policies that have become widespread during the last 25 years or so. Although the word is rarely heard in the United States, you can clearly see the effects of neo-liberalism here as the rich grow richer and the poor grow poorer.
>
> "Liberalism" can refer to political, economic, or even religious ideas. In the U.S. political liberalism has been a strategy to prevent social conflict. It is presented to poor and working people as progressive compared to conservative or Rightwing. Economic liberalism is different. Conservative politicians who say they hate "liberals"—meaning the political type—have no real problem with economic liberalism, including neoliberalism.
>
> "Neo" means we are talking about a new kind of liberalism. So what was the old kind? The liberal school of economics became famous in Europe

> when Adam Smith, an English economist, published a book in 1776 called *The Wealth of Nations*. He and others advocated the abolition of government intervention in economic matters. No restrictions on manufacturing, no barriers to commerce, no tariffs, he said; free trade was the best way for a nation's economy to develop. Such ideas were "liberal" in the sense of no controls. This application of individualism encouraged "free" enterprise, "free" competition—which came to mean, free for the capitalists to make huge profits as they wished.
>
> Economic liberalism prevailed in the United States through the 1800s and early 1900s. Then the Great Depression of the 1930s led an economist named John Maynard Keynes to a theory that challenged liberalism as the best policy for capitalists. He said, in essence, that full employment is necessary for capitalism to grow and it can be achieved only if governments and central banks intervene to increase employment. These ideas had much influence on President Roosevelt's New Deal—which did improve life for many people. The belief that government should advance the common good became widely accepted.
>
> But the capitalist crisis over the last 25 years, with its shrinking profit rates, inspired the corporate elite to revive economic liberalism. That's what makes it "neo" or new. Now, with the rapid globalization of the capitalist economy, we are seeing neo-liberalism on a global scale.[40]

The neoliberal ideology champions the superiority of unregulated markets to create more efficient and productive forms of economic growth that will produce greater economic well-being for all. Neoliberalism therefore calls for scaling back government social welfare programs and reducing government intervention into the economy. Yet, there is more to the neoliberal philosophy. It is an ideology of globalization in that it also suggests that unregulated markets will more easily be assimilated into the international political economy and will benefit from that assimilation. Neoliberalism is therefore an agent of consolidation of different economic systems, cultures, and peoples into the Western-based systems of power and exchange. Under neoliberalism, "development" by the Third World occurs via the deregulating of domestic markets so that they can be integrated into the Western-dominated global economy.[41]

Neoliberalism is most commonly associated with economic globalization. Yet the neoliberal ideology operates not so much simply to rationalize globalization as natural or inevitable as much as it operates, as Martinez and Garcia suggest, to instigate domestic public policy change that will facilitate integration into the global economy. Neoliberal welfare policies are a critical part of this package. The neoliberal welfare policy regime is one that has increasingly been elaborated not only in the United States but in the Anglo nation-states in particular. Jamie Peck has effectively highlighted the similarities and differences in what he calls "workfare states" in Canada, the United Kingdom, and the United States.[42] These workfare regimes have all been developed in recent years, in part in response to pressures concerning globalization. These policies are consonant with calls to reduce the size of government, decrease the welfare state, and free low-income heads of families, mostly single mothers, so they can be added to the pool of workers needed to take the growing numbers of low-wage jobs being created in the changing economy.

For Peck then, welfare reform is a preeminently neoliberal public policy. It is tied more to enforcing labor discipline than to imposing morality. It is more about serving economic purposes than about promoting family values. Peck agrees with Piven and Cloward when he suggests that the focus on moral regulation in welfare reform is largely a tool of stigmatizing the poor in order to send a message to the laboring population that they need to be compliant and take what work the emerging low-wage economy provides. It is either that or face the denigration that comes with moral condemnation when receiving public assistance. Peck writes:

> As Frances Fox Piven reminds us, "Political talk notwithstanding, welfare is not mainly an institution to regulate individual morality. It is also, and more important, a labor market institution." It follows that work-based welfare reforms bring about changes in rules and dynamics of the job market, or, as Piven puts it, they "alter the terms of the labor market, especially the lower tiers of the labor market where poor and unskilled women compete for work." The shadow of workfare therefore falls far across the labor market itself, where it helps set the terms and the tone of low-wage employment relationships. In conditioning access to the labor market, workfare also plays a part in determining who gets what, typically with regressive social-distributional consequences. This is one of the reasons why welfare reform is such a deeply politicized process: programs and benefits are often targeted at specific groups (such as lone parents or immigrants), with far-reaching consequences for patterns of labor-market participation. One of the paradoxes of the welfare/labor-market relationship is that those social groups with access to nonwage sources of support are typically treated by employers, unions, and labor-market institutions as semide-

> tached workers, leading to discrimination, exclusion from better jobs, and a pattern of reliance on unstable work that perversely reinforces the need for nonwage benefits while apparently confirming the perception that these are unstable *workers*. This underlines the fact that welfare/workfare politics are intricately bound up with the wider political, economic and institutional forces that reproduce the "contingent workforce," and the relations of the gender, ethnicity, and class that divide and define this workforce.[43]

And for Peck, workfare is at the core of an internationalizing logic of welfare reform. Welfare reform is spreading from the United States to Canada and the United Kingdom most especially to emphasize workfare programs and enforce labor discipline. Peck notes that in spite of the uneven effects, workfare programs are the piece of U.S. welfare reform that is being exported, indicating that the workfare model is central to what is of transnational relevance in welfare reform.[44] Welfare reform is part of globalization especially in its workfare dimensions. Welfare reform's emphasis on workfare is a neoliberal policy in good part because it works hand in glove with privatization, deregulation, and welfare state retrenchment to free markets, and it regiments workers into taking whatever low-paying jobs the new economy creates.

It may well be that something more ambitious than simply the promotion of worker discipline is operating here. Frances Fox Piven and Richard Cloward's own work has emphasized how welfare has historically included Durkheimian rituals of denigration and stigmatization of welfare recipients in ways that reinforced labor discipline among the laboring population more generally. Demeaning moral regulation regarding the family life of welfare recipients was as an important tool to discourage other families from forgoing low-wage work and relying on public aid. Yet Piven and Cloward also noted that welfare then operated to enforce labor discipline in ways that reinforced a commitment to traditional social and cultural values.[45] And today, it could well be that welfare reform's behavior modification regime is about disciplining the population in ways more than simply creating a compliant workforce. And that might be why welfare reform's behavior modification regime is not strictly about work but also concerns family.

Neoliberalism is therefore about more than freeing markets. The privatization of state services is an important dimension of neoliberalism that goes beyond simply scaling back government. This "privatization of public assistance" creates an ideal venue for the elaboration of what Michel Foucault called the practices of "governmentality."[46] Rather than regulate deviant populations and enforce work and family values through a centralized and coercive state apparatus, the artifices of governmentality work to diffuse regulatory power throughout civil society well beyond the walls of government. For Foucault, governmentality works its way throughout the civil society. It transmutes coercive state regulation into more insidious forms of discipline that are elaborated through the myriad social institutions and the professional practices of those who administer their services to the populations deemed to be in need of them. These include most especially the physically sick, the mentally ill, the drug-addicted, the criminal, the poor, and other so-named marginal and deviant aggregations.

Neoliberalism does the same today in its preoccupation with privatizing state services, getting around public civil servants, turning services over to private, often for-profit contractors, and contracting with them more and more on a performance basis that emphasizes increased contractual payoffs according to documented measured outcomes. As a result, such providers become ensnarled in the extenuating tentacles of power that in turn instigates the proliferation of a wide variety of client-management practices. These are geared to monitoring, surveilling, and disciplining their clients to comply with standards of behavior that will enable the agency to document outcomes. Neoliberal privatization therefore proliferates disciplinary practices across a wide swath of social institutions. The powers of subjectification and subjugation are entrenched throughout the citizenry, starting with the people who seek services and/or are required to get treatment from these agencies. Then they surely ramify throughout the lower rungs of the socioeconomic order to promote self-regulation among those who anticipate the hardship of having to endure such agency encounters and therefore seek to avoid being put in a category where they have to.

In this way, the governmentality of neoliberalism's privatization disseminates the "governing mentalities" as "emergent structures of feeling" and therefore does more than simply regulate labor.[47] The economic and cultural collude in neoliberalism's privatization. Symbolic and material effects combine, just like the passions and the reasons of a new regime of human service provision.

Privatization is more than economic policy; it is cultural policy. Neoliberalism's privatization instigates a governmentality diffused throughout civil society's social institutions and propagates a new cultural sensibility about providing services.[48] The social-control dimensions of social welfare unavoidably get inflected under these conditions if for no other reason that contracting with the state involves the disciplining of clients to demonstrate success rates in managing, if not solving, social problems.

All of this bulks large under welfare reform, which has accelerated privatization of state services much faster than any other area of public administration.[49] Welfare-to-Work contractors are increasingly popular, often for-profit providers, frequently operating under performance-based contracts. They find themselves elaborating an intricate set of client-management practices designed to engage in the surveillance and monitoring of clients to ensure they discipline themselves as good clients and engage in behavior that can be produce measured outcomes.[50] The number of job interviews completed or the number of days on the job become ways of tracking performance in many welfare-to-work firms. Clients are not so much empowered to create a meaningful life for themselves and their families but are instead supported just enough to meet obtuse performance criteria. Agencies are rewarded, for instance, for each client who stays on a job for thirty days, irrespective of the pay, the benefits, the work conditions, and the overall effect of the job on the well-being of the client and her family. After thirty-one days, even if the client no longer holds the job, it is no longer a concern for the agency.

The governmentality of neoliberalism includes its own depersonalization of the humans being served, forcing the people in question, in this case most often single mothers who are not necessarily ready, to immediately take on full-time work that can adequately support their families. Clients become units for producing measurable outcomes and their job is to discipline themselves to make the most of that situation. The most common result is continued poverty under conditions of the increased stress of trying to be both a breadwinner and a homemaker, with inadequate support for either.

The Antinomies of Welfare

Therefore, the neoliberal dimensions of workfare in welfare reform suggest still another debate. There is a debate about whether welfare reform is more about enforcing family morality or about the economic issue of labor discipline. I want to suggest that this is actually a false choice. Welfare reform reflects issues about both work and family and does so because they are in an important respect two sides of the same coin. Further, these are two sides of a coin that has global currency. I want to suggest that welfare reform promotes both work and family behaviors that are seen as needed by the emerging global order.

In other words, welfare reform reflects a series of antinomies that, upon closer examination, are more consonant than dissonant. Cultural versus economic, symbolic versus material, recognition versus redistribution, identity politics versus political economy, and even behavioral modification versus economic globalization: these are dichotomous distinctions that have been used to suggest that welfare reform is more about one side than the other of each divide. Yet, upon closer inspection one sees reasons to doubt that any of the distinctions holds much water. Instead, welfare reform indicates just how much one side of each divide is imbricated in the other. Welfare reform highlights its own hybridity as both a cultural and an economic policy that serves symbolic as well as material purposes. It is a policy that in the current period reflects an identity politics grounded in therapeutic interventions in service of economic globalization.

The 1996 law set strict time limits and work requirements for the receipt of aid. Yet, the first sentence of the law's preamble states that "marriage is the foundation of a successful society." In addition, the law included funding for abstinence-only education, "illegitimacy bonuses" for states that reduced the number of children born outside of marriage, and options for states to limit assistance to children born to mothers while they were receiving welfare. Therefore, there is no surprise that there has been much debate about whether morality or economics has been the driving force behind the push to reform welfare and eliminate welfare dependency.[51] Was welfare reform primarily about work or about family? This debate took on heightened significance as the 1996 welfare reform law began to come up for reauthorization. Some groups had felt that welfare reform had in its first five years emphasized reducing welfare dependency by getting single mothers to take paid employment outside the home, and they felt that more emphasis now needed to be given to reducing welfare dependency by discouraging the formation of single-parent families.[52] Act I of welfare reform was work; act II would be family. Economics was emphasized in the first round; in the second round morality would move to center stage.

Welfare reform's emphasis on the cultural, moral, and symbolic is imbricated in the economic, social, and material. The cultural dimensions of welfare policy that focus on issues of family morality are very much entwined with the economic dimensions that concentrate on issues of reinforcing the work ethic. This is because culture and economics are never in real life entirely separable. Economic systems are cultural formations, and culture is derived from the means of creating a livelihood in any one social order.

Welfare has never involved either strictly enforcing work or promoting family morality to the exclusion of the other. Instead, for much of the modern age, it involved reinforcing what Linda Gordon, Nancy Fraser, and others have called the "family wage system," which combines cultural issues of family morality with economic issues of work to reproduce the class, race, gender, and sexual hierarchies associated with the existing social order.[53] As Stephanie Coontz has emphasized, the traditional family was valorized as the foundation of society more in name than in fact since most families almost could never afford to conform to that ideal.[54]

The family wage system, founded as it was on this mythical ideal, is itself best seen as a cultural/economic hybrid. It is based on the relationship of the traditional two-parent family to the market and the state. This triad of family, market, and state is premised on the assumption that it will work best when these institutions are articulated smoothly. Their smooth articulation is premised on the idea that the implied subject position of this constellation of institutions is the male head of a traditional two-parent family. State social policies are primarily designed to insure the family against the temporary or permanent loss of income from the male breadwinner. Lineages of heteronormativity, as well as patriarchy and even white privilege, continue to run through this matrix even as it has had to adjust to changes that include women working outside the home, the emergence of dual wage-earning families, increased formation of alternative families, and other social changes.

The entire edifice of the existing political economy is sustained by the articulation of this institutional matrix involving the family, the market, and the state. The political economy's survivability through the crisis of social change in family and economic relations is contingent in no small part upon public policy that works to sustain the traditional family and work values in spite of the social changes that have been occurring. The creation of alternative families is seen as a threat to the family wage system, creating additional burdens on the market and the state. Also seen as equally threatening in terms of imposing additional costs are attempts to have the female-identified work of reproduction that is central to "homemaking" treated as important as the male-identified work of production that is central to "breadwinning." Public policy must therefore not only oppose these threats to the financial viability of family wage system, it must seek to reduce these threats. Otherwise, it will not be performing its role in the institutional triad that goes into reproducing the family wage system.

Today, welfare reform's highly invasive therapeutic regime intensifies this emphasis of the traditional family. It is a major example of how public policy works to reinforce both the cultural and economic dimensions of the family wage system in spite of the tumultuous social changes that have been taking place in work and family, at great cost of the well-being of low-income, mother-only families. In new ways, these families are being punished and forced to serve as denigrated examples to all other low-income families.

Therefore, while much is made of the idea that welfare encourages the formation of mother-only families, what is more often overlooked is that welfare does substantial cultural work reinforcing the traditional two-parent family ideal. The preoccupation with moral regulation of welfare recipients reinforces using the welfare population as a demonstration project for reinforcing the work and family values among the population more generally. By stigmatizing welfare recipients and holding them up for moral denigration, everyone else is reminded of the dangers of transgressing the standards of the family wage system. The regulation of welfare recipients sends the message to the whole low-income population that people in our society can only hope to be affirmed as full citizens if they play by the rules of the family wage system.

The relationship of regulating welfare recipients to reinforcing work and family values for the broader population points to another tie between the symbolic and the material. That is, there are larger symbolic purposes for regulating the population more generally that are served by the real material deprivation imposed on welfare recipients. For instance, the recent push toward the privatization of welfare administration includes allowing for-profit agencies to make large profits by placing welfare recipients in low-wage jobs.[55] This amounts to turning welfare recipients over to private corporations to be treated as commodities for making money. As a result, this privatization of welfare administration not only has real material consequences to welfare recipients in terms of how they are treated, it also demonstrates that welfare recipients can be treated as disposable commodities not worthy of being held onto and cared for by the state.

The imbrication of the symbolic and material as well as the cultural and economic shows that issues of identity and issues of political economy are entwined in welfare reform as well. A "politics of recognition" is entwined with a "politics of redistribution."[56] Issues of material redistribution involving economic resources are entwined with issues of symbolic recognition of various social identities. The reconstruction of welfare mothers as a pool of available low-wage workers highlights that identity politics is implicated in economic struggle.

Finally, the interrelationships between the cultural and economic, the symbolic and the material, and the identity politics with political economy point to still another connection. Much of welfare reform is focused on getting welfare recipients to change their behavior, and new procedures have been put in place to institute processes and programs for getting welfare recipients to change their behavior so that they will stop relying on public assistance for their family's survival. A significant dimension of the behavior modification in welfare reform is tied to getting recipients to think differently about who they are, about their personal strengths and weaknesses, and about their ability to live without welfare. Yet, much of this kind of intervention and therapy in welfare reform is pertinent to efforts to make social adjustments in the face of ongoing economic globalization.

Globalization calls for new subjects, new workers, a new proletariat. Economic policies that facilitate an ever more rapid flow of capital across national borders are tied to welfare reform policies that participate in the refashioning of the acceptable self called for by the changing global economy. As the nature of work in the global order changes, especially at the lower rungs of the occupational structure, the need for new and different recruits emerges, and welfare reform is one way in which such recruits get made. In particular, the rise in low-wage service work, personal-care assistants, security workers, and related fields calls for grooming a new class of docile workers who can cheerfully work under the more privileged elements of the population while accepting low pay for demeaning work. These are often old jobs, to be sure, but they take on new forms in the new economy, especially because they are often temporary and have a greater turnover. The new low-wage worker needs to be more adept at acclimating herself to new and different work conditions on a regular basis. Higher levels of docility are needed. Welfare reform's focus on converting single mothers with young children into workers who fit such a mold is entirely consistent with not only improving the employability of such mothers in a changing postindustrial, service economy.[57] It is also entirely consistent with dominant understandings of what that economy needs to thrive in an increasingly globalized context. Therefore, working on the "inner child" in welfare reform is connected to erecting the "outer behemoth" of globalization.

Global Knowledge Regimes: Decontextualizations

The ability to promote the cultural/economic behavior modification processes in service of the emerging global economy is facilitated by the proliferation of transactional knowledge regimes that articulate understandings of who people are and how they ought to behave in allegedly neutral terms decontexualized from considerations of culture and identity.[58] For instance, in discussing how workfare is being implemented in Canada, Kari Dehli notes new expert discourses on welfare operate so that "local and particular experiences are represented and transformed into an extra-local 'documentary reality,' thus facilitating the social organization of management and regulation. . . . [These] processes of policy formulation . . . transform people's experiences of work, economic upheaval and political struggle into administrative categories which can be put to work in state institutions."[59]

The decontextualized abstract quality of welfare policy discourse parallels that of development discourse, which has for several decades already forged ahead as the pioneer in this respect, disseminating its allegedly neutral understandings of economic development to places far and wide. The major consequence has been to further the integration of lesser-developed economies into the Western-dominated international political economy on terms most favorable to First World corporate interests. Arturo Escobar has effectively written that "development" is a artifact of discourse, an invention of the First World that is then imposed on Third World countries which, as a result, are expected to "develop" along lines laid out for them by the discourse of development.[60] International lending institutions and development agencies to varying degrees participate in the development process not just in the sense of actually achieving economic development—for worse as well as better—but also, perhaps more significantly, in terms of helping reproduce development discourse's artifactual effects.

An interesting artifactual effect that Escobar highlights well is the invention of the "village" as a site for development.[61] Communities in Third World countries are often positioned in development discourse not only as locales where people live, but as villages as sites of underdevelopment, as places that need to develop in very specific ways, consonant with the logic of First World development discourse and the interests of those who propagate it. The imputation of particular Third World needs by First World narrations of what is development helps reinforce power relationship between donor countries and agencies and their recipient countries and communities. Development discourse inevitably reinscribes "dependency." At the initial moment of encounter, the Third World locales are tutored to see their deficiencies and to refer to themselves as undeveloped, even primitive and uncivilized. Then, the Third World locales are told how to meet their needs by undergoing development that will facilitate their assimilation into the First World global political economy. Why integration into the global political economy is the solution for addressing the needs of Third World countries is not a question that is addressed by development discourse. These two disparate concerns—assimilation and the fulfillment of need—are assumed to be working hand in glove. The Third World actors in question may have already known that they had needs, but now they are taught that they have needs of a particular sort—ones that just happen to be the kind of needs that development agencies are organized to address. These needs tend to be not just ones about poverty, but more about a lack of development that must be remedied if Third World places are to be integrated into the First World political and economic systems.

In this way, development discourse reinscribes a hierarchy of privilege where the First World dictates to the Third World, where the goal is that the Third World learn to fit into the First World. This is most often done with a highly technical, specialized, and scientific terminology about the deficiencies of recipients vis-à-vis donors. The power of development discourse to manufacture problems and then impose solutions in ways that favor First World interests is masked under allegedly neutral technologies of development.

"Development," "village," "dependency," and a host of other objects of concern are therefore for Escobar best seen as first and foremost manufactured entities produced by development discourse. They are in this sense symbolic entities that have real material consequences, for they are used to reproduce power relationships between donors and recipients in the international arena. They are used to impose First World understandings of what is the problem and what is the solution for Third World activities and practices. It should come as no surprise, then, that when development activities are finally undertaken they often end up promoting economic growth that favors First World economic interests that at times actually undermine the protection of local values and the meeting of local needs.[62] The examples abound across the modern history of development in the Third World. In country after country where First World economic interests have identified resources they wish to acquire or exploit, development practices have encouraged changes such as the conversion to export commodity production of massive amounts of acreage that had been devoted to subsistence farming, often leaving the families that relied on the land even more economically vulnerable. In this sense, a First World knowledge operates as a form of power that marginalizes local knowledges. In the process, local concerns are swept aside as well. And all are left to ponder: development for whom?

The false neutrality of expert discourses are rampant domestically as well.[63] Nancy Campbell has similarly demonstrated that technical discourses mask power relationship and hierarchies of privilege in relationship to the making of drug policy in the United States.[64] Her primary concern focuses on drug policy discourse that reinscribes deficiency in women who use illegal drugs. Once again, an allegedly disinterested scientific discourse is working in favor of the privileged to reinforce structures of power that reproduce the social inequities along class, race, and gender lines. Campbell notes that women who use illicit drugs end up being "mis-"treated by the anti-drug policy regime. This mistreatment in no small part occurs not only in the harshness of penalties for illicit drug use, but also in the tendentious way in which drug policy discourse envisions treatment and in the kinds of treatment programs that are established. Both legalization and medicalization constitute expert-dominated discourses that position women drug-users in ways that are disabling and denigrating.[65] Drug-using women are positioned in drug policy discourse in ways that ignore the role of poverty, inequality, discrimination, and other broad structural forces beyond personal behavior and psychological outlook.[66] Drug policy discourse replicates this injustice in many treatment programs that are excessively committed to attributing blame and personal irresponsibility to the person. Even when women get treatment, it is often in demeaning and stigmatizing ways that reinforce their designation as personally irresponsible individuals.

The "needs talk" of drug policy discourse therefore erases opportunities to diagnose the sources of drug use and to treat them.[67] Instead, the focus is only on the client's personal attributes as the sources of her problems. Often the methods can be debilitating, provoking resistance and rebellion, and providing clients with yet another reason to drop out of treatment. Such a discourse of denial about the structural roots of drug use, particularly among low-income women, makes it seem plausible that drug-using women should simply change their behavior and they would never face the problems of drug use again. In fact, poverty and the hopelessness it breeds continue unabated when drug policy discourse is ascendant.

Drug policy in both its soft therapies and hard punishments becomes focused on "governing mentalities" at the expense of attending to the material practices that engender drug use.[68] Processes of class, race, and gender marginalization are ignored, while behavior and attitude are highlighted. Drug policy discourse becomes an agent in service of making social strain safe for the existing social order. People, not the social processes that grind them up, are the objects of treatment. Drug policy discourse puts these social processes beyond reach and out of sight, leaving the client as the only real object of concern.

Scientific and technical discourses of assistance for "developing" villages and "treating" clients, therefore, are but two instances in how allegedly neutral, objective, and disinterested ways of narrating encounters between the helping and the helped mask the power relationships involved. These connections are effectively articulated by Jenrose Fitzgerald:

> Development discourse, like welfare policy discourse, is a transparency narrative that both constructs poverty in a certain way and then obscures the processes of that construction through the mask of objectivity. . . . The problem of professionalization, for Escobar, is a problem because of the extent to which explicitly political debate about the benefits of growth are discouraged or relegated to the realm of "politics," separate from the realm of "science." Like the alternative visions of a war on poverty offered by the Black Panthers and the work of "Third World" economists, alternative approaches that do not work with the dominant professional model are rendered invisible. . . . The convergence of political, economic, scientific, and bureaucratic transparency narratives contains the politics of poverty, making it difficult for alternative visions to be heard or seriously engaged. It is for this reason that I have stressed the importance of challenging discourses of transparency. . . . How those alternative visions might take shape remains to be seen.[69]

Building on the insights of Fitzgerald, I want to suggest that there is merit in considering that the articulations of development and welfare reform discourses extend to helping create a frictionless global space when compliant populations are enlisted into an emerging global system. The power of expert discourse written in a decontextualized, abstract language of allegedly neutral science is that it can pretend to be without culture bias, even when it is profoundly biased. Now, as welfare reform discourse begins to spread from the United States across the First World, just as development discourse did a half-century ago across the Third World, there is even more reason to be alert to the operation of the behavior modification regime of welfare reform in reinforcing First World prejudices that consolidate privilege along class, race, and gender lines.

The False Dawn of Globalization

Detailing the economic processes of globalization and the therapeutic interventions of welfare reform still leaves them undertheorized about their connections. Several assumptions are necessary for theorizing one or another version of these connections. One set of assumptions is if globalization processes are actually occurring, and if so, how. John Gray has offered a nuanced reading of globalization that suggests it is indeed occurring but in a less than systematic and highly self-destructive way.[70] In its wake, globalization's helter-skelter disruption of social life creates an increased need for various forms of social control to substitute for the norm-enforcing effects of social institutions that are increasingly undermined by the processes of globalization. Gray sets himself against both the skeptics who deemphasize the significance of globalization and the proponents who glorify it as producing a new economic utopia.[71] He writes from the distinctive point of view of a "radical-conservative," deeply critical of global capitalism as destructive of traditional forms of life. For Gray, globalization is being promoted by a hegemonic, neoliberal ideology that glorifies the idea of a free, unregulated market on a grand scale, and does so in a way that is destructive of the very social institutions needed to sustain liberal democratic societies. Globalization is for Gray the end stage of one variant of the West's Enlightenment project of modernity run amok. He compares it to Soviet communism by suggesting that both are examples of the dangers that result from an excessive faith in utopian thinking about the capacity of individuals and societies to break out of their cultures, traditions, social institutions, and community commitments.

> A single global market is the Enlightenment's project of a universal civilization in what is likely to be its final form. It is not the only variant of that project to have been attempted in a century that is littered with false Utopias. The former Soviet Union embodied a rival Enlightenment Utopia, that of a universal civilization in which markets were replaced by central planning. . . . The Utopia of the global free market has not incurred a human cost in the way that communism did. Yet over time it may come to rival it in the suffering that it inflicts.[72]

For Gray, the United States is the leader in promoting globalization and has gone the farthest among Western industrialized countries in rolling back government interventions in order to free market forces to pursue globalization and allow U.S. society to be reorganized to fit into a new world order. Gray sees the growing inequality, increasingly social problems and the accelerating social dysfunction in the United States as signs of the destructiveness of economic globalization.[73] Gray writes:

> The result is the re-proletarianization of much of the industrial working class and the de-bourgeoisification of what remains of the former middle classes. The free market seems set to achieve what socialism was never able to accomplish—a euthanasia of bourgeois life.
>
> The imperatives of flexibility and mobility imposed by deregulated labour markets put particular strain on traditional modes of family life. How can families meet for meals when both parents work on shifts? What becomes of families when the job market pulls parents apart?[74]

Growing fundamentalism in the United States and other parts of the world also suggests that the destructiveness of globalization to cultures, traditional values, social institutions, and communities is leading to reactionary backlashes of increasingly violent sorts. September 11 is but one instance. While conservative proponents of globalization like to suggest that they are defenders of tradition, they are, for Gray, the vanguard that is pushing a laissez-faire globalization that is highly destructive of traditional ways of life. "The fate of the Right in the late modern age is to destroy what remains of the past in a vain attempt to recover it."[75] "The neoconservative ascendancy has identified the free market with America's claim to be the exemplary modern nation. It has appropriated America's self-image as the model for a universal civilization in the service of a global free market. For a public nurtured on such illusions the coming years will be traumatic."[76]

Gray's dystopian nightmare of globalization is compounded by the fact that, for him, it is far less than systematic. It does not develop the same way everywhere; nation-states are strengthened even as they are weakened; some populations do better than others; and definitely some classes prosper while others do not. "A universal state of equal integration in worldwide economic activity is precisely what globalization is not. On the contrary, the increased interconnection of economic activity throughout the world accentuates uneven development between different countries."[77]

> Few visions of the future have ever been so delusive as Herbert Marcuse's or Michel Foucault's perennially fashionable vision of perfected capitalist control of society. Late modern capitalism may incarcerate people in high-tech prisons and monitor them by video surveillance cameras at their work-place and in the high street, but it does not box them into an iron cage of bureaucracy or imprison them forever within a minute niche in the division of labour. It abandons them to a life of fragments and a proliferation of senseless choices.
>
> The dystopia we face is not a nightmare of totalitarian control. Intermingling the ephemera of fashion with an ingrained reflex of nihilism, *American Psycho* is a truer approximation to the later modern condition than Kafka's *The Castle*.[78]

For Gray, however, the uneven, discontinuous and dysfunctional character of globalization does indeed mean a growing use of forms of social control. Behavior regulation gains increasing emphasis as a substitute for the wearing away of social institutions. And for Gray, punitive and therapeutic forms of social control work hand-in-glove as increased incarceration rates lead to greater family dissolution among low-income populations, particularly African Americans and Latinos, requiring more therapeutic interventions to address the family problems that ensue.[79] He makes this most explicit when he notes that the 1996 welfare reform law in the United States was part of a larger effort to develop social control policies as surrogates for the social institutions that free markets have destroyed.[80]

Macro/Micro Articulations: The Global Behemoth and Welfare's Inner Child

Gray's trenchant critique of globalization suggests that its unsystematic and even unpredictable character increases the need of enhanced forms of social control that are not tied to, and can substitute for, the social institutions that globalization undermines. His analysis suggests that there is merit in theorizing welfare reform's behavior modification regime as part of more diffuse processes of promoting compliant subjects for the new world order.

I therefore want to build on Gray's vision of how the destructiveness of globalization creates needs for new forms of social control. I will suggest that this perspective indicates possible relationships between the therapeutic behavior modification regime of welfare reform and the economic processes associated with globalization. Yet, to do this, we may need to bracket his misleading statements about Michel Foucault. Foucault did not so much suggest that the new forms of power would be operating as some sort of centrally administered iron cage of bureaucracy.[81] Instead, his theorizing can be seen as more consistent with Gray's vision of the future, especially about articulations between microprocesses such as behavior modification in welfare reform and macroprocesses such as globalization. Theorists following Foucault's insights have suggested that globalization thrives on such diffuse networks of power relationships even as they develop without central coordination.[82]

We can relate Foucault's theorizing on new forms of power by focusing more explicitly on the terms "macro" and "micro." These terms have longstanding relevance in the social work profession, but they also point to a way in which the work of Michel Foucault is directly related to concerns in that field.[83] Foucault emphasized that the sources of power had changed with the development of modern "disciplinary society." For Foucault, by the time we arrive at modern societies as they have developed since the eighteenth century, power becomes no longer headquartered in a central sovereign or authoritative source.[84] Instead, it is more dispersed, moving through the capillaries of the social organism more so than its main arteries. For much of his years in writing on this subject, Foucault emphasized how power operates at the microlevel, more through a "micropolitics" of "biopower" whereby individual human subjects self-police themselves by virtue of internalization of the dominant understandings of who they are and how they should behave. In this sense, disciplinary power is not so much repressive as it is productive, working from the bottom up, in and through subjectivities so that people engage in practices of self-production, thereby producing the good citizens that they are called upon to be by the social order. For Foucault, this sort of twist to the uses of power provides a new ironic meaning to the idea of "self-governance." In fact, Foucault was to use this irony to question the extent to which democracy created a social order that was truly one in which people were self-determining in a way that was reflective of real autonomy and liberation.

Foucault referred to the dissemination and maintenance of these practices of self-policing as the process of "governmentality."[85] Eventually he focused on what he called "technologies of the self," which were the practices to which individuals subjected themselves in order to refine their capacity to act as particular subjects of the social and political order.[86] Since these technologies of the self were forms of power, they could, for Foucault, then very much be sites of resistance. Ultimately, Foucault focused on the idea that taking ownership of these technologies as much as possible was the most important way that individuals could resist, be political and "fight the power," anonymous, impersonal, and diffused such as it is in all its polymorphous diversity and ambiguity.

Gilles Deleuze extended Foucault's concern about disciplinary power, suggesting that in the late-modern or even postmodern society that was emerging, the disciplinary institutions, such as the family, the school, the factory, the community, were breaking down and discipline was being eclipsed by control.[87] The postmodern societies of control did not need formal institutions of discipline that promulgated power relationships via punctuated applications of surveillance to encourage self-regulation by the compliant subject populations in question, whether they were children, students, workers, or law-biding citizens. Instead, these formal institutions were passé, given that new "technologies of the self" were emerging that replaced periodic surveillance with continuous monitoring. The disciplined self was being surpassed by the continuously monitored self as the new preferred subject for the emerging postmodern societies of control.

Mitchell Dean has offered a novel extension of Foucault's concern about disciplinary social policies.[88] He has suggested, contrary to Gray, that the emerging forms of welfare policies in the globalizing era actually demonstrate the neoliberalism of the globalization ideology to be less the perfection than the perversion of the Enlightenment. For Dean, neoliberalism is its own counter-Enlightenment. The new welfare policies that emphasize disciplining the recipient population create new forms of compliance making "targeted populations" synonymous with "active citizens." Creating "active citizens" ironically by way of promoting abject, self-regulating subjects perverts the Enlightenment project, the basic premises of humanism, and the ideals of the liberal contractual society. The idea that science and reason can be used to perfect society is overextended so that it turns back on itself, undermining the idea that they can serve the promotion of human freedom and self-actualization.

For Dean, these new disciplinary policies, promoted by neoliberalism, displace modernist social policies of rationally organized and universally premised social welfare provision to install hyperrationalizing policies that glorify conformance to the dictates of the market over the promotion of individual autonomy. The counter-Enlightenment of the neoliberal welfare policies promotes self-regulating subjects needed for the emerging global order. Whether or not neoliberal welfare policies of self-regulation are the perfection or the perversion of the Enlightenment, there is an important confluence of thinking here across political perspectives about the hyperrationalistic disciplinary regimes that are coming into place.

There is one more source that effectively details these micropractices of welfare reform as integrally tied to the macroforces associated with the neoliberalism of the globalization ideology. Using the Foucaldian-inspired idea that postmodern power is lodged inside human subjects as they work to fashion identity and self, Michael Hardt and Antonio Negri have offered an ambitious attempt to theorize how this sort of "self-governance" is critical to the formation of the brave new world order created by economic globalization.[89] Hardt and Negri put the micro/macro relationship front and center in their analysis of what is the new global system, how it came about, how it operates, and what sustains it. They see the contemporary processes associated with globalization as leading to the development of a postmodern, post–nation-state system of "empire." And for Hardt and Negri, the new postmodern transnational global empire is one that is built from the bottom up via the art of "self-governance" and the politics of self-constitution associated with the systems of continuous monitoring and self-regulation as articulated by Foucault and Deleuze. The new world order is built on the back of the subjectivities of the people who populate it.

New subjects are needed for the new world order. In fact, what is new about the new world order is that it is one that is preoccupied with the creation of new subjectivities. It is an order of subjectivities. The new world order sustains itself through the people it creates. In particular, it thrives through the production of subjectivities that accept the need to make everything anew. In such a world, all is to be assimilated on its terms, even as those terms are constantly changing. The new systems of production are ones that emphasize artificiality, plasticity, the opportunity to remake things as needed, including people, their identities, and their self-understandings.

For Hardt and Negri, therefore, what is radically new about the new world order is that it represents the end of the "outside." The end of the outside implies the end of all that which is not incorporated into the systems of control operating within the new world order. This means the end of nature, the end of wilderness, the end of the primitive, the end of the uncivilized, the end even of the foreign, the alien, the unknown. The distinctiveness of the new world order lies in its break with the old binaries of the previous age. The symbolic/material, natural/cultural, the cultural/economic, the objective/subjective, the private/public, and so on, all dissolve in the face of the processes of incorporation. In place of the terms of inclusion and exclusion are the terms of incorporation promulgated by the systems of power operating to build and sustain the new world order.

These systems of power are also distinctive in a particularly postmodern way. Entirely consistent with Foucaldian theorizing, the power that fuels this system has no center and is not centralized in some sovereign source or central source of authority. Instead, it operates via networks that articulate relationships across a variety of nodes of communication and exchange. It works its way into social relations, including political and economic ones, via the arts of self-construction and the ways in which people are encouraged to fashion themselves as identifiable selves and subjects of the new world order, often in terms that do real violence to their lives, in particular by defining themselves as people who work more for less, and increasingly so. The empire of the new global economic order traverses national and cultural borders, cuts across social systems, and creates a smooth social space in which postmodern selves populate the new world order and arrive ready to fit into the emerging systems of global exchange. In its quest to conquer all by remaking it, the empire of the new global economic order creates its own "world" here on earth.

For Hardt and Negri, these networks of self-construction are forms of cooperative production in the sense that people collaborate and actively participate in these networks of self-construction. This is then both a distinctive strength and a weakness, for collaboration implicates people in their own self-definition, making their own subjection as subordinated subjects of the new world order something they have chosen. For instance, the choice to see oneself as worthy exclusively in terms of one's productive contributions to the new order makes such a delimiting self-definition seem to be one that is not imposed via power exercised by others, but a result of one's own choosing and not a form of power at all. Yet, the idea that the subjected must be enlisted in their own subjection ups the ante for power requiring it to work through networks of cooperation in order to reproduce the social life that the new order calls for.[90]

Since the new world order develops an interest in not just the manufacturing of goods but the manufacturing of subjectivities, the affective dimensions of life become an important public issue. Hardt and Negri also emphasize how a power of subjectivity must of necessity also be a power of affectivity as well as effectivity. Once the power for reproducing society comes to involve self-construction, then sustaining the system involves both attending to issues of care as well as work. It involves the arts of reproduction as well as those of production. The bioproduction of life involves caring for the self and others, not only working for the self and others. The system of biopower therefore involves breaking down the distinctions between the public sphere of productive relations and the manufacturing of material goods on the one hand and the private sphere of reproductive relations and the attention to affective dimensions of social life on the other. The system of biopower involves creating compliant subjects for the new world order, socially and culturally as well as economically. And the ability to practice the arts of subject construction becomes itself a valued commodity. From personal care attendants to job coaches, the emerging order proliferates occupations in care of the self.

Hardt and Negri build on Foucaldian analysis to suggest that the biopower of the new forms of self-governance are very much tied to the new emerging systems of economic production. Yet, the new systems of production of postmodern society are very much the new postindustrial ones. Postindustrial society has been termed an "informational society" where "symbolic analysts" assume a critical role in producing new forms of communication and knowledge.[91] The new forms of power then are focused on language, communication, and intellectual power—the sources for information critical to the new central forces of production in the computerized postindustrial society.

Therefore, as Marxists have emphasized for the industrial system, power is still very much tied to the ability to dominate the systems of production. Yet, now production has changed and is critically driven by systems of communication and the production of knowledge. The bioproduction of life flows from this concern and engenders the populating of the smooth space of global capitalism with a striated social order based on people's abilities to participate in the informational society. The smooth space of the economic empire is segmented increasingly in terms of those who produce the critical communications and information needed and those who serve them. Increasingly, global flows of information and resources are matched by global flows of people so that an underclass of servants can support the information elites in their toils in the new system of production.

For Hardt and Negri, then, the people most likely to pose a threat to the bioproduction of life under this new system are those who end up with self-constructions least needed by the social order. The unassimilated parts of the First and Third Worlds, the communities and peoples passed over by the emerging economic empire become sites of social resistance. These poor and unpossessed selves, the dispossessed, become the basis for a new militancy that can enable "the multitude" to constitute themselves as a new proletariat and resist their incorporation into the global economic empire and the hardship it implies for so many. Hardt and Negri remain optimistic that resistance to the emerging forms of self-governance can serve political ends:

> Militancy today is a positive, constructive and innovative activity. This is the form in which we and all those who revolt against the rule of capital recognize ourselves as militants today. Militants resist imperial command in a creative way. In other words, resistance is linked immediately with a constitutive investment in the biopolitical realm and to the formation of cooperative apparatuses of production and community. Here is the strong novelty of militancy today: it repeats the virtues of insurrectional action of two hundred years of subversive experience, but at the same time it is linked to a new world, a world that knows no outside. It knows only an inside, a vital ineluctable participation in the set of social structures, with no possibility of transcending them. This inside is the productive cooperation of mass intellectuality and affective networks, the productivity of postmodern biopolitics. This militancy makes resistance into a counterpower and makes rebellion into a project of love.[92]

Hardt and Negri provide us with a radical incrementalism for the new world order. For them, the resistance to domination by the macroprocesses of economic globalization begins with the resistance to the processes of micropolitics, biopower, and the production of life via the acts of subjectification built into the new forms of self-governance, self-regulation, and self-constitution called for by the new world order. Resisting the therapeutic interventions designed to get us to be the compliant subject of the new world order is the beginning of politics. Resisting such regimentation would be challenging the new forms of power at their most critical juncture. Micropolitics is macropolitics, and fighting therapeutic strategies to normalize the population is an important part of challenging globalization today.[93]

While there is much to debate about Hardt and Negri's ambitious analysis, they offer a rich perspective for examining how welfare reform's behavior modification program bears the traces of globalization. Welfare reform has heightened the emphasis on focusing on welfare recipients' behavior as the source of their poverty. It is reflective of a growing tendency in the culture to promote behavioral discipline as the source for achieving social and economic success and distinction. It echoes the concern that each family must find a way to be productive members of the emerging social order, relying as little as possible on assistance from the state. The first order of business is for all family heads to remake themselves in terms that will make them able to fit into the emerging system of production. If people cannot assume the role of privileged symbolic analysts, perhaps they can retrofit their identities to be seen as attractive for underlaborer positions in the service sector, whether it is as clerical assistants or personal-care attendants. We are all in recovery, and everyone is his or her own job coach.

In this sense, welfare reform is very postmodern. While there is much merit to the idea that welfare has always played a central role in promoting disciplined subjects for the modern political economy in Western societies, its role in enlisting welfare recipients into rituals of self-denigration for the purposes of disciplining the laboring population more generally has taken a distinctively postmodern turn in recent years.[94] Now, welfare reform represents a more self-conscious preoccupation with remaking oneself as a compliant subject, socially, culturally, economically, transnationally, and globally. Welfare reform's inflected therapeutic idiom emphasizes the importance of self-fashioning for inclusion in the new world order.[95] And Hardt and Negri emphasize that power operates in the new world order not by excluding people but by specifying the terms for their inclusion. Rather than exclusion, the oppressed and dominated suffer "differential inclusion" on terms less favorable than those who can assume more productive subject positions.[96]

In particular, First World narratives of globalization increasingly position women on welfare as racialized and gendered identities in liminal and vexed subject positions as "potential workers," erasing as it does the fact that these women are already workers of a very important sort, for they have primary responsibility for child rearing, nurturing, and homemaking. These narratives of globalization position women on welfare as "potential workers" not just to constitute them as a new pool of low-wage workers who are needed for the global economy that economic elites are hoping to build. These narratives of globalization serve not just to identify these women as the subaltern but also work to signify the universal role of the compliant subject for the new world order. The appropriation of women's bodies serves purposes of discipline on a more global scale.

Welfare reform therefore is not so much about disqualifying poor single mothers on welfare as undeserving of inclusion in the new world order as much as requiring all the poor to assume positions of inferiority in that order. Welfare reform works therefore on both these levels for the good of that new world order. Welfare reform provides aid and offers assistance to the needy on the basis of their willingness to make the transition to accepting positions of low-wage, servile work in the subordinate orders of the New Age economy, often slotting recipients into marginal positions in the service economy where they provide personal services for those who command the positions of privilege. This quid pro quo sends a signal across the economically marginal population more generally. As Peck himself aptly notes: "Stripped down to its labor-regulatory essence, workfare is not about creating jobs for people that don't have them; it is about creating workers for jobs that nobody wants. In a Foucaldian sense, it is seeking to make 'docile bodies' for the new economy: flexible, self-reliant, and self-disciplining."[97]

Fundamentally Excluded

Yet, as it was to be, the events of September 11, 2001, suggest ever so painfully that the new world order involves not just the regimentation of compliant subjects. It also involves the marginalization of the fundamentally excluded. While the leaders of the global economy were increasingly focused on fending off demonstrators at their periodic meetings in Seattle, Genoa, and other global sites, the growing ranks of the more extreme militants in parts of the Arab world were working desperately to take down the symbols of global power, as if that were their only recourse to the totalizing power of empire. In the process, thousands of innocent civilians died tragic deaths, murdered in cold-blooded, senseless acts of terror and violence, casualties for no other reason than that they worked at the sites from where global power emanated.

President George W. Bush told the whole world a week after high-jackers crashed airplanes into the World Trade Center and the Pentagon that they did it because they hate everything that the United States stands for—freedom, justice, and the American Way. Yet, many, many other Americans were willing to note that there were other reasons, including U.S. foreign policies toward the Arab world and U.S. dominance of a globalizing economy that has threatened traditional ways of life and instituted economic marginalization for many parts of the Arab world. U.S. foreign policies have supported oppressive dictators and not done enough to end the misery of Palestinians. The U.S.-led globalizing economy offered the unsatisfactory choice for many Arab regions (and other places as well) to be included on terms that will ensure the loss of one's traditional ways of life, culturally and economically; or be excluded and increasingly marginalized into extreme forms of destitution. So the seeds of radical fundamentalism were sown.

President Bush's response not surprisingly ignored the Hobson's Choice that faced so many of the dispossessed. Instead, as if to underscore the double-bind, he offered U.S. citizenship to those of the marginalized if they turned the terrorists in. Bush did not stop there in making the war a "clash of civilizations" because he had already trumpeted the superiority of the West when he called for a "crusade" to wage a "war on terrorism" in order to secure the "homeland" and achieve "infinite justice." Drawing from the rhetorical reserve of Western culture, the president invoked, consciously or not, troubling precedents in the Christian crusades and the Nazi's apocalyptic vision of the standing up for the homeland. All to mete out a justice that knew no bounds. This metaphorical war against a generalized condition created its own amorphous cloud of mystification. Calling to fight a "war" rather than to fight "crime" surely would mobilize many more resources, justify far more militaristic responses, and condone far greater incursions into civil liberties and personal freedoms. Many more people were bound to die.

In fact, the rhetorical responses to the events of September 11 underscored an important inversion: U.S. militarism had already been instigating terrorism for some time. As Foucault and others have reminded us, power creates its own resistance and does so in a variety of ways, serving multiple purposes.[98] Power breeds discontent; power elicits opposition so it can find out what needs to be conceded; power allows opposition to grow to the point that it can be repudiated; power creates a center that by definition marginalizes the periphery; power shapes the terrain over which resistance must traverse, specifying the conditions and forms of effective resistance. If power were a living, breathing, conscious being, it would know it can do these things; instead, it just seems that way. Militarism had led the world's superpower to oppress, often ignorantly, sometimes intentionally, large parts of the world that were marginalized by processes of globalization and superpower policies that were articulated with those processes. As marginalization of parts of the world intensified and as discontent over marginalization and the oppressive policies associated with it grew, the probability increased that some people would be open to responding to, participating in, or even just supporting the demagogic championing of violent reactions to globalization that were specified in particular ways. Madmen are not very predictable, but the conditions under which they find an audience are more so. Under these conditions, the war against terrorism could only be scripted—even rehearsing roles for a new President Bush to take similar advice that his father-president received before him, from the very same advisors—Dick Cheney, Colin Powell, and even Donald Rumsfeld.

President Bush's rhetorical onslaught, however, was designed not to highlight the tertiary conditions that give rise to the despair that breeds terrorism. Instead, it was designed to demonize the fundamentalist Taliban rulers of Afghanistan and their harboring of the alleged master-mind of the horrors of September 11, Osama bin Laden. Bush's father used the same tactics to connect Saddam Hussein with "Satan." Yet, the result is just more war all over again as the conditions that breed its plausibility in the minds of desperate people lived on.

The Taliban fundamentalists responded by insisting that if the United States attacked, the whole Arab world was obligated to rise up in its own *jihad* against the United States and all its allies. Crusade vs. Jihad. What goes around, comes around. Words were cycling back to escalate the rhetorical conflict, creating the conditions for higher and higher levels of military conflict. The terror of the word laid the groundwork for the terror of the deed.

As the world stopped to see how far this escalation would go, the new world order continued to grind on—including compliant subjects even as it excluded the fundamentally dispossessed. This double-work ensured that militants would continue to terrorize even as the multitude would resist. This double-play was to be fraught with its own troubling dynamics. Terrorism could make resistance more open to repression. The chances for positive change would have to live beyond this diabolical relationship.

Conclusion

The microprocesses of the behavior modification regime of welfare reform and the macroprocesses of economic globalization are possibly linked in ways that go beyond the specific needs of capitalism for more workers for emerging low-wage labor markets. The ties between the outer behemoth of globalization and the inner child of welfare reform may be more than strictly economic. Instead, there is possibly merit in thinking about how neoliberal, privatized welfare reform is symptomatic of new forms of "biopower" operating to produce not just low-wage workers but compliant citizens for a new world order, socially and culturally as well as economically. Welfare reform may well be a new global staging project for the "theatricality of power."[99] The ritualized denigration of welfare recipients under the therapeutic interventions of welfare reform may very well be a symbolic exercise designed to reinforce labor discipline more generally, this time regimentation into a new globalizing economy. It also may be a symbolic exercise to enforce an even larger discipline that enlists the populations into processes of self-governance and self-regulation, making for a new type of compliant global subject who flexibly adapts to the ever-changing systems of production in ways that remain consistent with "the rules of the game" concerning family as well as work. Welfare reform's tie to processes of globalization may be more than economic, even if one has good reason to suspect that economics is a good part of the connection.

The macro-micro tie between welfare reform's behavior modification regime and globalization suggests both the strengths and the weaknesses of the emerging order. Built from below, via the disciplinary arts of self-regulation, the multitudes of people caught up in the disciplinary web can both make and break the chains of power. The networks of domination can be disrupted by unruly subjects who choose to resist the demands for compliant selves. Globalization may be more or less real, but it is by no means a fait accompli. The product of politics, even micropolitics, it is vulnerable to political disruption. Neither natural nor inevitable, the forces of globalization are political constructions open to political contestation. In emphasizing this in the economic realm, Piven and Cloward have eloquently articulated how the current predicament points to still another instance of how hope lives on in the fundamental reality that politics is the constitutive force making our "world." They have written:

> [E]conomic change also creates concrete new possibilities for worker power. People work at new and different occupations, they have different skills, and in time they will see the power potential inherent in the interdependencies of a new and fabulously complex and precarious communications-driven economy that is as vulnerable to mass disruption as the manufacturing-driven economy was. In time, maybe only a little time, they will develop the awareness of commonalties and capacities for joint action which will make working-class power possible again. And they are also likely to find the imagination and the daring to break the new rules governing communications which are even now being promulgated to criminalize the exercise of power from below.
>
> It is the end of a power era. It is also the beginning of a power era.[100]

The craggy ground of social and behavioral regulation is the site on which some would build a new globalized system of production. It becomes the site of a radical incrementalism working to resist global power. Terrorists who may claim to represent the dispossessed may discredit radical incrementalism's nonviolent forms of resistance. The struggle against globalization must find ways to overcome such associations. For it is only beyond them that there lies the chance for nonviolent challenges to the creation of compliant subjects for a new world order.

Appendix: Sources and Measures for Data in Chapter 5

1. Government Ideology, 1996: Ideological score for each state government in 1996. Range = 1.3 to 93.9, on a 0 to 100 scale, with higher values indicating a more liberal government. Mean = 39.8; standard deviation = 26.4. *Source*: William D. Berry, Evan Ringquist, Richard Fording, and Russell Hanson, "Measuring Citizen and Government Ideology in the American States, 1960–93." *American Journal of Politics* 42 (January 1998): 327–348.

2. Interparty Competition, 1996: Based on the difference of proportions for seats controlled by each major party (Democrat and Republican) in each state's lower and upper house. Range = .30 to .97, on a 0 to 1.00 scale, with higher values indicating greater party competition. Mean = .74; standard deviation = .18. *Source*: U.S. Census Bureau, *Statistical Abstract of the United States*. Washington, DC: Government Printing Office, 1998.

3. Low-Income Voter Turnout, 1996: Based on the proportion of all individuals falling below the U.S. Census Bureau's poverty threshold who voted in the 1996 elections. Range = .34 to .62, with higher values indicating a higher proportion of low-income persons voting. Mean = .45; standard deviation = .06. *Source*: U.S. Census Bureau, *Current Population Survey: Voter Supplement File*. Washington, DC: U.S. Department of Commerce, 1996.

4. Per Capita Welfare Caseload, 1996: The average monthly number of AFDC recipients in each state as a percentage of the total resident population as of July 1, 1996. Range = 1.9 to 8.2, with higher values indicating a higher per capita caseload. Mean = 3.96; standard deviation

= 1.40. *Source*: U.S. Department of Health and Human Services, *Indicators of Welfare Dependence: Annual Report to Congress*. Washington, DC: Government Printing Office, 1997.

5. Percentage of Welfare Caseload African American, 1996: Based on the proportion of each state's AFDC caseload in 1996 that was classified by the government as African American. Range = .3 to 86.2, with higher values indicating that African Americans made up a higher proportion of the caseload. Mean = 32.07; standard deviation = 26.51. *Source*: U.S. Department of Health and Human Services, Office of Family Assistance, 1996.

6. Percentage of Welfare Caseload Latina, 1996: Based on the proportion of each state's AFDC caseload in 1996 that was classified by the government as Hispanic. Range = 0 to 57.4, with higher values indicating that Latinos made up a higher proportion of the caseload. Mean = 11.00; standard deviation = 14.73. *Source*: U.S. Department of Health and Human Services, Office of Family Assistance, 1996.

7. Unemployment Rate, 1996: Official unemployment rate for each state. Range = 3.1 to 8.1, with higher values indicating a higher percentage of the labor force was unemployed. Mean = 5.19; standard deviation = 1.13. *Source*: U.S. Bureau of Labor Statistics, Local Area Unemployment, 1996.

8. Unmarried Birthrate, 1996: Percentage of all births born to unmarried women. Range = 16.0 to 45.0, with higher values indicating that unmarried women accounted for a higher proportion of all births. Mean = 31.30; standard deviation = 5.69. *Source*: U.S. Census Bureau, *Statistical Abstract of the United States*. Washington, DC: Government Printing Office, 1998.

9. Policy Innovation: The year of each state's earliest AFDC waiver request. Range = 77 to 97, with higher values indicating a later starting date for waiver requests (97 indicates no waiver requests under the AFDC program through 1996). Mean = 87.5; standard deviation = 7.1. *Source*: Robert C. Lieberman and Greg M. Shaw, "Looking Inward, Looking Outward: The Politics of State Welfare Innovation under Devolution." *Political Research Quarterly* 53 (2000): 215-240.

10. Change in Incarceration Rate, 1990–1996: Based on the percentage change in the state prison population from 1990 to 1996. Range = -4.2 percent to 164.5 percent, with higher values indicating larger increases in incarceration. Mean = 44.9; standard deviation = 25.0. *Source*: U.S. Bureau of Justice Statistics, 1996.

11. Sanction Policy by State, 1997: Range = 1 to 3, where 1 is weak sanctions (delayed and not applied to the entire family's benefit), 2 is moderate sanctions (delayed but applied to the full family), and 3 is strong sanctions (full-family immediate sanctions). The frequency distribution is 31 percent (weak); 42 percent (moderate); and 27 percent (strong). *Source*: Vee Burke and Melinda Gish, *Welfare Reform: Work Trigger, Time Limits, Exemptions and Sanctions Under TANF*. Washington, DC: Congressional Research Service, 98-697, EPW. August 6, 1998.

12. Work Requirement by State, 1997: Range = 0 to 1, on a 0 to 1 scale, where 0 is a work requirement that is the same as the federal 24-month requirement and 1 is less than 24 months. While 51 percent of the states adopted stricter work requirements, 49 percent did not. *Source*: American Public Welfare Association, *Survey Notes* 1 (October 1997): 7–8.

13. Time Limit by State, 1997: Range = 0 to 1, on a 0 to 1 scale, where 0 is a time limit that is the same as the federal 5-year requirement and 1 is less than 5 years. While 41 percent of the states adopted stricter time limits, 59 percent did not. *Source*: American Public Welfare Association, *Survey Notes* 1 (October 1997): 7–8.

14. Family Cap by State, 1997: Range = 0 to 1, on a 0 to 1 scale, where 0 is no Family Cap is adopted and 1 is where the Family Cap is adopted. While 41 percent of the states adopted the family cap, 59 percent did not. *Source*: American Public Welfare Association, *State Survey on Welfare Reform*, 1997, p. 23.

Notes

Notes to the Introduction

1. Michael B. Katz, *The Price of Citizenship: Redefining the American Welfare State* (New York: Metropolitan Books, 2001).

2. Sanford F. Schram, *After Welfare: The Culture of Postindustrial Social Policy* (New York: New York University Press, 2000).

3. See Pamela Loprest, "How Families That Left Welfare Are Doing: A National Picture." B-1 in "New Federalism: National Survey of America's Families" Series. (Washington, DC: Urban Institute, 1999); and Sheila R. Zedlewski and Donald W. Alderson, "Before and After Reform: How Have Families on Welfare Changed?" B-32 in "New Federalism: National Survey of America's Families" Series. (Washington, DC: Urban Institute, 2001).

4. Martha F. Davis, *Brutal Need: Lawyers and the Welfare Rights Movement, 1960–1973* (New Haven, CT: Yale University Press, 1993).

5. See Alice O'Connor, *Poverty Knowledge: Social Science, Social Policy, and the Poor in Twentieth-Century U.S. History* (Princeton, NJ: Princeton University Press, 2001).

6. See Sanford F. Schram, *Words of Welfare: The Poverty of Social Science and the Social Science of Poverty* (Minneapolis: University of Minnesota Press, 1995).

7. See Frances Fox Piven and Richard A. Cloward, *The Breaking of the American Social Compact* (New York: New Press, 1997), pp. 65–72.

8. See Schram, *Words of Welfare*. For a historical perspective on how bureaucratization of social welfare programs encouraged the marginalization of critical social welfare scholarship, especially feminist work, see Camilla Stivers, *Bureau Men and Settlement Women* (Lawrence: University Press of Kansas, 2000).

9. See Richard J. Bernstein, *Praxis and Action: Contemporary Philosophies of Human Activity* (Philadelphia: University of Pennsylvania Press, 1971), p. ix, where Bernstein writes:

> Aristotle . . . uses "*praxis*" to designate one of the ways of life open to a free man, and to signify the sciences and arts that deal with the activities characteristic of man's ethical and political life. In this context, the contrast that Aristotle draws is between "*theoria*" and "*praxis*" where the former expression signifies those

sciences and activities that are concerned with knowing for its own sake. This contrast is an ancestor of the distinction between theory and practice that has been central to almost every major Western philosopher since Aristotle.

10. Ibid., p. xi, where Bernstein writes:

> [Y]oung left Hegelians in the 1840s . . . [embarked on] an urgent quest to go "beyond" Hegel. In this quest the concept of "*praxis*" arose on the horizon. Cieszkowski seems to have coined this "new" use of "*praxis*" and declared that the role of philosophy was "to become a practical philosophy or rather a philosophy of practical activity, of '*praxis*' exercising a direct influence on social life and developing the future in the realm of concrete activity." . . . What distinguishes Marx from other left Hegelians is that he soon grew impatient with vague talk about *praxis* and he went on to develop a thorough, systematic and comprehensive *theory* of *praxis*.

Marx's theory of praxis is perhaps best summed up by the last of his eleven theses on Feuerbach: "The philosophers have only *interpreted* the world in various ways; the point is, to *change* it." See Bernstein, *Praxis and Action*, p. 13.

11. See Brian Fay, *Social Theory and Political Practice* (London: George Allen and Unwin, 1975), p. 97. For additional considerations on the relationship of theory to practice, see Jeffrey Isaac, "The Strange Silence of Political Theory," *Political Theory* 23 (November 1995): 636–652; John G. Gunnell, *The Orders of Discourse: Philosophy, Social Science, and Politics* (Lanham, MD: Rowman and Littlefield, 1998); and Samuel A. Chambers, "Spectral History, Untimely Theory," *Theory & Event* 3 (2000) (http://muse.jhu.edu/journals/theory_and_event/v003/3.4chambers.html).

12. O'Connor, *Poverty Knowledge*, p. 31.

13. See Schram, *After Welfare*, pp. 178–182, for an initial discussion of "radical incrementalism."

14. See Rasto Eräsaari, "Why Recognition of Contingency Is Not Surrendering to Contingency," *Finnish Yearbook of Political Thought* 3 (1999): 132–146.

15. For a thorough analysis that recognizes the need to account for the politics in social welfare research but does not go very far beyond that, see O'Connor, *Poverty Knowledge*.

16. See Schram, *Words of Welfare*.

17. For an eloquent plea to allow problems to have priority over methods in the structuring of research, see Ian Shapiro, "Problems, Methods, and Theories in the Study of Politics, or: What's Wrong with Political Science and What to Do About It" (Charles E. Lindblom Lecture on Public Policy, Yale University, February 2001) (http://pantheon.yale.edu/~ianshap/Lindblom%20Lecture.pdf).

Notes to Chapter 1

1. See Theda Skocpol, *Boomerang* (New York: W. W. Norton, 1996).

2. Theda Skocpol, *The Missing Middle: Working Families and the Future of American Social Policy* (New York: W. W. Norton, 2000).

3. Ibid., p. 163.

4. See Nicholas Lemann, "Can Populism Be Popular?" *New York Review of Books*, November 16, 2000, pp. 48–52.

5. Skocpol, *The Missing Middle*, p. 165.

6. Ibid., p. 161.

7. Ibid., pp. 170–171.

8. As quoted in Lemann, "Can Populism Be Popular?"

9. Ibid., pp. 165–166.

10. John Schwarz, *America's Hidden Success* (New York: W. W. Norton, 1983). Also see John E. Schwarz with Thomas J. Volgy, *Forgotten Americans: Thirty Million Working Poor in the Land of Opportunity* (New York: W. W. Norton, 1992).

11. Theodore Marmor, Jerry Mashaw, and Phillip Harvey, *America's Misunderstood Welfare State* (New York: Basic Books, 1990).

12. E. J. Dionne, *They Only Look Dead* (New York: Touchstone, 1997).

13. Sheldon Danziger and Peter Gottschalk, *America Unequal* (Cambridge, MA: Harvard University Press, 1995).

14. Benjamin I. Page and James R. Simmons, *What Government Can Do: Dealing with Poverty and Inequality* (Chicago: University of Chicago Press, 2000).

15. Charles Murray, *Losing Ground: American Social Policy 1950–1980* (New York: Basic Books, 1984). It is interesting to note that *Losing Ground* and several other books that exemplify the attempt to connect welfare scholarship to politics have been published by Basic Books, whose explicit mission is to make "contributions to the public discourse." Basic Books' interest in connecting scholarship to politics was underscored when it sponsored a debate about "the future of the public intellectual." See "The Future of the Public Intellectual: A Forum," *Nation*, February 12, 2001, pp. 25–27.

16. See Sanford F. Schram and Philip T. Neisser, eds., *Tales of the State: Narrative in U.S. Politics and Social Policy* (Lanham, MD: Rowman and Littlefield, 1977), Introduction.

17. For a review of the many criticisms of the weak factual basis for the arguments in Charles Murray's *Losing Ground*, see Alice O'Connor, *Poverty Knowledge: Social Science, Social Policy, and the Poor in Twentieth-Century U.S. History* (Princeton, NJ: Princeton University Press, 2001), pp. 247–250.

18. There is even the need, I would suggest, to consider the possibility that at times the most politically potent scholarship is not immediately relevant to contemporary politics. See Samuel A. Chambers, "Spectral History, Untimely Theory,"

Theory & Event 3 (2000) (http://muse.jhu.edu/journals/theory_and_event/v003/3.4chambers.html).

19. Lemann, "Can Populism Be Popular?" p. 50.

20. See Margaret Somers and Fred Block, "From Poverty to Perversity: Markets, States, and Institutions over Two Centuries of Welfare Debate," unpublished manuscript, August 2001.

21. Murray, *Losing Ground.*

22. Thomas Malthus made his perversity argument about public assistance in *Essays on the Principles of Population* (London: Penguin Books, 1985) [1798 orig.].

23. Albert O. Hirschman, *The Rhetoric of Reaction: Perversity, Futility, Jeopardy* (Cambridge, MA: Belknap Press of Harvard University Press, 1991), pp. 27–42.

24. For an example of the attempt to provide facts that could combat the myths surrounding welfare use, see *The Basics: Welfare Reform* (New York: Twentieth Century Fund, 1996) (http://www.tcf.org/Publications/Basics/welfare/index.html). Also see *Welfare Myths: Fact or Fiction? Exploring the Truth about Welfare* (New York: Welfare Law Center, 1996) (http://www.welfarelaw.org/mythtoc.html).

25. Page and Simmons, *What Government Can Do*, p. 220, note that European countries have higher levels of public employment as a means of generating jobs. They do not discuss that these countries also have higher levels of unemployment.

26. See Stephen K. White, "Narratives of the Welfare State," *Theory & Event* 1 (1997) (http://muse.jhu.edu/journals/theory_and_event/v001/1.2white.html).

27. See Sanford F. Schram, *After Welfare: The Culture of Postindustrial Social Policy* (New York: New York University Press, 2000), pp. 80–81.

28. It is important to distinguish my version of "assuming the best" from the more commonly recognized polemical uses of this phrase by conservatives. Conservatives have had their own version of "assuming the best" as when they oppose affirmative action and other compensatory programs on the grounds that those programs allegedly are crafted from a patronizing perspective that assumes the people assisted are not capable of competing and achieving on their own. Yet this version of "assuming the best" is at its best only a thinly disguised veil for ignoring structural inequities in the socioeconomic order. My version of "assuming the best" is dedicated to intervening to help people overcome those structural inequities on the grounds that people can be assumed to make good use of that assistance.

29. Christopher Hitchens, in "The Future of the Public Intellectual: A Forum."

30. Michael J. Shapiro, *Reading "Adam Smith": Desire, History and Value* (London: Sage Publications, 1993), pp. xxix–xxx.

31. For explanation of the importance of learning how to work at a distance in order to be able to make a close connection to the lives of the people you study, see Charles Lemert's eloquent description of what he calls "global methods." See Charles Lemert, *Social Things* (Lanham, MD: Rowman and Littlefield, 2001), pp. 196–200.

32. Work at a distance to destabilize hegemonic discourse is not work that is limited to public intellectuals but is also an important activity practiced by front line activists themselves. This sort of "guerrilla wordfare" is an important part of the toolkit of activists in such movement organizations as ACT-UP in its fight against homophobia and neglect of the AIDS crisis. Other groups in other areas of struggle have also found countering discourse to be critical to their struggles. See Lisa Duggan, "Queering the State," *Social Text* 39 (Summer 1994): 1–14. I want to thank Jenrose Fitzgerald for making this point clear to me.

33. The phrase "heroes of their own lives" is from Linda Gordon, *Heroes of Their Own Lives: The History and Politics of Family Violence* (New York: Viking, 1988).

34. See chapter 3.

Notes to Chapter 2

1. See Nigel Parton, "Some Thoughts on the Relationship between Theory and Practice in and for Social Work," *British Journal of Social Work* 30 (August 2000): 449–463. In contemporary political theory there is an interesting debate about whether theory is alienated from practice and whether this is bad. See John G. Gunnell, *The Descent of Political Theory* (Chicago: University of Chicago Press, 1997). Also see Jeffrey Isaac, "The Strange Silence of Political Theory," *Political Theory* 23 (November 1995): 636–652.

2. Jane Addams is also used by Alice O'Connor to provide a counterpoint from the past to question the limitations of contemporary social policy research. See Alice O'Connor, *Poverty Knowledge: Social Science, Social Policy, and the Poor in Twentieth-Century U.S. History* (Princeton, NJ: Princeton University Press, 2001), pp. 29–32.

3. See Wendy Sarvasy, "Transnational Citizenship through Daily Life" (paper presented at the Annual Meeting of the Western Political Science Association, Seattle, Washington, March 25–27, 1999); Charlene Haddock Seigfried, "Socializing Democracy: Jane Addams and John Dewey" (paper presented at the Annual Meeting of the Midwest Political Science Association, Chicago, Ill., April 12–14, 1999); and Jean Bethke Elshtain, "Jane Addams: A Pilgrim's Progress," *Journal of Religion* 78 (July 1998): 339–360; idem, "Jane Addams and the Social Claim," *Public Interest* 145 (Fall 2001): 82–93; and idem, *Jane Addams and the Dream of Democracy* (New York: Basic Books, 2002).

4. Mary Jo Deegan, *Jane Addams and the Men of the Chicago School, 1892–1918* (New Brunswick, NJ: Transaction Books, 1988); and Elshtain, "Jane Addams and the Social Claim," pp. 84–94.

5. C. Wright Mills, *Sociology and Pragmatism*, Irving Louis Horowitz, ed. (New York: Paine-Whitman, 1964), p. 309. Alice O'Connor notes that while not all settlement house workers were by any means what we would today call multiculturalists

and were paternalistic in their approach to impoverished immigrants, Addams committed herself early on in her involvement in the settlement movement to a "bottom-up" strategy that learned from low-income immigrants and facilitated their realization of their own life goals on their own terms. See O'Connor, *Poverty Knowledge*, pp. 42–43.

6. For relevant commentary on this issue that contrasts Jane Addams to her close colleague and friend Charlotte Perkins Gilman, see Deegan, *Jane Addams and the Men of the Chicago School,* pp. 226–230.

7. See Parton, "Some Thoughts on the Relationship between Theory and Practice in and for Social Work," pp. 455–460.

8. See O'Connor, *Poverty Knowledge*, pp. 42–43.

9. While some have emphasized that Addams did not work with African Americans, this is not true. Although the neighborhood served by her settlement at Hull House was largely comprised of European immigrants, there were also African Americans among the families. Addams was to some extent limited by the racial thinking of her time, but she was by no means reluctant to push to racial justice. For instance, while many people hailed *Birth of a Nation* as a cinematic achievement when it was made, she was an early and vocally outspoken opponent calling for the film to be banned because of its prejudicial depictions of African Americans. See Louis Menand, *The Metaphysical Club: A Story of Ideas in America* (New York: Farrar, Straus & Giroux, 2001), p. 374.

10. Ian Shapiro, *Democratic Justice* (New Haven: Yale University Press, 1999).

11. See Nancy Fraser, "Recognition or Redistribution? A Critical Reading of Iris Young's *Justice and the Politics of Difference*." *Journal of Political Philosophy* 3 (June 1995): 166–180; and Iris Marion Young, "Unruly Categories: A Critique of Nancy Fraser's Dual Systems Theory," *New Left Review* 222 (March–April 1997): 36–40.

12. See Emmanuel Levinas, *Totality and Infinity/Philosophical Series* (Pittsburgh: Duquesne University Press, 1969).

13. Maria C. Lugones, "Playfulness, 'World'-Traveling, and Loving Perception," in *Making Face, Making Soul = Haciendo Caras: Creative and Critical Perspectives by Women of Color,* Gloria Anzaldúa, ed. (San Francisco: Aunt Lute Foundation Books, 1990), pp. 390–402.

14. Homi Bhabha, "DissemiNation: Time, Narrative, and the Margins of the Modern Nation," in *The Post-Colonial Studies Reader,* Bill Ashcroft, Gareth Griffiths, and Helen Tiffin, eds. (New York: Routledge, 1995), pp. 29–35.

15. William E. Connolly, *Why I Am Not a Secularist* (Minneapolis: University of Minnesota Press, 1999), pp. 51–53.

16. See Joe Soss, *Unwanted Claims: The Politics of Participation in the U.S. Welfare System* (Ann Arbor: University of Michigan Press, 2000).

17. See Parton, "Some Thoughts on the Relationship between Theory and Practice in and for Social Work," pp. 452–455.

18. Jane Addams, *Democracy and Social Ethics* (New York: Macmillan, 1911 [orig. 1902]).

19. Jane Addams, *Twenty Years at Hull House, with Autobiographical Notes* (New York: Macmillan, 1910).

20. Allen F. Davis, "Welfare, Reform and World War I," *American Quarterly* 19 (Autumn 1967): 516–533.

21. Ernest W. Burgess, "The Urban Community." Selected Papers from the Proceedings of the American Sociological Society, 1925. Chicago: University of Chicago Press, 1926, as described in Deegan, *Jane Addams and the Men of the Chicago School*, p. 147.

22. See Menand, *The Metaphysical Club*, pp. 306–324; Deegan, *Jane Addams and the Men of the Chicago School;* and Gioia Diliberto, *A Useful Woman: The Early Life of Jane Addams* (New York: Scribner, 1999).

23. See Deegan, *Jane Addams and the Men of the Chicago School*, pp. 226–230.

24. Addams, *Democracy and Social Ethics*, pp. 273–274.

25. On the relationship of theory to practice, see John Gunnell, *The Orders of Discourse: Philosophy, Social Science, and Politics* (Lanham, MD: Rowman and Littlefield, 1998).

26. Addams, *Democracy and Social Ethics*, p. 12.

27. Ibid., p. 223.

28. Ibid., pp. 5–6.

29. Addams, *Twenty Years at Hull House*, p. 183, as quoted in Sarvasy, "Transnational Citizenship through Daily Life," p. 6.

30. Addams, *Twenty Years at Hull House*, p. 270.

31. Jane Addams, "Education," in *Jane Addams: A Centennial Reader*, intro. Christopher Lasch (New York: Macmillan 1960 [reprint of 1902]), p. 146.

32. Menand, *The Metaphysical Club*, pp. 313–316, effectively highlights how Addams was in many respects an important teacher to Dewey about many things related to democracy, power, and knowledge. Yet, I think it is critical not to limit Addams's significance on how she influenced prominent thinkers such as John Dewey. Instead, it is more important to understand her own unique contributions to democratic theory and practice.

33. James Bohman, "Democracy as Inquiry, Inquiry as Democratic: Pragmatism, Social Science, and the Cognitive Division of Labor," *American Journal of Political Science* 43 (April 1999): 590–607.

34. Seigfried, "Socializing Democracy," pp. 2–3.

35. Addams, *Democracy and Social Ethics*, pp. 7, 11–12.

36. See Sarvasy, "Transnational Citizenship through Daily Life," pp. 16–22.

37. Ibid., pp. 17–22.

38. Addams, *Democracy and Social Ethics*, pp. 6–8.

39. Ibid., pp. 9–11.

40. On Addams's use of the male pronoun, see Seigfried, "Socializing Democracy," pp. 21–22. On woman as the model citizen, see Nancy Fraser, "After the Family Wage: Gender Equity and the Welfare State," *Political Theory* 22 (November 1994): 591–618.

41. Addams, *Democracy and Social Ethics*, pp. 72–73.

42. Ibid., pp. 207–208.

43. Seigfried, "Socializing Democracy," pp. 21–22.

44. Addams, *Democracy and Social Ethics*, pp. 14–16, 38.

45. Mills, *Sociology and Pragmatism*, p. 309.

46. In particular, see Deegan, *Jane Addams and the Men of the Chicago School*, pp. 147–149.

47. William Julius Wilson, *The Truly Disadvantaged: The Inner City, the Underclass, and Public Policy* (Chicago: University of Chicago Press 1987), p. 56.

48. Addams, *Democracy and Social Ethics*, pp. 68–69.

49. Ibid., pp. 94–101.

50. Ibid., p. 146.

51. Ibid., pp. 270–272.

52. For a discussion of how Addams thought it was most critical to reject the idea of antagonism as essential to life and thought, see Menand, *The Metaphysical Club*, pp. 313–316.

53. Lugones, "Playfulness, 'World'-Traveling, and Loving Perception," pp. 390–402.

54. See David Wagner, *What's Love Got to Do with It: A Critical Look at American Charity* (New York: New Press, 2000).

55. Cornelia Meigs, *Jane Addams: Pioneer for Social Justice* (Boston: Little, Brown, 1970), pp. 256–263.

56. Menand, *The Metaphysical Club*, pp. 313–316.

57. Randolph Bourne, the turn-of-the-century cultural radical, was critical of Jane Addams's resistance to conflict and saw it as a fetter on social activism. See Menand, *The Metaphysical Club*, p. 402. Yet, Bourne joined Addams as a pacifist in opposition to World War I.

58. Like Jane Addams in her day, Frances Fox Piven and Richard Cloward in theirs understood that the future of social science in social welfare grew from out of ongoing political struggle. See chapter 3.

Notes to Chapter 3

1. Frances Fox Piven and Richard A. Cloward, *Regulating the Poor*, rev. ed. (New York: Vintage, 1992).

2. Frances Fox Piven and Richard A. Cloward, *The Breaking of the American Social Compact* (New York: New Press, 1997).

3. Frances Fox Piven and Richard A. Cloward, *Poor People's Movements* (New York: Pantheon Books, 1997).

4. Frances Fox Piven and Richard A. Cloward, *Why Americans Still Don't Vote* (Boston: Beacon Press, 2000).

5. Sanford F. Schram, *After Welfare: The Culture of Postindustrial Social Policy* (New York: New York University Press, 2000), p. 178.

6. See Sanford F. Schram, *Words of Welfare: The Poverty of Social Science and the Social Science of Poverty* (Minneapolis: University of Minnesota Press, 1995), pp. 3–14.

7. Frances Fox Piven and Richard A. Cloward, *Regulating the Poor: The Functions of Public Welfare* (New York: Vintage Books, 1971), p. 338.

8. On the relationship of knowledge to power, Plato in Book V of *The Republic* has Socrates saying:

> Until philosophers are kings, or the kings and princes of this world have the spirit and power of philosophy, and political greatness and wisdom meet in one, and those commoner natures who pursue either to the exclusion of the other are compelled to stand aside, cities will never have rest from their evils,—no, nor the human race, as I believe,—and then only will this our State have a possibility of life and behold the light of day.

See *The Works of Plato*, Irwin Edman, ed. (New York: Modern Library, Random House, 1956), p. 431.

9. Dietrich Rueschemeyer and Theda Skocpol, *States, Social Knowledge, and the Origins of Modern Social Policies* (Princeton, NJ: Princeton University Press, 1996).

10. Harold D. Lasswell and Daniel Lerner, eds., *The Policy Sciences* (Stanford, CA: Stanford University Press, 1951).

11. Henry J. Aaron, *Professors and Politics Revisited* (Washington, DC: Brookings Institution, 1989).

12. David Ricci, *The Transformation of American Politics: The Rise of Washington Think-Tanks* (New Haven: Yale University Press, 1993).

13. Richard P. Nathan, *Social Science in Government: Uses and Misuses* (New York: Basic Books, 1988).

14. Hugh Heclo, "Issue Networks and the Executive Establishment," in *The New American Political System*, Anthony King, ed. (Washington, DC: American Enterprise Institute, 1978), pp. 87–124.

15. See John G. Gunnell, *The Orders of Discourse: Philosophy, Social Science, and Politics* (Lanham, MD: Rowman and Littlefield, 1998). Also see Jeffrey Isaac, "The Strange Silence of Political Theory," *Political Theory* 23 (November 1995): 636–652; and Samuel A. Chambers, "Spectral History, Untimely Theory," *Theory & Event* 3 (2000) (http://muse.jhu.edu/journals/theory_and_event/v003/3.4chambers.html).

16. See Michael Tomasky, *Left for Dead: The Life, Death and Possible Resurrection of Progressive Politics in America* (New York: Free Press, 1996), pp. 96–117. Other critics include Jim Sleeper, *Liberal Racism* (New York: Viking, 1997), pp. 58–60; and Fred Siegel, *The Future Once Happened Here: New York, D.C., L.A., and the Fate of America's Big Cities* (New York: Free Press, 1997), pp. 46–61.

17. Reinhold Niebuhr popularized the phrase "speak truth to power." See Reinhold Niebuhr, *Moral Man and Immoral Society: A Study in Ethics and Politics* (New York: C. Scribner's Sons, 1934).

18. While Max Weber emphasized impartiality and the need to understand society as it was, Karl Marx famously stated: "Philosophers have only *interpreted* the world, in various ways; the point, however, is to *change* it." See Karl Marx, "Theses on Feuerbach," XI, in *Marx & Engels: Basic Writings on Politics and Philosophy*, Lewis S. Feuer, ed. (New York: Anchor Books, 1959), p. 245.

19. Rueschemeyer and Skocpol, *States, Social Knowledge, and the Origins of Modern Social Policies*.

20. Ira Katznelson, "Knowledge about What? Policy Intellectuals and the New Liberalism," in *States, Social Knowledge, and the Origins of Modern Social Policies*, Dietrich Reuschemeyer and Theda Skocpol, eds. (Princeton, NJ: Princeton University Press, 1996), pp. 17–38.

21. Theodore J. Lowi, "The State in Political Science: How We Become What We Study," *American Political Science Review* 86 (March 1992): 1–7.

22. See Schram, *After Welfare*, pp. 19–25.

23. United States Department of Health and Human Services, Administration for Children and Families, Temporary Assistance for Needy Families (TANF) 1936–1998. Updated through June 1999 (http://www.acf.dhhs.gov/news/ caseload.htm); and Sanford F. Schram, "Introduction," in *Welfare Reform: A Race to the Bottom?* Sanford F. Schram and Samuel H. Beer, eds. (Washington, DC: Woodrow Wilson Center Press, 1999), pp. 4–8.

24. U.S. Department of Health and Human Services, Administration on Children and Families, *Temporary Assistance for Needy Families: Total Number of Families and Recipients, July–September 2000, July 27, 2001* (http://www.acf.dhhs.gov /news/stats/welfare.htm).

25. See Sarah Brauner and Pamela Loprest, "Where Are They Now? What States' Studies of People Who Left Welfare Tell Us," A-32 in the series, New Federalism: Issues and Options for States (Washington, DC: Urban Institute, May 1999).

26. On the deadlock over welfare, see Steven M. Teles, *Whose Welfare? AFDC and Elite Politics* (Lawrence: University Press of Kansas, 1996), pp. 1–18.

27. Martha F. Davis, *Brutal Need: Lawyers and the Welfare Rights Movement, 1960–1973* (New Haven, CT: Yale University Press, 1973).

28. Piven and Cloward, *Regulating the Poor*, pp. 249–282.

29. Jill Quadagno, *The Color of Welfare: How Racism Undermined the War on Poverty* (New York: Oxford University Press, 1994). Also see Michael Brown, *Race, Money, and the American Welfare State* (Ithaca, NY: Cornell University Press, 1999), p. 185: "By 1961, 40 percent of the ADC [Aid to Dependent Children] caseload was composed of black families, up from about 14 percent in 1939."

30. In particular, see Charles Murray, *Losing Ground: American Social Policy, 1950–1980* (New York: Basic Books, 1984).

31. See Michael B. Katz, *The Undeserving Poor: From the War on Poverty to the War on Welfare* (New York: Pantheon Books, 1989); and Herbert J. Gans, *The War against the Poor: The Underclass and Antipoverty Policy* (New York: Basic Books, 1995).

32. See Martin Gilens, *Why Americans Hate Welfare: Race, Media, and the Politics of Antipoverty Policy* (Chicago: University of Chicago Press, 1999).

33. Wahneema Lubiano, "Black Ladies, Welfare Queens, and State Minstrels: Ideological War by Narrative Means," in *Race-ing Justice, En-gendering Power: Essays on Anita Hill, Clarence Thomas, and the Social Construction of Reality*, Toni Morrison, ed. (New York: Pantheon Books, 1992), pp. 232–263.

34. For a critique, see Adolph Reed, Jr., "The Underclass as Myth and Symbol: The Poverty of Discourse about Poverty," in *Stirrings in the Jug: Black Politics in the Post-Segregation Era* (Minneapolis: University of Minnesota Press, 1999), p. 180.

35. See Joe Soss, Sanford Schram, Thomas Vartanian, and Erin O'Brien, "Setting the Terms of Relief: Explaining State Policy Choices in the Devolution Revolution," *American Journal of Political Science* 45 (April 2001): 378–395.

36. See Lawrence M. Mead, "The Rise of Paternalism," *The New Paternalism: Supervisory Approaches to Poverty*, Lawrence M. Mead, ed. (Washington, DC: Brookings Institution Press, 1997), pp. 1–38.

37. Jon Carroll, "Mr. Newt Explains It All for You," *San Francisco Chronicle*, November 27, 1995, p. B8.

38. The people who have criticized Piven and Cloward's efforts in the 1960s for producing the gridlock over welfare that reached into the 1990s is a diverse group that includes government officials as well as academics from New York City, Mayor Rudolph Giuliani, and self-proclaimed leftists such as Michael Tomasky. For Giuliani's criticisms, see Jason DeParle, "What Welfare-to-Work Really Means," *New York Times Magazine*, December 20, 1998, pp. 50–59, 70–74, 88–89. Also see Tomasky, *Left for Dead*, pp. 96–117; Sleeper, *Liberal Racism*, pp. 58–60; and Siegel, *The Future Once Happened Here*, pp. 46–61.

39. Richard A. Cloward and Frances Fox Piven, "A Strategy to End Poverty," *Nation*, May 2, 1966, pp. 510–517.

40. Piven and Cloward, *Regulating the Poor*, p. 338.

41. See Richard C. Fording, "The Conditional Effect of Violence as a Political Tactic: Mass Insurgency, Welfare Generosity, and Electoral Context in the American States," *American Journal of Political Science* 41 (January 1997): 1–29; and

Sanford F. Schram and J. Patrick Turbett, "Civil Disorder and the Welfare Explosion: A Two-Step Process," *American Sociological Review* 48 (June 1983): 408–414.

42. The suggestion that Piven and Cloward's efforts in the 1960s to overload the welfare system set the stage for the backlash against public assistance that came in the 1990s even crept into the obituary of Richard Cloward when he died in August 2001. See Stephanie Flanders, "Richard Cloward, Welfare Rights Leader, Dies at 74," *New York Times*, August 23, 2001, p. B9.

43. See Michael Wines, "White House Links Riots to Welfare," *New York Times*, May 5, 1992, p. A1. Myron Magnet explicitly connects welfare dependency and the liberalism of the 1960s in *The Dream and the Nightmare: The Sixties' Legacy to the Underclass* (New York: Morrow, 1993).

44. See Davis, *Brutal Need*, pp. 40–55.

45. Piven and Cloward went on to found Human SERVE in 1983, an organization that led the fight for the Motor Voter Bill that was enacted in 1993 as the National Voter Registration Act.

46. The need to find scapegoats looms large in Siegel, *The Future Once Happened Here*, pp. 46–61, but is apparent in others as well.

47. On the connection between hollow men that Nietzsche critiques and the need for scapegoats among critics of welfare, see Schram, *After Welfare*, pp. 52–55.

48. Tomasky, *Left for Dead*, pp. 96–117.

49. See Theodore R. Marmor, Jerry L. Mashaw, and Philip L. Harvey, *America's Misunderstood Welfare State: Persistent Myths, Enduring Realities* (New York: Basic Books, 1990), pp. 237–241.

50. Teles, *Whose Welfare?* pp. 84–89.

51. For a defense of "bottom-up" social science, see Schram, *Words of Welfare*, pp. 38–55.

52. See Jacob Heilbrunn, "The Moynihan Enigma," *American Prospect* 33 (July–August 1997): 18–24.

53. For a good example of Daniel Moynihan's use of his political experiences to pass as research or social science, see the essays collected in Daniel P. Moynihan, *Coping: On the Practice of Government* (New York: Vintage, 1975).

54. See Christopher Lasch, *The Revolt of the Elites and the Betrayal of Democracy* (New York: W. W. Norton, 1995), pp. 176–192.

55. Matthew A. Crenson, *Building the Invisible Orphanage: A Prehistory of the American Welfare System* (Cambridge, MA: Harvard University Press, 1998), pp. 118–121.

56. For an analysis of how research stripped of its complexity and uncertainty can influence public policy deliberations in misleading ways, see Joseph Gusfield, *The Culture of Public Problems: Drinking-Driving and the Symbolic Order* (Chicago: University of Chicago Press, 1981), pp. 83–108; and Joel Best, *Threatened Children: Rhetoric and Concern about Child-Victims* (Chicago: University of Chicago Press, 1990), pp. 45–64.

57. Daniel Patrick Moynihan, *The Negro Family: The Case for National Action*, reprinted in Lee Rainwater and William L. Yancey, *The Moynihan Report and the Politics of Controversy* (Cambridge, MA: MIT Press, 1967), pp. 74–75.

58. For an examination of how the Moynihan Report was in some respects based on the ascendant liberal view among social scientists that racial discrimination had led to the development of pathology among low-income African Americans, see Alice O'Connor, *Poverty Knowledge: Social Science, Social Policy, and the Poor in Twentieth-Century U.S. History* (Princeton, NJ: Princeton University Press, 2001), pp. 203–210.

59. Katz, *The Undeserving Poor*, pp. 44–52. Also see Stephen Steinberg, *Turning Back: The Retreat from Racial Justice in American Thought and Policy* (Boston: Beacon Press, 1995), pp. 119–123.

60. For an analysis that highlights how the Moynihan Report overlooked declines in black male labor-force participation, see William Julius Wilson and Katherine M. Neckerman, "Poverty and Family Structure: The Widening Gap between Evidence and Public Policy Issues" (conference paper) (Madison: Institute for Research on Poverty, University of Wisconsin–Madison, 1984), p. 72. Wilson, however, would subsequently choose to emphasize that Moynihan was prophetic in predicting the rise of a "black underclass"; see William Julius Wilson, *The Truly Disadvantaged: The Inner City, the Underclass, and Public Policy* (Chicago: University of Chicago Press, 1987), pp. 20–21.

61. Stanley Aronowitz, "On Intellectuals," in Stanley Aronowitz, *The Politics of Identity: Class, Culture, Social Movements* (New York: Routledge, 1992), pp. 125–174. Also see Lowi, "The State in Political Science," pp. 1–7.

62. For misleading praise of the research in "The Moynihan Report," see William Julius Wilson, *The Truly Disadvantaged: The Inner City, the Underclass, and Public Policy* (Chicago: University of Chicago Press, 1987), pp. 63–92 and 173–174. Wilson had previously noted that Moynihan had focused on the decline in the correlation between unemployment rates and welfare receipt while overlooking that as more and more low-wage workers dropped out of the labor force altogether, they were not included in the unemployment rate, making declines in the unemployment rate misleading indicators of economic improvement. See Wilson and Neckerman, "Poverty and Family Structure," p. 33. This analysis was dropped when the essay was published in *The Truly Disadvantaged* (see pp. 63–92). In that later volume, Wilson instead gives more emphasis to Moynihan's critique of the black family as "prophetic" (p. 173). For a critique of Wilson's analysis, see Schram, *Words of Welfare*, pp. 107–114.

63. Daniel Moynihan himself has contrasted his role in trying to improve social welfare policy with that of Frances Fox Piven and Richard Cloward by invoking their "Crisis Strategy" to overload the welfare system as a straw man. He has even joined others in the breathtaking claim that the Crisis Strategy led to gridlock in Washington over what to do about welfare to the point that after thirty years it

eventually made the welfare reforms of 1996 necessary. According to Moynihan, the Crisis Strategy had created such gridlock that welfare policy had to be "taken out of Washington" if anything was to be done to get people off welfare and into jobs. Devolution was a necessity given the gridlock in Washington caused by the Crisis Strategy. Moynihan made comments to this effect at a workshop on federalism at the Woodrow Wilson International Center for Scholars, Washington, DC, May 11, 2001.

64. In particular, see Laurence E. Lynn, Jr., "Ending Welfare Reform as We Know It," *American Prospect* 15 (Fall 1993): 90.

65. See Schram, *After Welfare*, pp. 130–148.

66. See Schram, *Words of Welfare*, pp. 3–19.

67. Jason DeParle, "The Ellwoods: Mugged by Reality," *New York Times Magazine*, December 8, 1996, p. 64.

68. See Schram, *After Welfare*, pp. 32–34.

69. David T. Ellwood, "Welfare Reform As I Knew It: When Bad Things Happen to Good Policies," *American Prospect* 26 (May–June 1996): 28–29.

70. See Schram, *Words of Welfare*, pp. 3–7.

71. DeParle, "The Ellwoods," p. 64.

72. Frances Fox Piven, "Was Welfare Reform Worthwhile?" *American Prospect* 27 (July–August 1996): 14–15.

73. See Schram, *Words of Welfare*.

74. DeParle, "The Ellwoods," p. 64. Italics added.

75. Ibid.

76. Ibid.

77. DeParle, "What Welfare-to-Work Really Means," p. 53.

78. Ibid., p. 56.

79. For instance, see Richard A. Cloward and Richard M. Elman, "The Storefront on Stanton Street: Advocacy in the Ghetto," in *Community Action against Poverty: Readings from the Mobilization Experience*, George A. Brager and Francis P. Purcell, eds. (New Haven: College and University Press, 1967), pp. 253–279; Richard A. Cloward and Richard M. Elman, "Poverty, Injustice and the Welfare State: Part 1: An Ombudsman for the Poor," *Nation*, February 28, 1966, pp. 230–235; and Richard A. Cloward and Richard M. Elman, "Poverty, Injustice and the Welfare State: Part 2: How Rights Can Be Secured," *Nation*, March 7, 1966, pp. 264–268. The theme of arbitrary denial of basic civil rights to welfare recipients by welfare workers is revisited in Richard A. Cloward and Francis Fox Piven, "Workers and Welfare: The Poor against Themselves," *Nation*, November 25, 1968, pp. 558–562.

80. See Tomasky, *Left for Dead*, p. 106. Also see Sleeper, *Liberal Racism*, pp. 58–60; and Siegel, *The Future Once Happened Here*, pp. 46–61.

81. Critics such as Tomasky tend to read Piven and Cloward's 1966 Crisis Strategy article and the theoretical argument by Piven and Cloward in their subsequent award-winning 1971 book, *Regulating the Poor* in isolation from each other. As a

result, the Crisis Strategy is read as a pro-welfare plan that uncritically sees welfare as an unmitigated good, while *Regulating the Poor* is read as an anti-state critique that sees welfare as an unredeemable form of social control. Reading the Crisis Strategy and *Regulating the Poor* together enables one to see more clearly that Piven and Cloward never argued either one of these extreme positions. See Cloward and Piven, "A Strategy to End Poverty," pp. 510–517; and Piven and Cloward, *Regulating the Poor.*

82. See Wendy Brown, *States of Injury: Power and Freedom in Late Modernity* (Princeton, NJ: Princeton University Press, 1995), p. 14.

83. DeParle, "What Welfare-to-Work Really Means," p. 58.

84. Teles, *Whose Welfare?* p. 17.

85. See Kathryn Edin and Laura Lein, *Making Ends Meet: How Single Mothers Survive Welfare and Low-Wage Work* (New York: Russell Sage Foundation, 1997), pp. 234–235.

86. For a discussion of the "politics of survival" versus a "politics of social change," see Joe Soss, *Unwanted Claims: The Politics of Participation in the U.S. Welfare System* (Ann Arbor: University of Michigan Press, 2000), pp. 87–89.

87. Siegel, *The Future Once Happened Here*, pp. 52 and 61.

88. For the relevant passages where Piven and Cloward discuss how work has been important for centuries as a source of instilling commitment to the moral values of the existing order, see Piven and Cloward, *Regulating the Poor*, pp. 3–8. In these passages, Piven and Cloward suggest that the vagaries of the economy at times work to deny jobs for the poor and that in turn undermines their commitment to the social order and the established values. Nowhere in their article proposing the Crisis Strategy do they suggest that they hope that the effort to enable people to receive welfare will have the same result.

89. Piven and Cloward, "A Strategy to End Poverty," p. 517.

90. Ibid., p. 511.

91. Tomasky, *Left for Dead*, pp. 96–117.

92. For a prominent example of how the argument on behalf of supporting those who "play by the rules" can backfire into public policies that marginalize poor single mothers with children, see Ellwood, "Welfare Reform as I Knew It: When Bad Things Happen to Good Policies," pp. 22–29. Ellwood had originally gone to Washington to work with President Clinton on welfare reform on the basis of his arguments for the need to reform welfare so that it rewarded people who "played by the rules." See David Ellwood, *Poor Support: Poverty in the American Family* (New York: Basic Books, 1988), pp. 231–236. He eventually resigned in protest because his ideas were coopted as the basis for the draconian welfare reforms of 1996. For an explanation that Ellwood should have known better, see Piven, "Was Welfare Reform Worthwhile?" pp. 14–15.

93. See Joel Rogers, "Why We Need an Independent Politics, and How to Build It," *Dissent* 43 (Spring 1996): 91–94, for a discussion of progressive electoral

politics and the need to build coalitions and avoid being overly identified with out groups. For an attempt to contextualize these concerns and the suggestion that defending welfare has become an important issue for standing up for the dispossessed in our society, see Frances Fox Piven, "Welfare and the Transformation of Electoral Politics," *Dissent* 43 (Fall 1996): 61–67.

94. In particular, see Ruy Teixeira and Joel Rogers, *America's Forgotten Majority: Why the White Working Class Still Matters* (New York: Basic Books, 2000). Also see Joel Rogers, "The Man From Elroy (Nomination of Tommy G. Thompson as Health and Human Services Secretary)," *Nation*, January 29, 2001, p. 15. For what remains still one of the very best analyses of the dilemmas of getting democratic majorities in a capitalist society to support inclusive social policies, see Joshua Cohen and Joel Rogers, *On Democracy: Toward a Transformation of American Society* (New York: Penguin Books, 1983).

95. Thomas Byrne Edsall with Mary D. Edsall, *Chain Reaction: The Impact of Race, Rights, and Taxes on American Politics* (New York: W. W. Norton, 1991), pp. 275–277.

96. Siegel, *The Future Once Happened Here*, p. 50.

97. Ibid., pp. 52–61.

98. Siegel, *The Future Once Happened Here*, pp. 7–13.

99. See Elliot Currie, "The Liberals Done It," *Dissent* 45 (Winter 1998): 114–117.

100. See Sean Wilentz, "The Rise and Fall of Racialized Liberalism," *American Prospect* (September–October 1998): 82–84.

101. Teles, *Whose Welfare?* pp. 12–17.

102. See ibid., pp. 34–40; and Siegel, *The Future Once Happened Here*, pp. 46–54. Actually, the most aggressive purveyor of this myth is not Fred Siegel or Steven Teles but Lawrence Mead. See Lawrence M. Mead, *The New Politics of Poverty: The Nonworking Poor in America* (New York: Basic Books, 1992), pp. 16–19.

103. See Schram, *After Welfare*, pp. 122–129. On the risks of appeals to middle-class values, see chapter 1.

104. Tomasky, *Left for Dead*, pp. 106–107.

105. Teles, *Whose Welfare?* p. 17.

106. See Frances Fox Piven and Richard A. Cloward, "Dissensus Politics: A Strategy for Winning Economic Rights," *New Republic*, April 20, 1968, pp. 20–24.

107. On the disparate racial impacts of welfare reform, see Jason DeParle, "Shrinking Welfare Rolls Leave Record High Share of Minorities," *New York Times*, July 27, 1998, p. A1. On the persistence of poverty among single mothers who leave welfare for work, see Jason DeParle, "Bold Effort Leaves Much Unchanged for the Poor," *New York Times*, December 30, 1999, p. A1.

108. Lisa Duggan, "Queering the State," *Social Text* 39 (Summer 1994): 1–14.

109. See Joshua Gamson, "Silence, Death, and the Invisible Enemy: AIDS Activism and Social Movement 'Newness'," *Social Problems* 36 (October 1989): 351–367.

110. For a discussion of the ways the symbolic and material politics are interrelated, see Schram, *After Welfare*, pp. 1–4.

111. See David J. Garrow, *Protest at Selma: Martin Luther King, Jr., and the Voting Rights Act of 1965* (New Haven: Yale University Press, 1978). Garrow argues that by the time of the protests at Selma in 1965, Martin Luther King, Jr., had moved away from a strategy of getting Christian southerners to see the sinfulness of their discriminatory practices and toward a strategy that was intentionally designed to highlight for a wider national audience outside the South just how unjust Jim Crowism really was. In an article they wrote shortly after King's death, Frances Fox Piven and Richard Cloward noted that King's strategy since Selma was more one of dissensus that created difficulty for a majority coalition than one of consensus that tried to fit into that majority. King also moved toward emphasizing poverty over civil rights as the critical issue, and this further heightened the significance of the dissensus strategy because the black urban poor, in particular, were an important part of the liberal Democratic coalition. More was to be gained by broadening the conflict, resisting assimilation into majorities, and focusing on the fundamental issues of economic injustice. See Piven and Cloward, "Dissensus Politics," pp. 20–21.

112. E. E. Schattschneider, *The Semi-Sovereign People: A Realist's View of Democracy in America* (New York: Holt, Rinehart, and Winston, 1960), p. 10.

113. See Gamson, "Silence, Death, and the Invisible Enemy," pp. 351–367.

114. William Julius Wilson, "Bridging the Racial Divide: A National Multiracial Coalition Is the Best Hope for Progressive Politics," *Nation*, December 20, 1999, pp. 20–21.

115. Brown, *States of Injury*, p. 14.

116. Barbara Cruikshank, *The Will to Empower: Democratic Citizens and Other Subjects* (Ithaca, NY: Cornell University Press, 1999), pp. 61–62.

117. See Nigel Parton, "Some Thoughts on the Relationship between Theory and Practice in and for Social Work," *British Journal of Social Work* 30 (August 2000): 449–463.

118. Cruikshank, *The Will to Empower*, pp. 86, 119–121.

119. Ibid., p. 86.

120. Michel Foucault, *The History of Sexuality*, vol. 1, *An Introduction* (New York: Vintage Books, 1980) pp. 10–12.

121. Cruikshank, *The Will to Empower*, pp. 81–82.

122. Nikolas Rose, *Powers of Freedom: Reframing Political Thought* (Cambridge, UK: Cambridge University Press, 1999), pp. 18–24.

123. Gayatri Chakravorty Spivak, *The Post-Colonial Critic: Interviews, Strategies, Dialogues* (London: Routledge, 1990); idem, *In Other Worlds: Essays in Cultural Politics* (New York: Routledge, 1988); and idem, "Can the Subaltern Speak?"

Colonial Discourse and Post-Colonial Theory, Patrick Williams and Laura Williams, eds. (New York: Columbia University Press, 1994), pp. 66–111.

124. Loti Volpp, "(Mis)Identifying Culture: Asian Women and the 'Cultural Defense,'" *Harvard Women's Law Journal* 17 (Spring 1994): 57, 95–96.

125. See Deborah Gray White, *Too Heavy a Load: Black Women in Defense of Themselves, 1894–1994* (New York: W. W. Norton, 1999), p. 236.

126. See Anne M. Valk, "'Mother Power': The Movement for Welfare Rights in Washington, D.C., 1966–1972," *Journal of Women's History* 11 (Winter 2000): 34–35.

127. Piven and Cloward, *Poor People's Movements.*

128. On the strategic uses of "the homeless," see Schram, *Words of Welfare,* chapter 2; Mark J. Stern, "The Emergence of the Homeless as a Public Problem," *Social Service Review* 58 (June 1984): 291–301; and Rob Rosenthal, "Dilemmas of Local Antihomelessness Movements," *Homelessness in America,* Jim Baumohl, ed. (Phoenix: Oryx Press, 1996), pp. 201–221.

129. See Sakari Hänninen, "Is Finland Going beyond the Age of Entitlement?" *Displacement of Social Policies,* Sakari Hänninen, ed. (Jyväskylä, Finland: SoPhi, 1998), pp. 244–247.

130. Nikolas Rose, "The Crisis of the 'Social': Beyond the Social Question," *Displacement of Social Policies,* Sakari Hänninen, ed. (Jyväskylä, Finland: SoPhi, 1998), pp. 58–68.

131. Piven and Cloward, "Dissensus Politics," p. 24.

132. Richard C. Fording, "The Political Response to Black Insurgency: A Critical Test of Competing Theories of the State," *American Political Science Review* 95 (March 2001): 115.

133. Piven and Cloward, *Regulating the Poor,* p. xv.

134. For a reaffirmation of their commitment for combining theory and practice in the name of enabling people to reduce oppression by responding to their concrete, historically specific circumstances, see Frances Fox Piven and Richard A. Cloward, "A Reply to Ellen Meiksins Wood," *Monthly Review* 49 (January 1998): 44–46.

135. Harold I. Wilensky and Charles N. Lebeaux, *Industrial Society and Social Welfare* (New York: Free Press, 1965), p. v.

136. Walter I. Trattner, *From Poor Law to Welfare State: A History of Social Welfare in America* (New York: Free Press, 1974).

137. In reaction to the growing attention given by scholars to *Regulating the Poor,* Walter Trattner arranged in 1980 a conference panel designed to rebut *Regulating's* thesis that welfare operated to serve political and economic purposes. The subsequently published collection of essays tried to use as refutation evidence that suggested that welfare increases, especially in the nineteenth century, often occurred without increases in political instability. Yet, many of the examples provided were actually instances of increases in more coercive forms of assistance, such as

rising numbers of residents in the local poorhouse. A particularly egregious example in this respect was the essay by John Alexander, "The Functions of Public Welfare in Late-Eighteenth Century Philadelphia: Regulating the Poor?" in *Social Welfare or Social Control: Some Historical Reflections on "Regulating the Poor,"* Walter I. Trattner, ed. (Knoxville: University of Tennessee Press, 1983), pp. 15–34.

138. For a particularly noteworthy example, see Eugene Durman, "Have the Poor Been Regulated? Toward a Multivariate Understanding of Welfare Growth," *Social Service Review* 47 (September 1973): 339–359. For good measure in prefacing his "scientific" analysis, Durman anachronistically refers to Piven and Cloward as "Machiavellians."

139. For a compelling analysis that highlights the cyclical modulation of state policies between social welfare and social control, see Fording, "The Political Response to Black Insurgency: A Critical Test of Competing Theories of the State," p. 115. Fording demonstrates that when political stability is re-created, welfare liberalization is replaced by more coercive use of criminal justice policies.

140. See Schram, *After Welfare*, pp. 70–78.

141. Shep Melnick, "The Unexpected Resilience of Means-Tested Programs" (paper presented at the American Political Science Association annual meeting, September 3–6, 1998, Boston, Massachusetts); and David Dodenhoff, "Is Welfare Really about Social Control," *Social Service Review* 72 (September 1998): 310–337.

142. Frances Fox Piven, "The Rich, the Poor, and American Politics," 1999 O'Leary Memorial Lecture, Ohio State University, Columbus, October 27, 1999.

143. See Christopher Howard, *The Hidden Welfare State: Tax Expenditures and Social Policy in the United States* (Princeton, NJ: Princeton University Press, 1997).

144. Deborah Stone, *The Disabled State* (Philadelphia: Temple University Press, 1984), pp. 169–170.

145. Ibid., pp. 15–18.

146. Ibid., pp. 18–20.

147. Ibid., pp. 172–179.

148. Ibid., pp. 186–192.

149. Kathryn Edin, "A Few Good Men: Why Poor Women Don't Marry or Remarry," *American Prospect* 11 (January 3, 2000) (http://www.prospect.org/archives/V11-4/edin.html).

150. Crenson, *Building the Invisible Orphanage.*

151. Deborah Stone has emphasized that "innocence" is critical as a legitimating basis for being exempted from the work system is critical to qualifying for benefits from the need system. See Stone, *The Disabled State*, pp. 172–179.

152. Crenson, *Building the Invisible Orphanage*, p. 5.

153. See Theda Skocpol, *Protecting Soldiers and Mothers: The Political Origins of Social Policy in the United States* (Cambridge, MA: Belknap Press of Harvard University Press, 1992); Michael B. Katz, *The Price of Citizenship: Redefining the American*

Welfare State (New York: Metropolitan Books, 2001); Michael B. Katz and Lorrin R. Thomas, "The Invention of 'Welfare' in America," *Journal of Policy History* 10 (1998): 399–418.

154. Piven and Cloward, *Poor People's Movements*, pp. 3–5.

155. Crenson, *Building the Invisible Orphanage*, p. 39. It is important to note that while Crenson easily assimilates social control theories of social welfare to the Foucaldian disciplinary perspective, others have stressed their difference. Barbara Cruikshank, in particular, has noted the way the social control orientation is more structuralist and emphasizes that control is imposed from the outside, say as in punitive social welfare practices. A disciplinary orientation is more poststructuralist and emphasizes that discipline is more an artifact of self-imposition from within, as, for example, in the enactment of desire for a more self-respecting self. Cruikshank, in fact, contrasts Piven and Cloward and Foucault in just this fashion. See Cruikshank, *The Will to Empower*, pp. 30–44.

156. Theda Skocpol, "Why I Am a Historical Social Scientist," *Extensions: A Journal of the Carl Albert Congressional Research and Studies Center* (Fall 1999): 16–19.

157. See Theda Skocpol, "A Partnership with American Families," in *The New Majority: Toward a Popular Progressive Politics,* Stanley B. Greenberg and Theda Skocpol, eds. (New Haven: Yale University Press, 1997), pp. 104–132.

158. Frances Fox Piven and Richard A. Cloward, "Eras of Power," *Monthly Review* 49 (January 1998): 23.

159. For a call to emphasize the historical institutionalism of Theda Skocpol, albeit with revisions, see Ira Katznelson, "The Doleful Dance of Politics and Policy: Can Historical Institutionalism Make a Difference?" *American Political Science Review* 92 (March 1998): 191–197.

160. See Schram, *After Welfare*, pp. 177–182.

161. Frances Fox Piven and Richard A. Cloward, "Disruption and Organization: A Reply to Gamson and Schmeidler," in *The Breaking of the American Social Compact* (New York: New Press, 1997), p. 343.

162. Schram, *After Welfare*, pp. 178–182.

163. For a thoughtful reflection on conventional incrementalism, see Charles E. Lindblom, *Inquiry and Change: The Troubled Attempt to Understand and Shape Society* (New Haven: Yale University Press, 1990), pp. 131–132.

164. "Radical incrementalism" has affinities with Andre Gorz's notion of "nonreformist reform." See Andre Gorz, *A Strategy for Labor: A Radical Proposal* (Boston: Beacon Press, 1964), pp. 6–8.

165. See Lindblom, *Inquiry and Change*, pp. 131–132.

166. See Theda Skocpol, "The Choice," *The American Prospect* 10 (Summer 1992), as quoted in Frances Fox Piven and Richard A. Cloward, "We Should Have Made a Plan!" *Politics & Society* 25 (December 1997): 526.

167. Piven and Cloward, "We Should Have Made a Plan!" pp. 527–528.

168. See Schram, *Words of Welfare*, chapter 1.

169. See "Report and Recommendations on the Case of Prof. Richard A. Cloward and Brandeis University" (Washington, DC: Committee on Freedom of Research and Teaching of the Council of the American Sociological Association, August 30, 1980).

170. See Piven and Cloward, *Poor People's Movements.*

171. See Piven and Cloward, *Why Americans Still Don't Vote.*

172. According to Frances Fox Piven, Stanley Aronowitz suggested an emphasis on electoral politics was in contradiction to an emphasis on protest politics. Personal interview, February 18, 2001. Wendy Brown criticized Piven and Cloward for switching from critics to defenders of welfare in *States of Injury*, p. 14.

173. Thanks to Joe Soss for clarifying this point.

174. Piven and Cloward, "Dissensus Politics," pp. 20–24.

175. For an analysis based on this critical insight, see Fording, "The Conditional Effect of Violence as a Political Tactic," pp. 1–29.

176. For an examination on how in every era structural conditions create capacities as well as constraints for mobilization from below, see Piven and Cloward, "Eras of Power," p. 23.

177. Frances Fox Piven and Richard A. Cloward, "Power Repertoires and Globalization," *Politics & Society* 28 (September 2000): 413.

178. See Piven and Cloward, "We Should Have Made a Plan!" p. 532.

179. On the importance of utopian thinking in mobilizing political action and creating the basis for a dynamic and iterative "politics of transfiguration," see Paul Gilroy, *Black Atlantic: Modernity and Double Consciousness* (Cambridge, MA: Harvard University Press, 1993), pp. 38–39.

180. Richard Cloward as quoted in DeParle, "What Welfare-to-Work Really Means," p. 59.

Notes to Chapter 4

1. For a discussion of the differences between "top-down" vs. "bottom-up" research, see Sanford F. Schram, *Words of Welfare: The Poverty of Social Science and the Social Science of Poverty* (Minneapolis: University of Minnesota Press, 1995), pp. 38–76. For a related discussion, see Nigel Parton, "Some Thoughts on the Relationship between Theory and Practice in and for Social Work," *British Journal of Social Work* 30 (August 2000): 449–463.

2. Alice O'Connor, *Poverty Knowledge: Social Science, Social Policy, and the Poor in Twentieth-Century U.S. History* (Princeton, NJ: Princeton University Press, 2001).

3. O'Connor's critique of poverty knowledge leaves open the possibility that her successor science will still be too conventional. See ibid.

4. Bent Flyvbjerg, *Making Social Science Matter: Why Social Inquiry Fails and How It Can Succeed Again* (Cambridge, UK: Cambridge University Press, 2001), p. 143.

5. See Barbara Cruikshank, *The Will to Empower: Democratic Citizens and Other Subjects* (Ithaca, NY: Cornell University Press, 1999), p. 2.

6. See chapter 3.

7. See O'Connor, *Poverty Knowledge*, pp. 127–129.

8. See John H. Ehrenreich, *The Altruistic Imagination: A History of Social Work and Social Policy in the United States* (Ithaca, NY: Cornell University Press, 1985), pp. 43–77.

9. In particular, see Richard A. Cloward, "The Decline of Education for Professional Practice," *Social Work* 43 (November 1998): 584–586.

10. Allen Rubin, "Reply to Cloward," *Social Work* 44 (July 1999): 394–396.

11. Allen Rubin, "Presidential Editorial: A View from the Summit," *Research on Social Work Practice* 9 (March 1999): 142–147, and idem, "Presidential Editorial: Do National Association of Social Workers Leaders Value Research? A Summit Follow-Up," *Research on Social Work Practice* 9 (May 1999): 277–282.

12. Cloward, "The Decline of Education for Professional Practice," pp. 584–585.

13. Rubin, "Reply to Cloward," p. 396.

14. For an interesting attempt to suggest how clinical social work can be related to the promotion of social justice, see Jerome C. Wakefield, "Psychotherapy, Distributive Justice, and Social Work: Part 1: Distributive Justice as a Conceptual Framework for Social Work," *Social Service Review* 62 (June 1988): 187–210, and idem, "Psychotherapy, Distributive Justice, and Social Work: Part 2: Psychotherapy and the Pursuit of Justice," *Social Service Review* 62 (September 1988): 353–382.

15. See Schram, *Words of Welfare*, p. 7.

16. See Harry Specht and Mark E. Courtney, *Unfaithful Angels: How Social Work Has Abandoned Its Mission* (New York: Free Press, 1994).

17. Ibid.

18. See Robert Kuttner, *Everything Is for Sale: The Virtues and Limits of Markets* (New York: Knopf, 1997), pp. 110–158.

19. Marsha Gold and Jessica Mittler, "Medicaid's Complex Goals: Challenges for Managed Care and Behavioral Health," *Health Care Financing Review* 22 (Winter 2000): 85–101.

20. See Specht and Courtney, *Unfaithful Angels*; and Karen S. Haynes, "The One Hundred-Year Debate: Social Reform versus Individual Treatment," *Social Work* 43 (November 1998): 501–509.

21. Peter Passell, "Like a New Drug, Social Programs Are Put to the Test," *New York Times*, March 3, 1993, p. C1.

22. On the need to appreciate how social science is different from the natural sciences, see Flyvbjerg, *Making Social Science Matter*, pp. 9–49.

23. Passell, "Like a New Drug, Social Programs Are Put to the Test," p. C3.

24. For a journal that actively recruits articles on "best practices" in social work and awards prizes for them, see "Best Practices in Social Work," *Social Services Abstracts*, Social Services InforNet (http://www.socservices.com/html/best.html).

25. "Evidence-based practice" is more centered on generalizable empirical studies than is "best practices." For thoughtful critiques of the "evidence-based practice" movement, see Stanley L. Witkin and W. David Harrison, "Whose Evidence and for What Purpose?" *Social Work* 46 (October 2001): 293–296; and Stephen A. Webb, "Some Considerations on the Validity of Evidence-based Practice in Social Work," *British Journal of Social Work* 31 (February 2001): 57–79.

26. The political dimension of the idea of "best practices" is summed up nicely in an analysis of how the idea can create serious impairments to effective representation of the indigent in the legal system. See Stephen Mortenson, "Best Practices for Whom?" *New Jersey Law Journal* 162 (October 30, 2000): 31. As the title of Mortenson's article indicates, the politics of "best practices" lies in the fact that what is a best practice is in the eye of the beholder and depends on which interests and what values are being served. Best practices are in no way strictly factual and objective realities.

27. For a good argument on the ways the ambiguities inherent in social work practice necessitate taking context into account, see Parton, "Some Thoughts on the Relationship between Theory and Practice in and for Social Work," pp. 457–461.

28. See Suniya S. Luthar, Dante Cicchetti, and Bronwyn Becker, "The Construct of Resilience: A Critical Evaluation and Guidelines for Future Work," *Child Development* 71 (May–June 2000): 543–562.

29. "One best way" was the slogan of Frederick Taylor's Scientific Management movement that sought to reduce all kinds of work to repetitive preplanned tasks in order to achieve optimum levels of efficiency. See Judith A. Merkle, *Management and Ideology: The Legacy of the International Scientific Management Movement* (Berkeley: University of California Press, 1980).

30. The "best-practice" movement is sweeping social work in ways that are deeply depoliticizing. The movement has even reached Congress, where proposed legislation would create a national social work research center that would research best practices and disseminate them throughout the profession. See John V. O'Neill, "Research Bill Gains GOP Support in House," *NASW News*, June 2000 (http://www.naswpress.org/publications/news/0600/research.htm). Similar developments are occurring in the United Kingdom regarding its new, national "Scie" "Social Care Institute for Excellence) center; see Kendra Ingram, "Society: Social Care: Sky-High Hopes: Kendra Inman on a New Institute for Excellence That Aims to Make Research Relevant to Those Who Put It into Practice," *The Guardian*, March 21, 2001, p. 103.

31. J. Chip Drotos, "A History of 'Best Practices,'" *Behavioral Health Management* 19 (May 1999): 40.

32. There are even attempts to catalog forms of "practice wisdom" and then to test them empirically to see which ones should be disseminated as best practices. This approach neglects to consider the problems of misappropriation that will come with decontextualizing the types of "local knowledge" represented by such practices. For an example, see Anat Zeira and Aaron Rosen, "Unraveling 'Tacit Knowledge': What Social Workers Do and Why They Do It," *Social Service Review* 74 (March 2000): 103–123. For a critical alternative perspective that effectively questions the wisdom of emphasizing "evidence-based practice" as the cornerstone of professional practice, see Parton, "Some Thoughts on the Relationship between Theory and Practice in and for Social Work," pp. 455–460.

33. Carol R. Swenson, "Clinical Social Work's Contribution to a Social Justice Perspective," *Social Work* 43 (November 1998): 530, 534.

34. What I am calling the "Strong Program" should not be confused with the "Strong Programme" as articulated by David Bloor, *Knowledge and Social Imagery* (Chicago: University of Chicago Press, 1991), which is very different.

35. Cloward, "The Decline of Education for Professional Practice," pp. 584–586.

36. See Allen Rubin and Earl Babbie, *Research Methods for Social Work*, 4th ed. (Belmont, CA: Wadsworth, 2001).

37. See Wilfrid Sellars, "Empiricism and the Philosophy of Mind," in *Minnesota Studies in the Philosophy of Science, Volume I: The Foundations of Science and the Concepts of Psychology and Psychoanalysis,* Herbert Feigl and Michael Scriven, eds. (Minneapolis: University of Minnesota Press, 1956), pp. 253–329; and Wilfrid Sellars, *Science, Perception and Reality* (London: Routledge & Kegan Paul, 1963).

38. See Jeffrey Pressman, "Preconditions of Mayoral Leadership," *American Political Science Review* 66 (June 1972): 515. Jeffrey Pressman and Aaron Wildavsky, *Implementation: How Great Expectations in Washington Are Dashed in Oakland; Or, Why It Is Amazing That Federal Programs Work at All: This Being a Saga of the Economic Development Administration as Told by Two Sympathetic Observers Who Seek to Build Morals on a Foundation of Ruined Hopes* (Berkeley: University of California Press, 1973), pp. xi–xviii.

39. Michael B. Katz, *Improving Poor People: The Welfare State, the "Underclass," and Urban Schools as History* (Princeton: Princeton University Press, 1995).

40. See Sanford F. Schram, "In the Clinic: The Medicalization of Welfare," in *After Welfare: The Culture of Postindustrial Social Policy* (New York: New York University Press, 2000), chapter 3.

41. As of September 2001, there were 5,333,887 recipients receiving Temporary Assistance for Needy Families. See U.S. Department of Health and Human Services, Administration on Children and Families: http://www.acf.dhhs.gov/news/stats/welfare.htm.

42. See Ruth A. Brandwein, ed., *Battered Women, Children, and Welfare Reform: The Ties That Bind* (Thousand Oaks, CA: Sage Publications, 1999). Linda Gordon has emphasized that women who escaped abusive relationships and used welfare to do it were best seen as "heroes of their own lives." See Linda Gordon, *Heroes of Their Own Lives: The Politics and History of Family Violence: Boston, 1880–1960* (New York: Viking, 1988).

43. See Schram, *After Welfare*, chapter 3.

44. See Margaret Somers and Fred Block, "From Poverty to Perversity: Markets, States, and Institutions over Two Centuries of Welfare Debate," unpublished manuscript, August 2001.

45. Albert O. Hirschman, *The Rhetoric of Reaction: Perversity, Futility, Jeopardy* (Cambridge, MA: Belknap Press of Harvard University Press, 1991), pp. 27–42.

46. See Anu Rangarajan and Tim Novak, *The Struggle to Sustain Employment: The Effectiveness of the Postemployment Services Demonstration* (Princeton, NJ: Mathematica Policy Research, Inc., April 1999) (http://www.mathematica-mpr.com/strug-rpt.pdf); and Demetra Smith Nightingale, *Program Structure and Service Delivery in Eleven Welfare-to-Work Grant Programs* (Princeton, NJ: Mathematica Policy Research, Inc., January 2001) (http://www.mathematica.org/PDFs/wtwstructure.pdf).

47. See O'Connor, *Poverty Knowledge*, pp. 251–257.

48. Joel Fischer, "Has Mighty Casework Struck Out?" *Social Work* 18 (July 1973): 107–110, and "Is Casework Effective? A Review," *Social Work* 18 (January 1973): 5–20.

49. The issue of single-subject designs and the related issues concerning combining research and practitioner roles have expanded greatly over time as clinical social workers have sought ways to document their effectiveness. For just one poignant example, see Jerome C. Wakefield and Stuart A. Kirk, "What the Practitioner Knows versus What the Client is Told: Neglected Dilemmas of Informed Consent in an Account of Single-System Experimental Designs," *Journal of Social Work Education* 33 (Spring–Summer 1997): 275–291.

50. William M. Epstein, *Welfare in America: How Social Science Fails the Poor* (Madison: University of Wisconsin Press, 1997).

51. For an explanation of epistemic privilege, see John G. Gunnell, *The Orders of Discourse: Philosophy, Social Science, and Politics* (Lanham, MD: Rowman and Littlefield, 1998), p. 120; and see Victoria Davion, "Listening to Women's Voices: Rape, Epistemic Privilege, and Objectivity," in *Daring to Be Good: Essays in Feminist Ethico-Politics*, Bat-Ami Bar On and Ann Ferguson, eds. (New York: Routledge, 1998), pp. 100–113.

52. Rubin and Babbie, *Research Methods in Social Work*, pp. 327–354.

53. See Sally Kaplan and Ruth Alsup, "Participatory Action Research: A Creative Response to AIDS Prevention in Diverse Communities," *Convergence* 28 (1995): 38–55; Sloane Dugan, "Reflections on Helping II: A Perspective on Participatory

Action Research," *International Journal of Public Administration* 16 (1993): 175–188; Bernita Quoss, Margaret Cooney, and Terri Longhurst, "Academics and Advocates: Using Participatory Action Research to Influence Welfare Policy," *Journal of Consumer Affairs* 34 (Summer 2000): 47; Max Elden and Morten Levin, "Cogenerative Inquiry: Bringing Participation into Action Research," in *Participatory Action Research*, William F. Whyte, ed. (Newbury Park, CA: Sage Publications, 1991); and Karen Healy, "Participatory Action Research and Social Work: A Critical Appraisal," *International Social Work* 44 (January 2001): 93–105.

54. Rubin, "Presidential Editorial: Do National Association of Social Workers Leaders Value Research? A Summit Follow-Up," pp. 279–281.

55. Ibid., p. 280.

56. Flyvbjerg, *Making Social Science Matter*, pp. 166–168.

57. Ibid., p. 143.

Notes to Chapter 5

1. A more methodologically diverse, politically engaged welfare policy research community would be a major change from the current situation, dominated as it is by the government, foundations, think tanks, university research institutes, and other funding sources that push for quantitative studies to better manage the deviant behavior of those living in poverty. For a historical analysis on the welfare policy research that emphasizes how its depoliticized character has contributed to stifling public consideration of the structural roots of poverty, see Alice O'Connor, *Poverty Knowledge: Social Science, Social Policy, and the Poor in Twentieth-Century U.S. History* (Princeton, NJ: Princeton University Press, 2001).

2. I first raised these issues in *Words of Welfare: The Poverty of Social Science and the Social Science of Poverty* (Minneapolis: University of Minnesota Press, 1995).

3. See Nikolas Rose, *Powers of Freedom: Reframing Political Thought* (Cambridge, UK: Cambridge University Press, 1999), pp. 197–232.

4. Ibid.

5. See O'Connor, *Poverty Knowledge*.

6. Joe Soss, Sanford F. Schram, Thomas P. Vartanian, and Erin O'Brien, "Setting the Terms of Relief: Explaining State Policy Choices in the Devolution Revolution," *American Journal of Political Science* 45 (April 2001): 378–395.

7. Audre Lorde, "The Master's Tools Will Never Dismantle the Master's House," in *Feminism and 'Race'*, Kum-Kum Bhavnani, ed. (New York: Oxford University Press, 2001), pp. 89–92.

8. See Rose, *Powers of Freedom*, pp. 215–232.

9. For an excellent examination of the politically constructed character of social statistics as well as their importance in public policy debates, see Deborah Stone, *Policy Paradox: The Art of Political Decision Making* (New York: W. W. Norton, 1997).

10. See various chapters in Sanford F. Schram, Joe Soss, and Richard Fording, eds., *Race and the Politics of Welfare Reform* (Ann Arbor: University of Michigan Press, forthcoming).

11. Dante Chinni, "States Waver on Welfare Reform's Next Step," *Christian Science Monitor*, March 19, 2001, p. 2.

12. See Richard P. Nathan, *The Newest New Federalism for Welfare: Where Are We Now and Where Are We Headed?* (Albany, NY: Rockefeller Institute, State University of New York, October 30, 1997); John D. Donahue, *Disunited States: What's at Stake as Washington Fades and the States Take the Lead* (New York: Basic Books, 1997), p. 13; and Sanford F. Schram, "Introduction," in *Welfare Reform: A Race to the Bottom?* Sanford F. Schram and Samuel H. Beer, eds. (Baltimore: Johns Hopkins University Press, 1999), pp. 1–12.

13. See Larry L. Orr, "Income Transfers as a Public Good: An Application to A.F.D.C.," *American Economic Review* 66 (June 1976): 359–371; and Gerald C. Wright, Jr., "Racism and Welfare Policy in America," *Social Science Quarterly* 57 (March 1976): 718–730.

14. Wright, "Racism and Welfare Policy in America," pp. 718–730.

15. Christopher Howard, "The American Welfare State, or States?" *Political Research Quarterly* 52 (June 1999): 421–442.

16. Martin Gilens, *Why Americans Hate Welfare: Race, Media, and the Politics of Antipoverty Policy* (Chicago: University of Chicago Press, 1999).

17. Jill Quadagno, *The Color of Welfare: How Racism Undermined the War on Poverty* (New York: Oxford University Press, 1994).

18. Gilens, *Why Americans Hate Welfare*, p. 71.

19. See *Explaining the Decline in Welfare Receipt, 1993–1996* (Washington, DC: Council of Economic Advisors, May 9, 1997).

20. See James P. Ziliak, David N. Figlio, Elizabeth E. Davis, and Laura S. Connolly, "Accounting for the Decline in AFDC Caseloads: Welfare Reform or Economic Growth?" (paper presented at the Association for Policy Analysis and Management Annual Research Conference, Washington, DC, November 1997). This paper found that

> the decline in per capita AFDC caseloads is attributable largely to the economic growth of states and not to waivers from federal welfare policies. In the 26 states experiencing at least a 20 percent decline in per capita AFDC caseloads from 1993–1996, we attribute 78 percent of the decline to business-cycle factors and 6 percent to welfare waivers.

21. Robert E. Rector and Sarah E. Youssef, *The Determinants of Welfare Caseload Decline*, Report No. 99-04 (Washington, DC: Heritage Center for Data Analysis, Heritage Foundation, 1999).

22. U.S. Department of Health and Human Services, Administration on Children and Families: http://www.acf.dhhs.gov/news/stats/recipientsL.htm.

23. Elizabeth Lower-Basch, "*Leavers" and Diversion Studies: Preliminary Analysis of Racial Differences in Caseload Trends and Leaver Outcomes* (Washington, DC: U.S. Department of Health and Human Services, December 2000) (http://www.aspe.hhs.gov/hsp/leavers99/race.htm).

24. Ibid.

25. The sources for all data presented in this chapter are detailed in Soss et al., "Setting the Terms of Relief," 392 and in the Appendix.

26. Andrew Cherlin, Linda Burton, Judith Francis, Jane Henrici, Laura Lein, James Quane, and Karen Bogen, *Sanctions and Case Closings for Noncompliance: Who Is Affected and Why*. Policy Brief from Welfare, Children and Families: A Three-City Study (Baltimore: Johns Hopkins University, 2001), p. 5 (http://www.jhu.edu/~welfare/18058_Welfare_Policy_Brief.pdf).

27. See David T. Ellwood, "The Impact of the Earned Income Tax Credit and Social Policy Reforms on Work, Marriage, and Living Arrangements," *National Tax Journal* 53 (December 2000): 1063–1105.

28. Lower-Basch, "*Leavers" and Diversion Studies*. Lower-Basch writes:

> Exits from TANF may be an unalloyed good, when they are due to increases in income which allow a family to achieve self-sufficiency, or may be a matter of concern, particularly when they are due to sanctions for non-compliance and when the family does not appear to have a replacement source of income. One disturbing finding is that those studies which examined reason for exit found that minorities were generally more likely than Whites to have their cases closed due to sanctions rather than earnings (according to administrative data). In Arizona, African-Americans were 13 percent of cases closed due to sanctions, and just 9 percent of cases closed due to earnings. Hispanics were 39 percent of cases closed due to sanctions and 33 percent of cases closed due to earnings. Interestingly Native Americans were just 8 percent of cases closed due to sanctions and 15 percent of cases closed due to earnings. The report notes that Native Americans are more likely to live in extremely high unemployment areas (greater than 50 percent unemployment) and therefore to be exempted from the job search requirements, which sometimes lead to sanctions. Similarly in Illinois, cases closed due to non-cooperation are more likely to be minority (61.6 percent African-American, 10.6 percent Hispanic, and 26.8 percent Non-Hispanic White) compared to cases closed due to increased income (52.4 percent African-American, 8.7 percent Hispanic, and 28.3 percent Non-Hispanic White).

29. Cherlin et al., *Sanctions and Case Closings for Noncompliance*, p. 5.

30. See Schram, Soss, and Fording, eds., *Race and the Politics of Welfare Reform*, "Introduction."

31. For documentation on the data, see Soss et al., "Setting the Terms of Relief," p. 392.

32. For data sources, see Appendix.

33. These predicted probabilities were calculated using the method detailed in Gary King, Michael Tomz, and Jason Wittenberg, "Making the Most of Statistical Analyses: Improving Interpretation and Presentation," *American Journal of Political Science* 44 (April 2000): 347–361.

34. The change in probability associated with each significant variable is determined by holding all other variables at their means.

35. Soss et al., "Setting the Terms of Relief," p. 390.

Notes to Chapter 6

1. For a thoughtful attempt to counter the idea that all welfare recipients are black, see Deborah R. Connolly, *Homeless Mothers: Face to Face with Women and Poverty* (Minneapolis: University of Minnesota Press, 2000).

2. Linda Williams, *Playing the Race Card: Melodramas of Black and White from Uncle Tom to O. J. Simpson* (Princeton, NJ: Princeton University Press, 2001), uses Leslie Fiedler's distinction to suggest that in the United States historically race relations have unavoidably been dramatized in melodramatic terms of either "Tom" or "Anti-Tom" (as in "Uncle Tom"). Williams suggests that the entirety of race relations is always at risk of being plotted in melodramatic narratives that do real injustice to its subject matter. She suggests that Americans to a great degree cannot talk about race without melodrama. Americans are continually narrating race in melodramatic ways if for no other reason than because race itself is a melodramatic construction of questionable politics. This makes the choice in either case fraught with political pitfalls that must be negotiated.

3. For an analysis that underscores how preexisting prejudice and mass media depictions interact to racialize welfare attitudes in the mass public, see Tali Mendelberg, "Executing Hortons: Racial Crime in the 1998 Presidential Campaign," *Public Opinion Quarterly* 61 (Spring 1997): 134–157.

4. See Nicholas Lemann, *The Promised Land: the Great Black Migration and How It Changed America* (New York: Knopf, 1991), pp. 172–179.

5. For an insightful analysis on the reception of the Moynihan Report, see Alice O'Connor, *Poverty Knowledge: Social Science, Social Policy, and the Poor in Twentieth-Century U.S. History* (Princeton, NJ: Princeton University Press, 2001), pp. 203–210.

6. William Ryan, *Blaming the Victim* (New York: Random House, 1971).

7. O'Connor, *Poverty Knowledge*, p. 207.

8. See Michael B. Katz, *The Price of Citizenship: Redefining the American Welfare State* (New York: Metropolitan Books, 2001), p. 327.

9. See Michael B. Katz, *The Undeserving Poor: From the War on Poverty to the War on Welfare* (New York: Pantheon, 1989), pp. 44–48; and O'Connor, *Poverty Knowledge*, pp. 205–206.

10. See Daniel Patrick Moynihan, "We Can't Avoid Family Policy Much Longer" (interview), *Challenge* 35 (September–October 1985): 11. For a discussion of how Moynihan himself championed his own work as important, see Nicholas Lehman, *The Promised Land: The Black Migration and How It Changed America* (New York: Knopf, 1991), pp. 172–177.

11. For a review of the criticism of the "Moynihan Scissors," see O'Connor, *Poverty Knowledge*, pp. 205–206; Katz, *The Undeserving Poor*, pp. 44–48; and Sanford F. Schram, *Words of Welfare: The Poverty of Social Science and the Social Science of Poverty* (Minneapolis: University of Minnesota Press, 1995), pp. 109–112.

12. See William Julius Wilson and Katherine M. Neckerman, "Poverty and Family Structure: The Widening Gap between Evidence and Public Policy Issues" (conference paper) (Madison: Institute for Research on Poverty, University of Wisconsin–Madison, 1984), p. 72; and Schram, *Words of Welfare*, pp. 109–114.

13. William Julius Wilson, *The Truly Disadvantaged: The Inner City, the Underclass, and Public Policy* (Chicago: University of Chicago Press, 1987), pp. 20–21.

14. Adolph Reed, Jr., *Stirring in the Jug: Black Politics in the Post-Segregationist Era* (Minneapolis: University of Minnesota Press, 1999), p. 193. Also see Schram, *Words of Welfare*, p. 31 and p. 197, n. 73.

15. O'Connor, *Poverty Knowledge*, p. 204.

16. For an example of a publication that debunked welfare myths without ever discussing the race issue at all, see *The Basics: Welfare Reform* (New York: Twentieth Century Fund, 1996) (http://www.tcf.org/Publications/Basics/welfare/index.html).

17. See *Welfare Myths: Fact or Fiction? Exploring the Truth about Welfare* (New York: Welfare Law Center, 1996) (http://www.welfarelaw.org/mythtoc.html).

18. Ibid.

19. Not all studies examining first-time receipt of welfare produce the same results on the demographic composition. For research finding that from 1983 to 1991, four of every ten first-spells on welfare were black, see Johanne Boisjoly, Kathleen Mullan Harris, and Greg J. Duncan, "Trends, Events, and Duration of Initial Welfare Spells," *Social Service Review* 72 (December 1998): 466–492.

20.

> The PSID is a longitudinal survey of a representative sample of U.S. individuals and the families in which they reside. It has been ongoing since 1968. The data were collected annually through 1997, and biennially starting in 1999. The data files contain the full span of information collected over the course of the study. PSID data can be used for cross-sectional, longitudinal, and intergenerational analysis and for studying both individuals and families. The PSID sample, originating in 1968, consisted of two independent samples: a cross-sectional national sample and a national sample of low-income families. The cross-sectional sample was drawn by the Survey Research Center (SRC). Commonly called the SRC sample, this was an equal probability sample of households from the 48 contigu-

ous states and was designated to yield about 3,000 completed interviews. The second sample came from the Survey of Economic Opportunity (SEO), conducted by the Bureau of the Census for the Office of Economic Opportunity. In the mid-1960's, the PSID selected about 2,000 low-income families with heads under the age of sixty from SEO respondents. The sample, known as the SEO sample, was confined to Standard Metropolitan Statistical Areas (SMSA's) in the North and non-SMSA's in the Southern region. The PSID core sample combines the SRC and SEO samples. From 1968 to 1996, the PSID interviewed and reinterviewed individuals from families in the core sample every year, whether or not they were living in the same dwelling or with the same people. Adults have been followed as they have grown older, and children have been observed as they advance through childhood and into adulthood, forming family units of their own.

See http://www.isr.umich.edu/src/psid/.

21. The PSID's representativeness is subject to some debate since some families over time leave the study and the PSID did not include new immigrants arriving after its start in 1968. Yet, John Fitzgerald, Peter Gottschalk, and Robert Moffitt have concluded "we find no strong evidence that attrition has seriously distorted the representativeness of the PSID . . . and considerable evidence that its cross-sectional representativeness has remained roughly intact." See John Fitzgerald, Peter Gottschalk, and Robert Moffitt, "An Analysis of Sample Attrition in Panel Data," *Journal of Human Resources* 33 (1998): 251–299.

22. U.S. Department of Health and Human Services, Administration on Children and Families, Office of Family Assistance, National Emergency Tanf Datafile as of 4/14/2000: http://www.acf.dhhs.gov/programs/opre/characteristics/fy99/tab06_99.htm, last updated 8/27/2000.

23. See Kathryn Edin and Kathleen Mullan Harris, "Getting Off and Staying Off: Racial Differences in the Work Route Off Welfare," in *Latinas and African American Women at Work*, Irene Browne, ed. (New York: Russell Sage Foundation, 1999); and Elizabeth Lower-Basch, *"Leavers" and Diversion Studies: Preliminary Analysis of Racial Differences in Caseload Trends and Leaver Outcomes* (Washington, DC: U.S. Department of Health and Human Services, December 2000) (http://www.aspe.hhs.gov/hsp/leavers99/race.htm).

24. See Rebecca M. Blank, *It Takes a Nation: A New Agenda for Fighting Poverty* (Princeton, NJ: Princeton University Press, 1997), p. 154; and Greg J. Duncan, Kathleen Mullan Harris, and Johanne Boisjoly, "Time Limits and Welfare Reform: New Estimates of the Number and Characteristics of Affected Families," *Social Service Review* 74 (March 2000): 55–75.

25. Blank, *It Takes a Nation*, p. 154.

26. Martin Gilens, *Why Americans Hate Welfare: Race, Media, and the Politics of Antipoverty Policy* (Chicago: University of Chicago Press, 1999).

27. Boisjoly, Harris, and Duncan in "Trends, Events, and Duration of Initial Welfare Spells," Table A1, find, using the PSID, that the percentage black of all children receiving welfare in any one calendar year gradually moved upward from 1973 to 1990 from the low 40 percent range to 52 percent, suggesting that the black proportion of the welfare population was lower back when the press began to over-represent welfare as a "black program" in the 1960s and 1970s.

28. The issue of "whitewashing" the racial composition of the welfare population parallels the historic tendency in the United States to make blacks invisible—the topic of arguably the greatest American novel, *The Invisible Man* by Ralph Ellison (New York: Random House, 1952). On the issue of invisibility as it relates to African American women, see Patricia Hill Collins, *Black Feminist Thought: Knowledge, Consciousness and the Politics of Empowerment* (Boston: Unwin Hyman, 1990). Also see Maxine Baca Zinn and Bonnie Thornton Dill, "Theorizing Difference from Multiracial Feminism," *Feminist Studies* 22 (Summer 1996): 321–331. On the need to take race into account in litigation to defend welfare rights, see Naomi R. Cahn, "Representing Race Outside of Explicitly Racialized Contexts," *Michigan Law Review* 95 (February 1997): 965–1004.

29. See Michael K. Brown, "Ghettos, Fiscal Federalism, and Welfare Reform," in *Race and the Politics of Welfare Reform,* Sanford F. Schram, Joe Soss, and Richard Fording, eds. (Ann Arbor: University of Michigan Press, forthcoming).

30. *Characteristics and Financial Circumstances of TANF Recipients, Fiscal Year 1999* (Washington, DC: U.S. Department of Health and Human Services, Office of Family Assistance, 2000) (http://www.acf.dhhs.gov/programs/opre/characteristics/fy99/analysis.htm).

31. See Elizabeth M. Grieco and Rachel C. Cassidy, *Overview of Race and Hispanic Origin,* Census 2000 Brief, C2KBR/01-1 (Washington, DC: U.S. Bureau of the Census, March 2001), p. 10, table 10 (http://www.census.gov/prod/2001pubs/c2kbr01-1.pdf). Grieco and Cassidy (p. 10) note: "Nearly half (48 percent) of Hispanics reported only White, while approximately 42 percent reported only Some other race, when responding to the question on race." The remaining 10 percent indicated more than one race.

32. Lower-Basch, *"Leavers" and Diversion Studies,* Table 2 (http://www.aspe.hhs.gov/hsp/leavers99/race.htm).

33. *Characteristics and Financial Circumstances of TANF Recipients, Fiscal Year 1999* (http://www.acf.dhhs.gov/programs/opre/characteristics/fy99/analysis.htm#trends).

34. U.S. Department of Health and Human Services, *Indicators of Welfare Dependence Annual Report to Congress* (Washington, DC: Government Printing Office, March 2000) (http://aspe.hhs.gov/hsp/indicators00/index.htm).

35. For an alternative perspective, see Rosalee Clawson and Rakuya Trice, "Poverty As We Know It (Media Portrayals of the Poor)," *Public Opinion Quarterly* 64 (Spring 2000): 53. Clawson and Trice provide evidence that the mass media

continued to overrepresent blacks in news stories about poverty and welfare in the 1993–1998 period when welfare reform was being debated and assessed. Yet, while this is certainly correct for poverty, it is less so for welfare, if we compare their calculations to the various data presented in this chapter. One response is that the public tends to interpret stories about blacks in poverty as reinforcing negative stereotypes about blacks taking welfare. Yet, that suggestion itself implies that the audience relies on more than the pictures and stories to interpret how poor blacks are reported. The idea that the audience is already primed to interpret these stories in a less than salubrious way is therefore once again affirmed.

36. Duncan, Harris, and Boisjoly, "Time Limits and Welfare Reform," table 1.

37. For a discussion of how reticence to discuss differences between welfare recipients and others is part of a self-defeating "politics of euphemisms," see Schram, *Words of Welfare*, pp. 20–37.

38. For an informed analysis on how the national government led the way in cracking down on the manufactured "welfare fraud" crisis, see Frances Fox Piven and Richard A. Cloward, *Regulating the Poor: The Functions of Public Welfare,* updated edition (New York: Vintage, 1993), pp. 373–381.

39. See Kathryn Edin and Laura Lein, *Making Ends Meet: How Single Mothers Survive Welfare and Low-Wage Work* (New York: Russell Sage Foundation, 1997), pp. 143–191.

40. Benefits in under Aid to Families with Dependent Children fell 42 percent in real terms from 1970 to 1990. See Robert Moffitt, "Incentive Effects in the U.S. Welfare System: A Review," *Journal of Economic Literature* 30 (March 1992): 5.

41. Hortense Spillers as quoted in Wahneema Lubiano, "Black Ladies, Welfare Queens, and State Minstrels: Ideological War by Narrative Means," *Race-ing Justice, En-gendering Power: Essays on Anita Hill, Clarence Thomas, and the Construction of Social Reality*, Toni Morrison, ed. (New York: Pantheon Books, 1992), p. 323.

42. Slavoj Žižek, "Multiculturalism, Or, the Cultural Logic of Multinational Capitalism," *New Left Review 225* (September–October 1997): 28–29.

43. See Linda Gordon, *Heroes of Their Own Lives: The History and Politics of Family Violence* (New York: Viking, 1988). Also see Frances Fox Piven, "Women and the State: Ideology, Power, and Welfare," in *For Crying Out Loud: Women's Poverty in the United States,* Diane Dujon and Ann Withorn, eds. (Boston: South End Press, 1996), pp. 183–200.

44. Michael Rogin, *Blackface, White Noise: Jewish Immigrants in the Hollywood Melting Pot* (Berkeley: University of California Press, 1996), pp. 30, 112. Also see Williams, *Playing the Race Card*, pp. 154–158.

45. See, in particular, David R. Roediger, *The Wages of Whiteness: Race and the Making of the American Working Class* (New York: Verso Press, 1991); Ruth Frankenberg, *White Women, Race Matters: The Social Construction of Whiteness* (Minneapolis: University of Minnesota Press, 1993); and Noel Ignatiev, *How the Irish Became White* (New York: Routledge, 1995).

46. James Baldwin,"On Being 'White,' and Other Lies," *Essence*, April 1984, pp. 90–92.

47. David M. Halbfinger, "Judge Dismisses Main Charges in Suit by Ex-Chief of Troopers," *New York Times*, July 6, 2000, p. A1.

48. Steven Levine provided the point that Christie Whitman suffered from "e" envy. Lacking an "e" in her last name, she was prevented from being a "Whiteman."

49. See Iver Peterson and David M. Halbfinger, "New Jersey Agrees to Pay $13 Million in Profiling Suit," *New York Times*, February 3, 2001, p. A1.

50. W. J. T. Mitchell, *Picture Theory* (Chicago: University of Chicago Press, 1994).

51. Michel Foucault has emphasized that pictures become coherent only by virtue of a "cycle of representation" whereby a circuitry connects a picture to interpretations by the viewing subject that are needed to visualize the viewed object. Foucault goes on to stress that the cycle of representation necessarily combines the *image* of a picture with the *text* of interpretations to make the viewed object, which is therefore better conceived as a text/image or what Foucault calls a "calligram." See Michel Foucault, *The Order of Things: An Archeology of Knowledge* (New York: Vintage, 1973), p. 11.

52. Interview with John Tryneski, Executive Editor, University of Chicago Press, April 20, 2001.

53. Sanford F. Schram, *After Welfare: The Culture of Postindustrial Social Policy* (New York: New York University Press, 2000).

54. Paul de Man, *Resistance to Theory* (Minneapolis: University of Minnesota Press, 1986), pp. 3–20.

55. Schram, *After Welfare*, pp. 54–55.

56. I want to thank Maureen Whitebrook and Alexa Robertson for noting the significance of being at the front of the bus.

57. See Johanna Brenner, "Organizing around Welfare Reform: Activist Notes" (paper presented at the Work, Welfare and Politics Conference, University of Oregon, February 28–29, 2000).

58. See Greg Duncan and Saul Hoffman, "The Effect of Incomes, Wages, and AFDC Benefits on Marital Disruption," *Journal of Human Resources* 30, 1 (Winter 1995): 23; and Saul D. Hoffman and Greg J. Duncan, "Teenage Underclass Behavior and Subsequent Poverty: Have the Rules Changed?" in *The Urban Underclass*, Christopher Jencks and Paul E. Peterson, eds. (Washington, DC: Brookings Institution, 1991), pp. 155–174.

59. See Barbara J. Nelson, "The Origins of the Two-Channel Welfare State: Workmen's Compensation and Mothers' Aid," in *Women, the State and Welfare*, Linda Gordon, ed. (Madison: University of Wisconsin Press, 1990), pp. 123–151.

60. Frances Fox Piven and Richard A. Cloward, *The New Class War: Reagan's Attack on the Welfare State and Its Consequences* (New York: Pantheon Books, 1982), pp. 38–39. For an account on the ways that welfare reform of recent years

has continued the social policies that "othered" welfare recipients as less deserving in large part on racial grounds, see Kenneth J. Neubeck and Noel A. Cazenave, *Welfare Racism: Playing the Race Card against America's Poor* (New York: Routledge, 2001).

61. For a thoughtful attempt to demonstrate that welfare recipients are not different than others in terms of basic attitudes and behaviors, see Mark Robert Rank, *Living on the Edge: The Realities of Welfare in America* (New York: Columbia University Press, 1994), pp. 167–174.

62. Paul Gilroy, *Against Race: Imagining Political Culture beyond the Color Line* (Cambridge, MA: Belknap Press of Harvard University Press, 2000).

Notes to Chapter 7

This chapter is dedicated to Murray Edelman. Margaret Berman assisted with the data collection and analysis.

1. Administration for Children and Families, *Change in TANF Caseloads* (Washington, DC: U.S. Department of Health and Human Services, 2001) (http://www.acf.dhhs.gov/news/stats/recipientsL.htm).

2. Assistant Secretary for Planning and Evaluation, *Leavers and Diversion Studies: Summary of Research on Welfare Outcomes Funded by ASPE* (Washington, DC: U.S. Department of Health and Human Services, 2000).

3. Murray Edelman, *Constructing the Political Spectacle* (Chicago: University of Chicago Press, 1988).

4. See Deborah A. Stone, *Policy Paradox: The Art of Political Decision Making* (New York: W. W. Norton, 1997); and Roger W. Cobb and Marc Howard Ross, eds., *Cultural Strategies of Agenda Denial: Avoidance, Attack, and Redefinition* (Lawrence: University Press of Kansas, 1997).

5. Joseph Gusfield, *The Culture of Public Problems* (Chicago: University of Chicago Press, 1981), p. 51.

6. Michael Kelly, "Doves' Day of Reckoning," *Washington Post,* October 11, 2000, p. A31.

7. Ibid.

8. William H. Miller, "Surprise! Welfare Reform Is Working," *Industry Week,* March 16, 1998, pp. 27–30.

9. Jason DeParle, "The Welfare Dilemma: A Collection of Articles by Jason DeParle," *New York Times,* 1999 (http://www.nytimes.com/library/national/deparle-index.html).

10. We used a two-step process to identify relevant stories. First, we searched Lexis-Nexis to find all stories with at least one sentence that included both "welfare" and "reform" and at least one sentence that included one of four combinations: "roll" and "decline," "roll" and "drop," "caseload" and "decline," and "case-

load" and "drop." This procedure yielded a preliminary sample of 358 stories. Second, to limit our analysis to relevant media portrayals, we identified and removed all letters to the editors and news stories that were either irrelevant or made only passing reference to welfare. This procedure resulted in a loss of 108 cases, producing a final sample of 250 relevant stories.

11. The sample of 250 stories and prototypical articles representing each of the five coding categories is available from the authors on request. Coding reliability was evaluated by having two individuals independently code a random subsample of fifty stories. Applying the five categories described in the text, the two coders agreed on 82 percent of the cases in this subsample, a rate of agreement that meets conventional standards for inter-rater reliability. See Allen Rubin and Earl Babbie, *Research Methods for Social Work*, 4th ed. (Belmont, CA: Wadsworth, 2000), pp. 192–193.

12. Sanford F. Schram, *Words of Welfare: The Poverty of Social Science and the Social Science of Poverty* (Minneapolis: University of Minnesota Press, 1995).

13. Dennis Chong, "Creating Common Frames of Reference on Political Issues," in *Political Persuasion and Attitude Change*, Diana C. Mutz, Paul M. Sniderman, and Richard A. Brody, eds. (Ann Arbor: University of Michigan Press, 1995), pp. 195–224.

14. Mark Fishman, *Manufacturing the News* (Austin: University of Texas Press, 1988).

15. Leon V. Sigal, *Reporters and Officials: The Organization and Politics of Newsmaking* (Lexington, MA: D. C. Heath, 1973).

16. John Zaller, *The Nature and Origins of Mass Opinion* (New York: Cambridge University Press, 1992); and Daniel C. Hallin, "The Media, the War in Vietnam, and Political Support: A Critique of the Thesis of an Oppositional Media," *Journal of Politics* 46 (February 1984): 2–24.

17. Barbara Ehrenreich, "The New Right Attack on Social Welfare," in Frances Fox Piven, Richard A. Cloward, Barbara Ehrenreich, and Fred Block, *The Mean Season: The Attack on the Welfare State* (New York: Pantheon Books, 1987), pp. 161–193.

18. Frances Fox Piven, "Globalization, American Politics, and Welfare Policy," *The Annals* 577 (September 2001): 26–38.

19. Jean Stefancic, Richard Delgado, and Mark Tushnet, *No Mercy: How Conservative Think Tanks and Foundations Changed America's Social Agenda* (Philadelphia: Temple University Press, 1996).

20. Stanley Feldman and John Zaller, "The Political Culture of Ambivalence: Ideological Responses to the Welfare State," *American Journal of Political Science* 36 (April 1992): 268–307.

21. Martin Gilens, *Why Americans Hate Welfare* (Chicago: University of Chicago Press, 1999), p. 37.

22. Ehrenreich, "The New Right Attack on Social Welfare," pp. 165–173.

23. Gilens, *Why Americans Hate Welfare.*

24. Daryl Michael Scott, *Contempt and Pity: Social Policy and the Image of the Damaged Black Psyche, 1880–1996* (Chapel Hill: University of North Carolina Press, 1997).

25. See Schram, *Words of Welfare*, pp. 3–19.

26. For instance, see Mary Jo Bane and David Ellwood, *Welfare Realities: From Rhetoric to Reform* (Cambridge, MA: Harvard University Press, 1994).

27. Kristin Luker, *Dubious Conceptions: The Politics of Teenage Pregnancy* (Cambridge, MA: Harvard University Press, 1996).

28. Murray Edelman, *Political Language: Words that Succeed and Policies That Fail* (New York: Academic Press, 1977), chapter 3. In the 1960s, liberals used such crisis language in tandem with the militaristic metaphor of a "war on poverty"—a construction that cued anxieties about the costs of inaction while also suggesting the state's capacity to use its arsenal of weapons to achieve victory. See Stone, *Policy Paradox.*

29. Mark R. Rank, *Living on the Edge: The Realities of Welfare in America* (New York: Columbia University Press, 1994).

30. See Sheldon H. Danziger and Daniel H. Weinberg, "The Historical Record: Trends in Family Income, Inequality, and Poverty," *Confronting Poverty Prescriptions for Change*, Sheldon H. Danziger, Gary D. Sandefur, and Daniel H. Weinberg, eds. (Cambridge, MA: Harvard University Press, 1994), pp. 18–50.

31. Assistant Secretary for Planning and Evaluation, *Leavers and Diversion Studies.*

32. Chuck Collins, Betsy Leondar-Wright, and Holly Sklar, *Shifting Fortunes: The Perils of the Growing American Wealth Gap* (Washington, DC: United for a Fair Economy, 1999).

33. Joe Soss, *Unwanted Claims: The Politics of Participation in the U.S. Welfare System* (Ann Arbor: University of Michigan Press, 2000).

34. Sanford F. Schram, *After Welfare: The Culture of Postindustrial Social Policy* (New York: New York University Press, 2000), pp. 73–84.

35. Gwendolyn Mink, *Welfare's End* (Ithaca, NY: Cornell University Press, 1998), pp. 9–20.

36. Joe Soss, Sanford F. Schram, Thomas P. Vartanian, and Erin O'Brien, "Setting the Terms of Relief: Explaining State Policy Choices in the Devolution Revolution," *American Journal of Political Science* 45 (April 2001): 378–395.

37. Robin M. Dion and LaDonna Pavetti, *Access to and Participation in Medicaid and the Food Stamp Program: A Review of the Recent Literature* (Washington, DC: Mathematica Policy Research, March 2000); and Lissa Bell and Carson Strege-Flora, *Access Denied: Federal Neglect Gives Rise to State Lawlessness* (Seattle: Northwest Federation of Community Organizations, 2000).

38. Steve Schultze, "Lawmakers Want Maximus Fired: Six Legislators say W-2 Contractor Has Broken Faith," *Milwaukee Journal Sentinel*, October 27, 2000, p. B3;

and David S. Hilzenrath, "N.Y. Judge Shelves Welfare Contracts Won by Maximus; Procurement Process Ruled 'Corrupted,'" *The Washington Post,* August 22, 2000, p. D13.

39. DeParle, "The Welfare Dilemma."

40. Laura A. Wilson, Robert P. Stoker, and Dennis McGrath, "Welfare Bureaus as Moral Tutors: What Do Clients Learn from Paternalistic Welfare Reforms?" *Social Science Quarterly* 80 (September 1999): 485.

41. Gusfield, *The Culture of Public Problems*, pp. 53–54.

42. "Welfare Reform Fails Poorest: Many Who Are Eligible Don't Get Food Stamps," *Chicago Tribune,* August 22, 1999, p. C10.

43. U.S. Department of Health and Human Services, "Welfare Reform: Implementing the Personal Responsibility and Work Opportunity Reconciliation Act of 1996," (Washington, DC: HHS Fact Sheet, February 2, 2001) (http://www.hhs.gov/news/press/2001pres/01fswelreform.html).

44. For an alternative reading, see Peter Edelman, "The Worst Thing Bill Clinton Has Done," *Atlantic Monthly,* March 1997, pp. 43–58.

45. Rebecca M. Blank, "What Goes Up Must Come Down? Explaining Recent Changes in Public Assistance Caseloads," JCPR Working Paper 78 (Chicago: Joint Center for Research on Poverty, Northwestern University, March 1, 1999).

46. Laura Meckler, "Welfare Caseload Drop Slowing around U.S.," *Philadelphia Inquirer*, April 4, 2001 (http://inq.philly.com/content/inquirer/2001/04/04/national/WELFARE04.htm).

47. Bane and Ellwood, *Welfare Realities.*

48. LaDonna Pavetti, "The Dynamics of Welfare and Work: Exploring the Process by Which Women Work Their Way Off Welfare," Ph.D. diss., Harvard University, 1993.

49. Congressional action in 2000 restored some efforts to collect data on welfare entry and exit. It will be some time, however, before enough data will be available to support trend analyses of caseload dynamics under TANF.

50. Gene Falk, *Welfare Reform: Trends in the Number of Families Receiving AFDC and TANF* (Washington, DC: Congressional Research Service, Domestic Social Policy Division, 2000).

51. Ibid. Long-term recipients were defined in this analysis as those receiving welfare for sixty or more months; new recipients were defined as those who had been on the rolls for three months or less.

52. Kathleen A. Maloy, LaDonna A. Pavetti, Peter Shin, Julie Darnell, and Lea Scarpulla-Nolan, *Description and Assessment of State Approaches to Diversion Programs and Activities under Welfare Reform* (Washington, DC: George Washington University Center for Health Policy Research, August 1998) (http://aspe.os.dhhs.gov/hsp/isp/diverzn/).

53. Bell and Strege-Flora, *Access Denied.*

54. Pamela J. Loprest and Sheila R. Zedlewski, *Current and Former Welfare Recipients: How Do They Differ?* (Washington, DC: Urban Institute, 1999).

55. Gilens, *Why Americans Hate Welfare*, pp. 184–187.

56. Robert E. Rector and Sarah E. Youssef, "The Determinants of Welfare Caseload Decline," Report No. 99-04 (Washington, DC: Heritage Center for Data Analysis, Heritage Foundation, 1999).

57. Heidi Goldberg and Liz Schott, *A Compliance-Oriented Approach to Sanctions in State and County TANF Programs* (Washington, DC: Center on Budget and Policy Priorities, 2000).

58. Assistant Secretary for Planning and Evaluation, *Leavers and Diversion Studies*; General Accounting Office, *Welfare Reform: Information on Former Recipients' Status* (Washington, DC: U.S. General Accounting Office, 1999); and Pamela Loprest, *Families Who Left Welfare and How They Are Doing* (Washington, DC: Urban Institute, 1999).

59. Assistant Secretary for Planning and Evaluation, *Leavers and Diversion Studies*; and Loprest, *Families Who Left Welfare and How They Are Doing.*

60. Loprest, *Families Who Left Welfare and How They Are Doing.*

61. Pavetti, "The Dynamics of Welfare and Work."

62. See Frances Fox Piven and Richard A. Cloward, *Regulating the Poor: The Functions of Public Welfare*, updated edition (New York: Vintage Books, 1993).

63. Assistant Secretary for Planning and Evaluation, *Leavers and Diversion Studies.*

64. Loprest, *Families Who Left Welfare and How They Are Doing.*

65. During the last decade of the AFDC program, the nominal transition benefits for exiting families included ongoing access to Food Stamps for those who qualified, one year of Medicaid coverage for those who qualified, and one year of child care for those leaving AFDC for a job.

66. Loprest, *Families Who Left Welfare and How They Are Doing.*

67. Ibid.

Notes to Chapter 8

1. See the debate between Frances Fox Piven and Richard A. Cloward and Ellen Meiksins Wood. Ellen Meiksins Wood, "Modernity, Postmodernity, or Capitalism?" *Monthly Review* 48 (July–August, 1996): 21–39; Frances Fox Piven and Richard A. Cloward, "Eras of Power," *Monthly Review* 49 (January 1998): 11–24; Ellen Meiksins Wood, "Class Compacts, the Welfare State, and Epochal Shifts: A Reply to Frances Fox Piven and Richard A. Cloward," *Monthly Review* 49 (January 1998): 24–43; and Frances Fox Piven and Richard A. Cloward, "A Reply to Ellen Meiksins Wood," *Monthly Review* (January 1998): 44–46.

2. See Frances Fox Piven, "Welfare and Work," *Social Justice* 25 (Spring 1998): 67–83.

3. See Frances Fox Piven, "Women and the State: Ideology, Power, and the Welfare State," *Gender and the Life Course*, Alice S. Rossi, ed. (New York: Aldine, 1985), pp. 265–287, for the argument that under capitalism ordinary women's concerns about an everyday "moral economy of domesticity" led to mobilization for social welfare policies to compensate families in the face of the injuries inflicted by the vagaries of the market system.

4. The terminology of "micro vs. macro" is popular in the profession of social work. It is also a way of referring to the important work of Michel Foucault, who emphasized that the sources of power had changed with the development of modern "disciplinary society," where power operates from below via a "micropolitics" of "biopower" such that individuals are enlisted in constructing themselves as compliant subjects of the existing macro social order. See Michel Foucault, "Governmentality," in *The Foucault Effect: Studies in Governmentality with Two Lectures by and an Interview with Michel Foucault*, Graham Burchell, Colin Gordon, and Peter Miller, eds. (Chicago: University of Chicago Press, 1991), pp. 87–104.

5. Daniel P. Moynihan, "Toward a Postindustrial Social Policy," *Public Interest* 96 (Summer 1989): 16–27.

6. See Frances Fox Piven, "Globalization, American Politics, and Welfare Policy," *Annals of the American Academy of Political and Social Science* 577 (September 2001): 26–37.

7. For an ambitious attempt to connect the contemporary micropractices in self-construction to the macropractices of fashioning a new global economic order, see Michael Hardt and Antonio Negri, *Empire* (Cambridge, MA: Harvard University Press, 2000).

8. See Susan George, "A Short History of Neoliberalism" (Conference on Economic Sovereignty in a Globalising World, March 24–26, 1999) (http://www.globalpolicy.org/globaliz/econ/histneol.htm). Also see James K. Galbraith, "The Crisis of Globalization," *Dissent* 46 (Summer 1999): 12–16.

9. Jamie Peck, *Workfare States* (New York: Guilford Press, 2001), pp. 16–21.

10. Ibid.

11. See Piven, "Welfare and Work," pp. 67–83. Also see Stephen Gudeman, *Economics as Culture: Models and Metaphors of Livelihood* (London: Routledge and Kegan Paul, 1996).

12. See Linda Gordon, *Pitied But Not Entitled: Single Mothers and the History of Welfare* (New York: Free Press, 1994), pp. 53–59; and Nancy Fraser, "After the Family Wage: Gender Equity and the Welfare State," *Political Theory* 22 (November 1994): 591–618.

13. See Frances Fox Piven and Richard A. Cloward, *Regulating the Poor: The Functions of Public Welfare* (New York: Vintage 1992), pp. 3–8.

14. Peter M. Hass, "Introduction: Epistemic Communities and International Policy Coordination," Special Issue on Knowledge, Power, and International Policy Coordination, *International Organization* 46 (Winter 1992): 1.

15. See Arturo Escobar, *Encountering Development: The Making and Unmaking of the Third World* (Princeton, NJ: Princeton University Press, 1996), pp. 35–39.

16. On "narratives of transparency," see Jenrose Dawn Fitzgerald, "Rationalizing Welfare Reform: Citizenship, Knowledge, and the Politics of Transparency," Master's thesis, Comparative Studies, Ohio State University, 2000.

17. For an examination of how public policy promotes and is promoted by "governing mentalities," see Nancy D. Campbell, *Using Women: Drug Policy and Social Justice* (New York: Routledge, 2001), pp. 33–54.

18. John Gray, *False Dawn: The Delusions of Global Capitalism* (London: Granta Books, 1998).

19. Hardt and Negri, *Empire*, pp. 22–41.

20. See note 1.

21. For a discussion about the evidence for globalization in trade, finance, and foreign direct investment, see Andrew Glyn, "Egalitarianism in a Global Economy," *Boston Review* 22 (December–January 1997–1998).

22. See Gray, *False Dawn*; and Hardt and Negri, *Empire*.

23. Wood, "Modernity, Postmodernity, or Capitalism?" pp. 21–39.

24. See Karl Polanyi, *The Great Transformation* (Boston: Beacon Press, 1944); and Joseph A. Schumpeter, *Capitalism, Socialism and Democracy* (New York: Harper and Brothers, 1942).

25. See Andrew Gamble, "The Last Utopia," *New Left Review* 236 (July/August 1999): 117–127.

26. Frances Fox Piven and Richard A. Cloward, *The Breaking of the American Social Compact* (New York: New Press, 1997), p. 9.

27. Ibid.

28. Piven and Cloward, "Eras of Power," p. 20.

29. See Piven, "Globalization, American Politics, and Welfare Policy," p. 28.

30. Ibid., p. 26.

31. See the comments of Theda Skocpol in the symposium "Welfare: Where Do We Go from Here?" *New Republic,* August 12, 1996, pp. 19–22. Skocpol suggests that the 1996 law's repeal of AFDC is not so significant in part because when it was originally created by the Social Security Act of 1935, AFDC did not radically revise the state public assistance programs that predated it. States had substantial discretion before AFDC and they still did after. Repealing AFDC therefore also still leaves intact a system that relies heavily on the states for the provision of public assistance. See Theda Skocpol, *Protecting Soldiers and Mothers: The Political Origins of Social Policy in the United States* (Cambridge, MA: Belknap Press of Harvard University Press, 1992), pp. 525–526.

32. See Gwendolyn Mink, *Welfare's End* (Ithaca, NY: Cornell University Press, 1998), p. 50.

33. See Sanford F. Schram, *After Welfare: The Culture of Postindustrial Social Policy* (New York: New York University Press, 2000), pp. 59–88.

34. See Michael B. Katz, *The Price of Citizenship: Redefining the American Welfare State* (New York: Metropolitan Books, 2001), pp. 317–359.

35. Schram, *After Welfare*, pp. 59–88.

36. Jodie Levin-Epstein, *The IRA: Individual Responsibility Agreements and TANF Family Life Obligations* (Washington, DC: Center on Law and Social Policy, August 1998) (http://www.clasp.org/pubs/TANF/ira.htm).

37. Ibid.

38. Ibid.

39. Ibid.

40. Elizabeth Martinez and Arnoldo Garcia, "What Is Neoliberalism? A Brief Definition for Activists" (*Corporate Watch*) (http://www.corpwatch.org/issues/glob101/background/2000/neolib.html).

41. Escobar, *Encountering Development*, pp. 93–94.

42. See Peck, *Workfare States*, p. 21.

43. Ibid., pp. 21–22.

44. Ibid., p. 16.

45. See Piven and Cloward, *Regulating the Poor*, pp. 3–8, for an analysis of how the vagaries of the economy at times work to deny work to the poor, and this in turn undermines their commitment to the social order and established values. Piven and Cloward note that work has been important for centuries as a source of instilling commitment to the moral values of the existing order.

46. "Privatization of public assistance" is from Sanford F. Schram, *Words of Welfare: The Poverty of Social Science and the Social Science of Poverty* (Minneapolis: University of Minnesota Press, 2001), pp. 59–76. On "governmentality," see Michel Foucault, "Governmentality," pp. 87–104; and Mitchell Dean, *Governmentality: Power and Rule in Modern Society* (London: Sage Publications, 1999).

47. "Governing mentalities" is from Nancy D. Campbell, *Using Women*, pp. 33–54; and "emergent structures of feeling" is from Susan J. Shaw, "Neoliberalism at Work: Contemporary Scenarios of Governmental Reform in Social Work and Public Health" (paper presented at the annual meeting of the American Anthropology Association, Washington, DC, November 28, 2001).

48. See Schram, *After Welfare*, pp. 70–73.

49. See Barbara Ehrenreich, "Spinning the Poor into Gold," *Harper's* 295, August, 1997, pp. 44–52.

50. For rich detail showing how neoliberalism's privatization under welfare reform has helped proliferate a panoply of disempowering client-management practices, all in the name of disciplining subjects to produce measurable outcomes of questionable value to the women in welfare-to-work programs, see Shaw, "Neoliberalism at Work."

51. For reviews of these debates, see Frances Fox Piven, "The Welfare State as Work Enforcer," *Dollars & Sense* (September 1999): 32, and "Welfare and Work," pp. 67–83.

52. Robert Rector, "Implementing Welfare Reform and Restoring Marriage," in *Priorities for the President*, Stuart M. Butler and Kim R. Holmes, eds. (Washington, DC: Heritage Foundation, 2001).

53. See Gordon, *Pitied But Not Entitled*, pp. 53–59; and Fraser, "After the Family Wage," pp. 591–618.

54. See Stephanie Coontz, *The Way We Never Were: Family and the Nostalgia Trap* (New York: Basic Books, 1993).

55. See Schram, *After Welfare*, pp. 70–75.

56. Ibid., pp. 1–3.

57. See Miriam Ching Yoon Louie, *Our Sweat, Our Fight* (Boston: South End Press, 2001); and Pierrette Hondagneu-Sotelo, *Doméstica: Immigrant Workers Cleaning and Caring in the Shadows of Affluence* (Berkeley: University of California Press, 2001).

58. On the value of decontextualized, abstract knowledge for purposes of domination that can be exported transnationally, see Peck, *Workfare States*, pp. 88–89.

59. Kari Dehli, "Subject to the New Global Economy: Power and Positioning in Ontario Labour Market Policy Formation," *Studies in Political Economy* 41 (Summer 1993): 87.

60. Escobar, *Encountering Development*, pp. 12–14.

61. Ibid., pp. 47–52.

62. See James C. Scott, *Seeing Like a State: How Certain Schemes to Improve the Human Condition Have Failed* (New Haven, CT: Yale University Press, 1999), pp. 342–358.

63. See Murray Edelman, *Political Language: Words That Succeed and Policies That Fail* (New York: Academic Press, 1977).

64. Campbell, *Using Women*, pp. 14–18 and 33–54.

65. Ibid., pp. 14–18.

66. See Elliot Currie, *Reckoning: Drugs, the Cities and the American Future* (New York: Hill and Wang, 1993).

67. On the sources of domination that arise from when the "needs talk" of expert discourses misreads low-income women, see Nancy Fraser, "Women, Welfare and the Politics of Need Interpretation," in *Unruly Practices: Power, Discourse, and Gender in Contemporary Social Theory* (Minneapolis: University of Minnesota Press, 1989), pp. 144–160. For an emphasis on needs that are not so much misread as manufactured by expert discourses, see Barbara Cruikshank, *The Will to Empower: Democratic Citizens and Other Subjects* (Ithaca, NY: Cornell University Press, 1999); and Nicolas Rose, *The Powers of Freedom: Reframing Political Thought* (New York: Cambridge University Press, 1999), pp. 51–60.

68. Campbell, *Using Women*, pp. 33–54.
69. Fitzgerald, "Rationalizing Welfare Reform," pp. 167–171.
70. Gray, *False Dawn*.
71. Ibid., pp. 53–77.
72. Ibid., p. 3.
73. Ibid., pp. 114–119.
74. Ibid., p. 72.
75. Ibid., p. 38.
76. Ibid., p. 131.
77. Ibid., pp. 53–54.
78. Ibid., p. 38.
79. Ibid., pp. 116–119.
80. Ibid., pp. 109–110.
81. See Foucault, "Governmentality," pp. 87–104.
82. See Hardt and Negri, *Empire*, pp. 22–41.
83. See Adrienne S. Chambon, Allan Irving, and Laura Epstein, eds., *Reading Foucault for Social Work* (New York: Columbia University Press, 1999).
84. For a poignant example of the disciplinary practices of the micropolitics of slavery, see Saidiya V. Hartman, *Scenes of Subjection: Terror, Slavery, and Self-Making in Nineteenth-Century America* (New York: Oxford University Press, 1997).
85. Foucault, "Governmentality," pp. 87–104.
86. Luther H. Martin, Huck Guttman, and Patrick H. Hutton, *Technologies of the Self: A Seminar with Michel Foucault* (Amherst: University of Massachusetts Press, 1988).
87. Gilles Deleuze, "Postscript on the Societies of Control," *October* 59 (Winter 1992): 4–6.
88. Mitchell Dean, "Neo-Liberalism as Counter-Enlightenment Cultural Critique," in *Displacement of Social Policies*, Sakari Hänninen, ed. (Jyvaskyla, Finland: SoPhi, 1998), pp. 198–226.
89. Hardt and Negri, *Empire*, pp. 22–41.
90. For a related analysis, see James C. Scott, *Domination and the Arts of Resistance: Hidden Transcripts* (New Haven, CT: Yale University Press, 1990).
91. The term "symbolic analysts" was coined by Robert Reich. His ideas are discussed in Hardt and Negri, *Empire*, pp. 291–292.
92. Ibid., p. 413.
93. The continuing importance of mass protest politics even on today's global stage is underscored by the diverse but coordinated efforts of the protesters of the World Trade Organization. See Michael Hardt and Antonio Negri, "What the Protesters in Genoa Want," *New York Times*, July 20, 2001, p. A18.
94. In particular, see Mitchell Dean, *The Constitution of Poverty: Toward a Genealogy of Liberal Governance* (New York: Routledge, 1991); and idem, *Governmentality*.

95. Peck, *Workfare States*, pp. 16–21.

96. Ibid., pp. 198–201.

97. Peck, *Workfare States*, p. 6.

98. For a consideration of the variety of ways in which power creates its own opposition, see Howard Winant, *The World Is a Ghetto: Race and Democracy since World War II* (New York: Basic Books, 2001), pp. 33–35.

99. On the "theatricality of power," see William E. Connolly, *Identity\Difference: Democratic Negotiations of Political Paradox* (Ithaca, NY: Cornell University Press, 1991), pp. 206–208.

100. Piven and Cloward, "Eras of Power," p. 21.

Index

Addams, Jane: and African-Americans, 250n. 9; on antagonism, 46–47; bottom-up approach, 4–5, 24, 34, 113; on citizenship education vs. character education, 38; and cosmopolitanism, 38; democratic rights vs. relationships, 39–41; and Dewey, 251n. 32; and feminism, 33–35; on local and global connected, 39; and M. Carey Thomas prize, 46; and Nobel prize, 33, 46; in contrast with Piven and Cloward on dissent, 47; and pragmatism, 38–39; and priority to practice, 37; on George Pullman as a "modern Lear," 44; on "us" and "them" as related, 41
Advocacy: and global social justice, 239–240; on race in welfare, 180–182; and social science, 4–6, 29–30, 132–134
Agitation from below, 96–100, 233–236
Aid to Families with Dependent Children (AFDC): as assistance for children, 95; and end of entitlement, 1, 54, 141; and entry and exit rates, 195–196; and exit due to employment, 198; and increased state discretion under TANF, 141, 209; repudiated as encouraging depedency, 191
American dream, 174
American Sociological Association, and report on Brandeis Universityís tenure decision concerning Richard Cloward, 104
Analysis paralysis, 130
Antagonism, 46–47
Aronowitz, Stanley: and critique of Piven and Cloward's electoral strategy, 105; on social science and the state, 61
Assuming the best: as conservative discourse, 248n. 28; as counterdiscourse, 24–26
Assuming the worst, 25–26

Backlash, 87
Baldwin, James, 174
Basic Books, and public discourse, 247n. 5
Bernstein, Richard, 245n. 9, 246n. 10
Best practices, 119–123
Bhabha, Homi, on anxiety of signification, 35
Bifurcated welfare state, 77–78, 182
Big bang theory of welfare state growth, 96–100
bin Laden, Osama, 238
Biopower, 82, 229
Blackface and assimilation, 173
Block, Fred, on the perversity thesis, 22
Boisjoly, Johanne, 170

Bottom-up approach, vs. top-down approach: and affinities between Jane Addams and Piven and Cloward, 4–5, 24; as basic to settlement, 34; and contrast between Piven and Cloward and Daniel Moynihan and David Ellwood, 65; and research, 109; and research in Jane Addams's work, 113; and research in Piven and Cloward's work, 128; as resistance to globalization, 234–235
Bourne, Randolph, on Jane Addams, 252n. 57
Brandeis University, 104
Breadwinner, 182, 205
Brief treatment, 122
Brown, Wendy, criticism of Piven and Cloward, 68, 80, 105
Bryn Mawr College, 46
Bush, George W., 236, 238

Calligram, 278n. 51
Campbell, Nancy, 224, 286n. 47
Case advocacy vs. policy advocacy, 95
Caseload declines: and debate over cause for the decrease, 145; and diversion, 194–197; and the economy, 145, 271n. 20; and end of welfare gridlock since the 60s, 55–56; and state policy options under TANF, 144–49
Charitable choice option, 141
Charitable effort, 41–45
Cheney, Dick, 238
Chicago School of Sociology, 33
Child support, 95
"Children," as a middle class appeal, 30
Chong, Dennis, 189
Citizenship education vs. character education, 38
Civil rights movement, 78
Class-based appeals, 13, 212
Classical liberal economic theory, 23, 212–213
Clawson, Rosalee, 276–277n. 35
Clinton, Bill: and "end welfare as we know it," 1; and failed health plan, 12; and welfare reform, 63–64, 187
Cloward, Richard, 49, 104; critique of research elitism in social work, 115–117. *See also* Piven and Cloward
Cold War, and end of communism, 56
Columbia University School of Social Work, 117
Common frame of reference, and welfare reporting, 189
Community Action Program, 81
Comparative analysis, 24–25
Comprehensive policymaking, 101
Conflict theory, 91–92
Connolly, Laura, on economy and caseload declines, 271n. 20
Connolly, William: on politics of becoming, 35; on theatricality of power, 238–239
Conservative welfare policy, as self-fulfilling prophecy, 25
Contingency, 106–107, 111–112
Contradiction, in welfare, 80, 88–93
Coontz, Stephanie, 219
Corporate attack on welfare, 191
Corporate fraud, in welfare reform, 194
Cosmopolitan neighbors, and multiculturalism in Jane Addams, 38
Counterdiscourse, 24–26
Crenson, Matthew: on children as legitimation for welfare, 95; on historical institutionalism, 98–99; on orphanages as precursor to the modern welfare state, 96–99
Crisis Strategy, 50–51, 57, 65–70

Critical connectedness, 248. *See also* Global methods
Critical distance, 28–29. *See also* Critical connectedness
Cruikshank, Barbara: and social control vs. self-discipline, 264n. 155; and will to empower "the poor," 80–83
Cultural values, and welfare, 201–202, 217–221
Cycle of representation, 278n. 51
Cyclical theories of welfare change, 87–95

Danziger, Sheldon, 16
Davis, Elizabeth, 271n. 20
de Man, Paul, on reading as an act of supplementation, 177
Dean, Mitchell, 230
Dehli, Kari, 222
Deleuze, Gilles, 230
Democratic justice, 34–37
Democratic rights vs. relationships, 39–41
DeParle, Jason: on Ellwood and Bane's "dynamics study," 64; on Ellwood being "mugged by reality,"104; on Giuliani and Piven and Cloward's "perverted social philosophy," 66; on the logic of the Crisis Strategy, 68–69; and in-depth reporting on welfare reform, 188
Dependency: and conservative campaign to repudiate AFDC, 190–194; and contestability of facts, 125–127; and Ellwood and Baneís "dynamics study," 64; and perversity thesis, 22–23; and postindustrial social policy, 202; and therapeutic approach to welfare, 209–210
Deserted mothers vs. widows, 77–78
Deserving poor, 78
Development, individual and national, 223–226
Devolution, 141–43
Dewey, John: on democracy, 39; on education, 38; and Jane Addams, 251n. 32; and pragmatism, 5
Dilemma of intelligibility, 28
Dilemmas of accessibility, 26–28
Dionne, E. J., 16
Disability, 94
Discrimination, in state welfare programs, 141
Disentitlement, 1, 63, 198–199
Dissensus politics, 72–79; and Martin Luther King, Jr., 86, 261n. 111
Diversion programs, 90; and lack of media coverage, 196–97
Divorce, and welfare use, 180–181
Docility, and globalization, 221, 236
Drug crisis, 192–193
Duggan, Lisa, on queering the state, 78
Duncan, Greg, 170
Durkheimian rituals, 205

Earned Income Tax Credit (EITC), 195, 197
Edelman, Murray, 192
Edin, Kathryn, 70; on marriage rates for welfare mothers, 95; on unreported income, 170
Edsall, Thomas and Mary Bryd, 73
Elitism vs. populism, 27–28
Ellwood, David: in Clinton administration, 62–65; as public intellectual, 50; and resignation, 63; and top-down research, 65
Emergent structures of feeling, 216
Empowerment, 81–82
Empty clichés, 21

Enlightenment, 226, 230–231
Entry and exit rates, and effects on caseload decline, 196
Epistemic privilege, 129–130
Epstein, William, 129–130
Escobar, Arturo, 222–223, 225
Ethic of alterity, 34–35
Evidence-based practice, 122

Facts vs. values: and advocacy in social work, 132–134; and "facts never speak for themselves," 19–20; and the myth of the given, 122–129
Faith-based programs, 141
False neutrality, 78
Families first project, 129
Family cap, 142, 145–146; and racial composition of the rolls, 150–153
Family life obligations, 210–212
Family violence option, 126–127
Family wage system, 204–205, 219–220
Fiedler, Leslie, on "Tom" vs. "Anti-Tom" discourse, 273n. 2
Figlio, David, on economy and caseload declines, 271n. 20
Fischer, Joel, on single subject designs, 129–130
Fitzgerald, Jenrose: on guerrilla wordfare, 249n. 32; on transparency narratives, 225
Flyvbjerg, Bent: on phronesis and social science, 133–134; on rationality and power, 111
Food Stamp program, 17, 63, 198
Foucault, Michel: on biopower, 82, 229; on calligram, 278n. 51; on cycle of representation, 278n. 51; on governmentality, 83, 216, 229–230, 233; on power and resistance, 237; on repressive hypothesis, 82–83
Framing, 189
Fraser, Nancy, 219; on "needs talk," 287n. 67
Functionalism, 90–91
Futility thesis, 23

Garcia, Arnoldo, 212–213
Garrow, David, on Martin Luther King, Jr. and protest politics, 261n. 111
Genealogy, 97–99
Gilens, Martin, on race and opposition to welfare, 144, 165–167, 176
Gilman, Charlotte Perkins, 36
Gilroy, Paul, 185
Gingrich, Newt, on welfare as a sign of a sick society, 56
Giuliani, Rudolph: on Crisis Strategy 66–67; as critic of Piven and Cloward, 255n. 38; standing up for work and family, 74
Globalization: and conservatives, 227; and docility 221, 236; and Enlightenment, 226, 230–231; as hoax, 207–208; and Hobson's choice, 237; and low-wage labor, 55; as real threat, 207–209; and therapeutic welfare reforms, 228–229, 235–236; and transformed subjects/citizens, 221
Global methods, 248n. 31
Gordon, Linda, 219
Gore, Albert, 21
Gottschalk, Peter, 16
Governing mentalities, 216, 224
Governmentality, 83, 216, 229–230, 233
Gray, John, 206, 226–228
Gridlock, over welfare, 57, 85–87
Guaranteed income, 55, 69–70
Guerrilla wordfare, 249n. 32
Gusfield, Joseph, 186–87

Hardt, Michael, 206, 231–236
Harris, Kathleen, 170
Harvey, Phillip, 16
Hirschman, Albert, perversity thesis, 23, 127
Historical institutionalism, 98–99
Historical materialism, 5
Hitchens, Christopher, 26–28
Hobson choice, and globalization, 237
"Homeless," as strategic, 85
Homemaker, 182
Howard, Christopher, on race and state welfare policies, 143
Hull House, 36, 46
Human SERVE, 49, 105–106
Hussein, Saddam, 238

Incrementalism, 100–101
Individual responsibility plans, 142, 210–212
Innocence, and welfare eligibility, 94
Issue networks, 51

Job-ready: and advocacy for those who are not, 180–181; and compensatory programs, 95; and obtuse welfare reform, 183; and self-esteem, 127–128
Jolson, Al, 173

Katz, Michael: and critique of Moynihan Report, 61; on improving the poor, 125; on poorhouse, 96–97
Kelley, Florence, 36
Kelly, Michael, 187, 188, 199
King, Martin Luther, Jr., 86, 261n. 111
King, Rodney, riots, 57
Kissinger, Henry, as public intellectual, 59
Laboratories of democracy, 141
Lasch, Christopher, on public intellectuals, 60
Latinos: geographically concentrated, 169; and welfare, 168
Leavers, 188, 194; earnings of, 198; and lack of access to entitlements, 198–99
Lebeaux, Charles, 88
Lein, Laura, on unreported income, 170
Lemann, Nicholas, 21
Lemert, Charles, on Global methods, 248n. 31
Less eligibility, 90
Levinas, Emanuel, 34
Levine, Steven, on Whiteman, 278n. 48
Levin-Epstein, Jodie, 210–211
Lorde, Audre, on the Master's tools, 140
Lower-Basch, Elizabeth, 272n. 28
Lowi, Theodore, on social science in service of the state, 53
Low-wage labor: and globalization, 55; and "globalization hoax," 207–209; and welfare reform as a neoliberal policy, 214–215
Lugones, Maria, on politics of loving, 35, 45

Macro vs. micro, 203, 229
Malthus, Thomas, on perversity thesis, 23, 127
Managed care, 118–119, 121–123
Marmor, Theodore, 16
Marshaw, Jerry, 16
Martinez, Elizabeth, 212–213
Marx, Karl: and historical materialism, 5; and theory of praxis, 3; and thesis 11, 246n.10
Mass media, and welfare, 187–189
McKenzie, Richard, on orphanages, 60

McWilliams, Carey, and critique of welfare, 67
Mead, George Herbert, 36
Mead, Lawrence, 2
Medicaid, 63, 198
Medical model, and social work, 119
Metapicture, 176–77
Methodological agnosticism, 7
Methodological pluralism, 139–140
Micropolitics, 82, 229
Middle class appeals, 12–15, 29
Mills, C. Wright: and criticism of Jane Addams, 33; and C. Wright Mills Award to Piven and Cloward, 49
Mitchell, W. J. T., on metapictures and visualization, 176–78
Moral tutoring, and welfare, 194
Moral vision, 14
Motor voter bill, 49, 53, 105
Moynihan, Daniel: and *The Negro Family*, 61–62; on Piven and Cloward, 257n. 65; as public intellectual, 50, 59–62; and top-down research, 65
Moynihan Scissors, 159
Multitude, as new proletariat, 235
Murray, Charles, 2; popularity of *Losing Ground*, 18, 67, 127
Mutual aid, 37–38, 41, 45–46
Myth of the given, 124–128

National Association of Social Workers, 115–116, 132–133
National Voter Registration Act, 49
National Welfare Rights Organization, 2, 114
Natural order, 23
Negri, Antonio, 206, 231–236
Neoliberalism, 204, 212–217
New Deal, 54
New Jersey State Troopers, 174
New social movements, 79
New York City: and the Crisis Strategy, 66–67; and economic decline with deindustrialization, 71–72; and whether welfare bankrupted the City, 74
Nietzsche, Friedrich, on personal responsibility, 58
9/11, 236
1960s, and relationship to 1990s, 57–58, 66–67
Nixon, Richard, 70, 86
Nobel prize, 33, 46

O'Connor, Alice: on Jane Addams and bottom up approach, 249–250n. 5; and Piven and Cloward, 113–114; on relationship of social science to politics, 109–110
Ohlin, Lloyd, 113
Orphanages, 60, 97–99
Orr, Larry, on race and state welfare policies, 143
Otherness: in Jane Addams' theory of democratic citizenship, 33–42, 45; in dissensus politics, 76; in racial representations, 173–175, 183

Pack journalism, 190
Page, Benjamin, 15–17
Panel Study of Income Dynamics (PSID), 163–164, 274n. 20
Participatory action research (PAR), 131
Peck, Jamie, 214–215, 236
Personal Responsibility and Work Opportunity Reconciliation Act: and caseload decline, 54–55; and cyclical theory of welfare policy, 92; as milestone, 1; and relationship to the Moynihan Report, 159; as postindustrial social pol-

icy, 202; and the issue of welfare dependency, 126
Perversity thesis, 22–23, 127, 159
Phronesis, 133–134
Piven and Cloward: in contrast with Jane Addams on dissent, 47; and bottom-up approach, 65; and conflict theory, 91–92; on context and contingency, 106–107, 120; on contradictory character of welfare, 88–93; and Crisis Strategy, 51, 57, 65–70; and C. Wright Mills Award, 49; on cyclical character of welfare, 87–93; on differential treatment of rich and poor by the state, 182–183; on dissensus politics, 72–79; on dissent and Martin Luther King, Jr., 86, 261n. 111; and electoral strategy, 105–107; and functionalism, 90–91; on globalization hoax, 207–208; on globalization reality, 208, 239; on "less eligibility," 90; on low-wage labor, 55, 207–209, 214–215; as "Machiavellians," 263n. 38; on moral regulation in welfare, 215; on organizing poor people's movements, 84–85; and radical incrementalism, 100–107; on the relationship of scholarship to politics, 30, 50, 103–107; and self-discipline, 264n. 155; as structuralists, 99; and theory of praxis, 2–5, 24, 30; on universal vs. targeted programs, 101–102; on "us" and "them," 182–183
Piven, Frances Fox, 49, 105; on David Ellwood, 64; on increased spending to recommodify labor, 92–93. *See also* Piven and Cloward
Plato, on relationship of knowledge to power, 51, 253n. 8
Playing by the rules, 72–74, 78, 259n. 92
Polanyi, Karl, 206
Policy subsystems, 51
Policy triangles, 51
Politics of becoming, 35
Politics of loving 35, 45
Politics of spectacle, 78
Politics of survival vs. politics of social change: combined in the Crisis Strategy, 70; as part of dissensus politics, 74–75; as part of Piven and Cloward's model for combining scholarship and politics, 50; parallels symbolic politics vs. substantive policy distinction, 78; and the relationship of social work to politics for Jane Addams, 35
Poor people's movements, and organization, 84–85
Postindustrial social policy, 202
Poverty, and welfare leavers, 198
Powell, Colin, 238
Practice: priority over theory, 3, 29–30, 35–37; priority over research, 103–104, 110–115
Pragmatism, 38–39
Praxis theory, 2–4
Preaching to the choir, 18
Primus, Wendell, 195
Privatization: and corporate welfare fraud, 194; and governmentality, 215–217; and neoliberalism, 204–205
Protest: and contrast between Jane Addams and Piven and Cloward, 30; and contrast with middle class appeals, 47; and Crisis Strategy, 67–70; and dissensus politics, 72–79; and Martin Luther King, Jr., 86, 261n. 111; and welfare growth in the 1960s, 57–58; and welfare rights movement, 2; and World Trade Organization, 236, 288n. 93

Protest politics vs. electoral politics, as interrelated, 105–107
Public facts, 187
Public goods, 16
Public intellectual: and Christopher Hitchens, 26–27; and Christopher Lasch, 60; and Daniel Moynihan, 59–60; needs more than facts, 19; and Benjamin Page and James Simmons, 16; and Piven and Cloward, 50–52; and Piven and Cloward's model for combining scholarship and politics, 103–107; and Joel Rogers, 73; and Theda Skocpol,19; takes a critical stance toward prevailing discourse, 26
Public opinion: as manufactured, 27; on welfare, 191
Public sector functions, 16
Public sphere, as realm of action, 85
Pullman, George, as modern "Lear," 44

Quantification, advantages and disadvantages for welfare advocacy, 140
Queering the state, 78

Race: and the American dream, 174; and melodrama, 273n. 2; as social construction, 56, 167
Race to the bottom: among nation-states, 208–209; among states, 141–142
Race-neutral policy, 79
Racial composition of welfare caseload, 161–177, 191, 272n. 28
Racial profiling, 174–175
Racial representations: and welfare advocacy, 180–182; and welfare reform, 276–277n. 35
Racism and welfare reform: as associated with changing composition of the rolls, 167; as evidenced by state policy choices, 194; as highlighted by quantitative analysis, 154–55; as part of conservative campaign to retrench public assistance, 191; as related to public opinion surveys, 276–277n. 35; as return to past practice, 141–143
Radical incrementalism: of addressing prevailing modes of representation, 158; as bottom-up strategy, 51; in contrast with conventional incrementalism, 100–102; for a new world order, 206, 234; as Piven and Cloward's praxis, 5–6, 100–107; of statistical inquiry, 140
Recognition vs. redistribution, 34, 220
Rector, Robert, 147–148
Reed, Adolph, Jr., critique of William Julius Wilson's theory of self-censorship in the wake of the Moynihan Report, 160
Research models, dynamic vs. linear, 111–112
Reuschemeyer, Dietrich, on social science and the founding of the modern welfare state, 53
Riots, as related to welfare growth, 57
Risk and resilience, 120–121
Roberston, Alexa, on the front of the bus, 278n. 56
Rogers, Joel, 73
Rogin, Michael, 173
Role models, 43–45
Rose, Nikolas, on governmentality, 83
Rubin, Allen: critique of Richard Cloward, 115–118; on adjusting research methods to fit practice needs, 131
Rumsfeld, Donald, 238

Sanctions, 142–143; and family life obligations, 212; and racial composition of the rolls, 150–153; and roll declines, 146–149
Schattschneider, E. E., and socialization of conflict, 79
Scholarship, and social change, 30–32
Schumpeter, Joseph, 207
Schwarz, John, 16
Self-discipline, 216, 228–233; versus social control, 264n. 155
Self-esteem, 127–128
Sellars, Wilfrid, on the myth of the given, 124
September 11th, 236
Settlement house work, 45–46
Shapiro, Michael, on dilemma of intelligibility, 27–28
Shaw, Susan: on client-management practices under neoliberalism, 286n. 50; on "emergent structures of feeling," 286n. 47
Siegel, Fred, on critique of Piven and Cloward, 70–72
Siegfried, Charlene Haddock, on Jane Addams's style of writing, 41
Simmons, James, 15–17
Single mothers: and effectiveness of policies that reduce poverty, 17; and false neutrality of pro-family policies, 77–78; and the family wage system, 218–221; as focus of welfare reform, 1; marginalized by sameness arguments, 180–181; and "the poor," 84; and reduced support for staying home with children, 93; as vulnerable to marginalization by middle class appeals, 13–14; and welfare queen rhetoric, 191
Skinner, B. F., 129
Skocpol, Theda: on historical institutionalism, 98; on middle class appeals, 12–15, 29; on mothers' pensions, 96–97; social science and the founding of the modern welfare state, 53
Social control vs. self-discipline, 264n. 155
Social control vs. social assistance, 89
Social justice, as ineffable, 112
Social safety net, 15–18
Social Security Act of 1935, 98
Social Security, as solvent, 17
Social science: and advocacy, 4–6, 29–30, 103–104, 132–34; as founding the modern welfare state, 53; as underlaborer for practice, 130
Social work, 35, 43–46; and managed care, 115–123, 125; and medical model, 119; and national research center, 135; and research elitism, 115–116
Society of Social Work and Research, 115
Somers, Margaret, and the perversity thesis, 22
Soss, Joe, 186, 265n. 17
Speenhamland, 92
Spiller, Hortense, on appropriation of black women, 172
Spivak, Gayati Chakravorty, on strategic essentialism, 84
Starr, Roger, 70–71
Statistics, 20; and the state, 139–140
Stereotypes, reinforced by racialized images, 171–175
Stone, Deborah, on cyclical tensions between work-based and need-based systems, 93–95, 186
Strategic essentialism, 84
Structure/agency relationship, 5; in Marx, 85
Suture, in race and welfare policy, 172

Swenson, Carol, on managed care, 122
Synecdoche, and welfare dependency, 192–193

Taliban, 238
Taylor, A. J. P., on mass intellectuals, 59
Technologies of the self, 228, 230
Teles, Steven, on critique of Piven and Cloward's dissensus politics, 76–77
Temporary Assistance for Needy Families (TANF): abolished entitlement, 54; caseload decline, 54, 186; as covered in the mass media, 188; introduced state options for "get-tough" welfare policies, 141–142; and reassessment of the related research, 193–200; replacing AFDC, 1; as an therapeutic program to attack dependency, 209
Therapy, as hegemonic in social work, 118–123; in welfare reform, 210, 212
Think-tanks, 51
Thomas, M. Carey, prize for excellence in American living, 46
Time limits, 142, 145–146; and racial composition of the rolls, 150–153
Tomasky, Michael, and critique of Piven and Cloward, 67–72, 75
Transnational knowledge regimes, 205, 222
Transparency narratives, 205
Trattner, Walter, 88–89
Trice, Rakuya, 276–277n. 35

Universal welfare state, 15, 17, 25; and political strategy by Piven and Cloward, 102–103, 106–107
Universalism, 34
"Us" and "them," 41, 182–183

Values vs. facts: and advocacy in social work, 132–134; and "facts never speak for themselves," 19–20; and the myth of the given, 122–129
Visualization, 176–178

Wagner, David, on charity, 46
War on poverty, 81
War on welfare vs. war on poverty, 56
Weber, Max, on relationship of social science to politics, 51–53, 103–104
Welfare: as a "black" program, 55–56, 171, 191; and causes of caseload decline, 145–149, 194–197; and cultural values, 201–202, 217–221; as cyclical, 87–93; and dependency, 22–23, 55, 64, 125–127, 142, 178–179, 190–194, 202; as Durkheimian rituals, 205; and increased surveillance, 193–194, 216; and Latinos, 168; as postindustrial social policy, 202; as postmodern, 235; and public opinion, 191; and racial composition of caseload, 161–177, 276–277n. 35. 191; and racism in reform process, 141–143, 154–55, 191; as a secondary institution, 88–93; as therapy, 210, 212, 235
Welfare fraud, 170
Welfare Law Center, 161
Welfare "mess," in Nixon Administration, 58, 86
Welfare queen, 56, 172, 177
Welfare rights movement: and mobilizing "the poor," 81, 84; and Piven and Cloward's involvement, 57–58; and push for a guaranteed income, 2; and the strategy of emphasizing targeted welfare programs, 102; and symbiotic relationship with Piven and Cloward's welfare scholarship, 30
Welfare stigma, 55
Whitebrook, Maureen, on the front of the bus, 278n. 56

Whitman, Christie Todd, and racial profiling, 174–175
Wilensky, Harold, 88
Williams, Linda, 273n. 2
Wilson, William Julius: and critique of the data in the Moynihan Report 160, 257n. 62; on role models, 43; on self-censorship among scholars, 161; on universal programs, 79
Work requirements, 142,145–146
Workfare states, 214–215
Working families, 13–15, 21
World Trade Organization, and mass protests, 236, 288n. 93
Wright, Gerald, on race and state welfare benefit levels, 143

Youssef, Sarah, 147–148

Ziliak, James, on economy and caseload declines, 271n. 20
Žižek, Slovoj, on welfare queen, 172

About the Author

Sanford F. Schram teaches social policy and social theory in the Graduate School of Social Work and Social Research at Bryn Mawr College. He is the author of *After Welfare: The Culture of Postindustrial Social Policy* (New York University Press, 2000); and *Words of Welfare: The Poverty of Social Science and the Social Science of Poverty* (University of Minnesota Press, 1995), which won the Michael Harrington Award from the American Political Science Association. He is also co-editor with Samuel H. Beer of *Welfare Reform: A Race to the Bottom?* (Johns Hopkins University Press, 1999); and, with Philip Neisser, *Tales of the State: Narrative in U.S. Politics and Public Policy* (Rowman and Littlefield, 1997). He has published articles on the politics of welfare in the *American Sociological Review*, the *American Journal of Political Science, Polity, Rethinking MARXISM, Social Text*, and other journals.